KU-035-323

Contents at a Glance

CONTENTS

PART ONE Begin With the Basics

CHAPTER 1 Planning Ahead 22

CHAPTER 2 Be a Soil Detective 38

PART THREE Woody Plants

PART FOUR Exploring Edibles

PART FIVE *Tying It All Together*

APPENDICES

Foreword

I MEET A LOT OF WOULD-BE GARDENERS who hesitate to get going on their own gardens because they feel that they do not know enough to get started. I think that this is a real shame because it is almost entirely false. Gardening is what you do outside in your garden. No more and no less. But it need never be just that. Gardening should, first and foremost, be a pleasure. If you are not enjoying it then you can be pretty sure that you are doing something wrong. But I know that kind of thing is easy to say if you have been gardening for years and know what you are doing. The first few steps are always the hardest.

In fact I started gardening at a very young age. I had little choice in the matter: gardening was one of a series of daily chores, rather like the laundry and the washing up. My brothers and sisters and I were all allocated jobs according to the season, and for my part I loathed it. But one day, when I was about 17, a key turned in my head and I began to love it. I found the thing that gave me more consistent pleasure than anything else in my life. That pleasure has never gone away and continues to grow.

So, if you have not had gardening drummed into you from childhood, where do you start? Certainly by keeping it simple. Gardening is not complicated. The basic principle is to make a beautiful place outside using living plants. Simple. But there are two essential elements in that.

The first is that, however functional or small, a garden must be beautiful in your eyes. Each gardener has to please only themselves – or at most their household – but it means working out what you really like and then setting about creating the garden to fulfil your own personal standards of beauty. The real fun in gardening is in making it exactly as you want it. This takes no special skills, need not cost much money, and can be done surprisingly quickly.

The second factor that is essential is that every garden is ultimately based around plants. In my own experience, the greatest pleasure to be had from gardening is in planting, handling, and caring for plants. Even if you just have a few pots outside the back door or a window-box, by tuning into the needs of your plants you are connecting directly with the natural world. In our modern, urban, stress-filled lives, this has deeply therapeutic value. The weather takes on a new significance, and you start to notice the rhythm and moods of the seasons. Instead of being a passive bystander, you are becoming part of the natural world. This, not makeovers or quick "lifestyle" transformations, is the great secret of gardening.

Gardening is not a competition. We do it to make beautiful private spaces attached to our homes. This book opens the door to that private, beautiful space. If you enjoy the process of making and tending it half as much as I enjoy my garden, then it also guarantees you a very good time indeed.

MONTY DON

Introduction

It seems as if everybody these days is gardening, or wants to garden, "as soon as they have the time". There is something quite spiritual about working as a companion to the earth, helping to provide flowers, trees, and scented herbs, as well as offering our families the practicality and health of fresh fruits and vegetables. It's a pleasurable option for most of us today, but it is an option that has evolved over time.

ENCOURAGING GROWTH

The garden of our ancestors was a transient place. The men searched for meat with primitive weapons. The fallback against hunger were the grains and fruits found in the forests and open lands. Groups didn't stay long enough in one place to develop their own controllable plot of land. When humans finally did band and settle, land was the common property of the group. There was more than enough for everybody.

Gradually, this changed too. As groups or tribes discovered the comforts of staying on one site for a long time, certain lands became parts of tribal domain. While the men hunted, women and children could go out into the surrounding area and bring back grain seeds and edible roots for eating and also for planting. These early gardens would ensure there was food for the coming year, even if no game was brought in that day, that week, or even that month. For in some hidden corner of the village, each woman had a well-concealed stash of edibles to tide her family through the leanest days.

It was a lot of work, with sharpened sticks and strong branches, to prepare the ground for planting. When the grains and early vegetables emerged, they had to be protected. Materials were certainly at hand. Early fences were thorny hedges or tree branches thrust into the ground and woven into sturdy barriers with thick vines.

The gardens became more polished, through increasingly effective equipment and greater knowledge. And so, in accordance with a hierarchy of needs, there was a tad of leisure. The garden provided foodstuffs, as well as a friendly, safe haven and the opportunity to create beauty and order in a disorderly world.

Many of the earliest pleasure gardens contained a versatile assortment of herbs. Some were grown for energy, others purportedly cured or ameliorated disease and distress. Anthropologists have found papyrus records dating back to about 1550 BC that include prescriptions containing garlic, peppermint, anise, and other heartily fragrant herbs. Eventually, various plants became a necessary import. Spices, medicinal plants, fruits, and plants used for dye were carried long, dangerous distances for commercial profit.

All so different from today – or is it? Perhaps only the outward facade has changed. New foodstuffs are constantly under development and herbs have undergone a tremendous resurgence, not only in tea bags, but also in modern pharmacopoeia. As our places of escape become more crowded, a little personal plot of land takes on increasing importance.

I wrote this book to help you with the practical aspects as well as the pleasure of gardening. Not everything you plant will grow, but even the tiniest success will spur you onwards. To put a seed or plant in the soil and tempt it to flowering is, to me, the essence of creativity, even if the plant is doing most of the work.

L. PATRICIA KITE

Dedication
This book is dedicated to
Sarah Rose Raney.
Happy sunshine and many roses.

A PRIVATE REFUGE FROM THE OUTSIDE WORLD

What's Inside?

THE INFORMATION IN THE K.I.S.S. Guide to Gardening is arranged so that you learn the basics, then swiftly progress to the rewarding challenges of creating the garden you've always wanted – and keeping it that way.

PART ONE

In Part One I'll start with the basics: planning your garden, assessing and improving the soil, choosing and using the right tools, and how and when to water.

PART TWO

In Part Two I'll introduce you to some of my favourite annuals, perennials, and bulbs, and show you how to make the most of their unique characteristics.

PART THREE

In Part Three I'll reveal how big woody plants – ornamental trees, shrubs, roses, and vines – can make a real statement in the garden.

PART FOUR

In Part Four I'll whet your appetite with tempting fruit and vegetables as well as berries and herbs, and show how easy they are to grow, whatever the size of your garden.

PART FIVE

In Part Five I'll show you how to use the unifying elements of a garden – groundcovers, lawns, and container plants – to create a beautiful and harmonious environment.

PART SIX

In Part Six I'll encourage you to experiment and learn some new techniques. I'll explain how to grow your own plants, attract wildlife, and deal with weeds, pests, and diseases. I'll also suggest various projects and activities for different times of the year.

The Extras

I KNOW THAT YOU'RE BUSY, so this book has special titbits, marked with little pictures, to help you along.

Very Important Point
This symbol indicates directives to perform a task in a particular way.

Complete No-No
When you see this symbol, just don't do it!

Getting Technical
For you very thorough sorts, I've included these technical pointers to keep you happy.

Inside Scoop
These are special hints from me and other gardening gurus.

Throughout the book, you'll also find little boxes – some for facts, some just for fun.

Trivia...
My favourite boxes share minutiae about gardening, which is, above all, joy, and a link to the past and present.

DEFINITION
*Here I'll **explain** fancy gardening words and terms. You'll also find a simple Glossary at the back of the book with all the gardening lingo.*

INTERNET
www.internet.com

Boxes marked www send you to informative web sites pertinent to gardening and related subjects. The Internet is a great resource for gardeners.

PART ONE

RICH, CRUMBLY LOAM, THE IDEAL SOIL FOR PLANTING

BEGIN WITH THE BASICS

EVERY GARDEN requires some planning, even if you prefer an "unplanned" garden. That's because what goes in your garden is determined by the space itself (How big is it? Is it windy or hilly?), the type of soil it contains, and the amount of light and water it gets. With these factors in mind, *it's a simple matter* to start planning what you want to plant, and where.

In this part I'll walk you through the planning stages of your garden. My idea is to help you start off on the right foot, so that your first efforts are *successful*. And the greater your success, the more you'll want to know about creating a *gorgeous* garden. So before you start to dig, read.

Chapter 1

Planning Ahead

BEFORE YOU CAN MAKE a garden, you have to plan. It's the same with any kind of journey: you must start with a map. There are many ways to approach the planning and basic landscaping. This should take into account the interests and needs of your entire family, including pets.

In this chapter...

✓ Who should do the planning?
✓ Landscape components
✓ The front of the house
✓ The flower garden
✓ The four seasons
✓ Some questions to ask yourself
✓ Climates and microclimates
✓ Dealing with difficult sites

Who should do the planning?

MAYBE YOU BOUGHT YOUR HOUSE just for the big garden and have been looking forward to planning everything out yourself. Perhaps you already have some garden ideas in mind and can't wait to start work on implementing them. This is going to be fun! However, not everyone feels comfortable making all the decisions. Perhaps you wish you could get a little advice. Perhaps you wish you could just turn the whole project over to someone else. There is plenty of help available.

Call in the professionals

A landscape architect has a degree in landscape architecture and should be able to show you a specific degree from an accredited school. Budget constraints may deter you from considering a landscape architect or a landscape consultant, but do think about it before you automatically say no. A licensed professional with many years of experience can prevent you from making expensive mistakes – not only immediate ones, but those that come later when you have to pay several hundred pounds to take down a tree that simply shouldn't have been there in the first place. A professional will not only help you plan, but also may be able to recommend contractors and nurseries that will do the best job.

INTERNET

www.gardens-at-home.com/lanscape-gardening.htm

This website promotes planning your garden yourself. It offers useful suggestions on what questions to ask yourself initially. There is also an address to email for advice if you have further questions.

Garden centres

Some garden centres employ a specialist who can help customers plan their landscapes, or at least will be able to recommend a local professional. Using a garden design service, you can choose from a wide variety of options, from a complete design and build programme to a simple planting plan for you to do the work yourself.

Before you begin, decide exactly what you expect from your garden, whether it's to be an outside entertainment area, somewhere safe for children and animals to play, a haven for birds, bees, and butterflies, or whatever. Make a list of your needs. Your final garden design should meet all of them, and the designer should have a copy of your list. He or she should have a great deal of plant knowledge and should be able to recommend planting schemes that will work well in your garden.

Don't be shy about asking to see examples of other gardens that your designer has created. You can look at the paper plans in their portfolio, or even go round to visit other gardens that he or she has designed locally.

Simply plan it yourself

There's no reason why you can't draw up your own plan. Just remember to think of your garden as a whole, and not as the patch behind the house, the area by the fence, and so on. Don't create a hodgepodge.

Before you sit down with drawing paper and pencil, study your neighbourhood. Look for houses that are similar to yours. This includes the house size, one or two stories, which way the front of the house faces, doorways, windows, the garden path, and distance from the road.

I like to look around wealthy neighbourhoods and see what their landscape architects have accomplished. It gives me lots of great ideas for free.

When you're walking around a neighbourhood, try chatting to people who are outside gardening. Ask them what grows well "around here". What doesn't? How about local weather? Gardeners are often quite willing to share information on plants, especially if you admire their pretty plot. They may even give you a cutting or two.

■ **Having a look** *at other people's gardens may give you some useful ideas. For example, if you want your patio to receive maximum sunshine, why not site it away from the house?*

Making a scale drawing

How does an amateur plan? First, roughly measure your front and back gardens. Then buy some graph paper, the kind with little squares on it that perhaps you may remember from school. Paper with 10 squares per centimetre is a good size. Decide on the scale you will use to measure your garden.

An easy scale is one square on the paper equals 10 centimetres of your site. If your paper has 10 squares per centimetre, 1 centimetre on your graph paper will equal 1 metre of your garden.

Sketch your garden on the graph paper according to your scale. Draw your house, paths, existing trees, and any other permanent fixtures on the paper in approximate scale.

Now spend a few days in spring or summer observing sun and shade patterns in your garden. Mark these on the graph paper with a line that shows the sunny and shady portions. In the margins, write down when the sun strikes: "morning sun from 7 a.m. until 10 a.m." or "no sun due to shadows from neighbour's trees". This will give you some guidance in selecting your plants.

Some areas may receive sun for only part of the day such as in early morning

EARLY MORNING

A few areas receive sun for most of the day and can be planted with sun-loving plants

NOON

Some parts remain in shade for most of the day and will need quite deep shade-tolerant plants

EARLY EVENING

■ **When moving to a new house** *you'll probably have a good idea of whether the garden is quite sunny or shaded. Before you start to plan in earnest, though, take time to fully assess your site. For example, a north-facing garden (shown above in summer) will be colder all year round than a south-facing one. Plants will therefore grow more slowly because the soil will take longer to warm up.*

Now start searching the colour supplements of Sunday newspapers for plant advertisements. Collect catalogues. Start cutting out those little pictures and placing them on your graph. It helps if you also have in front of you a few pictures of your home's exterior. Even if you are not artistically inclined, concepts seem to form themselves when you've got pictures to shuffle around.

Landscape components

NOVICES TEND TO THINK ABOUT GENERIC *green plants when they're planning a garden. But there's a great deal more to be considered. Landscaping components can include fencing, trees, shrubs, privacy hedges and walls, paths, steps, and patios, a pool or pond, and lawns.*

You also have to decide whether you want a formal, informal, or deliberately wild garden. Should there be a special place for roses? Vegetables? Herbs? Fruit trees? Standard trees or dwarf varieties? What about a rock garden? Do you want a lot of flowers, which require some fussing, or a cool panorama of green? If that sounds like a lot to consider, there's more.

Where will you put the rubbish bin? Unless you like to stare at it (I don't), you will need a screened corner next to the back or front of the house. Do you want to build something? Plant something? Where will you put your tools, including the lawn mower? If you need a tool shed, where will it go? Tool sheds are not the most attractive items, so you have to conceal them somewhere or plant to enhance their appearance.

Will you eventually want a greenhouse? You may say no now, but as you get into the many pleasures of gardening you may change your mind. And if you live in a place where the winters are cold, a greenhouse may almost become a necessity. Even a

■ **In a smaller garden** *you don't want to be restricted by too many landscaping components, so keep them to a minimum. Rather than building a permanent barbecue, for example, you might do better to purchase a portable one that can be moved out of sight when it's not being used.*

child's sandpit or paddling pool should be planned for. And then there's the barbecue and gazebo. No matter what you ultimately decide about any of these items, you should at least consider them when you're in the planning stage.

The front of the house

PLAY A LITTLE GAME around your area. Try guessing the personality of the home owners just by looking at the front of their houses. How many times do you think "yuk"? Which homes just look so interesting that you want to meet the people living there?

■ **For a smart impression,** *a carefully chosen tree that won't overshadow the house, together with a few key shrubs, are all that are needed.*

In addition to reflecting the taste of its inhabitants, the external appearance of a building can increase or decrease its value.

Foundation plantings, those around the base of the house, are important. Use trees to frame the house like a picture frame, with the house itself clearly visible. Consider the eventual size of a tree when you buy it. A small tree can become a huge tree in 15 years, and do you truly want it in front of your picture window, or its roots doing wonders for your lawn or path?

Do seriously consider shrubs, rather than a plethora of flowering plants, for your home's exterior. Not that flowers shouldn't be included, but lots of them festooning the spring and summer months aren't quite as elegant as shrubs that change colour with the season, and provide fruit and flowers, too. There's a temptation here to buy one of every type of shrub to give variety. Do that in the back garden if you like. In the front, repetition, using just a few carefully selected shrub varieties, is the key to an organized and tidy appearance. Start with smaller ones towards the street and grade upwards so the eye follows the plantings. Again, remember that plants grow. Use a reference book to determine the eventual height and width before you buy a shrub.

The flower garden

YOU CAN HAVE ALL PERENNIALS, *all annuals, or a kaleidoscope that includes some of each plus flowering vines and bulbs. (I'll talk about all these kinds of plants in Part Two.) A mixed garden has many advantages, including design flexibility, longer-lasting colour, and easier maintenance.*

Trivia...

The earliest gardens were strictly practical and were used to grow food and medicinal herbs. But in Egypt, by 1500 BC the first decorative gardens appeared. They had walls, pools, trees, and plants grown just for their beautiful flowers.

Styles change. Right now, cottage gardens, full of old-fashioned varieties, are in. So are tropical gardens. But that can alter almost overnight. You must plan for what you like best, after doing your homework via neighbourhood scouting, reading catalogues, and visiting local nurseries. If you can visit some public gardens as well, that's a real bonus.

Tall and short

As a general rule, taller plants go in the back of a garden, medium ones (those between 45 and 90 centimetres high) in the middle, and shorties up front. That way you can see everything. If you use a lot of bulbs, you need to consider ways to camouflage their browning foliage with other plants, rocks, or other landscape features.

When considering garden design, make sure you can get to the plants at the back without having to trample on others in passing. Consider placing a stepping stone pathway for large areas, to make meandering easier. Stepping stones can be very inexpensive, but give a polished look to the garden.

■ **Colourful flowering perennials** *can be combined with a variety of shrubs and bushes to great effect. As well as planting with height and size in mind, think about choosing textures and different hues of foliage to create added interest.*

The four seasons

WHEN YOU'RE CHOOSING plants, think how you can have flowers for most of the year. If you pick plants that flower in each season, you'll have colour almost year round. Here's a list of some popular flowering plants. Note that some plants flower through more than one season. Removing faded flowers can prolong the blooming period.

■ **Canna flowers** *from mid-summer to early autumn.*

Spring

- Alyssum (*Aurinia*)
- Bergenia (*Bergenia*)
- Bugle (*Ajuga*)
- Columbine (*Aquilegia*)
- Crocus (*Crocus*)
- Daffodil (*Narcissus*)
- Evening primrose (*Oenothera*)
- Fleabane (*Erigeron*)
- Forget-me-not (*Myosotis*)
- Grape hyacinth (*Muscari*)

- Honeysuckle (*Lonicera*)
- Lily-of-the-valley (*Convallaria*)
- Phlox (*Phlox*)
- Primrose (*Primula*)
- Rose (*Rosa*)
- Speedwell (*Veronica*)
- Thrift (*Armeria*)
- Violet (*Viola*)
- Sweet woodruff (*Galium*)
- Tulip (*Tulipa*)

Summer

- Amaryllis (*Lycoris*)
- Arum (*Zantesdeschia*)
- Baby's breath (*Gypsophila*)
- Bee balm (*Monarda*)
- Canna (*Canna*)
- Clematis (*Clematis*)
- Cornflower (*Centaurea*)
- Dahlia (*Dahlia*)
- Dame's violet (*Hesperis*)
- Daylily (*Hemerocallis*)
- Gladiolus (*Gladiolus*)
- Honeysuckle (*Lonicera*)
- Iris (*Iris*)
- Jasmine (*Jasminum*)
- Joe Pye weed (*Eupatorium*)
- Lantana (*Lantana*)

- Lavender (*Lavandula*)
- Lily (*Lilium*)
- Montbretia (*Crocosmia*)
- Pinks (*Dianthus*)
- Purple coneflower (*Echinacea*)
- Rose (*Rosa*)
- Sage (*Salvia*)
- Sea lavender (*Limonium*)
- Snow-in-summer (*Cerastium*)
- Spurge (*Euphorbia*)
- Stonecrop (*Sedum*)
- Tiger lily (*Lilium*)
- Trumpet vine (*Campsis*)
- Tuberose (*Polianthes*)
- Verbena (*Verbena*)
- Yarrow (*Achillea*)

Autumn

- Aster (*Aster*)
- Cardinal flower (*Lobelia*)
- Catmint (*Nepeta*)
- Chrysanthemum (*Chrysanthemum*)
- False chamomile (*Boltonia*)
- Japanese anemone (*Anemone*)
- Purple coneflower (*Echinacea*)
- Rose (*Rosa*)
- Sneezeweed (*Helenium*)
- Stonecrop (*Sedum*)
- Trumpet vine (*Campsis*)
- Verbena (*Verbena*)

■ **Sneezeweed's daisy-like** *flowers bloom over a long period.*

Winter

- Christmas rose (*Helleborus*)
- Snowdrop (*Galanthus*)
- Snowflake (*Leucojum*)

- Winter-blooming bergenia (*Bergenia*)
- Winter jasmine (*Jasminum*)
- Witch hazel (*Hamamelis*)

Some questions to ask yourself

IT'S ALMOST IMPOSSIBLE, when you're visiting a colourful garden centre in spring, to resist buying plants. However, if you can restrain yourself, here are some things to consider before you make a purchase:

1. Is the plant an annual or perennial?

2. Does it need sun or shade?

3. What are the water and soil requirements?

4. How high and wide will it grow, and how fast?

5. Is it *invasive*?

6. When does it flower, and for how long?

7. Is it bothered by a plethora of diseases or insects and is it hardy in my area?

DEFINITION

An **invasive plant**, *also known as an aggressive or a rampant grower, is one that tends gradually to take over the surrounding territory. Some bamboos, for example, will crowd out everything in their path. Some ivies can cover buildings. Russian vine can take over a fence. If you want a rampant grower, confine it to a container.*

31

Climates and microclimates

TO SAVE MONEY AND TIME, and to avoid disappointment, you should know which garden plants suit your area. The United Kingdom has many and varied growing regions. As temperature and rainfall change, so does plant life. Additional modifying factors include the soil's ability to retain and distribute water, proximity to the sea, wind, mountain barriers, frost, and the length of the growing season. It's easy to see different climate areas when you're travelling by car. Consider how the wild trees and shrubs change from southern Cornwall northwards to Scotland.

The weather in the south-west of England can be so much milder than in places further north. For example, rhododendrons may be at their best in Cornwall in May, but don't really get going until much later in, say, Scotland. Rely on temperature as your guide, rather than the calender month.

What is a microclimate?

Simply put, microclimates are changes in climate that may occur only a few kilometres, or even metres, apart. As an example, suppose one portion of your garden is very shady and another is in full sun. The general climate is the same, but the microclimate will vary even though the sections of the garden are just a few metres apart.

Here's another example: you live at the foot of a hill and another house is near the fog-shrouded hill top. The microclimate may be different in each site. A third example: if you live near the beach, the sun and wind may be different to what it would be if you lived half a mile away, where the wind is blocked by buildings. And finally, suppose the nearest town to yours gets 5 centimetres more rainfall per year than your home town. Or the city 16 kilometres away has average summer temperatures that are 5 degrees higher. All these situations, and many others, create different plant-growing conditions that must be considered when making your plans and purchases.

Why are microclimates important?

While there are many plants native to the United Kingdom, many more have been imported from all over the world. They may come from tropical humid forests. They may come from mountainous areas or deserts. The innate structure of a specific plant is based on its origin. Although modern hybridization has provided some leeway, you still can't grow a desert cactus in a bog, and you still can't grow a water lily in a temporary puddle in the Gobi Desert.

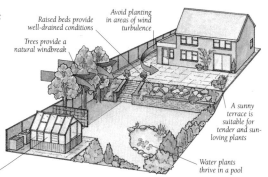

■ You can create *different microclimates, or growing environments, in even the smallest of gardens. Simply exploit or manipulate your garden features, as necessary, to provide the kind of conditions that plants from many different regions enjoy.*

Avoid planting in areas of wind turbulence

Raised beds provide well-drained conditions

Trees provide a natural windbreak

A sunny terrace is suitable for tender and sun-loving plants

A greenhouse provides a suitable environment for tender plants

Water plants thrive in a pool

THE PROS AND CONS OF CLIMATE ZONES

Some of the reference books you see about gardening will provide a climate zone map. The thinking behind this is that you find the climate zone you live in and look to see if every plant you like is right for your area. If it is, great! If it's not, too bad. You'll have to choose a different plant. The idea is that if you follow the recommendations for your climate zone, you'll have green fingers after all.

I have found, however, that using climate zones to plan your garden often isn't quite as simple as it seems. It's not that your climate is unimportant, it's just that the maps can't really tell the whole story. To be honest, it seems to me that every map is different, so I'm never really sure which zone is which, anyway. And the recommended plants for particular zones vary from reference to reference. Who's right?

In my years of gardening, I've discovered that a plant's specific needs – for a certain type of soil, to be in a sunny spot, or to be located where there is good drainage, for example – are more important to success than what climate zone you live in. That's why I prefer to focus on the microclimates that exist in your garden.

One last tip: when in doubt, visit your local garden centre. The retailer wants your business, and it's in his or her best interests to sell you plants that will do well. If the store sells a lot of plants that don't thrive in your area, you and your fellow gardeners won't be shopping there very much.

How microclimates change

Even within an established garden, microclimates don't always remain the same.

If your nextdoor neighbour builds an extension, the shadow may change the microclimate on your side of the fence. Another neighbour may install a wide-ranging sprinkler system, affecting drought-tolerant plants in your garden. If your local area loses a windbreak of tall trees because of a shopping centre development, wind patterns will now need to be considered.

You might change the microclimate yourself, either intentionally or otherwise. If you remove a huge tree from your garden, the microclimate in the immediate area will inevitably change. Conversely, if the tiny cypress sapling you planted some years ago reaches 10 metres tall, the microclimate around it changes along with the growth. All this affects which plants you will choose and which plants will succeed in your garden.

■ **A solid brick wall** *can provide shelter and shade for non sun-worshippers, or if it's exposed to the sun, can create a haven for heat-loving plants.*

Modern gardening is really wonderful, because you can create a specific microclimate for a plant that you really want to grow. A greenhouse is a microclimate. Fencing built to deter prevailing winds also creates a microclimate. Planting against a sun-reflecting white cement wall increases heat reflection, and so that's another microclimate. Even putting container plants outside under shelter in spring and summer, and then moving them indoors in the autumn to help protect them from the cold, is a managed microclimate.

■ **Fencing acts** *as an effective windbreak, providing a protected environment for more vulnerable plants.*

Dealing with difficult sites

YOU WILL SOON RECOGNIZE DIFFICULT *sites because plants may find it hard to grow there. However, it's a lot easier on your wallet to recognize difficult sites before you begin buying your garden plants. Then you can buy plants that will thrive in the face of horticultural adversity.*

Slopes

It may not look like much of an incline to you, but slopes of any kind can be water wasters. Not only are some difficult to water adequately, but when you do water it runs downhill, taking good topsoil with it. Mowing is also difficult, sometimes impossible, on a slope. Nor do you want to do your weeding at a 45-degree angle. How much extra work your slope demands depends on how steep the slope is. The most difficult situation is where the garden has literally been carved out of the hillside.

What to do? If you have a minimal maintenance mentality, put in groundcover. Plant it during a rainy period so you don't have to worry about watering while the plants are in the fragile get-started phase. On steep slopes you will need a fast and thorough groundcover.

If your slope is very sharply angled, you may wish to create a terrace arrangement. Terracing means creating narrow, flat shelves of land (terraces), and then bordering the terraces with wood or brick to keep the soil from sliding downhill – making what are basically large containers. Terracing is a lot of work, but once it's done you have made ample room for a selection of lovely plants and a vegetable garden, too.

Of course, even with terraces the garden is still sloped. Sprinklers will encourage water run-off. The best solution, if you put in any plant that needs regular watering, is to use a drip irrigation system. (You'll find more about irrigation in Chapter 4.) Slow watering allows water to soak in before it gathers enough weight to start running downhill. If sprinklers are already in place, create a basin around each plant by digging a shallow trench around it. The water will pool in this basin and seep in more slowly.

Trivia...

One of the oldest garden plans, that of the St. Gall monastery in Switzerland, dates back to AD 820.

Wind

Wind spreads airborne diseases, tears plant leaves, turns their edges brown, and speeds up water evaporation, causing drought stress even in plants that are regularly watered. Strong winds can uproot plants and snap branches. While you cannot stop the wind, you may be able to alleviate some of its harmful effects. For example, prune trees regularly and fewer branches will break off.

Wind in combination with steady rain will cause big trees to topple. If you live in a windy area, look around the neighbourhood and see which trees are thriving. To protect smaller plants, place them where the house blocks the wind, or create a windbreak. A windbreak can be a hedgerow of shrubs or a fence. If it's a fence, it needs to be constructed so some wind can pass through. Slats will do, or lattice. With a solid fence, the wind goes over the fence and then drops to the ground, creating a disturbance on the other side.

Shade

It may not be so obvious where the shady parts of your garden are. A neighbour's tree or two-storey house may create shade during part of the day. Your own home may create shade in part of the day, and so may a fence. Plants that need full sun won't thrive here.

When thinking "shade", one tends to think "cool". But that's not always true. Shaded areas adjacent to concrete may actually receive quite a bit of heat. However, there are many plants that thrive in shade, warm or cool.

■ **Tall plants that are susceptible** *to damage from strong winds, or small plants that need more protection, can benefit from the shelter afforded by the side of a house or enclosed fencing.*

Soggy soil

Another name for this is waterlogged soil. By any name, very little will grow here due to a lack of oxygen available to the plant. There are only a few trees, such as willows, that will grow in soil that is always wet. So you will have to take action. Action means correcting the water drainage so the soil has the chance to dry out. Either that or install a bog or water garden. If there are just a few plants you're concerned about, create a mound of drier soil and plant within this for better drainage.

A simple summary

✓ To plan your garden, you can hire a landscape architect, consult a specialist at a garden centre, or tackle the job yourself.

✓ In addition to the plants, think about fencing, trees, shrubs, privacy hedges and screening, walls, pathways, steps, patios, lawns, a barbecue, a greenhouse, and anything else that might appear in future when you're planning your garden.

✓ Plantings in front of your home will increase its value. Consider using a few key shrubs rather than a plethora of flowers at the front of the house. To get an idea of what will look nice, why not drive around and see what the neighbours have done?

✓ When you're choosing flowering plants, try to pick some that will bloom in each season so you have colour in your garden for as long as possible.

✓ Consider both your local climate and the microclimate when planning your garden. Microclimates are localized areas where the climate may vary, such as a very shady spot in a garden, a house near the sea, or an area that's protected by a wall.

✓ Slopes, windy areas, shady spots, and patches that are always wet can create problems in your garden. Make sure you plan for plants and other garden features that can withstand these difficult conditions.

Chapter 2

Be a Soil Detective

IT WOULD BE WONDERFUL if all gardeners had perfect soil that didn't need anything added to it for perfect plant growth. However, very few garden sites do. Depending on where you live, clay or sand may be a main soil ingredient. The pH may be a little too acid, or too alkaline. But you can always improve on what nature gave you.

In this chapter...
✓ The particle particulars
✓ Analyzing your pH
✓ Doing the groundwork
✓ Comprehending composting
✓ Deducing drainage woes
✓ Masterminding mulch
✓ Fertilizer finesse

39

WELL-ROTTED COMPOST, A GREAT SOIL CONDITIONER

The particle particulars

SAYING A SOIL HAS A LOT OF CLAY, or calling it silty or sandy, refers to the size and proportion of certain mineral particles present in the soil. These mineral particles can determine how well your plant survives – a factor that can be quite frustrating to the long-time gardener as well as the novice. But don't despair. Horticultural scientists and dedicated amateurs continue to locate, and hybridize, plants suited to specific sites in all but the most extreme terrain. Or, if you are willing to put in a bit of extra work, you can alter most soil types to fit your needs.

DEFINITION

Hybridize *means to cross or interbreed different plant varieties to produce a new plant, called a hybrid.*

Clay

Clay, also called heavy soil, has a significant proportion of very, very tiny mineral particles.

Each clay particle measures only about 0.002 of a millimetre. To see a single particle you'd need a special microscope. Because clay particles are so minute, they tend to stick together when wet.

If you pick up a handful of moist clay soil and squeeze it, you get a sticky, heavy, hard lump. However, when clay soil dries out, as in hot weather, the particle groups separate. The soil then cracks and more moisture evaporates, making the situation even worse. Many gardeners who have predominantly clay soil will grumble that it's very difficult to grow plants in it.

When the minute clay particles stick together, they can become dense enough to prevent full water and air movement. Instead of reaching roots, water puddles on or below the soil surface. If it puddles on the surface, little water reaches the plant roots. If it puddles below the soil surface, the roots may drown. Air does not circulate through dense, compacted soil, either. Air, sunlight, and the right amount of water are essential requirements for plant survival and healthy growth.

CLAY SOIL

Plant roots, which can be as thin as threads, have difficulty reaching down through hard clay soil. And since clay soil does not absorb sunlight easily, in spring when new plants need light and warmth, clay soil is slower to meet their needs.

Clay does have advantages, when you know how to work with it.

Nutrients, whether natural or added with fertilizer, often leach quickly out of other soil types. But the heavy density of clay tends to hold nutrients in place.

Many well-selected plants simply thrive in clay soil. But you must work with the soil a bit. That's where organic matter comes in. This crumbly material keeps the clay particles from sticking together. With it, air, water, and plant roots can easily make their way throughout the soil surrounding the plants.

Sandy soil

Sandy soil is also called light soil. Sand particles are visible to the naked eye. They vary in size, from 5-millimetre coarse sand particles to microscopic sand particles. When rubbed between your fingers, sand particles feel gritty. They don't stick together the way clay soil particles do. While soil containing ample sand warms up quickly in spring, drains well, and is easy to work with, it does have drawbacks.

A matter of air

The major drawback of sandy soil is limited water retention. Sandy soils have large air spaces between the particles. Water tends to run quickly through these air spaces, dispersing beyond the reach of the plant's roots. Fertilizers leach or wash quickly out of sandy soil along with the water, so plants don't get their full benefit. And very sandy soil may not contain sufficient organic matter to sustain healthy plant growth.

SANDY SOIL

You need to fill up those air spaces between sand particles. How? By adding plenty of organic matter.

Organic matter improves a sandy soil's ability to retain moisture and nutrients in the root zone. It acts like a sponge to hold water.

Many homes on the coast manage to have beautiful gardens because the gardeners have added organic matter to their soil. However, because organic material tends to wash away, it must be supplemented every few years. If you live in an area like this, always add organic matter to the soil when you're putting in new plants.

Silty soil

Silt particles are between clay and sand in size. When a sample of silt is held in your hand, it feels like flour.

Silty soil is subject to a problem called capping, where a crust or cap forms on the soil when soil crumbs on the surface are damaged by heavy rain or watering, or by walking on the soil when it is wet.

If your soil tends to crust, it will keep air from reaching the plant's roots, and also prevent seeds from germinating.

Silty soil can be improved by adding small amounts of clay to improve the soil structure and incorporating organic materials to encourage the soil to form crumbs.

SILTY SOIL.

Loam

Loam is a rich, dark soil that feels crumbly. It is a balanced mixture of about 40 per cent clay, 40 per cent sand, and 20 per cent silt particles, in combination with ample organic material. Loam is porous, providing good drainage. It retains moisture. It has humus, which provides good growing conditions for soil bacteria, which are essential to plant nutrition. Loam is the soil type you want to try to create.

TESTING YOUR SOIL TYPE

If you want to find out what sort of soil you have, there is a test you can do yourself, but it's not always accurate. Fill a large jar ⅔ full of rainwater (don't use tap water because it's too hard). Add dry soil, no lumps, almost to the top of the jar. Cover tightly and shake to mix well. Then set the jar on a level surface and observe the changes that take place.

Sand particles will sink to the bottom. The smaller silt and clay particles will remain suspended in the water. Within 2 hours, the silt particles will settle but the clay particles may take 2 weeks to settle. You will then see the layers: sand on the bottom, silt next, then clay on top. If you see ¼ sand, you have sandy soil. If you see more than ¼ silt, that's the answer. If you see ⅔ clay on top, you have clay soil. Use soil samples from different areas of your garden.

Analyzing your pH

THE MEASURE OF ACIDITY OR ALKALINITY *is the pH. You will see the term pH used in many gardening books. (You'll also see it in aquarium and chemistry books, and on some shampoo bottles.) It is used because some plants grow best in an alkaline soil, others in an acidic soil, and still others in a neutral soil that is somewhere between acidic and alkaline.*

Trivia...
The term pH comes from the French pouvoir hydrogène, *which means "hydrogen power". It is a measurement of hydrogen ion concentration.*

pH is measured on a scale from 0 to 14. Zero is the most acidic, 7 is neutral, and 14 is most alkaline. This is a logarithmic scale, which means that each numeral on the pH scale actually represents a tenfold change. That is, a pH of 7 is ten times more alkaline than a pH of 6.

I know these chemical terms can be intimidating to some people, but all it means for a gardener is that pH determines what organisms in the soil will thrive and what types of nutrients contained in the soil will be available to resident plants. The pH numbers depend, basically, on the amount of calcium (lime) present in the soil. In general, plants prefer a pH between 6.1 and 7.8.

pH tests

Most plants prefer to maintain their neutrality, but there are those that like life a little on the acidic side, and those that prefer things a bit more alkaline. If pH is very important to a specific plant's success, you will want to test it.

There are two kinds of tests available. The first are the do-it-yourself kits available at most garden centres, or through mail order garden catalogues. They are easy to use, and generally indicate pH by changing colour. For a more accurate test, private soil-testing laboratories will analyze soil samples for you. These tests are more expensive, but can provide information on soil contaminants as well as remedial advice. Enquire at your local garden centre or telephone your local horticultural college for details of your nearest laboratory.

After settlement, a yellow or orange colour indicates an acidic soil

A green solution indicates a neutral soil

Dark olive-green solution indicates an alkaline soil

■ **Soil acidity or alkalinity** *is measured on the pH scale, which runs from 0 to 14: above 7 is alkaline; below 7 is acidic. You can buy an easy-to-use kit to test your own soil: colours are matched against a chart to give you a numerical reading.*

pHiddling with your pH

What if you find out your soil is not what your plant prefers? Additives are available at most garden centres that can change the pH. You must follow the specific instructions on each container.

In general, to lower soil pH (that is, make alkaline soil more acidic), use soil sulphur, iron sulphate, or aluminium sulphate. Or you can fertilize with acid-type fertilizers. You can also make the soil pH more acidic organically by working in peat, leaf mould, sawdust, bark chips, or decayed pine needles. Plants that prefer very acidic soil (pH 4 to 6) include azalea, camellia, ferns, heather, lily, marigold, pine, radish, rhododendron, and yew.

If there's a lot of rain where you live, the chances are you have acid soil. The calcium in the soil, which would make it more alkaline, has probably been washed away by the rain. Areas where the soil is very high in organic material, or sandy soils, also tend to be acidic. In some regions, acidic soil is called sour soil.

■ **Rhododendrons** *prefer acidic soil (pH 4 to 6)*

To raise soil pH (that is, make it more alkaline) for your vegetable garden, add lime – which is a form of calcium.

Be careful when adding lime to the soil, because too much can harm instead of help.

Follow the directions on the container precisely. You can add wood ashes instead, but just a little bit at a time. Plants that prefer a somewhat neutral to alkaline soil (pH 6.8 to 7.5) include asparagus, carrots, brassicas such as broccoli and cabbage, cucumbers, lettuce, onions, peas, pumpkins, spinach, sweet corn, and courgettes.

Flowers such as carnations and irises also prefer soil that tends to be more alkaline. However, if your soil is quite alkaline, sometimes it's easier to garden in raised beds, where you can bring in better soil.

INTERNET

www. maigold.
co.uk/soil.htm

This site provides straightforward advice on identifying your soil type, and raising or lowering your soil pH.

Salty soil

A variety of minerals form salts that can build up in your garden soil. Many plants will not grow well, or grow at all, if the soil is salty. There may be one or several causes, including animal manures, chemical fertilizers, soft water from a home water softener, and salty irrigation water. Coastal areas often get buffeted by winds that bring a lot of salt with them from the sea. It's also possible that the soil in your home area is naturally high in salts. In high rainfall areas this salt would pass through the soil. But in low rainfall areas salt concentrates in the upper soil layer.

Testing for salty soil

Soil salt causes several problems. It slows or stops seed germination. It also harms plant roots, which, in turn, results in slow growth. Salt burn may also occur, where leaf edges looked burnt. Saline soil may also harm beneficial organisms in the soil. Testing for soil salt levels requires special equipment – a soil-testing laboratory should be able to help. If you have salty soil, always use fertilizers that have a low salt content and water well with salt-free water. But when you're giving lots of water, make certain your soil drainage is good. Puddles of salt-laden water are not an improvement.

Doing the groundwork

A VARIETY OF SOIL IMPROVERS IS AVAILABLE. Your choice will depend on the type you can find nearby and the needs of your soil. In general, you combine the improver with soil in a 50-50 mix. That means you have half soil and half additive. That can add up to a lot of additives.

Improving your soil

If you're faced with less-than-perfect soil, although there is no "magical cure", any small improvements that you can make will produce noticeably better plants. Giving a bed a good digging over will break up compacted soil and expose it to frost and drying winds, which in turn will help improve its structure. In this way, drainage is improved, air is introduced, and the natural process of organic-matter breakdown is speeded up.

Manure

Animal waste, or manure, is a good source of nitrogen. If you buy it already bagged at a garden centre, the bag should be labelled "dried" or "dehydrated". This means it has been pasteurized, or heat-treated, to destroy any harmful elements, including weed seeds. There are various types of animal manure. Fresh manures, whether horse, sheep, chicken, pig, pigeon, or rabbit, must be very well composted for at least a year before using. That's because fresh manure releases heat as it decomposes, and will burn adjacent plant roots. It may contain a great deal of salt, depending on the animal's diet, and it probably carries weed seeds.

Some commercially produced manures have been treated with chemicals to reduce odour. These chemicals are not good for plant roots. It's better to put up with the smell and choose manure au naturel.

Trivia...

In 1529 author Thomas Hill, in The Gardener's Labyrinth from Oxford University Press, wrote that of all the animal dung, or manure, doves' dung was the best. After that he recommended the dung of hens and other "foules", excepting water "foules". He also gave commendations to asses' dung, "goates" dung, then "oxe", cow, and swine, in that order. Horse dung was "the vilest and the worst". Mr. Hill did not recommend the use of human dung.

You may find that sewage sludge is available in your area. This is usually safe if it is packaged commercially, but you may prefer to use dried sewage sludge. Just make sure that you compost it correctly first (I'll tell you how later in this chapter). However, home composting may not eliminate metallic and other chemical substances that end up in sewage.

Always wear protective gloves when touching human or animal waste products, and clean your hands thoroughly with soap and warm water afterwards.

If you are dealing with animal waste products, make certain your tetanus booster shots are up-to-date.

Wood by-products

Wood by-products include sawdust and bark chippings. Because all wood by-products decompose, they take necessary nitrogen from the soil, sawdust more so than other products. Wood by-products purchased at garden centres have usually been fortified with nitrogen, but if you get wood by-products directly from a timber yard, you will have to add nitrogen fertilizer.

If the by-product is mostly sawdust, you must let it decompose first before you add it to the soil. If you don't, it will form a solid mass that doesn't let rainwater penetrate.

Compost

Compost can be made from fallen leaves, grass clippings, fallen fruit, aged flowers, manures, commercial leftovers, and kitchen organic leftovers. It makes an excellent soil improver, and some gardeners also use it as a mulch.

Leaf mould

Leaves should be left to rot for a year or more before being used as a soil improver. They take longer than other vegetable matter to decompose because they are broken down by fungi rather than bacteria. For this reason, it's a good idea to keep them in a separate heap until they do rot down. You can also buy leaf mould in bulk at some garden centres. Leaf mould especially benefits acid-loving plants and vegetable gardens.

Peat

Peat is more expensive than the other soil improvers, because it must be gathered from ancient wetlands. Peat is basically decayed sphagnum moss that has been compacting for hundreds of years. It is often used with indoor or container plants that demand a true acidic soil environment. Peat is lightweight, holds moisture well, and drains well.

However, peat has its drawbacks as an outdoor conditioner. First, it does not contain any nutrients, so in the garden you may want to mix it with other improvers, particularly those containing nitrogen. Second, peat sheds water when it's dry, rather than letting water soak in.

■ **Perlite and vermiculite** *are very useful if you have a lot of container plants, as they help with soil drainage and allow air to reach into the plant roots more easily.*

Perlite and vermiculite

These inorganic, porous, mineral, white or grey granules are often used for indoor plants. The granules are sterile, lightweight, and constructed so that air passes easily to plant roots. If you use perlite or vermiculite outdoors, mix it with compost and peat to provide essential nutrients. Do not use vermiculite to break up clay soil outdoors or indoors. The clay conjoins with vermiculite, making it sturdier than before. Although attractive, perlite and vermiculite contain little in the way of beneficial elements.

Sand

If you need just a little bit of sand for potted plants such as cacti, it can be purchased in small bags at most garden centres. If you want larger amounts, consider buying "builder's sand", which is available at builder's merchants and DIY stores.

Do not collect your sand from a beach. Legalities aside, beach sand is unsieved and contains a mixture of sand particle sizes as well as salt.

Commercially purchased sand is usually quartz sand that has been washed and sifted through a sieve, so you get larger particles. Sand is most often used to help aerate clay soil, and larger particles are the best for this. However, you must use a mixture of 80 per cent sand to 20 per cent clay soil, or you will create concrete soil, which is worse than the clay you started with.

Comprehending composting

COMPOSTING IS QUITE TRENDY TODAY. *Many gardeners have purchased inexpensive composting bins. Bins are designed for both large and small gardens and instructions come with each bin. If you have an out-of-the-way corner in your garden, you don't need a special bin to start composting.*

Composting basically takes leftover organic material and leaves it to rot or decompose. This decaying organic material turns it into a great soil conditioner. It's the ultimate in recycling. Use a mix of wet materials, such as leafy material and grass clippings, with dry, such as shredded paper, bark, or straw.

■ **Compost bins** *should start with a layer of twiggy materials, building up with waste matter. When the contents reach a height of about 10 to 12 centimetres, add a little manure to the top and leave to decay. Use when well rotted.*

HOW DOES COMPOSTING WORK?

Although leftover organic material just looks like leftovers, it contains micro-organisms, such as bacteria and fungi. Give these minute creatures some fresh air in a compost pile and they quickly go to work.

Earthworms

Earthworms soon enter the picture. As earthworms eat their way through the compost, the tunnels they make create spaces for air to enter, further aiding the bacteria and fungi. The by-products of all this activity are extremely beneficial to plants. So are earthworm waste products, called casts. Some people purchase composting wormeries just for the casts the worms inside generate.

The free-standing compost heap

If you have a large garden and can create a free-standing compost heap in an out-of-sight corner, try the following.

Make a flattened pile of green material such as weeds, leaves, small twigs, rotted sawdust, shredded branches, straw, kitchen vegetable and fruit leavings, eggshells, coffee grounds, farm animal manure, and cut grass. You can add some garden soil too.

Do not pile a whole batch of grass in the compost heap without mixing it with some other compost ingredients first, because grass tends to clump up and turn into smelly slime if it's put into the compost heap in bulk. Slimy grass encourages flies to lay eggs in your compost heap. Do not put herbicide-treated weeds in the compost heap, either, because they will just recycle the herbicide back into your plants.

About once a month, sprinkle a small amount of all-purpose fertilizer over the heap. Water afterwards, and keep the heap moist. The leftovers in the compost heap must be moist to decompose properly. Moist does not mean soggy, though. A soggy compost heap doesn't let air through, and the bacteria, fungi, and earthworms can't grow without air. A compost heap without air gets smelly, like rotten eggs. If this happens to you, stir and turn the heap, adding some dry leftovers as you do.

INTERNET

www.hdra.org.uk

You'll find frequently asked questions on compost here.

49

Piled high and deep

The minimum height for a free-standing compost heap is 1 metre, with a maximum of about 1.5 metres high. You can make it as wide as you want. If you can, use a spade or fork to turn the material so the bottom stuff moves near the top and the top stuff goes underneath. That encourages everything to heat up properly (heat is a by-product of decomposition), which will kill weed seeds and young insects. If everything is done correctly, in about 3 months in warmer climates (6 months where the winters are cool) you should have wonderfully aromatic, brown, crumbly, usable compost.

Some gardeners cover their compost heap with black polythene, canvas, or garden soil to encourage it to heat up faster. If you do, don't forget to pull the covering back occasionally to add the necessary water.

If you don't like turning the compost heap, you don't have to. It just takes longer to decompose all the materials.

Some people, concerned with appearances, build a fence around their free-standing compost heap. Others like the look of leftovers rotting in the sun. It's all a matter of perspective.

The container compost heap

A container compost heap is ideal for the smaller garden, because you can hide it behind some pretty, tall-growing perennial plants. The ingredients for a container heap are the same as for a free-standing one: a little of this, a little of that. The easiest way is to use a ready-made bin, available at most large garden centres and DIY stores for about £45 to £60. They hold about 1 cubic metre of compost and have ventilation holes in the sides and a removable cover.

You can use a large plastic dustbin. Drill holes in its sides, from bottom to top, to provide the air necessary for decomposition. It's hard to stir a big dustbin, so some people add a long piece of sturdy plastic pipe right in the middle before they start adding leftovers. Then they use this as a stirring spoon.

Uninvited guests?

Some people worry that a compost heap will attract pests. However, insects will not meander to your compost heap if it is properly constructed. A good compost heap generates heat as it decomposes. Insects are not usually crazy about this.

Rodents, dogs, and other invaders will not bother your heap unless you have added meat products or bones.

Deducing drainage woes

IF WATER COLLECTS AROUND YOUR PLANTS, *you need to improve the drainage. Plant roots, unless they have adapted to live in marshes, will not survive in soil that's usually soggy. Sometimes it takes a while to realize that your plant's bedraggled look is due to poor drainage, but here's a clue: poor drainage seldom occurs in sandy soils; if you have clay soil, suspect this problem. Other things can also cause this problem. Let's take a look at the symptoms and possible causes of poor drainage.*

Early clues

The earliest clue of poor drainage is water puddles that remain visible for some time after rain or watering stops. Simple! Another clue is which types of plants survive and which don't. If mint, mosses, spruce, and willow thrive and normal grasses disappear as if by magic, you probably have a moisture problem. Trees that do well when they're small but die as they get older and larger are another symptom, as are any size trees or shrubs that die seemingly without any reason after a wet winter.

Do not underestimate the damage and expense that poor drainage can cause.

Plant roots need oxygen. When soil is waterlogged, oxygen is not fully available. Wet soil tends to be low in vital plant nutrients, such as nitrogen. Soil that is constantly wet or damp is colder than dry soil. This slows plant growth in spring, when growth is all important. Wet soil encourages the proliferation of fungus diseases that attack plant roots.

Trivia...

Hundreds of years ago, local legends abounded about why some areas just wouldn't grow anything. Some bad deed was said to have taken place at the site. There is, for example, a hill in Oxfordshire where St. George is said to have slain the Dragon. Known as Dragon Hill, it was said grass never grew where the dragon's blood was spilled. Other barren sites included those where fatal duels had taken place.

Investigating hardpan

Hardpan is a condition of some clay and silt soils in which the particles are so tightly packed that water cannot drain through. A layer of hardpan below the surface can be the sole cause, or a major contributing cause, of drainage problems. To find out if you have a hardpan problem, take a spade and try to dig a hole about 45 centimetres deep in your garden. That should be pretty easy, but sometimes it isn't. If, by 15 to 20 centimetres down, you start scraping at the earth instead of digging, and if it's become a lot of slow, hard work, you've hit hardpan.

You can eventually get pretty far down with hardpan, particularly if you put some muscle into it. Gardeners who want plants to put down deep roots or who want to put in a tree but don't want to dig and scrape for what seems like forever can rent a power digger or hire a professional to do this sweaty job.

B is for bedrock

In some areas, not even scraping the soil gets the hole deeper. It is possible that you have bedrock – a layer of some type of rock underneath the soil.

It is tempting to try to plant in the softer soil above hardpan or bedrock. But it's not wise. When water comes in – hose water or rain – it sits above the hardpan or bedrock almost as if it's contained in a bowl. The roots reach down until they are blocked by the hardpan or bedrock. Then they become waterlogged, and if the situation continues, the roots will eventually rot.

In warm weather, hardpan and bedrock cause additional problems. Plant roots, instead of reaching deep into the soil, are confined above the hard layer, in a shallow layer of soil. Being shallow, the soil dries out very quickly and plants wilt very soon after being watered.

How high is the water table?

Natural water under the earth can be very deep down or almost just below the surface. When it rises above the surface, as in streams or floods, you can easily see it. But if the water is just below the surface you don't notice it or even think about it. That is, until you start digging a planting hole. In addition to other drainage problems, you may see water seeping into your hole. You will either have to plant in another way (in a pot or a sunken container, for example) or consider installing some type of drain line.

Basically, a drain line is a downhill trench with the high point at your targeted planting area and the low point where you want the water to emerge. The trench will have to be lined and pipes installed. You may prefer to use a professional landscaper for this job.

Dealing with drainage problems

Dealing with drainage problems depends on what you want to plant. If you have hardpan, dig down to a minimum of 30 centimetres for a small plant and 1 metre for a small tree. Replace all soil with good topsoil. For a deep-rooted plant such as a tree, you may want to dig down as far as possible, fill the hole with good soil, and then create a raised mound about 60 centimetres high. Alternatively, use containers or raised beds.

Masterminding mulch

MULCH IS ANYTHING *that can be put on the surface of the soil without injuring the plants. Mulch reduces topsoil erosion, helps keep soil from baking in the sun and drying in the wind, and discourages the sprouting and growth of many weeds. Mulch also helps limit soil movement during the winter. Sudden frosts, alternating with sudden thaws, make the soil shift, disturbing plants. In the vegetable patch, mulch scattered underneath such plants as cucumbers, marrows, or unstaked tomatoes acts as a cushion. This cushion decreases vegetable contact with damp ground, a situation that encourages rot.*

When to mulch

To deter weeds, apply mulches in early spring before seeds sprout, or germinate. To control water loss during hot summer months, apply mulches after the ground warms up in spring. If you place a mulch too early, the soil stays cool and plant growth slows. This particularly affects vegetables such as corn, cucumbers, melons, and early-ripening tomatoes, which need warmth for a good start. To protect more delicate plants from winter frosts, apply mulch straight after the first hard frost of the season.

Do not apply mulch on seeded areas or around emerging seedlings. This will encourage damping off, eliminating your tiny new plant growth almost overnight.

If you're growing seedlings, wait until they have become reasonably sturdy before you start mulching around them.

DEFINITION

Damping off *is the collapse of a young plant as a result of fungal disease that destroys the plant's roots.*

Picking the perfect mulch

As with soil improvers, lots of different substances might be used as a mulch. Some are organic and some are not. The best mulches are inexpensive, easy to get, and easy to use. Organic mulches disintegrate over time, but you can then dig them into the soil, which is quite beneficial.

Mulches can be made from all manner of substances, such as spent mushroom compost, rotted garden compost, chipped bark, shredded bark, and coconut shells. There are even decorative mulches, such as gravel, pebbles, or glass beads. I'm going to go into a bit more detail about mulches on the next few pages.

Pebbles

Gravel, pebbles, or crushed rock make an elegant mulch, and they are often used for the front of the house, where looks are everything. Colours include white, grey, shades of beige-brown, and a dark auburn of volcanic rock. These colours can be selected to blend with your home or patio.

Be careful when putting stone mulches close to a lawn, because mowers can pick up and throw the pieces. This can cause very serious injury to the person mowing and to passers-by. Rock mulches don't integrate into soil over time, the way organic materials will. They tend to scatter onto adjacent pathways, so put down more rock about every 5 years.

■ **The muted shades** *and smooth texture of pebbles look particularly attractive next to plants of different hues of green, such as golden creeping jenny and bugle. The effect looks very natural.*

Black polythene

PLASTIC MULCH

I call this black bin-liner plastic, which, to me, describes it better. Sold in rolls from about 30 to 120 centimetres wide, black plastic makes a functional, if unattractive, mulch. Sunlight doesn't penetrate the plastic, so weed germination (and thus weed survival) is minimal. An added benefit is its heat-holding capacity.

Planting within black plastic is simple. You carefully cut a hole in the plastic where you want your plant to grow. Then you dig a planting hole, backfilling with a mixture of soil and organic matter. Plants sited within a plastic mulch stay about 5 degrees warmer than their plastic-free neighbours. Those few degrees can mean the survival of tender plants when the weather fluctuates.

Many gardeners use black plastic covered with a layer of bark chippings or gravel. The covering enhances the plastic's appearance, endurance, and safety. Plastic without a covering can be slippery when wet. Covered, it is less exposed to the elements and to damage caused by foot traffic. If you do decide to use this lightweight material alone, you will have to weight it down. You can do this with either soil or rocks.

Black plastic will shred after a few years. If unprotected, plan on replacing it in 2 to 3 years. Note that plastic is not the best choice on poorly drained areas, because it holds the moisture in the ground.

Wood products

Bark chips, usually brown or reddish-brown, often come from pine, cedar, fir, or Scandinavian redwood trees. Quite natural looking, bark chips make a very attractive mulch. Some gardeners put a layer of black plastic beneath the bark to help keep weeds away. Bark chunks, available in various sizes, tend to scatter or thin after a while. Plan on augmenting them every 2 to 3 years. The larger the size initially, the longer bark chips last and the less they tend to scatter.

BARK CHIPS

Another option is to use small wood chips in various sizes. Spread them in a generous layer that is around about 7 centimetres deep. If these small wood chips are used continually and not mixed with anything else, you may need to add a bit of extra nitrogen fertilizer.

If you're considering sawdust, use only well-composted sawdust. If you simply can't wait, you can mix it with shredded fallen leaves or straw bits to break it up. As with chipped wood, some gardeners like to add some extra nitrogen fertilizer to their sawdust mulch.

In some areas there is a plethora of pines, and therefore pine needles. They are quite useful as a mulch if you have acid-loving plants, such as azaleas, camellias, chrysanthemums, and rhododendrons. However, you must remember never to smoke a cigarette or use a match around dry pine needles. They are extremely flammable. Old, shredded, oak leaves are also useful around acid-loving plants.

■ **Bark chunks and chips** *help to control weeds by blocking out the light. The mulch will need augmenting, but should last for several years.*

Your recycled garden

Fallen leaves and dried lawn clippings must be used as a team in order to make an effective mulch. Using just leaves, or just lawn clippings, will eventually result in a matted, smelly, damp blanket.

Straw

Many years ago, straw was commonly available, and in some areas, especially if you live near farmland, you may still be able to get it. It usually makes a good, clean mulch that eventually decomposes to benefit the soil internally as well as externally. When using straw as a mulch, aim to spread it about 15 centimetres deep, where practical. Make sure the straw you buy doesn't contain any weed seeds or grain, however, or you'll live to regret it. And, of course, never smoke a cigarette or use a match around straw. It is extremely flammable.

■ **A straw mulch** *provides a thick layer of light and airy protection around delicate flowering strawberry plants. It also helps improve the soil when it decomposes.*

How much mulch?

Mulch depth depends a lot on what type of mulch you are using. With chipped wood, shredded leaves, or grass clippings, your mulch should not be more than 5 centimetres thick after it settles down. Any thicker than that, especially around shallow-rooted plants, and you may suffocate the roots. If you are using coarser materials, such as bark chips, you can mulch up to about 10 centimetres thick. The open texture allows for good air movement. When mulching around young trees, make a mulch circle that is at least 60 centimetres wide. Continue enlarging the area as the tree grows.

Regardless of plant type, keep all organic mulches about 2.5 to 5 centimetres away from the trunks of trees, shrubs, and other plants. And mulch perennials at the end, not at the beginning, of a damp period.

Mulches hold moisture and, when they're next to the base of a plant, this can lead to crown rot, which is caused by bacterial and fungal organisms.

INTERNET

www.hdra.
org.uk

This site has tips on how to mulch, what to use, and the benefits of each type of mulch.

Fertilizer finesse

FERTILIZERS PROVIDE *nutrients for your plants, keeping them strong and healthy. The fundamentals of fertilizing follow.*

Even if chemistry was your worst subject at school, you must understand that successful plant growth requires the presence of certain elements.

To grow successfully, plants need boron, calcium, carbon, chlorine, copper, hydrogen, iron, magnesium, manganese, molybdenum, nitrogen, phosphorus, potassium, sulphur, and zinc. They also require these key elements in specific amounts. It's just like the measuring you do when you're baking a cake: so much flour, so much sugar, so much salt, so much fat.

Take heart. Although all of the elements are required, you really need to know about only three – nitrogen, phosphorus, and potassium. Nitrogen is part of each plant cell. It helps leaves and stems grow, and helps leaves turn green. Phosphorus encourages root growth. Potassium is very important for good flower and fruit production. It also helps plants resist disease organisms and balances the actions of nitrogen and phosphorus. Potassium is sometimes called potash.

Reading the label

Different types of plants need different amounts of nitrogen, phosphorus, and potassium. That's why you must read the container label when purchasing fertilizer. Generally, nitrogen will be abbreviated as N on a fertilizer label, phosphorus as P, and potassium as K. The amount of each element in the fertilizer is usually expressed as a number. Nitrogen always goes first, then phosphorus, then potassium. So a 10-6-4 fertilizer, for example, has 10 per cent N, 6 per cent P, and 4 per cent K. These numbers usually add up to 20 per cent. What's in the other 80 per cent? Filler material and small amounts of the other elements, which are needed for various plant growth processes.

In general, lawns require a fertilizer high in N and perennial flowers or fruiting plants require a fertilizer high in K. Annuals often don't require fertilizer if they're planted in enriched soil.

Different fertilizer types

Liquid fertilizers are most often used for container plants, but you can use them in the garden too. Just follow the directions and place the desired amount of liquid into a specific amount of water. Liquid fertilizers in solution can be used in a watering can or sprayed on plant leaves as foliage fertilizer. They are high in nitrogen.

Combined fertilizers are fertilizers mixed with weed killers, fungicides, or insecticides. This is stated on the package. If you're a beginning gardener, it is best to purchase each item separately, using each as needed.

Always read labels carefully before you buy a product, and again before you use it in the garden.

Organic fertilizers are, of course, fertilizers that are natural or organic. Because packaged fertilizers are made up of chemicals, they are sometimes called "inorganic" fertilizers. Organic fertilizers include manures, bone meal, and wood ashes. Bone meal is high in phosphorus and doesn't burn seeds the way inorganic fertilizers might. It is often used when planting bulbs, because it releases phosphorus slowly.

Wood ashes are a good organic potassium source, but go lightly, because wood ashes can raise the soil pH. Blood meal, which is powdered blood obtained from abattoirs, is high in nitrogen. Use it lightly and always handle it wearing gloves, washing your hands well with warm water and soap afterwards.

Trivia...

Many years ago, farmers thought rotting leather was a great fertilizer for peach trees. They would travel for long distances seeking discarded boots and other leather items, which they would then bury as close as possible to their peach trees. You can try it if you like, but it will probably just give your dog something to dig up.

Perfect timing

There are two prime times to fertilize. The first is when the garden is full of spring flowers and trees are starting to fruit. The second is after plants have stopped growing in the autumn. This allows the fertilizer to become available as root growth begins anew in spring. Do not fertilize newly installed plants. They're shocked enough. Wait a few weeks.

And technique

The simplest way to disperse fertilizer for small areas is with your gloved hand, or with a hand-held *broadcast spreader*. For lawns, a *drop spreader* does a more even job. There are also fertilizer attachments for your garden hose, and mechanical spreaders. A good garden centre will have a whole range of tools to choose from.

Fertilizer must reach the roots to be effective. Around plants, try to work in the fertilizer 2.5 to 5 centimetres deep, and water well after fertilizing. For big trees and shrubs, root feeder spikes are available at most garden centres. Avoid fertilizing seedlings until they have at least three true leaves – the leaves that form above the two baby leaves. Remember, a little fertilizer goes a long way – too much can burn and over-stimulate plants.

DEFINITION

Broadcast spreaders *consist of a container, a disc, and a crank. You put the fertilizer in the container and turn the crank, which turns the disc to disperse fertilizer evenly.* Drop spreaders *consist of a container mounted on wheels and no disc. As you push the container along, the fertilizer falls from holes in the bottom. You can adjust the size of the openings on the holes.*

A simple summary

✓ Clay and silt soil particles stick together, preventing full air and water movement. Sandy soils have problems holding water.

✓ You can alter most soil types to fit your needs. If possible, you want to create a balanced soil mixture of clay, sand, and silt with lots of organic matter.

✓ Some areas of the garden may have drainage problems. This can be caused by clay soil, hardpan, bedrock, or a high water table. Drainage problems should be fixed.

✓ The pH and salinity of your soil will greatly affect the health of your plants.

✓ If possible, do a soil analysis of various parts of your garden to determine what type of soil you have. You can then choose plants accordingly, or do what you can to improve the soil quality.

✓ Ingredients that can be dug into soil as improvements include well-rotted farmyard manure, garden compost, wood by-products, leaf mould, peat, and sand.

✓ Composting means taking organic material and letting it decompose to form a soil improver or a mulch. This can be done in an open heap or in a container.

✓ Mulches are placed on top of the soil to protect nearby plants. They include bark chips, chipped wood, sawdust, pine needles, gravel, crushed rock, black polythene, and straw.

✓ Most soils aren't perfect. Adding proper amounts of fertilizer at the right time is very beneficial to plants. Nitrogen (N), potassium (K), and phosphorus (P) are the most common ingredients in fertilizers.

✓ Fertilization adds important nutrients for plant health. It is best done in early spring, and then again in the autumn.

Chapter 3

Tool Talk

THE VARIETY OF TOOLS offered at a large garden centre or ironmonger can make your head spin! When it comes to tools, you really can keep it simple, or you can go all out and buy a whole range of fancy tools. But plan ahead so you know what you're likely to need.

In this chapter...

✓ Hand-held tools

✓ Long-handled cutters and pruners

✓ Digging big holes

✓ Raking it in

✓ Hoe ho

✓ Lawn mowers

✓ Gardening extras

✓ Where to put the tools?

Hand-held tools

EVERY GARDENER NEEDS some simple hand-held tools. Get ready for some grass stains on your knees!

In my suburban garden, I use hand-held pruning shears, a garden trowel, curved-blade lopping shears, and a long-handled spade with a pointed blade. These are my basics, and I don't need more. You may.

The size and type of garden you have should determine what type of tools you buy. However, some people are gadget-happy, and if that's your thing you may end up with an entire shed full of special tools. You may even buy a huge tool shed to store your collection. That's fine. Gardening can be fun!

Dig those trowels

One of the most important tools is a hand, or garden, trowel. The garden trowel is shaped like a long, narrow scooper, and is used to dig and to place small plants. It may be made entirely of metal, or have a metal scoop with a plastic or wooden handle. Usually the handle is about 12 centimetres long. However, if you search, you can find garden trowels with 30-centimetre (or even longer) handles. These are designed for people who can't easily bend or kneel.

A bulb trowel, also known as a planting trowel or bulb planter, is quite useful. It is used to move seedlings as well as dig and place bulbs. The trowel is narrower than the garden trowel, and tapers to a rounded point. Unless it's very inexpensively made, it will have markings on the blade telling you how deep into the soil you've dug.

Highly recommended by a friend is a dibber, or dibble, a little metal or plastic cone with a handle. You stick it in the earth and give a little twist, and you've got a planting hole. Simple!

BULB
TROWEL

Trowel tips

Buy the sturdiest steel trowel you can afford. Don't skimp here. A cheap trowel may bend the first time you dig into hard earth and break by the third time you use it. It is neither cost effective nor effective.

There are inexpensive trowels, in the £4 range, and trowels priced as high as £25.

If you have a choice, buy one narrow and one wide trowel. There are also ergonomic designs for people with hand problems such as arthritis. You may have to search a bit for the unusual, but in today's innovative market you can usually find what you want. Keep your trowels clean and oiled for maximum efficiency.

Hand-held secateurs

Secateurs are another gardening essential. They are used to cut small branches, such as those on roses, and are also good for taking cuttings for propagation. They come in an amazing variety of styles and a wide range of prices, from about £10 to £50. Note that the price often reflects the tool's cutting efficiency.

Secateurs are designed to cut stems and branches that are about the thickness of a pencil. They should open easily after each closing, and have a firm closing catch to store them safely when not in use. Test several varieties to see how each fits in your hand. For lefties, there are left-handed models available if you look hard enough.

Choosing secateurs

For the general-needs gardener, the best secateurs to buy have curved by-pass blades that work the way scissor blades do. Get the best you can afford. Inexpensive secateurs have a tendency to fall apart at the connecting mechanism, especially if you use them on too large a branch – and you will. The blades also dull very easily.

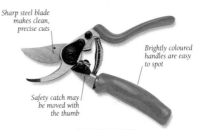

Sharp steel blade makes clean, precise cuts

Brightly coloured handles are easy to spot

Safety catch may be moved with the thumb

BY-PASS SECATEURS

Before buying your secateurs, make sure that they are not too big and heavy for you. Play around with them for a bit in the shop to see that the handles fit neatly into the palm of your hand as you open and close the blades. Make sure you give the blades a good clean with a brush after use, and keep the spring mechanism well oiled. It is a good idea to get yourself a secateur holster, which will keep them safe and handy between pruning cuts.

I was always losing my secateurs and trowels in the garden, until I started tying red ribbons around the handles.

Some gardeners paint the handles of their secateurs red or bright yellow to make them stand out amidst the garden greenery.

Hand forks

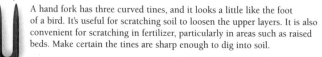

A hand fork has three curved tines, and it looks a little like the foot of a bird. It's useful for scratching soil to loosen the upper layers. It is also convenient for scratching in fertilizer, particularly in areas such as raised beds. Make certain the tines are sharp enough to dig into soil.

You can also get hand forks with straight tines. These are designed to turn over soil in a small area.

Weeders

A hand-held weeder helps you dig weeds all the way out, including the roots. There are many types on the market, including a fishtail weeder, a dandelion digger, and a prong-hoe.

HAND FORK

Long-handled cutters and pruners

NO DOUBT ABOUT IT, *gardeners tend to spend a lot of time on their knees. But when you're tired of bending, you get a chance to stretch. And every real gardener knows that stretching without the right tool in hand is nothing but a warm-up wasted. So make sure you're prepared.*

Lopping shears

Lopping shears resemble secateurs, but have 60- to 90-centimetre long handles and either a curved or an *anvil-type* cutting head. Some have expandable, or telescoping, handles. You'll use lopping shears to cut branches and to trim rose or other thorny bushes from a safe distance.

DEFINITION

Anvil-type shears have a single cutting blade and a solid, non-cutting opposing part. They produce a slicing action.

Since you may be working with your arms straight out or over your head, take the time to lift the shears overhead and make sure you can handle them comfortably. It's quite possible that you'll be using these shears for a long period, and they seem to get heavier by the second.

LOPPING SHEARS

Hedge shears

If you have a hedge, you'll eventually need hedge shears. While their length varies, the most common hedge shears are about 60 centimetres long and usually have straight blades.

HEDGE SHEARS

Hedge shears are for soft-stemmed hedges and those people who enjoy a *topiary* hobby. Gardeners who like perfect lawn edges may use them to get at otherwise inaccessible areas.

> **DEFINITION**
>
> *Clipping trees or shrubs into ornamental shapes, such as squares or animal figures, is called* **topiary***. This is an art form practised since early Roman times. You'll find good examples in many formal gardens, such as some National Trust properties.*

Hedge shears should not be used for pruning branches. This will break the hedge shears, and will not do a very good job on the branches either.

Saws

A saw is used to cut branches that are too thick to be cut with lopping shears. Saw blades may be straight or rounded. A tremendous variety of saws may tempt you, but if you want to keep things very simple, the general-purpose pruning saw is a good choice. It's lightweight and easy to manipulate at awkward angles. A nice second saw to have around is the double-edged pruning saw. While somewhat unwieldy and requiring some arm strength, it works well on branches that are close to the ground.

For upper branches, and/or treasured trees, call a tree surgeon to do your pruning. Large branches are heavy and may not fall where you want them to. Cutting randomly can decimate a tree, preventing flowering, fruiting, and growth, and can slowly kill your tree. Look under "Tree Work" in the Yellow Pages for a qualified tree surgeon and get a few different price quotes before you commit yourself. Estimates are usually free, but do get them in writing.

Your tree surgeon should be licensed and fully insured, and willing to show you written proof of both.

Digging big holes

THE RIGHT TOOLS FOR SERIOUS DIGGING will do a lot to make
your gardening experience a pleasure. Make sure you test-drive each piece of
equipment so you know you'll be happy with it when you get it home.

Spades

A good-quality spade will last for a decade or longer. I'm still using my
father's wooden-handled spade 30 years after he bought it. Get
one with a blade of forged steel, even though it costs a bit
more than the other kinds. An inexpensive spade may bend, or
even snap, with hard use.

Spade handles come in various sizes, as do people. A long
handle may prove easier on your back, but make sure you try
before you buy to find one that suits your height. The handles
can be long, medium, or short, and the
blades can be wide, narrow, rounded,
pointed, or square. A narrow blade
penetrates the ground more easily
when you're digging. The wider blade is
best for moving earth from one place to another. The square one is
best used for construction projects. Whichever you use, don't try
to lift an entire mountain with one shovel-load. After use, clean
and oil the spade for premium performance.

Border spades

The difference between this and an ordinary spade is simply its
size. A border spade is narrower, lighter, and much easier to
manipulate in tight corners and in between plants. It's also a
better tool to use if you have had any back problems. A border
spade is normally sold with a matching border fork.

*When digging, use the ball of your
foot to drive in the spade. Don't
press down with the arch of your
foot on the blade top. You can
injure your foot, as well as slip
and fall.*

■ **Make your legs** *do the work
when you are digging. Keeping your
back straight will avoid back strain.*

Raking it in

IF YOU DON'T have a grass catcher on your lawn mower, you will need a lawn rake, also called a leaf rake. Come October, you may need one anyway. Lawn rakes are also handy for keeping mulch evenly spread. There are large ones for the lawns and leaves, and smaller ones to help you get behind bushes.

SPRING-TINED
LAWN RAKE

Garden rakes have many short tines set on a square or curved back. Some gardeners never buy one. Others like them for levelling and breaking up soil while preparing a seedbed. A garden rake can be useful for spreading compost and cleaning up general garden debris. If you have a large area, a rake with 16 tines is preferable.

INTERNET

www.homeandgarden
ing.co.uk

Search for "choosing tools" on this website for reports on gardening tools and accessories.

Garden forks

A garden fork is a long-handled fork with four long, flat tines. It comes in a variety of sizes, but the main two are the standard fork and the smaller border fork. Forks are used for extracting and lifting vegetables that a spade might damage. Obviously, you won't have any vegetables to dig when you first start your garden, so this tool might be added to your collection later. Garden forks are also helpful for turning compost heaps.

Hoe ho

GARDEN HOES ARE AVAILABLE with a wide variety of bases. The standard draw hoe, or common garden hoe, is quite adequate for most garden needs. This type of hoe is used to chip away at weed patches, as well as general cultivating. Make certain the handle is appropriate for your height and body type, so you don't have to bend over awkwardly to work.

DUTCH HOE

Other hoes include the triangular, digging, combination, and Dutch hoe. If you want two hoes, the Dutch hoe is good for removing surface weeds without damaging plant roots. There are also hoes for specific purposes, such as the onion hoe and the eye hoe.

TAKE CARE

Always hang up hoes, rakes, and shovels. When you take a rest while gardening, do your best to prevent anyone from tripping over, or stepping on, your tools. Place them upright, out of the way, with blade or tines facing away from passers-by. Should it be absolutely necessary to temporarily put a garden tool down flat, place tines, rake, or blades face down. This makes it less likely that an unsuspecting neighbour will inadvertently step on the face-up blade and get clobbered by the handle. This may be funny in tv sit-coms, but in real life it's not.

Lawn mowers

IF YOU HAVE A LAWN, you are going to need a lawn mower. Some mowers run on petrol, some on electricity. You can still find manual push mowers, too, especially at car boot sales. Because your needs and those of your lawn are quite specific, it would be unwise for me to try to advise you on what type of mower to get.

INTERNET

dspace.dial.pipex.com/ town/square/gf86/

The site of the Lawn Mower Museum in Southport, Lancashire. It has the largest collection of vintage lawn mowers in the world, as well as toy lawn mowers and lawn mowers of the rich and famous.

If you buy a petrol-powered lawn mower, you'll need to have petrol on hand when you want to use it. These mowers can be difficult to start unless they have an electric ignition.

Electric mowers require an outlet and the dexterity to avoid running over the cord when you're mowing (although there are battery-powered ones available). All are designed for ease of use on flat surfaces. You cannot use electric mowers on wet grass, and, like all mowers, you must keep them away from children and pets.

ELECTRIC MOWER

In addition to testing for pushing ease, starting efficiency, and safety, you may want to read up on the various models in a Consumer Report. Mowers require regular maintenance, including professional servicing once a year.

Gardening extras

IN ADDITION TO MOWERS, there are many mechanical devices, such as hand trimmers, lawn sweepers, leaf blowers, rotary edgers, and strimmers. There are hand tools in every shape and size. Should you buy any of these things? You may decide you should. Just wait until you know your precise needs. Until then, keep it simple. However, there are a few items you really should have.

Gloves

Unless you like hands pricked by rose thorns and fingernails with dirt under them, gloves are a garden must. They're also useful if you don't like picking up worms and beetles with your bare hands. There are all sorts of gardening gloves. Some are made specifically for dealing with thorny branches. A pair of these heavy-duty gloves, which have long arm extensions, is great if you intend to do a lot of pruning. If you buy roses or pyracantha, you will need them.

Soft cotton gloves are suitable for many ordinary garden tasks. They're inexpensive enough (about £2 a pair) to replace as needed.

If you're handling chemicals, you must use heavy-duty rubber or vinyl gloves. Read the package to see if they are suitable for the job.

Gardening gloves basically come in small, medium, and large. Make sure you buy the right size.

Padding

If you're going to be kneeling or sitting on the ground while gardening, get a soft, rectangular sitting and kneeling pad made specifically for garden use. That means you can hose it off with no harm done.

Wheelbarrow

Eventually, you'll need a wheelbarrow. It is helpful when you're transporting large plants or moving earth, rocks, or compost. You can push the kids around in it, too. Get a good one. You will have it for many years.

■ **A sturdy wheelbarrow** *with long handles will make light work of shifting heavy loads around the garden.*

Broom

For general sweeping and cleaning, horizontal, heavy-duty brooms are indispensable. Make certain yours is reinforced where the handle fits into the broom head. If you don't, you will find that the handle keeps coming out as you sweep – a constant nuisance.

Garden hat

You shouldn't have to think twice about wearing a garden hat or sun visor. You'll avoid skin cancer, and also keep your skin looking younger and healthier. If you're outdoors when the sun is shining strongly, consider using a sunscreen too.

Where to put the tools?

YOU CERTAINLY DON'T WANT YOUR *tool collection to get wet, pilfered, or misused. Although a special corner of the garage is fine for storing tools, as you amass merchandise you may want to consider a tool shed. Sheds come in vinyl, aluminium, steel, or wood. Some tool sheds are quite large and come equipped with windows and doors. Others are quite small. Unless you like stooping over and peering around in the dark, get a shed in which the tallest adult in the family can stand upright.*

Some assembly may be required, or you can buy tool sheds ready-made. If you have young children, the tool shed should have a secure lock.

Wooden sheds are probably the most popular choice, since they tend to blend in more easily with any style of garden. Aluminium sheds are also a good buy. Usually small and requiring minimal maintenance, they may have a door and even a window.

■ **A wooden tool shed** *has a certain rustic charm, as well as being useful for storing your precious garden tools safely.*

Stainless steel sheds are bit more expensive, partly because they must be plastic-coated to deter rust. Here again, the quality of what you get is reflected in the price.

The premium, in terms of visual appeal, are the wooden sheds. As with the steel sheds, quality usually improves with price. But shop around. Prevent deterioration by buying a shed made of hardwood, such as cedar, which is rot resistant. If that's too pricey, look for pressure-treated softwood. Paint the shed with a preservative as soon as you get it, and line it with waterproof building paper from an ironmonger or builder's merchant. Add gutters to keep the rain off the sides. Get the highest quality roofing material you can afford.

A simple summary

✓ Always buy the best quality garden tool you can afford. It really is cost effective. Cheap tools break easily.

✓ For small areas of hand digging, a hand trowel is a necessity. Buy both a slim and a wide version. Tie a red bow to the handle so you can easily find it when you leave it in the garden.

✓ Secateurs are useful for general duty, such as cutting roses or other flowers, as well as trimming wide stems.

✓ Lopping shears have long handles, and some stretch even further with expandable handles. Loppers are used for cutting relatively small branches.

✓ There are power saws and people-power saws for larger branches. For major pruning on large limbs or old cherished trees, consult a tree surgeon. Find one under "Tree Work" in your local Yellow Pages.

✓ Consult consumer reports before purchasing a power mower.

✓ Don't leave garden tools lying around. Someone could trip on them or step on them and be severely injured.

✓ Consider a tool shed to keep your equipment clean, safe, and dry. Make sure there's a lock on it if you have children. You don't want them playing with the shears and saws.

Chapter 4

Water Wisdom

ALL PLANTS NEED WATER, even a cactus in the middle of the desert. But different plants need different amounts of water. Some thrive on just a tiny amount every once in a while. Others practically insist on swimming. And you don't want to drown a dry-loving plant, or deprive one that thrives in damp soil. You have to add water somehow, but how and how much are not always clear. That's what I'll talk about in this chapter.

In this chapter...
✓ Watering methods
✓ When to water?
✓ Meeting the watering needs of every plant
✓ What's in the water?

73

Watering methods

HOW TO WATER YOUR PLANTS *sounds so simple that it's not even worth discussing. But in fact, there are lots of ways to get water into your garden, and your plants will appreciate a little knowledge on your part.*

Watering can

Watering cans are your simplest option, and they're great for adding water to container plants and even raised beds. Some are highly decorative and are used more for ornament than function. Others are made from plain plastic or metal, and either material is fine. A long spout comes in handy when you have to reach into corners at home or in the garden.

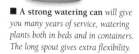

■ **A strong watering can** *will give you many years of service, watering plants both in beds and in containers. The long spout gives extra flexibility.*

If you have overhead plants, try a hanging-plant waterer. This is a plastic bottle with a very long tube attached. You put the open end of the tube into the soil around the plant. A few squeezes of the bottle and your job is done. It beats standing on a chair to water, and is ideal for people with limited mobility.

When selecting a watering can, keep in mind that small containers require many trips to the tap. However, if you choose a larger can, it may be difficult to fit under a tap, and it's heavy when filled. Overfilled, it tends to slosh.

Watering can tips

When hand watering, remember that you must give the plant enough water to wet its roots, not just the top layer of soil. Sprinkle slowly so that the water has time to soak into the soil. Look for a can with a strainer, called a "rose," at the base of the spout, as the flow from these cans is more even and more gentle.

Never use a watering can to distribute weed killer. The potent chemicals can leach into the can material or remain in seams. If you have no other way to get weed killer into your garden, get a special can in a bright colour, mark it distinctively, and place it away from the can you use to water.

Hoses

Buy the best hose possible. It's cheaper in the long run, and a leaky hose will be a tremendous annoyance.

There are several lengths and widths of hose available. The length you need depends on how many taps you have in your garden, where they are sited, and the size of your garden. While it's a nuisance to drag a super-long hose across an entire garden, it's more of a nuisance to be a few centimetres short of your favourite tree. Yes, you can get a hose extender that can be screwed onto the original, but it's easier to get the right length to begin with. Measure the distance from your tap to the furthest spot in your garden, then add 3 metres. This gives you some slack, and allows for the hose to wrap itself around garden furniture, corners, and bushes.

Hoses tend to come in a standard width, but you can get extra-wide ones. While they cost a lot more, the wider ones don't kink as easily as their skinnier counterparts. If the rubber hoses sold at your ironmonger or garden centre aren't too pricey, this should be your choice. The more common nylon or vinyl hoses won't last as long as a rubber hose. A good hose has a great life span and is cost effective. Should you actually have a choice of colours, green goes best with plants, black is a basic, and red makes it easier to see, thus, hopefully, avoiding the trip-and-fall phenomenon.

INTERNET

happygardener.com/text/chap8/ch8doc10.htm

Click here and you'll be taken straight to a site that provides step-by-step information on repairing your garden hose.

The hose connection

If you don't have a lot of taps, you'll want to consider buying a double hose connector, also called a Y-connector. A Y-connector enables you to put two hoses on one tap. You can then drag one hose to the left and another to the right, covering the whole garden. Little switches on the connector allow you to control each hose individually.

Hoses shouldn't be left lying around, because sunlight damages the material. If you can't roll yours up and tuck it in a corner, consider buying a hose reel so you can roll and unroll the hose. Some hose reels are designed to be attached to a wall. Others come equipped with wheels, so you can take them for a walk around the garden. Look at quite a few in a major garden centre before you make any purchase.

■ **A hose reel** *keeps your hose tidy and conveniently rolled up. Two lengths of hose may be joined with a connector to extend its range.*

Nozzles and sprinklers

If you like to stand and water your domain, an adjustable general-purpose nozzle is the single best device you can buy for your hand-held hose. Just keep it simple. Get one for each hose, plus a spare. Use the finer spray for seedlings, the moderate spray for most other jobs, and the really strong spray to hose down your car.

I like nozzles that you twist to adjust the spray. After a while, the trigger types tend to stick or break.

Other types of nozzles are available, including an overhead extension for watering hanging baskets and a root irrigator that is ideal for watering trees.

If you also want to use your hose as a sprinkler, hose sprinkler heads are available in a multitude of designs. Some rotate, some swing left then right, and others spout straight up, then out, like a fountain. Most heads screw onto the end of your garden hose and are placed on the ground, but a spike sprinkler has a base you stick into the soil. I've tried all kinds of sprinkler heads, and now just get the cheapest with little holes that shoot the water up fountain style. They don't jam or rotate the wrong way, and are inexpensive to replace. Keep it simple, right?

SPIKE SPRINKLER

Soaker hoses

If you can leave a flat hose in place, consider using a soaker hose. Water seeps out slowly and isn't wasted into the air or deposited on leaves to encourage fungus growth; instead it goes straight down to the roots. It's necessary to leave soaker hoses in place, because pulling them along or moving tends to twist them, and then the water doesn't go where you want it to.

■ **A soaker hose** *runs along your garden delivering water across its entire length. Some are made of a porous material that lets water seep through; others have tiny holes in them.*

For cosmetic reasons, some gardeners bury the soaker hose under a light layer of soil. If you do this, cover the far end with a small plastic bag to prevent dirt from entering and clogging the system. Should you later install an automated system, soaker hoses can then be integrated.

Sprinkler systems

Many people have sprinkler systems professionally installed. Others tackle this intricate installation job with the aid of how-to books, relatives, and neighbourly advice. Sprinkler systems are great if you have large expanses of garden to cover, or don't want to be tied to regular lawn or garden watering. Depending on the sprinkler system, you can set it on an automatic timer, or turn it on and off by hand.

It's very important that the sprinkler systems are arranged to water the targeted area evenly. Remember that on a windy day, sprinklers deliver water in the direction that the wind is blowing.

Remember that sprinklers wet plant leaves as well as the ground, which may encourage mildew and fungus growth on some plants.

■ **Sprinklers are ideal** *for lawns or large borders – but they do use a lot of water, so an automatic timer may be a good investment if you are likely to forget to turn yours off! Water early in the morning or in the evening for maximum benefit.*

Drip irrigation

Drip irrigation systems are above-ground pipes placed around the perimeter of the garden and adjusted by a central tap. They deliver water just a drop at a time. Some can be adjusted for misting and other special needs. They are excellent for most garden areas, and the preferred choice for slopes that have been planted with plants that really need substantial water. Drip systems require about 30 per cent less water than other systems, and so are especially valuable for drought-prone areas. They do require some maintenance to keep the tiny holes open.

Some gardeners employ a professional to install drip irrigation, others do it themselves. It helps to be handy or to have the advice of someone who has accomplished the job successfully.

INTERNET

www.sutton.com/ resourcecentre/home_ maintenance/project_ one.html

Information about drip irrigation and soaker hoses.

When to water?

SEVENTY TO NINETY PER CENT *of a healthy plant is composed of water. This water evaporates through a plant's leaves, and does so quickly in warm weather. All plants need to replenish this lost water in order to survive. Some plants need a lot of water and some need less. You'll want to pay a lot of attention to water demands when you purchase plants for your garden. This is especially true if you have a very busy schedule and tend to be forgetful about watering, or if you are away from home a lot. In that case, buy plants that won't wither if they get a little dry.*

In general, early morning is the best watering time. As the day progresses, light and sunshine will help dry the leaves. Why do you want the leaves to dry?

Overhead or high sprinkler watering can splash fungus spores from one plant to another. If the leaves dry out quickly, the fungus doesn't get a chance to take hold.

If you can't water in the early morning, early evening is the next best choice. Water early enough in the evening so that plants get a chance to dry off before evening damp and dew appear.

How much water?

So many variables come into play when determining how much to water your garden that it's impossible to answer this question simply. You must consider plant type, soil type, soil slope, time of year, length of day, available light at the site, mulching practices, and, of course, the weather. I don't just mean rain, but also the impact of temperature, humidity, and wind. That said, I'll try to answer the question anyway.

In general, each time you water, soak the soil deeply. In hot weather, of course, you'll need to pay extra attention to your plants. Just looking at their leaves often tells you the story. As temperatures rise, plants lose increasing amounts of water through their leaves. The leaves then start to sag. If garden plant leaves are sagging in the evening, you can wait until morning before taking action. If the leaves haven't perked up, this is the plant's message that it definitely needs more water. Other water deprivation symptoms include flowers that fade rapidly, flowers that fall off, poor plant growth with no other discernible reason, and older leaves turning brown and dropping early in the season.

Meeting the watering needs of every plant

IT SHOULD COME AS NO SURPRISE that different types of plants have different watering needs. I'll give you more detailed advice about specific plants in later chapters about the plants. For now, you should have a basic understanding of how to address the needs of every member of your garden.

Plants in pots

Pay extra attention to the needs of any plant in a container. Don't wait overnight to water a thirsty potted plant. If it looks like it needs water, it does – now!

Unlike plants in open garden soil, container plants have no way of sending out roots to find more water. They rely solely on what you give them.

Flowers

How frequently you need to water your flowers will depend, in large part, on your type of soil. Your goal is for the water to reach the plant's roots, not just slide over the surface or run downhill. If you have good loamy soil, it will absorb and distribute water well. So perhaps you can just water once a week. If you have sandy soil, water tends to pass right through. The soil therefore dries out quickly and you'll probably need to water more often. Clay soil tends to let water enter slowly, retains water due to poor drainage, and has a tendency to puddle if over-watered. Depending on the amount of clay, you may want to let the soil dry out a bit before watering again.

Poke a stick down about 5 centimetres a few days after you have watered, and see what the soil moisture looks like at that level.

■ **A wilting** *potted plant or hanging basket needs prompt first aid. Immerse it temporarily in a bowl of water so that it can absorb moisture through the roots.*

Trivia...

If you like cut flowers to display in your home, avoid watering your flowering plants from above. This can bend the flower stalks and damage the blossoms.

Lawns

Water lawns before they look dried out.

Water-stressed lawns change colour, taking on odd shades of blue-green or green-brown. When you water, make certain the water reaches 15 centimetres into the soil. If you're not sure how long that takes with your watering system, put clean, empty 150- to 225-gram tins at various places on your lawn. When these are filled with water, you've probably accomplished your goal.

If you use an attachable sprinkler on your garden hose, be sure to move it so that all parts of the lawn get an equal and sufficient share of the water.

Trees and shrubs

Newly planted trees and shrubs must be watered regularly. Older trees and shrubs can usually withstand some drought, but when the weather is dry for a long period, you'll have to water. The water must reach the tree and shrub roots, which can go quite deep. Rather than sprinkling or hose watering, you can use a root irrigator, or deep root waterer. This is a long steel tube with holes at the end. You push it into the soil at the **drip line**, and attach the top end connector to a hose. Turn on the hose, and water is forced downward into the root zone.

> **DEFINITION**
>
> A **drip line** is an imaginary circular area around a tree based on where the tips of the outermost branches end and where rainwater normally drips off the leaves.

Another method of watering trees is to let the water trickle slowly at the base of the tree. If you really want to do it right, dig a trench around the base to hold the water in. The trench should be about 7 centimetres deep and 15 centimetres wide.

■ **To ensure that the water** *stays where you want it to stay — around the roots of the tree or shrub being watered — create a basin at the base of the stem and water into it.*

Seeds and seedlings

Seeds must have water, and you will want to keep the soil slightly moist at all times. If you are sowing seeds in very dry soil, water it very well before planting the seeds. Water reaching a depth of 15 to 20 centimetres is not too much. After you have planted the seeds and covered them with the recommended amount of soil, water again very lightly. Use the fine spray on your garden hose or a watering can with a rose on the spout. If the weather is warm, you may want to do this every day, preferably in the morning. Conscientious gardeners put a light mulch over the seed bed to conserve water. Don't worry – the blanketed seeds will grow through this mulch.

Monitor your seedlings closely and never let the soil totally dry out. The roots formed by seedlings are thinner than fine thread. They are extremely delicate and don't have much resilience. Once they dry out, it's unlikely they'll resuscitate even if you water them abundantly.

Be aware that wind is as much a culprit in soil drying as sun. Early morning water, followed by a hot, windy afternoon, can decimate seedlings by evening.

Vegetables

Waving a garden hose several times over the area where your vegetables are planted will not do a bit of good. You really want the water to reach deep into the plants' roots. Shallow watering results in plants that have roots only at the surface. The first dry spell and the plants die. Plants with deep-reaching roots can survive a brief dry spell, because they have more space from which to draw moisture. But they'll only develop deep roots with regular deep watering – going to a depth of about 12 centimetres. You'll get the best results by letting the water soak in gradually, rather than using overhead sprinkling.

While spring is a favourite sowing time, many vegetables can be planted throughout the summer. These late-planted seeds need special care, as heat causes extremely rapid water evaporation.

When putting out late-seeded vegetables, initially cover them with a light mulch to reduce evaporation. Remove the mulch as the seedlings start to appear.

Trivia...

In ancient Egypt the prime source of water was the River Nile, which rose and fell quite a bit every year. As a result, water shortages were common. To obtain a steady supply, the Egyptians used a shaduf, or swipe. This is a long pole supported on a pivot. It has a bucket at one end, and an opposing weight, such as a stone, on the other.

The operator dipped the bucket into the water, then pushed just hard enough on the stone to get it to drop – which lifted the bucket. The pivot allowed for a swivel action. This mechanism was invented by the Assyrians some time before 2200 BC and is still in use in some places.

What's in the water?

AS A RULE, the water out of your tap should be perfectly safe for your plants – you let your kids drink it, don't you? Still, there are some precautions to be taken when watering your gorgeous new garden plants.

Hard water

As water travels through rocks and soil, it picks up particles of calcium, magnesium, iron, lead, and other minerals. Water that is "hard" contains a fair amount of dissolved minerals. If your tap water is hard, you have to scrub harder to work up a lather in the shower, and you may see mineral deposits on your shower heads or taps.

Hard water in areas with alkaline soil isn't much of a problem, unless you want to grow acid-loving plants such as azaleas, camellias, and hydrangeas. You can try adding fertilizers that create a more acidic environment, or dig in a substantial amount of peat when you're putting plants in place.

If you use a water softener, you should obtain your plant water from another source or find a way to by-pass the softener. Continued use of softened water is harmful to all plants, particularly container plants and others with slow drainage. The softener ingredient replaces soil calcium with sodium. This sodium accumulates in the soil. It can cause leaf burn, and also block water transmission through the soil layers.

Distilled water

Rainwater is distilled water, because it hasn't passed through the earth, picking up minerals along the way. If you live in a rainy area, you may want to collect it in a waterbutt to save some money. Or, if you live in a drought-prone area, you may want to collect rainwater to save the environment. Either way, make sure the butt you use has a lid to keep out dirt and insects. It should also have a tap at the bottom. It helps to put the waterbutt on a little platform, so the tap is easily accessible.

Unfortunately, rainwater in some areas is full of impurities from air pollution. If your local weather forecast gives frequent warnings about the air quality, you may want to pass on the rainwater.

Grey water

Grey water is the water from the rinse cycle of washing machines or dishwashers, or water from showers and sinks. Special piping is installed to transfer this water outdoors instead of into the sewer system. Gardeners in areas with frequent hosepipe bans are often interested in the possibilities of grey water. But opinions vary. The biggest problem is that it has soap residue, which contains sodium, and too much sodium kills plants.

If you live in an area with restrictions on the use of water and you need to use grey water, try adding gypsum to the soil. Gypsum is sold in containers at larger garden centres. Just follow the instructions on the container.

A simple summary

✓ For small jobs you can use a watering can. But even if you have a drought-tolerant garden, you will probably need some other type of watering mechanism.

✓ When selecting watering equipment, buy the best quality you can afford. While hoses aren't expensive, drip irrigation and sprinkler systems can be. It's better to put off the purchase until you can afford a bit better quality.

✓ When putting in a drip irrigation or sprinkler system, consider hiring a professional to do the job. If you want to do it yourself, read how-to books, consult with other do-it-yourselfers, talk to garden centre staff, and get some help with the manual labour.

✓ Water early in the morning if at all possible, to give leaves a chance to dry off throughout the day. This helps prevent fungal infections from taking hold of your plants.

✓ Water deeply each time, except if you have hardpan, which requires shallower and more frequent waterings.

✓ Seeds and seedlings require special care. Water them daily, because even a little thirst can quickly kill them.

✓ Plants tolerate most types of water, but avoid the additives in softened water and grey water. If grey water use is unavoidable, add gypsum to the soil.

PART TWO

CHRYSANTHEMUMS FOR SUMMER TO AUTUMN COLOUR

FLOWERS FANTASTIC

SPRING ALWAYS SEEMS to begin when you can cut a bouquet of fresh flowers from your garden. It's amazing that, come April in many areas, the ground is already alive with yellows, reds, and purples. Colour stretches until autumn in the well-planned floral garden.

It may seem a difficult job to plan and place this panorama of colour and beauty. But you can *keep it simple*. Selecting the right plant

for the right place is a challenge most gardeners come to enjoy.

Flowering plants are usually divided into three major categories: annuals, which bloom in their first year and then die; perennials, which come back year after year; and bulbs, which are in a class by themselves.

Chapter 5

Ample Annuals

YOU CAN BUY ANNUALS as seed packets, as six-pack youngsters, or in full bloom. Give the requisite amount of water, the proper sunlight or shade, and a little soil assistance, and simple! Success is yours. In this chapter, I'll concentrate on easy-to-grow annuals for general garden use. I'll discuss flowering annuals that grow best in containers in Chapter 18.

In this chapter...
✓ Let's shop!
✓ Lightly shaded annuals
✓ Drought-tolerant annuals
✓ Damp-site annuals
✓ Fragrant annuals

A MAGNIFICENT DISPLAY OF VIOLAS

Let's shop!

YOU MIGHT FIND your first flowers right outside a supermarket in the early spring. A shop like this will usually feature the most popular *annuals*, bulbs, or *perennials* just starting to bloom. The sight of primrose pinks and reds, or pots of early golden daffodils cheering up the day, often compels you to buy them on the spot. Go ahead! You'll get weeks of beauty from your purchase.

It won't be long, however, before you find yourself spending some serious time at a garden centre. You'll find a wide selection of the most popular plants that tend to thrive in your area (as well as those that are a bit more challenging). If you look around thoroughly, you'll be amazed at the variety of plants and equipment you'll find. Because these big retailers purchase in quantity from growers and distributors, their prices are usually fair, too.

■ **Pink and white** *spring tulips interplanted with annual bedding plants provide a colourful spring display against a background of burgeoning foliage.*

Once you discover the joys of gardening, you'll start reading gardening books and catalogues, too. And sooner or later, you'll make the grand leap to the true garden nursery. Here there may be an acre of plants, many different varieties of the same species, and a bewildering array of choices. Unless you have a gigantic garden (and a gigantic bank account), you won't be able to buy everything that catches your eye. So how do you choose?

Selecting sensible plants

The true novice often visits a garden centre, sees some attractive blooming plants, brings them home, puts them in the ground, and watches them wilt. Disappointed but not discouraged, the novice returns to the garden centre. This time the new gardener asks some questions: "Does this need a lot of water?" "I have a shady area; what do I plant?", and "Do you have something that smells nice?"

If you recognize yourself in this scenario, wait a minute before you leave home. Stand in the garden, be it large or small, and write down something based on the following: "I need plants that are so many centimetres or so many metres tall. The place I want to put them is sunny. Or shady. Or semi-shady. I need drought-tolerant plants because I tend to forget to water. I want (or don't want) bees in my garden. I do (or don't) want plants that demand a lot of attention." Take that list with you when you go shopping. (You might want to go in with just a mental list, but how many times have you come back from the supermarket with everything except the milk?)

If you are really serious about getting the correct plant, take a generic garden book with you that has a fairly complete plant identification list and description. Garden centre descriptions can be a bit over-enthusiastic, giving scant information on whether a plant will survive in less than ideal conditions, and garden books are often more practical.

Pick a pack of plants

When you're at the garden centre, you'll find many plants in 1-litre pots, usually priced at £3 and up.

Purchase only plants that look healthy.

If they are sickly in the container, they are going to have an extremely difficult time surviving the move from one place to another. Plants in 1-litre containers and larger should not have dying leaves, roots desperately pushing their way out of the can, or little insects having a meal.

A popular way to buy plants is to get an inexpensive six-pack. These trays of six little plastic cubicles containing young plants are the best way to purchase annuals – which look best in small groupings. Again, look for healthy plants, just as you look for healthy green vegetables in the supermarket. You don't buy wilted lettuce or parsley, so don't buy a wilting green plant, regardless of its size.

Healthy, green top-growth

Sturdy new shoots

Compost just moist

Roots just visible around the root ball, but not congested

A HEALTHY CONTAINER-GROWN PLANT

When you're buying a six-pack, make certain you get all the plants you are paying for. Count them.

And while you're at the garden centre, buy a large sack, or two, of soil improver. Pick the one that's best for your soil (remember, we talked about that in Chapter 2). You're probably going to need it. Keep your shopping simple, too.

Bringing home the blooms

Make your trip to the garden centre your last stop. Do not leave your plants in the car while you run other errands. Remove your plants from the car as soon as you get home and place them in a shady, cool site. Give your purchases a drink of water while they are in the container. Plant them promptly. While plants can sit a day or two in 1-litre containers, those little six-packs will not hold a plant for very long. Hopefully, you have already dug the site and integrated some organic soil. No? Do it now.

INTO THE GROUND

1 Transplant as gently as possible

Remove your plant carefully from its container, keeping the roots and soil in one ball. Place in the hole you've made in the ground, and fill in with good, organically enriched soil.

2 Give your new plant extra care

Gently press down the soil with your fingers and water thoroughly. Over the next 2 weeks, don't let the soil dry out: lack of water, combined with the shock of being moved, can kill new plants.

UNDERSTANDING SCIENTIFIC NAMES

Throughout this book, and in many gardening books, you'll see plants referred to by their scientific names. Although you may not be into learning Latin just to garden, these names are actually quite useful. Common names, such as "pansy", vary greatly from region to region. Even your nextdoor neighbour may use a different name for a particular plant than you do. To add some uniformity to how we refer to plants, scientists developed a universal naming system using Latin words. Of course, not all scientists agree about what the correct Latin name for a plant is, and plants are often reclassified. Be that as it may, a basic understanding of how to read the Latin names will help you select the plants you want.

Dividing large groups into smaller ones

Science divides all living things into large groups, which are then divided into smaller and smaller groups. Eventually, each living thing is classified into a genus, and that group is further broken down into specific species. Humans, for example, are classified in the genus *Homo* and the species *sapiens*.

Genera and species

Latin names are written in italic type. The genus name is capitalized but the species name is not. Some genera (plural for genus) include a tremendous number of species, while others include only one. So when you see the name *Myosotis sylvatica* alongside the flower forget-me-not, you're reading the Latin name for a particular flower. The genus *Myosotis* contains over 50 species of flowers, including the species *sylvatica*. A short form for the name would be *M. sylvatica*. So what?

Latin names can help

Well, perhaps you're browsing through a seed catalogue, and can't find the forget-me-not *Myosotis sylvatica*. You might find another species in the *Myosotis* genus that appeals to you. Or perhaps you only want the *sylvatica* species. Knowing the Latin name will help ensure that you select the right flower. On occasion, I'll give just the genus name for a group of similar plants, because that is enough information to get you on your way. You'll also see that lots of plants are known only by their Latin name – irises, for example, are simply members of the genus *Iris*.

Lightly shaded annuals

THERE AREN'T MASSES OF ANNUALS that truly thrive in the sort of shade you get under an established tree, but you can still pick and choose what to plant if your area has light to medium shade.

Canterbury bells

Most flowers in the genus *Campanula* are perennials – plants that live on year after year – but the Canterbury bell (*Campanula medium*) is a delightful biennial/annual. Blue, lavender, pink, or white flowers have a bell-like appearance, dangling in clusters among slightly hairy leaves from stems that are about 60 centimetres tall. This plant does like good soil, although it doesn't have to be perfect. Water Canterbury bells regularly. While you can grow them from seed, it's a lot easier to buy a potful at a garden centre. Get them started as early in the season as possible for June and July blooms.

Forget-me-nots

Prolific self-seeders, forget-me-nots (*Myosotis sylvatica*) will turn your garden into a sea of blue wherever you plant them. Just about 15 centimetres tall, they're great towards the front of any bed. They do best in light semi-shade, and are one of the few annuals that tolerate fairly consistent moist soil. In addition to the traditional blue flowers, there are pink and white varieties, but you may have to search for these in garden catalogues. Sow seeds in very early spring (you may never need to buy seeds again) for flowers from mid-spring until mid-summer.

> ### Trivia...
> In the Victorian era, a codified language of flowers was developed to serve as a guide for appropriate flower use. A flower's symbolic meaning was taken quite seriously, and books were written that explained the language. A gift of a bouquet of forget-me-nots, according to the language of flowers, signified friendship and fidelity.

■ **Dainty forget-me-nots,** like this variety of Myosotis sylvatica known as Victoria Rose, will cover a bed with tiny pink flowers every spring for years to come.

Balsams

Many people simply use the Latin name *Impatiens* when referring to this genus of annuals. From the word for "impatience" in Latin, *Impatiens* has the habit of propelling its seeds outwards when its seedpods are touched. This is an annual that tends to have a lot of offspring for you to enjoy each summer. I like the balsam variety (*I. balsamina*) and the busy Lizzie (*I. walleriana*), *a perennial that is usually grown as an annual*. Busy Lizzie gets its name from the plant's determination to be the one with the most blooms.

> **DEFINITION**
>
> **A perennial usually grown as an annual** *is a plant that has a very short life span. Instead of trying to get it to grow from year to year, as a perennial does, most gardeners re-seed or replace it every year.*

BUSY LIZZIE
(*Impatiens walleriana*)

Colours include pink, white, orange, salmon, and red, with both single- and double-flowering varieties widely available. Size ranges from 15 to 90 centimetres high, depending on the variety. The flowers can reach 5 centimetres wide, so space the plants accordingly. *Impatiens* likes semi-shade and shade, in that order. You will have to keep the soil slightly moist to keep the plants happy. If you're going to plant from seed, sow in early spring. Don't put them out in the garden until after the last frost, as they are not frost tolerant.

Pansies

Although pansies (*Viola* x *wittrockiana*) don't object to some sun, they do best in semi-shade with regular watering. Loamy soil should be provided. Colours, and colour combinations, are so striking, especially close-up, that you will want them in masses along pathways as well as in window boxes closer to eye height.

When you put pansies out depends on where you live. For those in cold winter areas, set out nursery plants in spring, after the last frost, to enjoy summer blooms. For those in mild climates, you can purchase nursery-grown pansies in the autumn and have blooms through the winter and into the spring. You'll want to pick these delicate flowers for table decorations. The more you pick, the more new flowers will appear.

PANSIES (*Viola x wittrockiana*)

More annuals for shade

Among the other visual delights that will tolerate some shade are flowering tobacco (*Nicotiana*), larkspur (*Consolida*), love-in-a-mist (*Nigella*), mignonette (*Reseda odorata*), and wishbone flower (*Torenia fournieri*). Coleus (*Solenostemon scutellarioides*) have tiny flowers that are not much to look at, but their spectacular patterned leaves, in colours ranging from white to green to red to purple, will brighten your garden from the time you plant them until the first frost.

Drought-tolerant annuals

THERE ARE ANNUALS *that will live on less water. But "less" does not mean no water at all. Even if you decide to plant drought-tolerant annuals because of water shortages, water bills, or a dislike for watering, you still must water for a few weeks to get the plants started.*

CREEPING ZINNIA (*Sanvitalia procumbens*)

Creeping zinnia

This looks like a miniature zinnia or daisy that happens to be trailing on the ground. Flowers are bright yellow or orange, single or double, with dark purple centres. Plant seeds in mid-spring, or buy young plants in six-packs (but be aware that flowering plants don't transplant well). Place the plants about 12 centimetres apart to leave room for them to creep outwards.

Because it doesn't grow to more than 15 centimetres high, place creeping zinnia (*Sanvitalia procumbens*) along a path or in another spot where you'll be sure to see it. Once you get creeping zinnia started, it needs very little water. You should see blooms from mid-summer until the first frost.

Four o'clocks

If you have children who would like to have their own little garden, four o'clocks (*Mirabilis jalapa*) are a great choice with their large, easy-to-handle seeds. Flowers can be scarlet, white, yellow, or *variegated*, and they appear in profusion from late spring until autumn.

The hard, round, black seeds fall to the ground, and if they land in a suitable spot, you'll have new plants next year. Underground tubers may also provide a plant resurgence. I have grown four o'clocks successfully in clay soil and against a white wall. Although they need water to start, they tolerate dryness and just adore heat.

■ **For evening scent** *choose* Mirabilis jalapa's *fragrant, trumpet-shaped flowers that open later in the day, hence its name four o'clock.*

Globe amaranth

When buying globe amaranths (*Gomphrena globosa*), make sure that you get the type that you want. There are dwarf varieties, 15 centimetres high, that are suitable for edging; and taller ones, up to 45 centimetres high, that make great cut flowers. The flowers can be white, yellow, scarlet-purple, or rose. Give these flowers full sun and average soil.

Globe amaranths are one of the few flowering annuals that don't mind a bit of wind. In fact, the wind may scatter seed at the season's close, so that you have more amaranths next year.

Trivia...

You can create stunning dried flower arrangements with globe amaranths. Pick the flowers as they begin to open. Hang groups of five stems upside down in a cool, shady place until they are dry. Unlike many dried flowers, these will keep most of their colour.

Sweet alyssum

Sweet alyssum (*Lobularia maritima*) is a low-growing (10 to 20 centimetres high) edging plant with the most delightful honey-sweet fragrance. This is an easy annual to grow from seed. It thrives in just about any soil if it's given enough water to get it started. Then water a bit from time to time for the most flowers.

Most often seen in white, there are also pinks and purples, but they don't seem to be as hardy or prolific. Some varieties, such as carpet of snow, will self-seed, cropping up in the oddest garden places, but always lovely. In mild climates, you may have alyssum almost throughout the year. If you like the sight of a roving bumblebee (or three), you'll discover that this hardy annual seems to send out an invitation to visit.

SWEET ALYSSUM (*Lobularia maritima*)

Statice

Not only does this papery-flowered plant do best when in dry soil, but it thrives in seaside gardens. This, no doubt, accounts for its other common name – sea lavender. Colours include blue, lavender, and rose, with lavender being the most common.

Statice (*Limonium sinuatum*) will grow to about 60 centimetres high. Plant seeds early in the spring for mid-summer blooms, or buy six-packs at the garden centre.

STATICE (*Limonium sinuatum*)

Do not put statice near plants that get a lot of water. Over-watering can be quickly fatal.

More drought-tolerant annuals:

- African daisy (*Arctotis*)
- Cape marigold (*Dimorphotheca*)
- Rose moss (*Portulaca*)

- Scarlet sage (*Salvia*)
- Sunflower (*Helianthus*)
- Zinnia (*Zinnia*)

Damp-site annuals

THERE IS A DIFFERENCE, *of course, between damp and soggy. If you have soggy soil, think perennials rather than annuals. There are few annuals that truly thrive in constant moisture. But if things are just a little damp, try the forget-me-not, Madagascar periwinkle (Catharanthus), pansy, spider flower (Cleome hassleriana), or one of the following annuals.*

Poached-egg plant

Try planting poached-egg plant (*Limnanthes douglasii*) in a spot like this in spring or autumn. Once you have it growing and it's happy, it will self-seed. This small annual measures only 15 centimetres high, at most, but it's quite appealing, and suits its nickname of poached-egg plant. From summer until autumn, yellow-green leaves are crowned with yellow-centered white flowers.

INTERNET

www.e-garden.
co.uk

This gardening site features lots of articles, problem solvers, glossary, diary dates, and on-line shopping.

Monkey flower

This colourful plant is technically a perennial, but is usually grown as an annual. For some, the 5-centimetre wide flowers resemble a smiling monkey. Colours include browns, yellows, rose, orange, and scarlet, usually with a lot of maroon spotting. Monkey flowers (*Mimulus hybridus*) must have shade, a lot of water, and rich soil with ample organic matter. They are not, in my experience, the easiest plants to grow, but it's not always easy to find plants that enjoy sitting in quite moist soil. They grow to about 60 to 120 centimetres high. Ferns make nice companion plants.

Snow-on-the-mountain

A member of the extensive spurge family, snow-on-the mountain (*Euphorbia marginata*) is more of a background than a foreground plant, since the light green leaves take precedence over the minute white **bracts**. Use it to frame brightly coloured plants, such as some of the vivid dahlias, sages, and zinnias.

DEFINITION

A **bract** *is a group of modified, or changed, leaves. While most are green, bracts are sometimes quite colourful.*

In warmer climates this plant will need some shade, but it does well in full sun in more temperate areas. The coloured bracts appear in summer on plants growing to about 60 centimetres high.

The sap of all euphorbias is a skin and eye irritant, and is poisonous if swallowed.

Wishbone flower

WISHBONE FLOWER (*Torenia fournieri*)

This delicate yellow and purplish, trumpet-shaped flower gives summer and autumn colour. It needs lots of water, so put it where you will remember to sprinkle regularly. A short period of drought will kill it quickly. Wishbone flowers (*Torenia fournieri*) do best in light to medium shade. They grow to about 30 centimetres high, and thus are suitable for quite visible borders. They also look nice in pots. The name "wishbone" derives from the wishbone-shaped pollen-carrying **stamens** nestled in the flower's throat.

> **DEFINITION**
>
> **Stamens** are usually located inside the flower petals. They are usually a slim stalk topped by an anther. An anther contains pollen grains, and is usually yellow.

Fragrant annuals

SOME ANNUALS ARE BEST KNOWN for their fabulous fragrance. If you really want to engage passers-by, try planting some of the following flowers.

Heliotrope

Trivia...

The leaves and flowers of heliotrope turn towards the sun. The name heliotrope is from the ancient Greek: helios for sun and trepos, which means "turning to go into it".

In its native Peru, heliotrope (*Heliotropium arborescens*) grows year-round, sometimes to enormous size. But here it usually acts as an annual, and seldom gets over 30 centimetres tall. The aroma, reminding some of vanilla, is absolutely delicious up close. It is not one of those fragrant plants that grabs you by the nose from quite a distance – a plus for some, a minus for others.

While the scent of heliotrope is world-famous, the entire plant is poisonous if ingested. Contact with leaves may irritate skin and eyes of sensitive people, so this is a plant to keep away from youngsters.

Heliotrope requires a bright, sheltered site in rich soil full of organic material, and needs regular watering. Even if you can't find a suitable site in your garden, think about putting it in a pot by the front door.

Mignonette

This North African native wins accolades as the most fragrant of all garden annuals. Plant it right next to your patio doors, or next to windows that are opened on cool summer evenings. Then sneak some more here and there in the garden, and tuck a few in good-size pots. Mignonette (*Reseda odorata*) needs part shade, good soil, and regular watering. It likes cool summers, and does not bloom well in hot, dry weather. This plant grows about 30 centimetres tall, and small, drab, greenish-yellow flowers appear in groups about 15 centimetres long.

Mignonette heartily resents transplanting, so if you can sow seeds in early spring, do it. Otherwise, move from six-pack to garden quite gently, and do not move it again.

MIGNONETTE (*Reseda odorata*)

Stock

This *biennial* is usually grown as an annual. Stock (*Matthiola incana*) has a spicy aroma that's best in the evening and on cool, overcast days. There is also an evening version called night-scented stock (*Matthiola longipetala*), for those who enjoy their gardens after dusk. Native to the Mediterranean coast, stock likes you to reproduce a similar climate – moist, quite well-drained soil that is high in organic matter. It does best in very light shade, and is best when it blooms before the weather gets hot. Colours include ivory, shades of red, and shades of purple. Stock can grow as high as 85 centimetres, although most plants don't get that tall. You must give stock regular water, but be very careful not to over-water, which often results in rotted roots.

DEFINITION

*A **biennial** is a plant that takes two years to complete its life cycle. The first year it grows from seed to a leafy plant, but no flowers appear. The second year, the plant flowers, develops seed, and dies. If you buy biennials already started at garden centres, you are buying a plant in its second year. In the garden, they'll behave just like annuals, which also die at season's end.*

■ **The spice-scented stock** – Matthiola incana – *has soft, grey-green foliage that surrounds the fragrant flower spikes.*

Sweet pea

Every Victorian garden had sweet peas (*Lathyrus odoratus*), and the delicate, papery, sweet-scented flowers of these plants are just as popular in our gardens today. There are bush sweet peas that reach 75 centimetres tall, and climbing sweet peas, and both are excellent for cutting. If you grow the climbing variety, you will need to provide some type of support. Make sure that you give them full sun, ample water, plenty of fertilizer, and good soil.

The scent was bred out of many sweet pea hybrids to obtain more flamboyant flowers.

Make certain your sweet pea packet says "scented", or look for this variety in a catalogue of heritage-type plants.

Sweet peas are relatively easy to grow from seed, so do try it. Unless you want to wait seemingly forever, soak the hard seeds for 24 to 48 hours before planting.

SWEET PEA (*Lathyrus odoratus*)

Sweet William

Sweetly fragrant, this low-growing annual does best in sun or light shade. Most often seen in the reds and pinks, there are also violet- and white-flowered varieties of sweet William (*Dianthus barbatus*). The flower clusters are about 7 to 12 centimetres wide, appearing in bouquet-like groups. The leaves are usually grass-like and tinged blue or grey. This charming plant looks best in an informal, natural setting. It will self-seed and then behave as a biennial if conditions are right, including good soil, regular watering, a sunny spot, and occasional fertilizer.

A simple summary

✓ There are lots of places to find plants, from the supermarket to the large garden centre. Take a small garden encyclopedia with you to help you pick the best choices for your garden and for unbiased advice.

✓ The least expensive way to grow annuals is to get a six-pack of young plants. These need to be planted in your garden as soon as possible. If you pay more, you can get larger, more established plants in individual pots. Either way, choose only plants that look healthy.

✓ Very few annuals like shade, but there are a few that enjoy semi-shade. Take a thorough look at your planting site to determine how much sunlight it actually gets – and at what time of day – before you buy your plants.

✓ There are a host of drought-tolerant annuals, most of which also need partial or full sun. If well-treated, many of these plants will self-seed, giving you lots of plants in the same area – which you can move or give away to friends.

✓ Not too many like damp soil, so you might try to correct it, or create raised beds. However, there are some that will do fine in soil that's fairly wet, as long as it's not wet all the time.

✓ Everyone enjoys fragrant flowers, and annuals can help add wonderful aromas to your garden. Put them near windows, doors, and patios, so that you can enjoy the fragrance both inside and out. Plant some near the front door to welcome you home in the evening.

Chapter 6

Perennially Perfect

PERENNIALS WILL APPEAR in your garden year after year, becoming like old friends. Some perennial flowers are short-lived, while others, such as the peony, seem to last forever. Keep in mind that most perennials go dormant, or take several month-long naps, during part of the year. If they don't disappear from sight, they may grow so slowly that you get worried about their health. Wait until spring, or mid-spring if you've had a frosty winter, and see if they revive. In this chapter I'll explore some of the best-known perennials, and explain what grows well in different types of gardens.

In this chapter...

✓ Perennial preliminaries

✓ Perennials for semi-shade

✓ Drought-tolerant perennials

✓ Perennials for moist soil

✓ Fragrant perennials

Perennial preliminaries

NATURE DOESN'T USE A RULER when designing a natural garden, and neither should you. On the other hand, you should put some thought into where you plant your flowers. For best results, group your perennials according to their flowering times. You'll want sections dedicated to spring, summer, and autumn flowers. (Remember, there's a chart in Chapter 1 detailing what blooms when.)

The groups should slightly overlap from side to side and from front to back.

It's very important to consider the watering needs of your flowers before you put them in the ground. Regardless of their season and height, plant drought-tolerant plants together, and separate from the water-lovers.

Timing your purchases

The simplest and most successful way to grow perennials, usually, is to buy young plants in pots. You should do this in late autumn or early spring, as soon as the variety appears at the garden centre. Put newly purchased young plants in prepared soil as soon as possible, water daily if necessary to keep the ground around them slightly damp, and then just let them grow.

■ **Planting in groups** is a highly effective way of using plants to fill a bed or border. The impact of mass plantings cannot be beaten.

One major reason flowers die soon after you bring them home is that the plant was bought too late in the season, when the bloom is at least half over, or almost finished. Your plant will not extend itself just because you bought it and popped it into a prime garden site. All is not lost, however, if you have some patience. Next year, at the right time, you'll get your flowers.

Size and shape matter

Place your taller perennials, such as coneflowers (*Rudbeckia*), delphiniums (*Delphinium*), or hollyhocks (*Alcea*), in the rear of your garden, and shorter ones up front so they can be easily seen. An exception would be if you have a very narrow planting site, as is true for many modern homes. You might then want to skip the taller perennials entirely, and instead plant the medium ones and the shorties. If your garden centre doesn't have what you need, check out the catalogues. Modern hybridizers have created miniatures of what were formerly only tall perennials.

If you're installing perennials that don't spread wide enough to make a good show, plant three to five of the same variety together. Repeat the variety planting at least once in a nearby area to avoid an artificial appearance. If you can repeat more than once, that's even better.

■ **Bright yellow and deep red** *coneflowers provide a welcome splash of colour at the back of a border, especially when planted in groups.*

DELPHINIUM
(*Delphinium*)

Considering colour

Colours that clash when you wear them, such as oranges and reds, clash in the garden too, so separate bright coloured flowers by those with mellow hues. Because flowering is seasonal, you'll want to intersperse your perennials with bulbs and annuals. This will help to fill in blank areas and supply continuing colour throughout the warm months. Don't forget tiny flowering bulbs right up front, too.

Perennials for semi-shade

EACH PERSON'S DEFINITION *of semi-shade varies. No perennial will truly thrive in constant deep shade, such as that created by a large tree. However, if they get some sunlight during the day, and you remember to water them, some perennials have a good chance of doing pretty well. What follows is a list of some of the most popular perennials that will tolerate some shade.*

BEAR'S BREECHES *(Acanthus mollis)*

Bear's breeches

This hardy, easy, relatively fast-growing perennial makes an attractive, dark green, stately display under trees that do not have shallow roots. Bear's breeches (*Acanthus mollis*) grows about 1 metre tall and is good as a **specimen plant**, standing alone for show or as part of a border. The underground roots eventually become parents of new plants. If you don't want them, simply pull them out and move them to another site. In late spring to early summer there are tall, dramatic spikes of usually white flowers that get many admiring glances.

> **DEFINITION**
>
> A **specimen plant** *is a single plant, usually medium or tall, that is planted individually. It's designed to serve as a focal point in the garden. The phrase is often used to refer to trees or shrubs.*

Bergenia

This is a plant that really knows how to keep it simple. All you really need to do is give the super-sturdy bergenia some water. It will repay you from winter's end to late summer with intermittent pink flowers on little stalks emerging from leathery, lettuce-like, medium green leaves. It is happy in just about any soil, and eventually forms multiple clumps. These are easy to break off, giving you more plants for free. Bergenia (*Bergenia*) is a great plant for the somewhat forgetful gardener, because once you get it going, it tolerates some neglect. There are all sorts of hybrids with flowers ranging from white to red. They are widely available.

BERGENIA *(Bergenia)*

LILY-OF-THE-VALLEY
(*Convallaria majalis*)

Lily-of-the-valley

Lilies-of-the-valley (*Convallaria majalis*) are super to plant under **deciduous** trees and evergreens that are not overly dense. As you will find out (if you haven't already) it isn't easy to find plants that will grow under trees. Tree roots tend to snatch away water and nutrients, and the foliage often provides too much shade. But lilies-of-the-valley are accommodating. This plant's needs are relatively straightforward – just give it regular water, plus a little extra if you do put it under trees.

> **DEFINITION**
>
> **Deciduous** trees shed their leaves annually at the end of the growing season. They're a reason why autumn is such a lovely season.

It will multiply cheerfully underground, sending up 20-centimetre-long green leaves in the spring that disappear in the autumn. White, waxy, highly scented, bell-like flowers appear in late spring. Lilies-of-the-valley are particularly pretty when potted and set on the patio, and their scent will sweeten an entire room when brought indoors as cut flowers.

If you have young children in the home, or even young visitors on occasion, it's best not to grow lilies-of-the-valley. As lovely as they are, all parts of this plant are poisonous if ingested.

Virginia bluebells

Virginia bluebells (*Mertensia pulmonarioides*) are one of the few perennials that will truly grow in almost full shade, although they prefer partial shade. In exchange for their tolerance, these woodland dwellers (sometimes also called Virginia cowslip) insist on good soil that is kept damp. They'll reach about 38 centimetres high, and pinkish buds appear in early summer. The buds open to sky blue, bell-like flowers.

These plants will multiply and self-seed. Tuck the seedlings here and there to attract bees. At season's end, Virginia bluebells die back. Good companion plants include bee balm (*Monarda*), maidenhair fern (*Adiantum*), or tobacco plants (*Nicotiana*).

More perennials for semi-shade:

- Aquilegia (*Aquilegia*)
- Aster (*Aster*)
- Bee balm (*Monarda*)
- Bleeding heart (*Dicentra*)
- Cardinal flower (*Lobelia cardinalis*)
- Japanese anemone (*Anemone japonica*)
- Jacob's ladder (*Polemonium*)
- Joe Pye weed (*Eupatorium purpureum*)
- Loosestrife (*Lythrum*)
- Plantain lily (*Hosta*)
- Primrose (*Primula*)
- Solomon's seal (*Polygonatum*)

Drought-tolerant perennials

IF YOU THINK *"drought-tolerant" means you can forget to water altogether, think again. It simply means the plant can survive with less water than many others. If you never want to water your garden again, consider paving it over! Bearing the need for some water in mind, here are some less-thirsty perennials.*

LAMB'S EARS (*Stachys byzantina*)

Lamb's ears

The temptation is to bend down and pet the leaves, soft like a lamb's ear, from time to time. These are among the few plants happily placed next to heat-baked concrete, provided you give them some water from time to time. Grey leaves are covered with downy, sun-protecting, silver hairs. The leaves appear on ground-hugging stems about 30 centimetres long. In mid-summer, if you peer closely, you'll see tiny pink flowers.

In winter, with the rain, the leaves turn mushy and you're sure the plant is finished. But in spring, there it is again. Lamb's ears (*Stachys byzantina*) grow into clumps that are extremely easy to separate and move elsewhere as needed. Red or pink poppies are good neighbours for the colour contrast they provide.

Sage

There are entire books, and entire gardens, devoted to sage (*Salvia*), and I think no garden is complete without at least one sage plant. Sage comes in perennial, annual, and shrub forms – well over 700 species in all – so there's something for everybody.

A super-simple perennial is Mexican bush sage (*Salvia leucantha*). The chances are that you'll start with just one in a sunny, dryish corner, and soon you'll be picking places to tuck in a few more. Mexican bush sage, also called velvet sage, has prolific white flowers with prominent bell-shaped, bluish-purple calyces. A pretty, slightly bushy accompaniment might be the perennial pineapple sage (*S. elegans*), which really does smell like pineapple and is festooned with attractive red flowers in autumn.

PINEAPPLE SAGE
(*Salvia elegans*)

Artemisia

Silver, feathery leaves are the main attraction of artemisia, although it does flower in late summer. Once you get one started and notice how nicely it does in that hot, dry space that most other plants shun, you'll think about filling similar garden niches with more. And all you have to do is clip off a few of the longer stems, stick them in a jar of water for about two weeks until they develop roots, and pop them in the ground, giving a little water until they adapt. That's about as simple as it gets!

Artemisia likes the simple life. Don't add fertilizer to your artemisia's soil.

There are several types of artemisia that you might find attractive. The most common is sometimes called wormwood (*A. absinthium*). It grows up to 60 centimetres high, but often stays shorter. Since silvery leaves are usually the main visual attraction, place this plant where it makes a nice contrast with a brighter companion – perhaps one with flagrant red or orange flowers.

■ **Silvery artemisia,** *with its delicate foliage, enjoys an open, sunny, well-drained site. Some species have the added attraction of a pungent fragrance.*

Stonecrop

Generally, stonecrop (*Sedum*) perennials need occasional watering to keep them nice and plump, although *S. spathulifolium* is extremely drought tolerant once it gets started. Usually low growing, from about 5 to 60 centimetres high, the various stonecrops are often used as a low-maintenance groundcover.

Use these sun-adoring perennials as border plants in an area where you don't want to have to work hard. For once, you'll have no soil worries. Flowers are often pink, but there is an abundance of reds, depending on the species. If you want yellow blossoms, they're available too.

INTERNET

expertgardener.com

Click here to join a free gardening club where fellow enthusiasts can share tips and ideas, chat online, search for the latest news and enter competitions.

To get the colours you want, visit the garden centre in summer for the stonecrops in bloom.

Many have leaves that turn reddish in autumn – a nice perk to finish off the year.

Yarrow

Ultra-hardy yarrow is a great choice for the person who claims not to be able to grow anything, but yearns for success.

Silvery yarrow leaves are fern-like and dainty. Of the many types of yarrow (*Achillea*), you're most likely to find common yarrow (*A. millefolium*). Common yarrow flowers come in a variety of colours, including red, yellow, white, and cream.

■ **Cerise Queen** *is a common yarrow* (Achillea millefolium) *with a mass of feathery leaves and flat heads of rich reddish pink flowers in summer.*

These plants will usually grow about 60 centimetres high. If your garden has a sunny background space to fill, try fernleaf yarrow (*A. filipendulina*), which will grow up to 1.2 metres tall. Yarrow will spread a bit, and sometimes a lot, looking quite nice in compatible colour groupings. You can tuck it in among the low-growing lamb's ears (*Stachys byzantina*) for an attractive contrast of leaf textures.

Yarrows are quite nice for flower arrangements, including dried arrangements. This is another plant that you can divide and use elsewhere in the garden.

> ### Trivia...
> *An old English nickname for common yarrow was "nose-bleed". Young women considering a potential husband would tickle the inside of a nostril with a yarrow leaf. While doing this, they would recite, "Yarrow, yarrow, bear a white bow, if my love loves me, my nose will bleed now."*

More drought-tolerant perennials:

- Adam's needle (*Yucca gloriosa*)
- Baby's breath (*Gypsophila paniculata*)
- Butterfly weed (*Asclepias tuberosa*)
- Cinquefoil (*Potentilla*)
- Coneflower (*Rudbeckia*)
- Cranesbill (*Geranium*)
- Globe thistle (*Echinops*)

- Iceland poppy (*Papaver croceum*)
- Maltese cross (*Lychnis chaledonica*)
- Milkwort (*Polygala calcarea*)
- Moss phlox (*Phlox subulata*)
- Ox-eye chamomile (*Anthemis tinctoria*)
- Sunflower (*Helianthus*)
- Tickseed (*Coreopsis*)

I know you're thinking, "But sunflowers were listed in Chapter 5 as annuals!" Yes, some are. And some are perennials.

Perennials for moist soil

REMEMBER that there are varying interpretations, and degrees, of moist, from slightly damp all the way to soggy. Much depends upon the amount of sunlight, fog, and wind that may accompany a moist area of your garden. Of the plants listed here, some will fit your site better than others. When in doubt, talk to an information assistant in a garden centre for advice.

Cardinal flower

In the cardinal flower (*Lobelia cardinalis*), dark green leaves surround summer spikes of bright, flame-red flowers. A group of 1-metre-high cardinal flowers creates a great background for a garden pond, and looks stately at the back of a mixed border of perennials and annuals. Wherever they're placed, cardinal flowers like boggy conditions, and need good soil and ample water. A sheltered site in light shade is preferred.

Marsh marigold

Full of vim and vigour, marsh marigolds (*Caltha palustris*) do well in those marshy garden places where more finicky plants have refused to thrive. The flowers are bright yellow, and appear in small clusters in spring. Plant them in a semi-shady area for best results, but they'll put up with fair amounts of sun or shade as well.

Also called water cowslip and kingcup, these 30 centimetre by 30 centimetre low-growers display best as a splash of colour among your ferns. Dot the backdrop with some of the irises that also enjoy constantly moist soil, such as blue flag (*Iris versicolor*).

Primrose

PRIMROSE (*Primula*)

So often found in old-fashioned gardens, primroses (*Primula*) have never lost their popularity. Modern colours include reds, pinks, salmon, white, and purples. There are *double* and *single* forms available, as well as miniatures. Their height ranges from 15 to 30 centimetres, and each can provide enough flowers for a small bouquet. They are relatively easy to grow, if you water them very regularly.

> **DEFINITION**
>
> *Flowers can be denoted as* **single**, **semi-double**, *and* **double**. *These phrases refer to the arrangement of a flower's petals. A single whorl of two to six petals is found on most wildflowers. A semi-double flower has two or three whorls, and a double flower will have three or more.*

Sweet woodruff

Fifteen-centimetre-high woodruff (*Galium odoratum*)
will survive in barely damp soil. But give it some shade
with ample moisture and it gets so enthusiastic that it
may spread to cover several metres. For the thrifty
gardener, this means division in the autumn or spring
and extra plants to move elsewhere, or to give to friends.
(For more on how to divide plants, see Chapter 19.)

This is a true old-fashioned plant, and you may still
find it listed as *Asperula odorata*, its old Latin name.
In late spring, small white flowers appear in clusters.
Interestingly, the "sweet" part of this plant's name derives not from the flowers but from
the leaves and stems, which, if dried, have a pleasant, hay-like aroma.

> ### Trivia...
> Long ago, sweet-smelling
> bunches of woodruff were
> hung in churches, along with
> dried lavender and roses, to
> improve the air quality.
> Because of its fragrance,
> woodruff was also used as a
> mattress stuffing.

WILLOW GENTIAN (*Gentiana asclepiadea*)

Willow gentian

The colour of willow gentian (*Gentiana
asclepiadea*) is so intense that the phrase
"gentian blue" has come to describe a hue that's
blue with a purplish undertone. In bloom from
late summer to early autumn, gentians are
fantastic in the midst of a garden border, by
a pond, or in a wildflower garden.

There are about 400 species in the *Gentiana*
genus, from very low-growing plants to ones that
are a metre or so tall. Although they need some
personal attention, willows are one of the least
demanding gentians. In time, they'll spread to
45 centimetres and grow to 60
centimetres tall, or even more.

*Ample water and good
drainage are absolute necessities
for willow gentian.*

More perennials for moist soil:

- Bee balm (*Monarda*)
- Dropwort (*Filipendula*)
- Evening primroses (*Oenothera*)
- Joe Pye weed (*Eupatorium purpureum*)
- Loosestrife (*Lysimachia*)
- Solomon's seal (*Polygonatum*)
- Swamp milkweed (*Asclepias incarnata*)

Fragrant perennials

THE LEAVES, RATHER THAN THE FLOWERS, *are the source of fragrance for some perennials. Of course, "fragrance" is a matter of taste. When in doubt, take a sniff test before you buy. Perfumes that are nasal ambrosia to some are bland or downright stinky to others.*

Carnation

Omitting carnations (*Dianthus*) and pinks (similar flowers in the *Dianthus* genus) from the spotlighted list of fragrant perennials would raise the instant wrath of devotees who love them for their distinctive clove-like aroma. Carnations and pinks come in many, many varieties, and so they are divided into several groups.

These favourite cut flowers are fairly easy to grow if you don't live in areas with very hot, dry weather or very cold, wet weather. They are adaptable to coastal sites, and tolerate some air pollution. They do well in full sun, although they appreciate some light afternoon shade at the height of summer. Give them regular watering and good drainage.

Although many plants like organic mulches, carnations prefer gravel or sand around the base, which keeps soil away from the stems and leaves. To prolong flowering, remove dead blossoms.

There are so many colours and *bicolours* available (and so many shapes) that it's best just to look at them in person and pick what strikes your fancy. When selecting, be sure to do the sniff test to ensure the presence of the famous clove-like fragrance, because it doesn't occur in all the groups of flowers.

CARNATION (*Dianthus*)

> ### Trivia...
> If you have young children, grow some white carnations. Cut them with long stems and place in a clear, tall glass to which some red or blue food colouring has been added. Watch the carnations slowly change colour. It's a fun garden lesson on how water and accompanying nutrients travel to parts of a plant.

> **DEFINITION**
>
> **Bicolour** *flowers have two very distinct and separate colours on each blossom.*

Dame's violet

Sun or light shade, good-enough soil, and regular watering are all this exceptionally hardy perennial requires. Also called damask violet and sweet rocket, Dame's violet (*Hesperis matronalis*) usually blooms in early summer with lilac flowers on slim, drooping stems that are up to 1.2 metres tall. Flowers are clove-scented at night, attracting pollinating moths.

If your goal is an informal (and oh-so-trendy) cottage garden, Dame's violet is a "must". It was commonly grown in 17th-century English cottage gardens. Pretty accompaniments to dame's violet are columbine (*Aquilegia*), hollyhock (*Alcea*), monkshood (*Aconitum*), and sweet William (*Dianthus barbatus*).

WALLFLOWER (*Erysimum cheiri*)

Wallflower

Often a bright orange-yellow, but also found in cream, red, and burgundy, these sweetly fragrant flowers are late spring visitors. This isn't a plant for hot, dry areas. It likes a cool climate and ample moisture. If you decide to sow seeds, you must do so very early in the season, or you won't get any flowers until the following year. Gardeners who prefer an easier path buy six-packs from the garden centre in late autumn or early spring. Wallflowers (*Erysimum cheiri*) are great container plants for seasonal colour.

Burning bush

The ultra-hardy burning bush (*Dictamnus albus*) has leathery leaves that exude an intense, lemony fragrance. It grows up to about 90 centimetres tall and 60 centimetres across.

The reason for the unusual name of burning bush is that the plant has glands containing an inflammable oil. If a match is held near the flowers on a warm, calm day or evening, this oil will ignite and burn quite brightly.

BURNING BUSH (*Dictamnus albus*)

Not surprisingly, this plant has the alternative nickname of gas plant. In addition to providing an adult diversion, burning bushes are great cut flowers, and are lovely in garden borders. They are especially long-lived in cool climates, preferring a dry, semi-sunny site. Flowers, appearing in early summer, are usually pink, but if you hunt around you can find purple and white.

Close contact with burning bush is not advisable. All plant parts, especially the seedpods, may cause mild to severe stomach upset if ingested. And bare skin coming in contact with the leaves may cause an allergic reaction. So be sure to handle them with your gloves on.

And some more:

- Common valerian (*Valeriana officinalis*)
- Evening primrose (*Oenothera*)
- Jupiter's beard (*Centranthus ruber*)
- Peony (*Paeonia*)
- Phlox (*Phlox*)
- Rockcress (*Arabis*)

A simple summary

✔ Always buy the right plant for the conditions in your garden. This requires some knowledge of your garden, and timing your purchases properly.

✔ Although definitions of shade and semi-shade may vary, there are many plants that will grow in some type of semi-shade if given sufficient water.

✔ There are plenty of drought-tolerant perennials, but even these plants need water from time to time. Some need a bit more than others, so do your homework if you don't like to water, or need to regulate water use.

✔ Moist soil doesn't mean soggy soil. If you truly have lots of water, you should think of pond plants instead.

✔ Fragrant plants are sometimes powerfully fragrant, while other plants must be enjoyed with your nose much closer to the blossom. If you want a plant to perfume a room or a garden site, do the sniff test before you buy it.

Chapter 7

Beautiful Bulbs

FLOWERS FROM BULBS are often the first harbingers of spring. Their foliage peeks up through the last melting layer of snow, bringing a bit of colour and a promise of your great garden to come. In this chapter I'll explain how to buy bulbs and start them, and make some suggestions for plants that are simple to grow.

In this chapter...

✓ When is a bulb not a bulb?

✓ Bulb basics

✓ Spring-flowering bulbs

✓ Summer-flowering bulbs

✓ Bulbs for fragrance

When is a bulb not a bulb?

YOU MAY BE CURIOUS about the difference between bulbs, rhizomes, corms, and tubers, all of which are often just called **bulbs**. The distinction is not extremely important, because growing methods are pretty much the same. In everyday conversation, you'll undoubtedly refer to all of these flowers as bulbs. That's fine. Still, I like to keep things straight from the beginning. It's so much simpler that way.

> **DEFINITION**
>
> A **bulb** is basically a plant's food-storage organ. It is a modified shoot, with layers of fleshy leaf bases and roots.

True bulbs

True bulbs are usually rounded, with a pointed tip, a round base, and an interior made of layers, similar to an onion. Mature bulbs – those that have been in the ground for more than a season – reproduce by a dividing process within the parent bulb. True bulbs include the allium (*Allium*), belladonna lily (*Amaryllis*), daffodil (*Narcissus*), grape hyacinth (*Muscari*), hyacinth (*Hyacinthus orientalis*), iris (*Iris*), lily (*Lilium*), scilla (*Scilla*), snowdrop (*Galanthus*), and tulip (*Tulipa*).

Corms

Corms are rounded, and are small to medium size. They're not composed of layers, like true bulbs, but are solid all the way through. After a season, corms may produce baby corms, or cormlets, around the parent corm. These baby corms may be very small – about the size of a pea. Each cormlet contains the ingredients to make a new plant exactly like the parent. The corn lily (*Ixia*), crocus (*Crocus*), freesia (*Freesia*), gladiolus (*Gladiolus*), montbretia (*Crocosmia*), and autumn crocus (*Colchicum*) are a few of the common plants springing from corms.

Rhizomes

A rhizome is a swollen section of an underground, horizontal plant stem. Roots grow from the underside of this stem, and plant buds develop on top of the stem. Plants growing from rhizomes include some of the irises, leopard lilies (*Belamcanda chinensis*), and cannas (*Canna*).

Tubers

Tubers are swollen sections of root. Tubers may be shaped like short sausages or be entirely irregular. Buds grow from the top of each tuber. Begonias (*Begonia*), buttercups (*Ranunculus*), dahlias (*Dahlia*), and daylilies (*Hemerocallis*) are grown from tubers.

Bulb basics

NOW THAT YOU KNOW WHAT A BULB IS, and what it isn't, let's talk about how to start them in your garden. Here again, it's best to avoid just buying, digging, and crossing your fingers. You're much more likely to enjoy success if you make careful purchases and know ahead of time where your flowers will go.

Choosing bulbs

Outer layer (tunic) intact

Undamaged tip, with no signs of growth

Firm base without new root growth

A HEALTHY DAFFODIL BULB

If you plant at the right time, a good-quality bulb will give you flowers the first year. Get the largest bulbs of each kind that you can, from a reputable dealer. Buy only bulbs that feel solid; never take soft ones.

Avoid bargain bulbs, whether half-price at season's end or advertised in magazines at very low prices. Bargain bulbs are inexpensive for a reason. They may be incorrectly labelled, undersize, improperly stored or transported, or diseased. There is no saving when half of what you buy doesn't flower.

Before planting

Bulbs are a lot less fussy than many other plants about their surroundings, but you can't expect bulb roots to tunnel through clay. You paid good money for the bulbs, so put a little more into their bedding, and provide them with some fertile, light-textured soil to grow in.

Simply put, bulbs like to be in the ground. Plant spring-flowering bulbs in autumn, and summer-flowering bulbs in spring or early summer. Plant as soon as you get the bulbs.

If you're ordering from catalogues, order early. If for some reason you cannot plant your purchases straight away, store them in an open bag in a cool, dry place.

INTERNET

bulbsonline.org

This International Flower Bulb Centre site is well worth a visit – here you'll find a wealth of information and advice on a wide range of bulbous plants.

PLANTING BULBS OUTDOORS

1 Make a planting hole

Dig a large hole in well-prepared ground and place the bulbs, tips upwards, at least twice their own depth and width apart.

2 Cover with soil

Draw soil over the bulbs gently by hand to minimize any risk of displacing or disturbing them. Firm down the soil to remove any air gaps.

After planting

Place little plastic markers or lolly sticks by each bulb grouping. Use indelible ink to indicate "daffodil", or "tulip", or whatever you've planted. Push the marker well into the ground so it doesn't fall over. Everybody believes they are going to remember where they put each bulb, even after the leaves die back and there's no aboveground sign of the plant anymore. But nobody ever does. And if you forget, you may slice through a favourite bulb when digging in the area for some other plant. Keep it simple and you'll do fine.

Water deeply just after autumn planting, and let spring rain take care of the spring bulbs. For summer-flowering bulbs, you must water regularly unless the package specifically says not to. But never over-water. A thick bulb will rot if it gets soggy. As a general rule, bulbs like dry feet. Fertilize lightly in spring before the plants bloom, and in autumn after the first serious cold spell. Use just a little bit of fertilizer.

After blooming

Remove the spent flowers and let the foliage die back. Spent flowers go to seed, which takes energy away from the bulb.

Foliage dieback is a process that provides food for the bulb underneath, and therefore next year's flowers. Remove leaves only after they have turned brown.

Spring-flowering bulbs

WHEN YOU CAN'T find a wide variety of bulbs to choose from at your local garden centre, visit a large nursery, or try a catalogue. Many specialize in bulbs.

Bearded iris

There are entire volumes written about the 300-plus varieties of iris, and there is no way to cover them all in a few paragraphs. Tall bearded iris (*Iris*) rhizomes are most commonly found in garden centres. The "beard" is the little fuzzy moustache on the flower. Colours are gorgeous and the choice bewildering: you may have 50 options. And that's before you've seen the catalogues featuring irises.

■ **Magic Man** *is a bearded iris that flowers in early summer. The beards are bright orange.*

Buy and plant bearded irises from July until September. When planting, the tops of the rhizomes must be just visible.

Place the rhizomes about 30 centimetres apart. Group similar colours together – you may find that some colours look better in your garden than others. These plants are easy to grow almost anywhere. Most insist on lots of sunshine and well-drained soil, preferably just on the dry side. If you don't have good drainage, the rhizomes will rot. So create a slight mound and plant there.

Baby irises

Irises multiply by increasing their rhizomes, so you will get more flowers every year. Flowers appear in May and June, and in mild areas you may receive a flower surprise in later months.

INTERNET

crocus.co.uk/shop/bulbs

Go shopping for spring bulbs at this site, which offers more than 100 varieties, from snowdrops to crocus to irises.

When a clump becomes crowded, after 3 or so years, the flowers become smaller. Dig up the rhizomes and divide them in summer and autumn. Separate and replant portions that have leaves attached. Your irises should ideally be replanted within a few days. For more details on the technique of dividing rhizomes, turn to Chapter 19.

Trivia...

Iris, the Greek goddess of the rainbow, has given her name to both the multi-hued iris of the eye, and to the iris flower, which blossoms in nearly all colours of the rainbow. This goddess carries messages of love from heaven to earth, using a rainbow as her bridge. Another job is transporting the souls of women to the Elysian fields – a happy place where good souls go after death.

Crocus

Because you may see crocus (*Crocus*) flowers as early as 14 February, the crocus is dedicated to St. Valentine. This lovely plant is a true harbinger of spring. While it likes good care, this corm will thrive in just about any soil or situation. Spring-flowering Dutch hybrids are most commonly found in garden centres. To get the longest lasting display, plant corms at intervals from September until November. Plant them 7 centimetres deep, and in clusters – a lot of crocuses look fantastic together.

Crocuses are available in a wide variety of yellows and purple-blues, and there are multi-coloured types, too. Although an area of mixed crocuses has a quite pleasing appearance, I like distinct groupings of colour for maximum impact. A nice plan is yellow at the edges of the group to define boundaries, and purples and whites within. Crocuses, just 7 centimetres high, should always be at the front of any planting.

■ **Spring-flowering** *Dutch hybrid crocus combines rich violet-purple flowers with bright yellow stamens for a colourful display.*

Daffodil

Even a complete novice can grow daffodils (*Narcissus*), as long as excellent drainage is provided. Put them indoors by a sunny window or outdoors in a pot by the front door, scatter them in a flower bed, or plant them *en masse* to create a show stopper for the local neighbourhood.

Purchase bulbs as soon as they appear in the garden centres, and plant them outside during autumn. A succession of plantings will result in a succession of blooms. How deep to plant them depends on the variety, so be sure you read the package carefully. By early spring, pointed leaves start poking their tips above soil line. Including hybridized varieties, there are now thousands of types of daffodils. They are available in all shades of yellow, cream, and pale pink, to crystalline white, with centres of contrasting colours and varying shapes. If you're interested in a particularly fragrant daffodil, try planting the wild jonquil variety, *Narcissus jonquilla*.

DAFFODIL
(*Narcissus Quince*)

Snowdrop

The common snowdrop (*Galanthus nivalis*) is one of the first bulbs to flower after mid-winter has passed and the days begin to get longer. Its pure white, single, pendent, bell flowers have distinctive green V-shaped markings on their inner petals.

Snowdrops will be happy in sun or partial shade as long as the soil doesn't dry out in the summer. Plant the bulbs 5 centimetres deep as soon as they are available in early autumn. They are difficult to establish, but once they have settled down they'll form good clumps. The snowdrop is the one bulb that can be planted "in the green", which is after they have flowered but their green leaves are still fresh.

SNOWDROP (*Galanthus nivalis*)

Tulip

Although most gardeners would love to grow tulips (*Tulipa*), these aren't the easiest of bulbs. You need a rich, sandy soil, good drainage, and sun. Don't attempt tulips in clay soil unless you have added plenty of soil improvers. Unimproved clay soil generally results in crooked, dwarfed stems and leaves with sad little flowers on the top. This doesn't mean you can't have tulips – just put them in pots where you can control the growing medium.

TROUBLE WITH TULIPS

Tulips are susceptible to a virus known as the mosaic virus. In infected plants, solid colour flowers develop odd, but often beautiful, markings. When these strange tulips appeared in Holland in about 1637, people thought they had discovered a new strain, or type, of plant. A tulip-buying craze developed. People thought they would have instant riches if they could breed just one of these unique bulbs. One of the prices paid for just a single bulb included a load of grain, 1,000 pounds of cheese, 12 sheep, 10 oxen, 5 pigs, 4 barrels of beer, 2 tubs of butter, 2 hogsheads of wine, a suit of clothes, and a silver cup. But nobody was able to breed these flowers.

The mosaic virus is still around. It is contagious to all tulips, and although some thrive despite it, others die quickly. So do not replant virus-infected tulips, or replant tulips in areas where the mosaic virus has appeared in the last 3 years.

There are so many kinds of tulips that the genus has been divided into 15 major groups, including Darwin hybrids, Triumph, Lily-flowered, and Parrot. These groupings are based on the characteristics of the flowers. There's a tulip in virtually every colour of the rainbow. Plant them in the autumn, 25 centimetres deep and about 15 centimetres apart, in groups of one type and colour. You can even plant as late as December if the ground isn't frozen. Around the tulip clusters, consider planting low, spring-flowering annuals.

TULIP (*Tulipa*)

More spring-flowering bulbs

- Allium (*Allium*)
- Anemone (*Anemone*)
- Bluebell (*Scilla*)
- Glory of the snow (*Chionodoxa*)
- Grape hyacinth (*Muscari*)

- Hyacinth (*Hyacinthus orientalis*)
- Star-of-Bethlehem (*Ornithogalum*)
- Striped squill (*Puschkinia scilloides*)
- True squill (*Scilla*)
- Winter aconite (*Eranthis*)

Summer-flowering bulbs

SPRING IS DEFINITELY *the main time for bulbs, but there are some rhizomes, tubers, and bulbs that will bloom for you in the summer. If you do a bit of research before you plant, you'll have better luck.*

BEGONIA (*Begonia*)

Begonia

Unless you live in a frost-free area, start your tuberous begonias (*Begonia*) indoors. Put one tuber in a pot containing rich soil. The pots must be at least 15 centimetres high and 15 centimetres wide, and they must have drainage holes or the tubers will rot. The growing site must be semi-shaded and warm. Press the tubers, round side down, into the soil until just their tops show. Water them well, just once, then water just a drop every now and then until green shoots appear.

Transplant the begonias outside, very carefully, when shoots are about 10 centimetres high, taking care not to disturb the roots. Some people leave begonias in the pot and just set them outdoors. Give these plants indirect light, ample water without over-watering, and fertilizer every 2 weeks as growth continues. If the weather temporarily gets hot and dry, lightly spray them with water.

Do not put tuberous begonias outdoors until the weather is reliably warm. Depending on where you live, "reliably warm" may be April, but it may also be as late as June.

I recommend planting tuberous begonias of the same colour and variety together, because I think this makes the nicest display. At season's close, usually before the first frost, remove the tubers gently from the soil. Let them sit a few days in a dry spot until they harden. Store them in a cool, dry, frost-free area until next planting time.

Blackberry lily

Flower arrangers love this charming August- and September-bloomer for its beige seed capsules that split to frame clusters of large black seeds. Another common name, leopard lily, aptly describes the sprays of small, red-spotted orange flowers on 60-centimetre-high stems. The flowers open daily, one after another, for 3 weeks.

Plant the rhizomes in groups of three, about 2.5 centimetres deep, in good soil. Blackberry lilies (*Belamcanda chinensis*) should be placed in sun or light shade and need regular watering. They are related to the iris and can be similarly divided after a while for more plants. Alternatively, they can be propagated by seed in spring.

Canna

Tropical flowers are trendy, and cannas (*Canna*) will make just the right statement. If you've inherited an old garden, you may still have some of the old-time cannas. These plants can reach 2 metres high, and are sometimes dull looking. With minimal attention, they multiply via tuberous roots into a tall, solid wall of large leaves and big, floppy flowers.

But times, courtesy of *hybridizers*, have changed. Now cannas come in an array of pinks, reds, yellows, and stripes, and in a delightful size range. You can find dwarfs only 45 centimetres high – ideal for the large patio pot, or as part of a small garden. There are mid-size plants at 90 centimetres tall, and the orchid-flowering varieties can reach over 1.5 metres.

DEFINITION

Hybridizers *spend their time creating new plants by crossing genetically different parent plants. Some of the most glorious flowers we grow today are hybrids. If you're concerned that there's something "artificial" about growing hybrids, relax. Hybrids occur in nature, too.*

Planting your cannas

The best times to plant canna rhizomes are May or June. Plant them about 12 centimetres deep and 25 to 50 centimetres apart. They will multiply slowly, so allow enough space between them. Of course, they're easy enough to dig and divide, so if they get a little dense, it's easily remedied.

Cannas like heat and sunlight. If you place them in semi-shade, they may have leaves but they won't flower. As they're tropical plants, you must regularly water them, although they do tolerate short dry periods. At season's end, they'll get bedraggled and you should cut them back to about 15 centimetres high. Cannas will come back amply the next year, unless you live in a really cold area. Then you have to dig up the rhizomes, let them dry, and store upside down in a cool, shaded area.

■ **Rosemond Coles**, *with its yellow-edged orange petals and large decorative leaves, is one of the more spectacular cannas.*

Daylily

The daylily (*Hemerocallis*) is one of the most popular rhizomes. It is hardy, grows in sun or light shade, and, while preferring organically enriched soil, will tolerate poor soil if given good drainage. You must be careful to avoid areas where the tuberous roots have to compete with groundcover or shallow-rooted trees. Regular watering and occasional fertilizing promote the best-looking plants.

■ **Fragrant daylilies**, *such as this* Hemerocallis *Little Rainbow, demand very little in the way of attention and provide a reliable display every year.*

Often fragrant, daylilies come back, increasing in size, year after year. The new hybrids (hundreds are appearing each year) have larger flowers than the originals, and the bloom is more profuse. The traditional yellow-orange daylilies may still be found, but usually in someone's garden – not at the nursery. If you plant early-, mid-, and late-season varieties, your daylilies will flower for about 3 months.

INTERNET

www.daylilies.org/
daylilies.html

Visit the site of the American Hemerocallis Society. Go to the frequently asked questions section to learn all about daylilies.

Montbretia

Plant five corms of this South African native, and unless you live where the weather is really cold, you'll have 25 next year and more the year after that. This plant is simple-simple if you give it mostly sun and occasional water. The most common variety has bright, funnel-shaped, orange-red flowers. and produces about 10 blooms per 30-centimetre stem, so is excellent for cutting. Other varieties have yellow or red flowers, although they may not be as hardy. Flowers open one after another, with the first appearing in summer.

Montbretias (*Crocosmia*) need a well-drained soil in an open, sunny site. If you live in a cold area, it's a good idea to cover the plants with a mulch of peat or straw, once the strap leaves have withered away in late autumn.

More summer-flowering bulbs

Some of the hardiest summer blooms include these plants (a few of which may continue blooming into early autumn):

- Allium (*Allium*)
- Foxtail lilies (*Eremurus*)
- Gayfeather (*Liatris*)
- Gladiolus (*Gladiolus*)
- Lily turf (*Liriope*)

- Magic lilies (*Amaryllis*)
- Peruvian lilies (*Alstroemeria*)
- Red-hot poker (*Kniphofia*)
- Wandflower (*Dierama*)

Allium will actually bloom in the spring, summer, or autumn, depending on the variety.

■ **The stunning purple flowers** *of* Allium giganteum *are packed together into tight balls that make excellent dried flowers. The leaves, when crushed, smell of onions.*

Bulbs for fragrance

THE NOSE MAY KNOW, *but every nose is different. One person will insist a certain flower has a marvellous scent, and another says it has no scent at all. Sometimes you have to put the flowers right under your nostrils to get the scent, sometimes it wafts through the air. The aroma may waft during the daylight hours, or it may do so only at night. The following bulbs would be my selections for fragrance, but you may discover others that you like more.*

Hyacinth

When first introduced to Europe, hyacinths (*Hyacinthus orientalis*) were only for the wealthy. Now bulbs are less than £1, and can be found in myriad colours, including red, white, and blue. Many people enjoy planting them in this "patriotic" combination, especially if there are three of each planted about 15 centimetres apart. The bulbs should be planted about 12 centimetres deep. For outdoor success, choose medium-size rather than large bulbs. While many other early-flowering bulbs are short stemmed, the 30-centimetre-high hyacinth displays its flower-studded stem quite effectively.

Some protection from the wind will help ensure the health of your hyacinths. Planting in groups helps them withstand inclement weather, which can snap the long stems. Stake the stems if you anticipate really bad weather.

Hyacinths need a minimum of half a day's sun, good drainage, and enriched soil. Plant in the autumn, when the bulbs appear in local garden centres. If there's no rain, water once a week for a month. After they bloom (in the spring), fertilize, water regularly, and put a light organic mulch on top of the area. With care, each bulb will give 5 years of bloom, and sometimes more. Plant some candytuft (*Iberis*) around your hyacinths to provide a nice cover when the foliage of the bulbs dies back.

Trivia...
In long-ago Greece, bridesmaids wore crowns of hyacinth and parsley. The flower is said to symbolize faith, wisdom, prudence, and resurrection.

HYACINTH (*Hyacinthus orientalis*)

FORCING THE BLOOM

Hyacinths are just as splendid grown indoors in pots, where just one plant can perfume a room. If you want to get sophisticated, you can "force" your hyacinths to bloom in the later winter. Forcing is the practice of inducing an unseasonal growth by manipulating the plant's environment.

1 Cover the bulbs with soil

Plant hyacinth bulbs in some potting compost, leaving just the noses showing, in September. Make sure the soil is moist but not waterlogged.

2 Expose them to light

Keep the bulbs in a cool, dark place until the shoots are 10 centimetres high, then gradually bring them into the light for January flowers.

Madonna lily

Madonna lilies (*Lilium candidum*) are known to be a bit finicky, but worth the effort. They require moist, organic, very well-drained soil for their roots. The base of the plants should be kept shaded, but the tops like to be in full sun. (This particular shade and sun combination is the favourite of almost all lilies.)

Plant the bulb in early autumn, not more than 5 centimetres deep. For a truly great effect, plant three at a time, about 25 centimetres apart. Water well after planting, and repeat if the weather is dry. You'll see leaves quickly, and then the 1.2-metre-high, white-flowered stem shoots up in August, with fragrant, funnel-shaped blooms. The plant disappears after blooming, with leaves reappearing in the autumn. These leaves remain throughout winter but die off in spring.

Often purchased in gift pots, Easter lilies (*Lilium longiflorum*) should be planted outside in an appropriate site after the flowers fade. Plant them about 15 centimetres deep. You may, or may not, get flowers the following autumn, or in the normal mid-summer blooming time.

Regardless of lily type, never move a plant if it can be avoided. If you must, handle very carefully and replant immediately.

Freesia

Often purchased by the bag in mixed or single colours, relatively hardy freesias (*Freesia*) will cheerfully self-sow if you don't remove faded flowers. Regardless of the original colour – purple, red, pink, white, or gold – the next generation or so tends to come up with cream-coloured flowers.

■ **The fragrant white** *trumpets of the Madonna lily (Lilium candidum) look so spectacular that it's well worth putting in a bit of extra effort to grow them.*

Purchase corms from August to November. By planting small groups every 2 weeks, you'll get a succession of blooms, since each plant flowers for about 6 weeks. Plant corms 5 centimetres deep and 5 centimetres apart, with the pointed end up. Freesias require mostly sun and regular water. You get healthier plants when you fertilize every few weeks. For the adventurous, try planting freesia from seed.

Freesias also make good 30-centimetre-high potted plants for the patio or balcony. If you have a truly sunny window, try them indoors, too, on the windowsill. Yellow and white flowers tend to be more fragrant than other hues.

Tuberose

These flower clusters are so aromatic that you'll need to be sure to put them where you can enjoy the scent. In fact, the scent is so exuberant, some people prefer not to bring tuberoses (*Polianthes tuberosa*) indoors, while others insist.

Tuberoses can be a bit fussy about producing their waxy, white, tubular flowers. You need to have a quite warm site for these Mexican natives, and they find any type of chill quite distressing. But they're certainly worth a try, even in a warm, sunny window if you live in an area with cold weather.

Don't take chances when you buy tuberoses – purchase good-size rhizomes. They go into rich soil, 7 centimetres deep and about 15 centimetres apart. Give regular watering in spring and summer, and fertilize every 2 weeks when in growth. Expect one-time flower clusters, on 60- to 90-centimetre-high stems, from late summer to autumn. In warm weather areas, rhizomes left in the soil may reappear the following year.

A simple summary

✔ When buying bulbs, rhizomes, tubers, or corms, get the largest and heaviest you can find. Don't purchase so-called "bargain" bulbs. They usually have more than one flaw, and are not true money-savers.

✔ Although the more common bulbs are found in local garden centres and nurseries, look for others in catalogues. There's a huge variety available.

✔ If you really like a certain type of bulb, such as a daylily or daffodil, and want to learn more about it, join a specific society. There are societies for many of the more popular bulbs.

✔ Plant as soon as you obtain bulbs, as early in the proper season as possible. Plant spring-flowering bulbs in autumn, and summer-flowering bulbs in spring or early summer.

✔ Always mark the place where you've planted your bulbs, so you don't accidentally slice into them later.

✔ Place bulbs at the recommended depth for best performance.

✔ After flowers fade, always let bulb foliage die back naturally. This dieback is part of the bulb's natural life cycle, and it gives it strength for next year's growth.

PART THREE

COLOURFUL FOLIAGE OF THE NORWAY MAPLE

WOODY PLANTS

O F COURSE, you'll want to grow more than just flowers in your garden. Big woody plants *make a statement*, as they have hard fibrous stems that remain

above ground all year. Included in this group are ornamental trees, shrubs, roses, and vines.

There are so many choices you can make: do you want flowers, berries, fragrance, foliage, colour? Do you want to hide a fence or tool shed with a climber? Do you want enough roses for cutting, or just a few to dot the

garden with spring and summer flowers and perhaps fill a vase or two? Sometimes it seems like you want all of everything you see, and just making the choice can be tough. So sit down with this part of the book and get a grip on your options.

Chapter 8

Ornamental Trees

EVERY GARDEN deserves some type of tree. Tree leaves dance in the wind, shade you from the sun, shelter birds. Some provide autumn colour and spring flowers. If your tree grows big enough, you may even become grandparents to a batch of baby birds. There are evergreen trees that keep their leaves all year around, while deciduous trees lose their leaves in autumn and develop new ones in spring. The idea is to present trees that will give you the best shade, colour, or fragrance possible.

In this chapter...

✓ Arboreal anatomy
✓ Buying your tree
✓ Shade trees
✓ Flowering trees
✓ Instant arbours
✓ Autumn colour

A STRIKING DECIDUOUS HIMALAYAN BIRCH

Arboreal anatomy

THE THREE MAIN PARTS of a tree are its roots, trunk, and crown or top. There are three types of roots: the big, easily seen ones near the trunk, the **tap root**, and the thousands of thread-like **root hairs** at the end of rootlets. The complete root system of a full-size tree can reach out 12 metres or more! The big roots anchor the tree within the surrounding soil and help it remain upright. Trees fall over in a flood because the soil turns to mud and the roots can't stay in place.

A tree's trunk is its food storage mechanism as well as its support. The tree trunk has three parts: bark, wood, and pith. The bark is the outside of the tree that you're familiar with. Beneath the bark is a thin layer called cambium. This is the growing part of wood, having cells that become either bark or new wood. Underneath the cambium is the wood itself. There may be a darker type of wood called heartwood, and a lighter type called sapwood. Underneath all this, in the centre, is the pith.

Buying your tree

Before you buy any tree, find out how large it will get. The size of a tree includes both its height and its width.

Look hard at the spot in your garden where you plan to put the tree. Do you have room for a tree that's 15 metres tall with an 8-metre spread? An 8-metre tree with a 5-metre spread? Will your neighbour appreciate the spreading branches? Think now, or possibly pay for a tree removal service later. This is expensive! Take it from one who has had her wallet emptied several times.

Even if you want your garden to look well established, it's best to buy trees when they're younger and smaller. Juvenile trees recover much more easily from the shock of being transplanted than more mature trees do. Because of this, younger trees will often catch up with larger trees of the same type planted at the same time.

In the bag or in the pot

You can purchase trees "bare root", or "rootballed", in which the roots are surrounded by soil held in place by hessian. When receiving bare root or rootballed trees, do dampen them a bit.

Some gardeners soak the roots in mud. I just plop them in a large bucket of water for at least an hour, although some soak them for 1 or 2 days.

ROOTBALLED TREE IN GOOD CONDITION

Firm rootball with covering intact

Bare vs. rootballed

Bare-root trees are those you see plonked directly into the soil at the garden centre, usually in groups. When you buy one of these dormant trees, the shop assistant takes it out of the earth and its roots are bare. There will be no soil mass around the roots. The shop assistant will wrap it up in plastic or a similar material, hopefully putting some damp shredded paper or sawdust around it so the roots don't dry out. Bare-root trees must be planted very promptly. Remove any wrapping just before you do so.

■ **When you buy a bare-root tree**, check that it has well-developed roots that spead out evenly. It should also have small, fine roots. These are a good sign because they indicate that the tree will grow well. The roots should not look dry and withered.

When you buy some trees, they're dug out of the ground with some original soil around their roots. This is covered and held in place by hessian that is fastened in some way around the trunk. This wrapped area has the appearance of a ball. Hence this type of tree is known as "rootballed". Don't worry about the hessian. Just loosen it at the fastened top and cut a few slits in the side. Then go ahead and plant the tree. The material will eventually disintegrate on its own.

More often than not, trees you buy will be sold in large containers. Get someone at the garden centre to partially cut the sides of the container for you, to make removing the tree easier. Add water to the soil in the container as soon as possible after bringing your new tree home.

137

PLANTING YOUR TREE

The best time to plant most trees is at the beginning of their dormant, or resting period, some time in the late autumn. The key is to wait until most of the leaves are gone, and complete the job before new leaves appear in spring. There are several trees, however, that prefer to be planted in the spring. These include birch, dogwood, magnolia, several of the oaks, and the tulip tree, among others.

1 Dig the hole

Dig a hole about 50 percent wider than the rootball, and one and a half times its depth.

2 Check the depth

Set your tree in the hole. Use a cane to check that the tree is planted at the same depth as it was in its pot, or that the rootball is just covered.

3 Knock in the stake

Choose a strong wood stake and knock it firmly into the soil with a mallet, about 10 centimetres away from the trunk of the tree.

4 Fill with soil

Fill in around the rootball and stake with soil, firming it gently as you go with hammer or foot.

5 Firm the soil

Check the tree is still upright and finish by treading the soil gently until the surface is level, which also removes air pockets.

6 Water in

Fasten your young tree to its stake with a tree tie, then give it a good drink of water to help it recover from planting.

Perfect positioning

After you've dug the planting hole, place your tree, stand back, and see how it looks. Also check it in relation to other plants or trees planted nearby. You do not want to traumatize it by digging it up and moving it elsewhere. If all is satisfactory, plant it.

Feeling hungry?

If you're tempted to fertilize the newcomer in the autumn (thinking to speed up its adjustment), don't. Wait until new leaves appear in the spring, and then use an artificial fertilizer as recommended on the container.

If you plant in spring, you can fertilize appropriately. Always double-check the label to be sure the fertilizer is right for your particular type of tree.

Prudent pruning

Should you prune? Well, to be honest, I've seen some pretty disastrous results when novices start hacking away at deciduous tree limbs. Be kind. You can always prune a little more, but it's tricky to paste the branches back on. I prune for shape, to remove any sickly looking material, and to thin, especially where branches cross each other.

Flowering trees should be pruned when the blossoms are just about gone. Evergreens seldom need pruning, although you may have to shape them a bit each year. When pruning evergreens, trim junipers and yews before new growth appears, and pines, firs, and spruces after new growth begins.

If you have purchased a selection of pruning tools and are eager to use them, take a course in pruning. Some untutored enthusiasm could be disastrous. A local garden centre may offer a class, or a staff member might be able to direct you to one. But do yourself a favour: if it's a big tree, or a prized specimen, call in a qualified tree surgeon.

CUTTING BACK A STEM

■ **For stems with alternate buds,** *make a slanting cut about 5 millimetres above a bud. This sloping cut allows drops of rain, which might cause disease, to drain away from the bud.*

■ **For stems with opposite buds,** *make a straight cut directly above a pair of healthy buds. Keep the pruners as close above them as you can without grazing or damaging the buds.*

Shade trees

WHEN YOU'RE GROWING TREES FOR SHADE *you want to choose trees that spread out a bit, covering a nice wide area with their leafy branches. A tall, thin tree simply won't do the job. Here are some of my favourites.*

Chinese elm

Elm varieties are plentiful, and include Scotch, white, cork, camperdown, Dutch, English, rock, and fluttering. The American elm and the English elm, both once extraordinarily popular, have had continuing problems with Dutch elm disease, although semi-resistant strains have been developed. Your local garden centre can advise you on this, as well as recommend the elm best suited for your part of the country.

CHINESE ELM (*Ulmus parvifolia*)

Chinese elm (*Ulmus parvifolia*), also called Chinese evergreen elm or lacebark elm, is often recommended for its hardiness. It survives nicely in poor, compacted soil, and sustains itself well in both heat and drought. It is also resistant to Dutch elm disease and the hungry elm leaf beetle, making it a super choice for the new gardener.

Do not confuse this sturdy, good-natured shade tree with the brittle Siberian elm, which is not recommended for gardens or street planting. Siberian elm is sometimes – incorrectly – sold as Chinese elm.

The layered look

Chinese elm gets its "lacebark" nickname from its *exfoliating* bark. As the tree matures, the outer layer of brown bark sheds here and there, showing jigsaw-puzzle displays of pale yellow inner bark. The result is quite attractive. The leaves of the Chinese elm are rather pretty too, giving a dark green display in spring and summer, and changing to purple and pale yellow in the autumn. This tree may keep its leaves throughout the winter, or drop them, depending on how cold it gets in your neighbourhood.

> **DEFINITION**
>
> *When anything exfoliates, it comes off in pieces. A tree can exfoliate bark.*

These elms grow big

Chinese elms grow quickly, sometimes 1.5 metres a year when young, to an eventual height of 12 to 18 metres. (Most elms grow much taller, reaching 30 metres. An exception is the mushroom-shaped camperdown elm, which reaches 6 to 12 metres.) Elms, in general, are for large, sunny, well-drained sites where the dappled shade they provide is a pleasure during the warm season, yet doesn't impinge on the rights of sun-loving plants nearby. They do need fairly regular watering.

Hackberry

Also called the nettle tree, this elm-like tree is useful for both shade and ornament. Tiny flowers appear in May, often followed by 5-millimetre orange-red fruit that later becomes dark purple. Birds love the fruit. Leaves on this tree, which reaches 18 metres high in its native America, are shiny, bright green on top and paler green beneath. The bark is a greyish-brown with prominent warty or bumpy areas.

A lovely relative of the hackberry (*Celtis occidentalis*) is the sugar hackberry or Mississippi hackberry (*C. laevigata*). Like the hackberry, its bark has little distinctive bumpy areas. Fruit, which follows rather insignificant May flowers, is tiny and turns from orange to dark purple.

All hackberries are tough trees, growing well in city conditions or with their roots in brackish water. They grow best in continental climates with hot summers. In Britain they usually form a smaller, multi-stemmed tree.

■ **Wide-spreading** *branches, colourful fruit, and a hardy nature make the hackberry (Celtis occidentalis) an excellent shade tree.*

Japanese pagoda tree

Known by some as the Chinese scholar tree (*Sophora japonica*), this moderate-grower will reach a pleasant 6 metres high, then spread out to 15 metres. Spreading branches provide pleasant, filtered shade. *Pinnate* leaves, divided into numerous leaflets, are dark green, turning yellow in autumn. After the first few years, long clusters of yellowish-white, sweet-smelling, pea-shaped flowers appear in the summer. This lovely flower display can last for up to 2 months, attracting lots of bees.

Here's a deciduous tree where you don't have to worry about soil. It doesn't need much water either, once it gets started, although some protection from the wind may be needed. Best of all, insect pests and diseases tend to go elsewhere.

■ **The hardy Japanese pagoda** *will thrive in most gardens. It is popular for both the shade it provides and its fragrant flowers.*

> **DEFINITION**
>
> A **pinnate** *leaf has little leaflets running along both sides of a main axis. It looks a bit like a feather, and, in fact, the Latin word* pinna *means feather. As a rule, a pinnate leaf will be shed in its entirety, with the leaflets attached.*

Silk tree

From late spring until summer, powder-puff pink flowers jostle to almost hide the silk tree's (*Albizia julibrissin*) light green, ferny-leafed branches. Not fussy about soil, a silk tree still prefers a sunny site, and does best if you give it enough water. If you're forgetful, it will still grow, but not as quickly. A silk tree will reach 12 metres high, and about 12 metres wide. Although silk trees will tolerate temperatures as low as −15° C, they may die down in the winter. If so, remove the dead stems to encourage new growth.

Silk trees grow either with multiple trunks, or as a single tree with an umbrella shape. When shopping for one, make sure the tree is large enough to have developed its final shape (unless you want to fiddle with it later). Also be aware that some people call a silk tree a Persian acacia, some know it as a pink siris, and yet others as a mimosa.

If you're considering adding a silk tree to your garden, think about placing it where you can really enjoy the blooms. Many people plant it so they can look down at the flowers from an upstairs window.

SILK TREE (*Albizia julibrissin*)

More trees for shade:

- Alders (*Alnus*)
- Arborvitae (*Thuja*)
- Ashes (*Fraxinus*)
- Canoe birches (*Betula papyrifera*)
- Dogwoods (*Cornus*)
- Flowering cherries (*Prunus*)
- Flowering crab apples (*Malus*)
- Franklinia (*Franklinia*)

- Hawthorns (*Crataegus*)
- Hemlocks (*Tsuga*)
- Lacebark pine (*Pinus bungeana*)
- Magnolias (*Magnolia*)
- Maples (*Acer*)
- Mountain ashes (*Sorbus*)
- Oleaster (*Elaeagnus angustifolia*)
- Yews (*Taxus*)

Flowering trees

FLOWERING TREES GIVE YOU *two pleasures for the price of one. Blossom in spring or summer complements the new leaves, and if you're lucky you'll get the benefit of autumn colour.*

Flowering dogwood

Noted for its spring colour, the flowering dogwood (*Cornus florida*) brings you ample pink- or white-clustered blossoms, for an extremely showy display that more-or-less covers the entire tree. Then, in the autumn, the bright green leaves blaze forth in crimson hues. Bright, shiny red berries appear too, delighting the local birds. The berries may remain even after the leaves of this deciduous tree have fallen for the winter. Look closely, however, and amid the branches you can see flower buds waiting for spring.

If you want to select the flower colour, you will have to wait until spring to buy your tree. Many people have several flowering dogwoods, all in differing flower hues. The trees will grow to approximately 6 metres high. Branches will generally take a pyramid or umbrella shape.

FLOWERING DOGWOOD (*Cornus florida*)

More dogwoods

Other dogwood trees are extremely beautiful too. I'm partial to the Cornelian cherry dogwood (*Cornus mas*), and the reddish-green-stemmed common dogwood (*C. sanguinea*). You might also want to try the pagoda dogwood (*C. alternifolia*), a tree that does particularly well in cold-winter climates. If possible, put dogwoods in a sheltered, wind-free site. And give them plenty of water, especially during the first year.

Southern magnolia

It's extremely difficult to choose which magnolia to spotlight, but I think I'd have to go with southern magnolia (*Magnolia grandiflora*). Also called bull bay, it is quite exquisite, with its dinner-plate-size, fragrant white flowers – so popular for floating in a display bowl on the dinner table.

■ **The Cornelian cherry dogwood** *has star-shaped yellow flowers appearing in early spring, followed by bright red fruits.*

Flowering begins in June and continues right through the autumn. Large leaves that are shiny green on top and fuzzy pale orange underneath provide the flowers with a beautiful framework. Once the flowers drop off, orange-green, 5-centimetre-long fruits will develop. It really is a spectacular tree and one that will give you a lot of pleasure.

Magnolias like moist, well-drained, rich soil of a slightly acidic nature. They don't do well in compacted soil. It's important to think about their eventual height when you select a spot, and then place them where they are to grow permanently. Magnolias don't like to be moved from place to place.

Magnolias do not transplant graciously. Because they also quite dislike people fiddling around their base, this is not a place to put support plants that you will be digging up for any reason. Put an attractive mulch there instead.

The falling leaves can be somewhat messy, so keep them away from your patio. In general, most magnolias aren't too tolerant of city conditions. Also, do avoid dry and windy sites when planting. Other than that, magnolias are hardy and rarely have serious disease or pest problems.

More magnolias

STAR MAGNOLIA (*Magnolia stellata*)

The southern magnolia is a tall tree. Growing slowly, it will eventually reach 25 metres high or higher, and it can fill up a small garden when it reaches 11 or more metres wide. But if you have the space, it is worth it for its sheer magnificence. If you don't have the space, look for the variety Little Gem, which reaches about 6 metres high. Other fabulous magnolias include the ear-leafed umbrella tree (*M. fraseri*), the willow-leafed magnolia (*M. salicifolia*), the sweet bay (*M. virginiana*), and the star magnolia (*M. stellata*), a hardy specimen plant that averages just 8 metres high. For a lovely tree that blooms nicely at a young age, plant the deciduous saucer magnolia (*M. x soulangeana*). Read mail-order catalogues if you can't find what you want on sale near you.

Ornamental cherry

Flowering cherry trees are one of the most popular street trees in the country, and are always a welcome sight in the spring when their dazzling displays of white, pink, or even red blossoms burst open on bare stems. There are more than 200 different varieties to choose from, all with different sizes, shapes, and colours of blossom. At one extreme, *Prunus* Kanzan produces lovely, over-the-top, and extravagant double pink flowers, while at the other there are the simpler single, saucer-shaped flowers of the Yoshino cherry (*P. yedoensis*).

A tidy tree, the Yoshino grows to just 6 metres tall. Other varieties may reach 12 metres. All are deciduous. Flowering cherry trees require a sunny site with excellent drainage, and good soil. Root rot will occur with poor drainage, so it's important to plant these trees on raised mounds if unredeemable clay or the like is a problem.

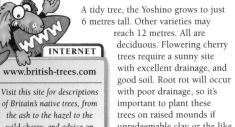

INTERNET

www.british-trees.com

Visit this site for descriptions of Britain's native trees, from the ash to the hazel to the wild cherry, and advice on how to grow them.

YOSHINO CHERRY (*Prunus yedoensis*)

Eastern redbud

Clusters of pink, purple, reddish, or white flowers are true eye-catchers as they bloom on the bare branches, and sometimes the trunk, in early spring. Soon, heart-shaped green leaves appear, which will turn lemon yellow in the autumn, accompanied by tan, bean-like seed pods that last into winter. Even in winter, the auburn bark on the open horizontal branches provides some visual interest.

Eastern redbuds (*Cercis canadensis*), which can reach 10 metres high at a moderate growth rate, are not fussy trees. They're happy in acidic or alkaline soil, damp soil, sun, or semi-shade. They need deep watering only about every 4 weeks during the growing season. This deciduous tree is tolerant of almost any type of garden condition. However, you do have to keep an eye out for insect pests.

■ *The distinctive leaves of Eastern redbud are preceded by pea-like flowers that are magenta in bud and open to pale pink.*

The eastern redbud is extremely popular, but the western redbud (*C. occidentalis*) gives it lots of competition. This is a much smaller tree, usually growing about 5 metres tall. It's often multi-trunked, and can also be grown as a shrub.

More flowering trees:

- Acacia (*Acacia*)
- Catalpa (*Catalpa*)
- Crab apple (*Malus*)
- Flowering almond (*Prunus triloba*)
- Flowering ash (*Fraxinus ornus*)
- Fringe tree (*Chionanthus*)

- Golden-rain tree (*Koelreuteria paniculata*)
- Golden rain (*Laburnum*)
- Hawthorn (*Crataegus*)
- Japanese snowbell (*Styrax japonicus*)
- Lilac (*Syringa vulgaris*)
- Smoke tree (*Cotinus*)
- Tulip tree (*Liriodendron*)

Instant arbours

IF YOU'RE EAGER to get your garden trees going quickly, you may want to plant some that are known for their rapid growth. These might be considered "temporary" trees, to be removed when slower-growing trees reach the height you want. Trees in the fast lane include the favourites I'm about to describe.

Ash

People seem to like to name ash (*Fraxinus*) trees after colours: red, claret, green, velvet, and white, among others. These are pretty much wash-and-go trees: none of the ashes demands a lot of attention. Among the hardiest of the hardy is the popular *F. pennsylvanica*, commonly known as both the green ash and the red ash. I'll call it the green ash here. This tree can survive severe cold (to –35° C!), semi-soggy soil, and drought conditions.

■ **Ash trees** *are popular for their foliage of paired leaves. Fraxinus angustifolia (shown here) has slender, dark green leaves that are attractively glossy.*

Like all ash trees, it's big, so even if you want a lot of shade really fast, buy only one. The tree is slim in youth, rounds out in middle age, and reaches at least 15 metres in height. In the autumn, the lance-shaped leaves turn a lovely yellow and the bark may develop a red tinge.

More eye-catching ashes

If you're feeling a little more flamboyant, consider the claret ash (*F. angustifolia*), whose dark green leaves turn wine red in autumn. For dry areas, the Arizona ash (*F. velutina*) grows from 10 to 15 metres high, depending on the variety. If you want lots of tree in a little time, the Arizona ash is a favourite among deciduous tree fans. At one time in the US, wood from the Arizona ash was used to make wagons. The bark is dark grey, and in the autumn the leaves turn bright yellow. Note, however, that with its shallow roots, you probably won't have much luck getting anything to grow under it, nor will you want to try to mow nearby for fear of damaging the roots.

Maple

Some of the maples (*Acer*) are bonsai material and some are towering specimens. There seem to be infinite varieties, most of which are breathtakingly beautiful in autumn, including the snakebark maple (*A. capillipes*). The giants are usually the ones that grow super quick, such as the red maple (*A. rubrum*) and sugar maple (*A. saccharum*), both reaching 20 metres. If you have limited space you'll want the smaller ones, but if you have enough land, the larger trees provide a brilliant seasonal prize. In general, maples make good shade trees. They do well in most good garden soils, and are seldom harassed by pests or diseases.

■ **The red maple** (Acer rubrum) *grows quickly to give a stunning display of red and bronze leaves, but it needs plenty of space.*

It's difficult to say which maple has the best autumn colour. The sugar maple, with its silver-grey bark, turns crimson, orange, and yellow, and is considered the most extravagant of the American maples. Leaves of the Norway maple (*A. platanoides*) and big-leaf maple (*A. macrophyllum*) turn a clear, deep yellow. In the shorter varieties, you'll get bright crimson red leaves from the amur or Tatarian maple (*A. tataricum*), the Japanese burgundy lace (*A. palmatum* Burgundy Lace), and the vine maple (*A. circinatum*). There are even maples with dark purple leaves.

INTERNET

www.totap.org.uk

Click here to find out about a millennium tree-planting initiative, Trees of Time and Place, which encouraged people to collect seeds from a favourite tree, sow them, and grow trees to plant out.

My advice is to buy any maple when you can see its autumn colour, even though the cost will be somewhat higher than when leaves are bare.

Even within the same variety there are variations in colour and leaf shape. If you can, make an autumn visit to a well-labelled **arboretum** before you buy. It's a simple matter to jot down the name of the tree you like, and then buy it in the following spring.

DEFINITION

An **arboretum** is a tree garden cultivated by horticulturists. Often open to the public, arboretums are a great way to learn about trees you may wish to plant in your own garden. They're also nice for a casual stroll.

Oleaster

The oleaster tree (*Elaeagnus angustifolia*) is a fast-grower that's very useful for erosion control on slopes. Even the tallest oleaster is not too imposing, reaching a maximum of 8 metres high. However, it also expands to 8 metres wide. This is a good background tree, with willow-like, olive green leaves. It is easily pruned to make a hedge.

This is a sturdy garden addition with fragrant, greenish-yellow flowers, even if it's not an eye-catcher like the maples. Site it in sun or light shade. It patiently tolerates dust, smoke, wind, and seashore exposure, and very cold or very hot, dry weather. The oleaster's only true nemesis is poorly drained soil, but it will withstand soil that's damp. Pests seem to avoid it, and transplanting is easy. Birds love its ample, yellow, olive-like berries in winter.

OLEASTER (*Elaeagnus angustifolia*)

Like anything else, the oleaster does have a drawback: messy berries and leaves. But its semi-thorny branches make it a good barrier plant, and on a slope, a bit of organic debris is only a minor distraction. There are other *Elaeagnus*, equally super hardy, that grow in shrub form. Keep an eye out for the attractive silverberry (*E. commutata*).

Weeping willow

Trivia...

In the first century AD, a Greek physician discovered that a concoction made from willow bark, despite causing an upset stomach, decreased both pain and fever. Native Americans brewed willow leaves into a bitter tea to cure headaches. Much later, researchers discovered that both the bark and leaves contained a chemical closely resembling aspirin.

Weeping-style trees with flexible, drooping branches provide a focal point for the garden, and for many people they seem to bring on waves of nostalgia. The weeping willow's (*Salix babylonica*) branches will cascade towards the ground, even from a height of 10 metres or more. If you decide this is a tree you simply must have, you will probably plant one despite known drawbacks. Yes, they drop leaves. Yes, they seem to send party invitations to bugs. Yes, the wood is brittle. And no, you can't garden around the roots – don't even try. So why bother?

Because they are beautiful, grow rapidly, tolerate almost any soil, and if you give them lots of water, weeping willows will thrive in any drainage conditions. If you have a stream on your property, this is definitely a tree to consider. Early American pioneers, moving westward over dry territory, were jubilant when they saw willows because it meant water was nearby.

The willow family tree

A relative, the golden willow (*Salix alba* var. *vitellina*), which tolerates both beach conditions and floods, is equally fast growing. Quite pretty, it has yellowish-brown bark, bright yellow stems, and leaves that are yellow-green underneath and bright green above. Of the hundreds of willow species, there are also shrub-like ones and small trees. Consider planting a decorative pussy willow (*S. caprea*), whose soft, silky, grey catkins are a popular feature in dried flower arrangements.

More instant arbours:

- Acacia (*Acacia*)
- Birch (*Betula*)
- Catalpa (*Catalpa*)
- Empress tree (*Paulownia tomentosa*)
- Eucalyptus (*Eucalyptus*)
- Honey locust (*Gleditsia*)
- Lime (*Tilia*)
- Pin oak (*Quercus palustris*)
- Poplar (*Populus*)
- Silk oak (*Grevillea robusta*)
- Silk tree (*Albizia*)

Autumn colour

CHOOSING A TREE *for its autumn colour can be a real challenge. Some provide brilliant displays of colour, but can be a little dull at other times of the year. Here I have listed those trees that really earn a place in your garden.*

Sweet gum

The sweet gum (*Liquidambar styraciflua*) originates from the eastern United States and Mexico. It provides autumn colours that are truly wonderful. I really like this tree, although by the time mine reached 10 metres high, it was too big for my suburban plot. It would have grown to 25 metres if I'd let it. But looking out of my window was really something! Even when the tree was young, it had great autumn colours: crimson, oranges, purples, and yellows.

■ **The sweet gum** (Liquidambar styraciflua) *is a conical, spreading tree with glossy, dark green leaves that turn to rich yellow-purple-red tones in the autumn.*

Each tree seems to have its own colour personality, so this is another example of a good purchase to make in the autumn.

Although the sweet gum doesn't have any flowers to speak of, the prickly, golf-ball-size fruits that follow hang on bare branches throughout most of the winter. Full sun and moderate water are all you need to nurture a sweetgum.

Birch

If you're into autumn yellows, try three birches planted in a triangle. Picturesque peeling bark, often white or grey, delicate branches and 2-centimetre cone-like fruits that follow the autumn leaf-fall will make the trio even more attractive.

Don't be afraid to try one of the more obscure species. Most commonly marketed are the 20-metre monarch birch (*B. maximowicziana*) and the 15-metre silver birch (*B. pendula*). The latter has weeping varieties, so if you like that sort of thing, shop around a bit. If one garden centre doesn't have it, another will.

Birches do demand lots of water in addition to sunlight. Some are susceptible to insect pests, including aphids – those tiny insects that drip sticky, sugary waste matter all over your new car.

My birches, which have never grown over 6 metres tall in 30 years, are a focal point of my back garden, and I've never had insect problems. The birds adore the little brown fruits that hang on throughout the winter.

■ **A graceful tree** *with a narrow crown, the Laciniata is a form of the silver birch (Betula pendula) that bears yellow-green catkins in spring.*

Smoke tree

If you have rocky or otherwise poor soil, this may be just the tree for you. It's simple to grow, multi-stemmed, and fairly small, growing only about 5 metres high and almost as wide. Leaves may be blue-green or purple throughout the spring and summer, changing to orange-red in the autumn. The name "smoke" comes from its greenish blooms, which, as they fade, send out stalks covered with fuzzy, greyish-purple hairs. This makes the tree seem as if it is in a smoky, almost surreal cloud. The appearance lasts through until late summer.

The smoke tree (*Cotinus coggygria*) grows in full sun or light shade, and although somewhat drought-tolerant, it prefers low to average water with good drainage. It can be grown as a shrub, or, if you don't mind a bit of pruning, as a small, single-trunked tree.

SMOKE TREE (*Cotinus coggygria*)

Washington hawthorn

Of all the hawthorns, this is truly the best one for autumn colour. The 8-metre-high deciduous *Crataegus phaenopyrum* dons an autumn ballgown of the most vivid orange-red. If you have the space for more than one, two make a real showstopper. In spring, pure white, grouped flowers appear. They are followed by clusters of scarlet berries that seem to cling to the branches forever, and are great for attracting birds. Hawthorn also grows well along roadsides, at salt-sprayed seashores, and in cities, including inner-city parks. Hawthorns come with and without thorns, the benefit of those with sharp spines being that they make a nice barrier.

What do they need in the way of conditions? Not much other than sun and an average amount of water. Other hawthorns include the cockspur (*C. crus-galli*), the May (*C. laevigata*), and the toba (*C. ¥ mordenensis* Toba) – a hybrid that performs exceptionally well in climates with cold winters.

INTERNET

www.gardening.about.com/library/weekly/aa100599htm

This U.S. site provides a good selection of trees for autumn colour, many of which will grow perfectly happily here in the United Kingdom.

More trees for autumn colour:

- Chinese pistachio tree (*Pistacia chinensis*)
- Chinese tallow tree (*Sapium sebiferum*)
- Horse chestnut
  (*Aesculus hippocastanum*)
- Katsura tree (*Cercidiphyllum japonicum*)
- Larch (*Larix*)
- Maidenhair (*Ginkgo*)

- Mountain ash (*Sorbus*)
- Poplar (*Populus*)
- Scarlet oak (*Quercus coccinea*)
- Snowy mespilus (*Amelanchier*)
- Sorrel tree (*Oxydendrum*)
- Tulip tree (*Liriodendron*)
- Tupelo (*Nyssa sylvatica*)

A simple summary

✓ Evergreen trees keep their leaves right throughout the year. Deciduous trees shed their leaves in the autumn and grow new ones in the spring.

✓ Before you buy any tree, learn how big it will grow and determine if this will realistically fit in your garden space. You don't want to have to move it later on when it is large.

✓ Buy younger, smaller trees, rather than those that are larger, to ease transplant shock, which could kill your tree. The smaller ones soon catch up in size.

✓ Plant deciduous trees during their dormant, or resting, season. Make the planting hole as big as you can – about 50 per cent larger than the extended rootball. Soak roots before, and water immediately after planting.

✓ You can buy trees to fill just about any niche in your garden: flowers, leaf shape, colour, seasonal beauty, size, protective barrier, camouflage.

✓ Part of the fun of gardening is doing some research. Study the trees you might want before you buy them.

Chapter 9

Successful Shrubs

SHRUBS SERVE MANY GARDEN FUNCTIONS. They are hedges, screens, boundaries, noise reducers, windbreaks, background plantings, garden dividers, prowler deterrents, and focal points. In addition to front and back garden shrubs that can be planted directly in the ground, you can buy shrubs to plant in big containers on your patio. There seems to be a size and style for just about every need.

In this chapter...
✓ What is a shrub?
✓ Too many choices
✓ Proper pruning
✓ Shrubs for hedges
✓ Scented shrubs
✓ Shrubs for visual fruit

GRACEFUL, ARCHING *NEILLIA THIBETICA*

What is a shrub?

WHAT'S THE DIFFERENCE between a shrub and a tree? That's a good question, and one that nobody has ever really succeeded in answering. You can say that a tree has one trunk and a shrub has several, but there are some trees with multiple trunks. You can say that trees are bigger than shrubs, but horticulturists have brought us trees that are quite tidy in size – unlike some shrubs, which grow wild and woolly.

In general, though, trees usually (but not always) have a single, woody trunk and are fairly to very tall, beginning perhaps at 6 metres high and ending at, well, towering. Shrubs usually (but not always) have several woody stems and may be from 30 centimetres to 5 metres high. There are also tree-like shrubs, tall shrubs pruned to look like small trees, and shrub-like trees. Phew! We definitely need to keep it simple. Even if you can't really define a shrub, will you know it when you see it? Probably.

The secret language of shrubs

When selecting a shrub, especially from a catalogue, you may see words that describe its shape. These words aren't always as clear as they should be, so let's go over them briefly:

- A **low-branching** shrub is one where the lowest branches come very close to, or touch, the ground.

- A **prostrate shrub** is lower than a low-branching shrub. Its branches grow sideways, and may even rest on the ground. A prostrate shrub is often used as groundcover.

- If a shrub is described as **pyramidal**, it has a pointed top and a wider base, like an Egyptian pyramid.

- A **columnar shrub** resembles a column, or a round pole.

- Like the columnar and the pyramidal shapes, the **compact shrub** has dense foliage, or leaves. It is, however, shorter, and almost square or rectangular in appearance.

- If you want a more airy touch, an **open shrub** is one that has all its branches spaced a bit apart.

- A **specimen**, or **focal point shrub**, is an open-style shrub.

- In **weeping-style shrubs**, the branches grow upwards and arch towards the ground.

Too many choices

THERE ARE SHRUBS that flower in early spring, some that flower a little later in the season, and summer and autumn bloomers. Some shrubs have fragrant flowers, many have berries. Although most have green leaves, others have leaves with yellow-green, blue-green, green-white, or purplish markings. Some are deciduous, others evergreen. The leaves of deciduous shrubs may change colours in autumn, becoming red, orange, or yellow before they drop. On some deciduous shrubs, the bark has its own fascination.

■ **The common holly** (Ilex aquifolium) *looks like a shrub before it becomes a tree.*

You may be tempted to select a little bit of everything. Try to resist. To create a successful garden picture, plant at least three shrubs of the same variety, so they form a little group. The exception is when you want a specimen, or focal point shrub. A plain old shrub is not a focal point, so choose your specimen plant carefully. You want a focal point to offer something special, such as colourful leaves, fantastic flowers, or delightful shape.

Planning first

Once again, just a little planning and a little bit of research before you shop will go far in helping you make the right choices.

The best advice I can give you is to look at a mature size specimen if possible, and visualize it in your selected spot. Then buy a smaller version of your chosen plant. Regardless of how small it looks when you plant it, it will grow.

To be extra-confident in your choice, do some background research on the plant's favourite habitat and any special needs, so you'll be sure it will do well in your garden.

Do not count on adapting the site to your shrub by changing the soil around it. Choose a shrub that is already suitable by its very nature.

How and when to buy your shrub

There are two best times to buy a shrub. One is in early spring, before new leaves appear on the branches. The other is in late autumn, approximately 6 weeks before the first heavy frosts. This allows for some root growth.

Most often, shrubs are sold in medium to large containers. Deciduous shrubs are sometimes sold early in the season with their roots bare, and this is the least expensive way to buy them. As the season moves on, the bare-rooted plants are placed in containers and the price goes up. Evergreens are sold in containers or hessian-wrapped. (You remember from Chapter 8?)

Picking a healthy shrub

Before you buy your shrub, make sure the soil is damp. If the rootball of an evergreen dries out, you are likely to be getting a half-dead plant. Chances are slim that you'll be able to help it recover. Whether it is deciduous or evergreen, always check to see if the roots are ramming their way through the container bottom or circling the trunk. If they are, the plant is root-bound. Shrubs grown in cramped surroundings like this are quite often water stressed. When you place them in the garden, the roots have limited capacity to reach out for moisture. A root-bound plant of any kind seldom adapts well when transplanted. Should you inadvertently buy one, loosen the roots and spread them out as best you can before planting.

PERFECT PLANTING

If you buy a container plant and haven't had the sides cut at the garden centre, loosen the rootball by dipping the entire container in a bucket of water and letting it soak for a few minutes. This will make getting it out of a tight container fairly easy. Regardless of the way your plant is packaged when you buy it, you must loosen the soil clinging to the roots so you can spread them out when you get ready to place the shrub in its planting hole. Roots tangled into each other will continue to grow that way. Spread-out roots anchor the plant and have more space for survival.

1 **Dig a big hole**

Dig a hole about 50 per cent larger than the size of the spread-out roots, and add some good organic material. If planting in spring, mix in a cup of general-purpose fertilizer (5-10-5).

Help it along

To protect the newly planted shrub from wind and sun while it adjusts to its new environment, place a cover (made from paper or a similar material) over it for a week or so. Don't forget to water.

If your new shrub is less than 1.2 metres high, you don't need to stake it. But if it's taller, put a solid stake in the hole before you plant the shrub. Fix the trunk to the stake with garden tape. Don't use wire, because as the shrub grows the wire will cut into it.

There is continuing (and heated!) discussion among experts about whether you should prune a new shrub. Some say not to prune the shrub in any way. Others say not to prune evergreens, but to prune deciduous shrubs. I say don't prune at first. The plant is traumatized enough by the moving, so keep it simple.

Heeling in your shrub

Plant your shrub within a few hours of buying it, and certainly within 24 hours of bringing it home. If this is not possible, you can heel the plant in to preserve its health, and your investment. This is really simple. In a shady spot, dig a trench about 45 centimetres deep. Place your shrub, tipped sideways about 45°, into the trench. Cover the roots with soil. In autumn, you can leave it this way for a week. In spring, leave it for a few days only, as it will start to grow and will be traumatized if you move it.

2 **Remove the pot**

Gently remove the shrub from its container. If necessary, water the pot first to make removal easier. Try not to disturb any of the soil around the roots while moving the plant.

3 **Plant your shrub**

Position the plant in the middle of the hole. Gradually fill around the plant with a mixture of local soil and organic soil. Give the plant a bit of a jiggle to fill any air pockets around the roots.

4 **Water it well**

Tap the soil down gently with your foot after each few spades of soil. Once it is stable in the hole, give your new purchase a hearty drink of water to help its roots get established.

Proper pruning

SOME PEOPLE LIKE SHRUBS with a natural look. Others want to clip them to look like hedgehogs or candelabra. You'll find the majority of people hacking away at the weekend. Whether inherited from a prior owner, or planted in great enthusiasm a decade ago, the pretty little shrub is now 5 metres tall and equally wide. It is perhaps blocking the view from their picture window, making midnight noises under their roof, or prolifically dropping leaves into their guttering. Eventually, they'll probably chop it down or try to dig it out. In between, they'll just keep pruning it.

Before you begin chopping away, do a little research about when your shrub should be pruned. Some shrubs should be pruned before they flower. Other shrubs should be pruned after they flower. If you don't do it at the proper time, you won't get many flowers or nice little berries for the birds.

When it's time to prune, give the about-to-be-trimmed plant a thorough watering. Now begin, using the proper equipment, such as secateurs or lopping shears. Make sure that you trim carefully and slowly.

Never cut a branch flush to the trunk. This is an invitation to decay.

Careful cutting

Remove dead wood and branches that don't have a healthy appearance, and any that are trying for the odd-growth Olympics. If you want to make a shrub more compact, cut where there is a bud pointing downwards. If you want to make a shrub taller, cut where there is a bud pointing upwards. After you have done just a bit of trimming, stand back and rest. Refocus. While indiscriminate cutting may work off human angst, you don't want to strip the plant, just shape it.

■ **Proper pruning** *needs proper tools. Always use sharp secateurs to cut back dead, diseased, or dying wood. When you have done this you can then prune for shape.*

General care

Deciduous shrubs need feeding about once a year. This is of greatest benefit if you do it in early spring or late autumn, after the plants have lost their leaves. Do not fertilize shrubs in late summer or early autumn. This will encourage new growth that is very susceptible to frost. Resist the temptation just to toss the fertilizer against the shrub trunk. Instead, see how far the roots fan out by looking at and poking into the soil. Water well afterwards.

■ **Spread fertilizer** *evenly around the plant so that none of your shrub's roots miss out on essential nutrients.*

INTERNET

www.doctorgreen
fingers.com

Click here for advice on all aspects of good plant care. This gardening"clinic" covers a wide range of topics from minor tree surgery to organic gardening. There's also advice on avoiding accidents in the garden. For details on correct and incorrect pruning methods, click on the "operating theatre" button.

New plantings need more regular watering than sedate, older plantings. After the first year, depending on the shrub, you can let it go almost dry between waterings. If you live in a cold area, lay some mulch around the shrub to keep the roots warm.

RESCUE FOR SAD SHRUBS

1. Is your shrub in a frost pocket? Tender shrubs dislike the cold. Try moving it.

2. Is your evergreen shrub in a windy spot? Wind increases water evaporation. Either create a way to break the wind, perhaps with a tree in the wind's path, or increase your watering.

3. Is your shrub under or near a tree with wide-spreading shallow roots? These roots absorb the water and nutrients in the soil around them, depriving your shrub. You must either move the shrub or remove the tree.

4. Is mulch piled high around the shrub trunk? A high blanket of mulch holds moisture that attracts rot fungi and causes other problems. Have a look and lower the mulch.

5. And the usual suspects: Is there enough sun for a sun-loving shrub? Have you put a shade-lover in the sun? The solution to these problems is obvious.

Shrubs for hedges

A HEDGE SERVES AS A PRETTY (and if it's thick enough, a prowler-deterring) boundary. Easy-to-grow shrubs favoured by hedge-lovers include the ones I'm about to describe.

Common privet

I have no great love for privets (*Ligustrum vulgare*), mostly because they tend to be seasonally messy. However, I have grown them for decades simply because they thrive in just about any soil, any place, sun or shade, never seem to contract disease, tolerate forgetfulness – you get the picture. You also will get dozens of little deciduous baby privets to keep or pull out, as the falling seeds seem to have a high birth rate. Should you want to make a really large hedge, plant these youngsters about 45 centimetres apart. Each heartily growing youth will reach about 1.5 metres high, although some grow as tall as 5 metres.

Privet is easily pruned, and some people do so to avoid the prolific, small, white flowers, which have a fairly unpleasant aroma. The flowers appear only for a short time in early summer, and pollinators do like them. When pruning young shrubs, make the shrub top slightly narrower than the broader base. This lets sun reach the base, promoting a preferred, bushy growth pattern.

There are several privets to choose from, including evergreens, and those are easily pruned and kept in small tree form. Simply put, if you want a shrub that ranks among the hardiest (and ranks highly with birds too), privets are for you.

Hedge cotoneaster

There are more than 50 species of cotoneaster, all with abundant small fruits that last well into the winter. The red, scarlet, yellow, or black ornamental fruits also attract birds, if you like a little wildlife. Some cotoneasters act as groundcover, others are upright, ranging in size from dwarf to 5 metres tall. The taller varieties are easily pruned to a desired shape.

Trivia...

Cotoneaster is so hardy, there are even cotoneasters that thrive by the sea, such as herringbone cotoneaster (Cotoneaster horizontalis).

Hedge cotoneaster (*Cotoneaster simonsii*) grows as a rounded evergreen shrub eventually reaching 2 to 2.5 metres high and equally as wide. When the plant's pinkish-white flowers subside, round black berries will appear. Cotoneaster is hardy and has no special soil requirements. It grows well in clay and even in deprived, stony soil. Although semi-shade tolerant, planting in full sun will yield the best results as far as flowers and fruits are concerned.

The only caution with cotoneaster is to plant it where it is to grow. Cotoneaster does not transplant cheerfully.

Deciduous varieties, such as cranberry cotoneaster (*C. apiculatus*), offer a nice alternative to the evergreens. Cranberry cotoneaster has dark green, glossy leaves turning reddish-purple at the season's end. Its flowers are small and white, but profuse in mid-summer. It grows to only 1 metre high, but will spread to 2.5 metres wide.

Japanese holly

Japanese hollies (*Ilex crenata*) make attractive informal or trimmed hedges. Densely packed leaves are dark green on a neat, rounded plant that grows slowly. Usually about 1.2 metres high, this plant can reach 3 metres or be as short as 30 centimetres.

JAPANESE HOLLY *(Ilex crenata)*

There are a fair number of varieties among the Japanese hollies, and the Convexa variety is one of the best of the group for hedge use. Its berries are black and inconspicuous. This holly adapts to sun or semi-shade, and to almost all climates. It will even put up with some pollution. Although it will adjust to most soils, there is a definite preference for fertile, moist, well-drained soil. If you want to prune Japanese holly into a formal hedge, do so after the new growth has matured in the spring.

Laurustinus

There's quite a choice of viburnums, including some with phenomenally fragrant white flower clusters. Some viburnums are evergreen, some are deciduous, and many are listed for general use. The evergreen laurustinus (*Viburnum tinus*) is brilliant for screens and hedges, reaching 2 to 4 metres high and almost as wide. Laurustinus leaves are dark green and the foliage adapts well to formal pruning. Its 7-centimetre-wide clusters of flowers are initially pink, later becoming white. It doesn't have the pleasant aroma of some of the other viburnums, but it does bear attractive, bright blue fruit. For informal hedges, pruning in alternate years is sufficient.

This shrub will tolerate a shady site, but if you want more flowers, you need to give it some sun. It's not fussy about soil – acidic or alkaline is fine. Planted near the sea, however, laurustinus' leaves may develop mildew.

Where it is marginally hardy, don't water laurustinus in late summer as this encourages lush growth that may not survive the winter.

Rosemary

If you'd like a short to medium-size hardy shrub, and fragrant flowers would be a plus, think rosemary (*Rosmarinus officinalis*). It grows most happily in fairly dry or gravelly soil, as long as it has good drainage. Full sun is fine, even against a white reflecting wall. Happy to −10° C in well-drained sites, as well as in warm winter areas, rosemary tolerates seaside areas reasonably well. And once the plant gets started, watering can be kept to a minimum. Moreover, rosemary rarely has pest or disease problems. It's hard to find something objectionable about rosemary. I've seen it grow healthily in gardens that, for one reason or another, are completely untended.

Choose carefully for the height you want, as some varieties are ground-cover plants and others, such as Tuscan Blue, grow to 2 metres tall. This variety has clear blue flowers, but other, smaller varieties have lavender-blue or violet flowers. You might want some of each.

■ **Rosemary not only** *looks pretty when in flower, it also smells wonderful, and, being a culinary herb, it's a useful shrub to have in your back garden.*

Trivia...

Rosemary symbolizes affection and remembrance. At one time, it played an emblematic role in weddings. Bridesmaids would present the groom with a ribbon-bound rosemary bouquet. The bride would bring a wreath of rosemary to her new abode, in remembrance of her former home and loving hearts that had cared for her so well. A bridesmaid would also plant a sprig of rosemary in the bride's new garden. When this rosemary grew, it would be used for the bride's daughters when they married. In a prelude to marriage, a young woman wishing to dream of her future husband would place a sixpence and a rosemary sprig under her pillow.

More shrubs for hedges:

- Arborvitae (*Thuja occidentalis*)
- Barberry (*Berberis thunbergii*)
- Box (*Buxus*)
- Burning bush (*Euonymus alatus*)
- Cherry laurel (*Prunus laurocerasus*)
- Evergreen honeysuckle (*Lonicera nitida*)
- False cypress (*Chamaecyparis*)
- Glossy abelia (*Abelia x grandiflora*)
- Great rhododendron (*Rhododendron maximum*)

- Juniper (*Juniperus*)
- Myrtle (*Myrtus*)
- Osmanthus (*Osmanthus*)
- Photinia (*Photinia*)
- Pittosporum (*Pittosporum*)
- Rose of Sharon (*Hypericum calycinum*)
- Scarlet firethorn (*Pyracantha coccinea*)
- Silverberry (*Elaeagnus commutata*)
- Yew (*Taxus*)

Scented shrubs

THERE'S AN ABUNDANCE *of sweet-smelling shrubs to choose from. Whether you are planting a whole border or just want one dramatic specimen plant to set off the rest of your plantings, there are shrubs ideally suited to your needs. Of course, they all have different care requirements, but you're bound to find one to suit you from the list of my favourites that follow.*

CLOVE CURRANT (*Ribes odoratum*)

Clove currant

Maybe you just want to grow something different. Great! If you like the scent of cloves, try this shrub. A deciduous shrub, clove currant, also known as buffalo currant (*Ribes odoratum*), likes quite dry soil and a somewhat shady spot – an alternative to many other shrubs that demand sunlight. It's multi-purpose, because besides the fruit and the spicy scent, there are cascades of tubular, sunny yellow flowers in spring, and leaves that transform into scintillating scarlet in autumn. Allow this plant ample garden space, as it enlarges by means of underground **suckers**. The better the quality of the soil, the faster this plant spreads.

> **DEFINITION**
>
> *Yes,* **sucker** *is a gardening term. Suckers are shoots springing from below the ground, typically from a plant's roots, instead of from its stem. They eventually push their way to the surface to make new plants.*

The young foliage of clove currant, like other Ribes species, is highly susceptible to aphids; if you spot these bugs, pick off affected shoots by hand, wash insects off with a hose, or use an insecticide.

To see if it is possible to grow a clove currant in your area, visit your local garden centre. If they sell it, it's probably safe to bring it home. Birds just love its small, black, sweet-tart fruits. Another bird attractor is golden currant (*R. alpinum* 'Aureum'). This hardy species likes full sun, does well in all soil types, and doesn't mind air pollution. It is often planted in groups and makes a good hedging shrub.

Daphne

In the language of flowers, daphne means "sweets to the sweet". Sweetness notwithstanding, daphnes (*Daphne*) are inclined to be prima donnas. If you simply must have that delicious fragrance next to your patio door or living room window, you'll just have to do the extra coddling to make these shrubs comfortable. Daphnes require very well-drained, neutral soil and full sun, although they tolerate partial shade. Always place some mulch around the shrub after planting and, once planted, do not move. Daphnes resent transplanting. Never over-water these shrubs, as their dislike for soggy soil is almost immediately apparent.

The winter daphne (*D. odora*) has a particularly beautiful scent. It grows from 1 to 1.5 metres high and almost as wide. Do note that all parts of this pretty shrub are poisonous if ingested, especially the berries.

WINTER DAPHNE (*Daphne odora*)

Gardenia

■ **The waxy beauty** *and sweet scent of gardenia (Gardenia augusta) once made it a popular buttonhole flower.*

The gardenia's (*Gardenia augusta*) fragrance is legendary, and while you can buy it in a perfume bottle, you can also grow it in your garden. One large, waxy, white cut flower can perfume a small room, and in mid-summer a mature shrub is covered with flowers. The plant's leaves are a shiny dark green. Native to China and Japan, this attractive evergreen is now available in many *cultivars* ranging in size from 60 centimetres to 2.5 metres. So you can keep a gardenia as a container shrub, giving it winter protection indoors.

> **DEFINITION**
>
> **Cultivar** *is a contraction of "cultivated variety". It's the progeny of a deliberate breeding effort which is known only in cultivation and produces plants with predictable, uniform characteristics.*

Gardenias demand very well-drained, acidic soil that's high in organic matter. They prefer full sun, but light shade may suffice. Avoid positioning gardenias in windy areas. Water regularly, and don't let the soil dry out completely. A 5-centimetre mulch of lime-free compost can help keep gardenias in good health.

This shrub must be regularly fertilized. Look for fertilizer that says "azaleas" on the label (it's also good for gardenias), and read the instructions carefully before applying. **Fish meal** is another fine fertilizer for gardenias.

Promoting new blooms on your gardenias is a piece of cake. Just take a moment to cut the faded flowers.

DEFINITION

*Because **fish meal** is an organic, or natural, item, it's popular with many gardeners who prefer to use natural products. It contains nitrogen in a form that is slowly released to plants. In the U.S., gardeners commonly use fish emulsion, which is a thick brownish liquid that also happens to smell quite strongly of fish.*

Lavender

If I could have only one type of plant in my garden, it would have to be lavender (*Lavandula*). I like this small evergreen shrub so much that I collect books about lavender, make lavender wands, put lavender in my cut flower displays, attempt to make lavender sachets, and order odd varieties from catalogues. Although some lavenders can be a bit sensitive, they make me happy, and their fragrance is fabulous.

Trivia...

For centuries, lavender has been used to scent soaps, bath water, and linen. According to some, the name derives from the Latin lavare, "to wash". Long ago people thought washing was unhealthy, and sanitary conditions were generally pretty awful. Because of this, people tended to have quite distinctive body aromas, some of which weren't very pleasant at all. To hide the unpleasant smell, they used to drench themselves in lots of home-made perfume, lavender included.

In general, the common lavenders, such as the French (*L. stoechas*) and Spanish (*L. stoechas pedunculata*), are quite hardy if you provide dryish, rather limy soil and bright sunshine. Frankly, lavenders like my clay soil, which is why we get along so well. Soil must be well drained, so if you have any problems whatsoever, including lengthy winter rains on clay soil, plant lavender on a mound. Depending on the variety, lavender will grow from 45 to 90 centimetres high. The narrow leaves and flowers are carried on slim, slender stalks, and the plant will bush out nicely if it can grow in the right soil.

■ **Spanish lavender** *doesn't need much attention in the right soil – and butterflies and bees absolutely love its fragrant purple flowers.*

The flowers are usually light to medium purple, but there are white, pink, and even green flowering lavenders. But these are not, in my experience, as hardy as the purple ones. If you live in a mild climate, lavender may bloom almost all year; otherwise you'll have spring and summer flowers. Experiment a bit to see what grows well in your climate. Given all the choices, you might try a more "exotic" lavender, which you can find from a catalogue. I have even heard about a type of lavender that has reddish flowers.

INTERNET

botanical.com

Botanical.com has details on a wide variety of medicinal herbs, including nine pages of historical and growing information on lavender, plus how to make some lavender concoctions.

Mock orange

Some people consider the orange blossom fragrance overly sweet, but most find mock orange (*Philadelphus coronarius*) a joy. In spring, white flower clusters transform this otherwise plain, deciduous shrub into a star. Unlike the more fussy gardenia or daphne, mock orange grows in just about any garden soil, and tolerates occasional drought. Give it full sun or light shade. The *P. coronarius* species is among the hardiest of the mock oranges, and in a sheltered spot may survive fairly cold winters. To avoid disappointment, select shrubs when they're in bloom, as some mock orange varieties don't have that famous fragrance.

VARIEGATED MOCK ORANGE (*Philadelphus coronarius*)

Mock orange is a great plant if you like butterfly visitors. In the language of flowers, it signifies "Remember me".

More scented shrubs:

- Allspice (*Calycanthus floridus*)
- American witch hazel (*Fothergilla*)
- Buddleia (*Buddleja*)
- Californian lilac (*Ceanothus*)
- Deutzia (*Deutzia*)
- False holly (*Osmanthus heterophyllus*)

- Glossy abelia (*Abelia x grandiflora*)
- Jasmine (*Jasminum*)
- Lilac (*Syringa*)
- Oleaster (*Elaeagnus angustifolia*)
- Star magnolia (*Magnolia stellata*)
- Sweetbox (*Sarcococca*)
- Virginia sweetspire (*Itea virginica*)
- Wintersweet (*Chimonanthus*)

Shrubs for visual fruit

VIVID FRUITS ARE THE SELLING POINT of some shrubs. As you probably know, the fruit of these plants is for visual (not internal) consumption. In fact, some can be poisonous, so make sure young children don't get their hands on them. Here are just a few of my favourites.

Barberry

The barberry (*Berberis*) is a low or medium-size shrub. It provides winter-persistent blue, black, or red super-showy berries, adored by birds. The berries follow yellow flowers that attract honeybees. The flowers do well in indoor arrangements, and appear during May and June amidst glossy, green leaves. The barberry's branches have thorns, so watch your fingers! All of the numerous barberry species are extremely easy to grow in average garden soil and several tolerate climate extremes. However, each has its own climate preference, so it's best to buy them from a local garden centre.

The most popular purchase is the wintergreen barberry (*B. julianae*), an evergreen from 1.2 to 2 metres high, but be aware that its blue-black berries don't last as long as those of some others. Of all the barberries, this is the thorniest, and hence is often used as a barrier shrub. Berries do last on the deciduous Japanese barberry (*B. thunbergii*). They're profuse and bright red, so they really stand out against winter snow. The leaves turn brilliant scarlet, orange, and yellow before they drop in the autumn from this 1.2- to 2-metre-high shrub. Barberries do well in full sun or light shade. They don't need very much water in order to thrive, and are generally a healthy, pest-free shrub.

Firethorn

I have 3-metre-high firethorn (*Pyracantha*) all along my back fence. Its bright red berries arrive in the autumn by what seems to be the thousands. Birds, especially robins, love the berries. Firethorn also has sharp thorns, so anybody who wants to crawl over my fence has to run a formidable gauntlet. In spring and summer pretty, small white flowers with an odd but mostly mild aroma attract foraging bees. I am always trying to get pollinators in my garden, so this is a great thing, and I just move my lounge chair away from the shrubs for a while.

There are many different types of firethorn, ranging from 1 metre to 5.5 metres tall. Berries might be yellow, orange, or red, and would last well into winter if the birds didn't eat them all. Purchase firethorn in the spring and place in a site that gets full sun. Water regularly but don't overwater or give a lot of fertilizer. Place this evergreen where it is to grow, as firethorn resents moving around. It grows extremely well against a house wall, especially if you prune it well back into the wall each year.

Usually very hardy, the only hazard that I've encountered is an occasional plant disease called fireblight. Literally overnight, the entire plant turns black with a scorched appearance.

Fireblight is caused by a bacterium that becomes particularly destructive when daily temperatures average above 15° C and when rains come during the blooming season. It may spread to nearby susceptible plants, such as apple trees, pear trees, hawthorn, and mountain ashes.

Sometimes the blackened plant is dead, at other times it only looks dead. I leave mine alone for a year, because the affected plant sometimes grows back, although never quite as hardy. Resistant varieties of firethorn are available. Look for those named Mohave and Teton.

■ **Orange Glow firethorn** *bears lots of orange-red berries. Enjoy the sight while you can, before birds devour the lot!*

Oregon grape

Also called grape holly, Oregon grapeholly, and Oregon grape mahonia, this good-natured shrub (*Mahonia aquifolium*) thrives in just about any garden soil, including clay and sandy. Plant several shrubs in a row and you have a nice, 1-metre-high hedge. The shiny evergreen leaves are holly-like, and are often used in bouquets and Christmas wreaths. In the winter, the leaves turn a reddish colour. From March to May, small golden-yellow flowers appear in dense clusters. When the flowers subside, purple-blue berries in grape-like clusters appear. The berries are quite attractive to birds.

OREGON GRAPE
(*Mahonia aquifolium*)

If you have a shady area, Oregon grape might just serve as a good fill-in. You do have to give it a moist, well-drained site, shelter from hot, dry winds, and an acidic soil. Although Oregon grape can be a bit fussy as to site, it isn't always easy to find a hardy shade-happy shrub, especially a disease-resistant one that has both pretty flowers and berries for the birds.

Purple beauty berry

Plant beauty berry (*Callicarpa dichotoma*) in masses to get the full October effect of its lilac berries appearing in enormous clusters, somewhat like small grapes. Each shrub grows about 1.2 metres high (even taller if it's in the shade), and develops a 1.2-metre spread. In the spring, pinkish-lavender flower clusters are carried on stalks above medium-green leaves. Purple beauty berry does well in full sun or light shade, needs only average garden soil, and requires below moderate water. In very cold winter areas, this deciduous shrub might die down to the ground. It will return in the spring, so don't worry. This one is easy to grow.

More shrubs for visual fruit:

- Baneberry (*Actaea*)
- Bearberry (*Arctostaphylos*)
- Beauty bush (*Kolkwitzia*)
- Californian lilac (*Ceanothus*)
- Cestrum (*Cestrum*)
- Cotoneaster (*Cotoneaster*)
- Dogwood (*Cornus*)
- Elaeagnus (*Elaeagnus*)

- Heavenly bamboo (*Nandina domestica*)
- Holly (*Ilex*)
- Photinia (*Photinia*)
- Snowberry (*Symphoricarpos*)
- Spice bush (*Lindera benzoin*)
- Spindle tree (*Euonymus*)
- Sweet box (*Sarcococca*)
- Viburnum (*Viburnum*)

A simple summary

✓ Shrubs have many garden uses. They serve as hedges, windbreaks, focal points, garden dividers, noise buffers, and, of course, decoration.

✓ Always consider the eventual size of the mature form of the shrub before planting.

✓ Unless you are using the shrub as a focal point, buying in groups of three is preferable from a design point of view.

✓ Shrubs are usually sold in containers, but you may obtain them with bare roots or wrapped in hessian.

✓ After purchase, always try to plant your shrub as soon as possible – in a hole that's at least 50 per cent larger than the spread-out roots.

✓ Select shrubs for their form, leaf colour, flowers, autumn hues, or pretty fruit.

Chapter 10

Rosier Roses

PEOPLE OFTEN THINK that roses are difficult to grow, but nothing could be further from the truth. There are few sites and soils that won't entertain roses. Even when the temperature drops to well below freezing, some roses, particularly old-timers, will make it through the winter.

In this chapter...
✓ Buying roses
✓ Sites made simple
✓ Planting for perfection
✓ Rose maintenance
✓ Rose diseases
✓ A rose by any other name
✓ Recommended roses
✓ Everything's coming up roses

THE ROSE: CLASSIC AND EASY TO GROW

Buying roses

THE EARLY SPRING *or autumn months are the best time to plant roses, and so these months are also the prime time to buy them. Should you choose to start in autumn, plant before the weather has started to cool down. If you're on a budget, be aware that many garden centres have a rose sale in the autumn.*

ELIZABETH HARKNESS ROSE

Choose your rose

When buying, start by doing your homework about what type of rose will best suit your garden site. Bare-root roses, the kind in the pretty plastic packages with a photo and brief description on the front, are usually the most popular. With bare-root roses, you generally don't get the widest selection, but they can cost less than container roses. Read the descriptions on the package. If this is not the rose that you came into the store to buy, go home empty-handed and do some more research. Of course, I know you'll never follow this advice and you'll just bring home the rose you like. It's still a good idea to know something about the plant, so get some information about the rose's requirements before you pop it into your garden.

Rescuing roses

You do not want a rose prone to black spot, rust, or mildew unless you are willing to give it extra care. You want roses that are hardy, vigorous, and disease free.

Look for roses with three to five canes coming off the enlarged main stem, plus a good fan of strong-looking roots. Do not buy leftover bare-root roses, the kind put in a pile at half-price.

Rose roots in plastic containers tend to dry out after a while, and roots really do need something to sink their teeth into for nutrition. So roses on sale for half-price could be substantially deprived and maybe not growing, or they might just need longer to adjust. Bear this in mind, particularly if you're a plant "rescuer" like I tend to be.

INTERNET

www.roses.co.uk/ harkness/rnrs/rnrs.htm

Visit this site to find out just about everything you'd ever want or need to know about roses, courtesy of the Royal National Rose Society. Founded in 1876, this is one of the world's leading specialist plant societies, with a flourishing worldwide membership. As well as helping to fund the development and promotion of the rose, it also plays a vital role in conserving part of our plant heritage.

Sites made simple

BECAUSE ROSES DON'T LIKE TO BE DISTURBED, *you should choose your site carefully. Every time I have to move an established rose (usually because I have placed it incorrectly), there's a 50 per cent chance I'll lose the plant. Besides, you're bound to be pricked – a lot – when you try to move a big, thorny rose bush.*

Air circulation

When selecting a site, in addition to ample sunlight, most roses, like most people, do best in an area with good air circulation. Poor air circulation encourages various debilitating fungus diseases such as powdery mildew, rust, and black spot. Good air circulation means just that; it does not mean placing the plant in a windy area. Heavy winds dry roses out and ruin the pretty flowers.

Water

Roses like to be watered regularly. If you plant them near trees or large shrubs, robber roots will steal water meant for your roses. So either don't plant them where there's competition underground, or plan on watering more often.

Soil

What do roses prefer in terms of soil? Well, there's preference, there's adaptability, and there's tolerance. Ideally, you want to provide your roses with fertile, well-drained soil. Dig it deeply the week before planting, turning it all over so fresh air eliminates any hiding diseases. Then, place your roses where they have ample sun but shelter from harsh winds.

Now that you know the preferred environment, let's talk about adaptability. Many roses will grow in any soil that has fairly decent drainage. As for tolerance, unless you are trying to grow on a bog site or a Sahara desert simulation, you can probably get roses to grow even in your rather inhospitable garden. Of course, if you do happen to have sandy or clay soil extremes, be kind. Before you plant, dig in a couple of buckets of organic matter: garden compost, well-rotted farmyard manure, or whatever is inexpensive and healthy.

INTERNET

www.classicroses.co.uk

Specializing in classic roses, Peter Beales offers an extensive online catalogue of shrub roses, ground-cover roses, classic ramblers and climbers, bush roses, and standard roses. There's also advice on rose care.

Planting for perfection

THE RULES FOR PLANTING roses are simple. *Just follow these instructions and you will get your rose plants off to a super start.*

Homecoming

When you bring a bare-root rose home, unpack it immediately and dunk the roots in a big bucket of cool water for an hour or more. I have left mine in a bucket overnight without them coming to harm and they seem to adjust better than if they had not been thoroughly soaked. If you've purchased container plants, give them a huge dose of water when they arrive home. Excess water will run out of the container holes. Water again if the container must stand about a bit. Before planting, place the rose in a wind-free, semi-shady site so you don't traumatize the plant.

Placement

Dig a planting hole that's big enough to hold all the roots comfortably. Don't skimp. You should fan out the roots of cramped bare-root roses. Container rose roots may remain as they are, unless they're root-bound. This may occur when the rose has been left in the container too long. The roots continue to grow but begin to curl around each other for lack of an alternative. In this scenario, you must ease them out before you place the rose in the ground. If the roots are all squashed together, they may continue to grow that way, vying with each other in a limited space instead of reaching outwards for nutrition and water.

■ **A container rose** should have a healthy root system. If it has been confined in its pot for too long, the roots can get tangled and may need to be cut back.

Set the plant in the hole so that the soil reaches the same level that it did in the container. Find this spot by looking for a slight colour change at the base of the stem. Backfill the hole with a mixture of 50 per cent good fertile soil and 50 per cent of whatever soil you already have. Tamp it down gently as you fill, or when you finish, to remove air pockets. Then water well.

Do not let the soil go dry on a newly planted rose. This is a major reason for new rose failure.

Rose maintenance

MAINTAINING ROSES is really no more demanding than keeping any other type of plant. You'll want your plants to be healthy and to look spectacular, so it's important to develop good maintenance habits. Keep reading for the essentials of good rose care.

Fertilizer

Although the hardier roses will do very well without regular fertilization, all roses benefit from a healthy snack in the spring. The easiest way to feed them is to buy fertilizers designed specifically for roses. These are widely available in garden centres and one box covers a lot of roses. Just follow the instructions, applying the fertilizer evenly around the plant base and then watering it in well.

PRUNING ROSES

Even if you don't do it the first year or two, after a while you'll begin to wonder about rose pruning. Generally, pruning of roses should be done in early spring, before the leaves emerge. Prune just above a bud with the cut sloping downwards. Why not any higher? The extra piece is likely to die and turn black, with the *dieback* perhaps progressing down the plant stem.

> **DEFINITION**
>
> **Dieback** *is exactly what it sounds like. It occurs when a shoot begins to die at the tip, either from disease or damage.*

a **Prune unwanted wood**

Prune out any diseased, damaged, or dead wood from the plant. Also, prune to thin out any crowded or crossed-over stems.

b **Prune for strong growth**

Prune just above a bud with the cut sloping downwards. This encourages the plant's energy to go into producing strong stems.

Support

General maintenance also includes checking to make sure trellises and other supports are well fixed, and any rose climber is well attached to it. I remember having a 2.5- by 3-metre climbing rose fall forwards off the fence, trellis and all. The wind displaced a lot of things that year, even re-siting a tree onto my roof. In order to save the climber, I had to cut it back to little stubs just to get it out of the pathway. It has since recovered, but it's never been quite the same.

Cold weather

Some roses are more winter-hardy than others. Generally, shrub and species roses withstand low temperatures better than other kinds. Even on a small island like Britain, different areas are more suitable for growing roses than others. For example, in Scotland, which might seem to have long, snowy winters, the influence of the Gulf Stream can mean that roses do better there than they do in East Anglia.

Why does cold cause problems? When the temperature drops below freezing, ice crystals form within the plant. The colder it is, the more ice crystals there are. These crystals begin to push at plant tissue and may tear it. When temperatures fluctuate, causing repeated thaw and frost, the damage is increased and can kill the plant.

One popular protection method is to mound soil around the plant's base right after the first killing frost. The mound should be at least 20 centimetres high. The soil helps to keep the plant as warm as possible, like a blanket, and also to prevent alternate freezing and thawing. This protects only the lower plant part.

However, even if the parts above are killed by frost, enough wood may survive to let the rose grow back. Remove the mounded soil in early spring unless a true cold spell is expected.

■ **A mound of soil** *around the base of your rose plant acts like a blanket to protect the lower stems in freezing weather.*

Suckering

You may see suckers coming from the plant base. Remove them immediately, or they will keep growing and use up energy-giving nutrients, at the expense of your roses. It's easy to spot a sucker as they look different from normal rose stems. They are a lighter green in colour, and rather than having thorns, they feel prickly. Always remove suckers completely, and keep an eye out for any new ones that appear. Some roses sucker more than others.

■ **Remove suckers** *regularly to prevent them from sapping strength from your roses. Grab the sucker firmly and tug it up from the root.*

A little history of hips

A rose hip is the cup-like receptacle that encloses rose seeds, or the rose fruit. Picture a small pomegranate and you'll have a mental image of a large rose hip. While many are light to vivid orange, ripe rose hips may be yellow, red, brown, scarlet, or black. Rose hips contain an enormous amount of vitamin C – about four times more than an orange. During World War II, when citrus fruits were scarce in Britain, the garden roses still had rose hips. These were collected and used to make syrup.

Although all roses make hips of some kind, letting the hips grow takes energy away from the flowers. Most people who want rose hips for culinary use grow roses specifically for this purpose. Rose hips, often collected from old-fashioned rugosa roses, have been used for many culinary purposes, including teas and wines. Some rose hips are larger (up to 4 centimetres) than others, and have a better taste.

If you want to find a recipe incorporating rose hips, you may have to search in a cookbook from your grandmother's or great-grandmother's day, or for reproductions of old-fashioned recipes. If you're thinking about collecting rose hips, make very certain they have not been treated with systemic or other chemicals before you pick them. A systemic is a chemical applied to the plant that travels throughout the plant for a specific purpose. A systemic may be a weed killer, a fungicide, an insecticide, or an insect killer. All systemics are poisonous, and unless you have grown the rose yourself, you truly have no idea what it may have been treated with.

Rose diseases

DISEASE IN PLANTS *will be discussed thoroughly in Chapter 21. But to select and keep healthy plants, you need to look out for signs of diseases that are somewhat common in roses. The following diseases, simplified and in order of importance, are the most troublesome.*

Black spot

Black spot is a fungal disease, characterized by circular black spots on the leaves. Leaf tissue around the spots may turn yellow. Black spot weakens the plant and may cause leaves to fall prematurely. Don't bring home a rose plant that shows signs of black spot, and look for plants stated as resistant to this disease. Do not water roses late in the evening, as water remaining on leaves encourages the spread of this disease.

BLACK SPOT

Mildew

Mildewed leaves are coated with a greyish-white powdery growth. The leaves become distorted. Mildew is most often found on plants growing in high humidity, which encourages the spread of the fungus. Purchase plants described as resistant to mildew.

Canker

Canker, which luckily is not too common in roses, appears as brown patches on the stems, and it is most visible in early spring and late winter. The patches may be several centimetres long, and may completely surround the stem. Depending on the canker type, the patches may appear sunken. All wood above the canker will eventually die.

Rust

Red-brown spots on the undersides of leaves are signs of rust. The leaf becomes deformed, and may develop cup-like depressions. Affected leaves may wilt, turn yellow, and drop off. Prolonged rain, or watering on overcast days or late evenings, encourages this fungal disease.

RUST

A rose by any other name

ROSES FALL WITHIN THE GENUS ROSA. *As a rule, roses are known by their trademark names, and that is how I'll refer to them here.*

You'll hear roses described as albas, bourbons, centifolias, Chinas, climbers, damasks, eglantine hybrids, floribundas, Gallicas, grandifloras, hybrid perpetuals, hybrid rugosas, hybrid teas, moss roses, noisettes, polyanthas, portlands, ramblers, and teas. Each of these is a group of roses. For the newcomer, it isn't important to memorize all the groups of roses. The desire for detail will come later, when roses begin holding you in their thrall.

What you will need to know, for starters, is type: miniature, bush, shrub, climber, or tree. Type, basically, represents height and width. And you'll want the fundamentals on the plant – how often it blooms, its fragrance, hardiness, and resistance to disease.

I now grow about 60 roses of various kinds. When I first started growing them, I didn't think type was important. I have changed my mind. When you put a tall plant next to a short one, the short plant is obliterated. It is also useful to know that a climber is a climber, so you don't have to risk moving a beautiful, healthily growing rose because it's begun to resemble Jack's beanstalk.

■ **Different types of roses** *can be grown together to create a stunning mixed rose garden. Here the roses* Stanwell Perpetual, De Rescht, *and* Marbree *take pride of place.*

Recommended roses

WITH THE MANY GROUPS OF ROSES and the *almost countless number of species, I will narrow the focus to those that are popular with new gardeners. The hybrid teas and the climbers, two of the groups I just mentioned, provide an ample and easy-to-grow assortment.*

■ **Double Delight** is a *hybrid tea with roses in red, white, and cream.*

Hybrid tea roses

If you've ever received a gift of a single rose, or a bouquet of roses, chances are the beauties were hybrid teas. Almost all the roses sold by florists are hybrid teas, and about 75 per cent of roses sold in garden centres are hybrid teas. They can be grown without formal protection throughout the winter months. However, if temperatures drop well below freezing, your plants will probably need shelter of some kind.

Hybrid teas are shrub roses. They generally have long, pointed buds carried singly on a stem. Flowers may be single, with one row of petals, but are usually double. Hybrid teas range from 60 centimetres to 2 metres tall, although most are in the 1.2–1.5-metre group.

The plants bloom on and off from mid-spring to late autumn, depending on your climate and general nurturing. Many hybrid teas are fragrant, and fragrance can be mild or intense. I have found that the printed description of a rose fragrance can be at marked variance to what my nose knows.

If the fragrance of a rose is important to you, it's worth spending a bit more to buy the plant when in bloom, rather than as a bare-root bush.

Hybrid tea history

Hybrid teas were developed long ago by crossing tender tea roses and the tough hybrid perpetuals, which themselves were a cross between oriental and European roses. The first officially recognized hybrid tea rose was La France, a pale pink flower appearing in 1867. After that, the hybrid tea population exploded with new varieties, and fresh ones continue to appear all the time.

The chart on the opposite page is far from complete, due to space limitations. All the hybrid tea roses listed here are considered hardy, and the word "durable" denotes vigour and partial or full resistance to disease. "Short" indicates a plant that grows from 60 to 90 centimetres high, "medium" indicates a plant that grows to about 1.2 metres, and "tall" indicates a plant that grows to the upper ranges, about 1.5 to 2 metres.

	Fragrant	Height	Repeat bloom	Durable	Comments
White					
Elina		short	■		
Elizabeth Harkness		short	■	■	
Mrs. Herbert Stevens		medium			
Pascali		medium	■	■	
Polar Star		medium			
Pristine		medium	■	■	
Pink					
Bewitched	■	tall		■	
Blessings	■	medium			
Century Two		medium			
Colour Magic		tall			
Confidence		medium		■	
Congratulations		medium	■	■	
Coral Bay		tall			
Duet		medium		■	
Eden Rose	■	medium		■	
Friendship		tall			
Sheer Elegance		medium		■	
South Seas		tall			
Tiffany	■	tall		■	
Lavender					
Blue Moon	■	short			
Heirloom		medium			*see lavenders in bloom*
Paradise		medium			
Yellow					
Allspice		tall			
Goldstar		short	■	■	
King's Ransom	■	medium		■	
Lowell Thomas		medium			
Oregold		medium			
Peace	■	tall		■	
Rio Samba		tall		■	
Sunblest		medium	■	■	

Continued . . .

	Fragrant	Height	Repeat bloom	Durable	Comments
Orange					
Fascination		medium		■	
Folklore	■	tall			
Futura		medium			
Mojave		medium			
Montezuma		medium			
Mrs. Oakley Fisher	■	short		■	
Mrs. Sam McGredy		short	■	■	
Red					
Ace of Hearts		medium			
American Pride		medium			
Flaming Peace		medium			
Forgotten Dreams	■	medium	■	■	
Fragrant Cloud	■	medium		■	
Gypsy		tall			
Ingrid Bergman		medium		■	
Kentucky Derby		tall		■	
Loving Memory	■	tall	■	■	
Mon Cheiri		medium	■	■	
New Yorker	■	medium			
Olympiad	■	medium			
Precious Platinum		tall			
Royal William		short	■	■	
Ruby Wedding		medium	■	■	
Wendy Cussons		medium			
Multicoloured					
Antigone	■	medium			
Barbara Bush		medium			
Brigadoon		medium			
Chicago Peace		medium		■	
Colorama		medium			
Double Delight	■	medium		■	
Shot Silk	■	short	■	■	some winter hardiness
Torville & Dean		medium			
Yankee Doodle		medium		■	

The peace rose

The Peace rose, originally known as #3-35-40, was first hybridized in 1937 in France by 23-year-old Francis Meilland. When Germany invaded France during World War II, **budwood** shipments of the plants were smuggled out. The last diplomatic pouch to leave Paris contained a shipment of this rose destined for America. For 5 years, Meilland did not know what happened to his beautiful rose. In 1944, he found out that it had survived and was thriving in various places under a host of different names.

The following year, the world-famous rosarian Robert Pyle gave #3-35-40 its official name, Peace. To symbolize the war's end, one Peace rose was given to each member nation of the United Nations. This rose, which the Duke of Windsor called "the most beautiful rose in the world", was also honoured as the World's Favourite Rose. There are colour variants of the original yellow Peace rose, and a climbing version. Every garden should have at least one Peace rose.

■ **Peace** *is the perfect rose, and a must for every rose grower.*

> **DEFINITION**
>
> **Budwood** *refers to strong young stems that have buds suitable for use in budding. When a professional decides to multiply a desired rose plant, growth eyes, or "buds", are sliced from the budwood of selected roses. These buds are inserted into cuts made in the bark of already-rooted cuttings, or understocks. Understocks are from roses known for their hardy root systems. Almost all bare-root rose bushes are budded plants.*

Climbers

Climbers can be found in medium, tall, and apparently never-ending sizes. The roses can be of any type, including floribunda, grandiflora, hybrid musk, hybrid tea, and polyantha.

Climbing roses can be used to cover old tree stumps, screen out neighbouring views, cover arbours, disguise garages, and hide fences. You will need to give all climbers firm support because wind and rain can pull them (and the support) to the ground. And remember, the plants get even heavier when laden with flowers. If you put them against a trellis, make certain the trellis itself is well anchored. To be sure, I always put some nails into the fence, and fix the trellis tightly with wire.

When planting roses, you don't need to be reminded that they have thorns. As you are pulling the thorns out of your hands, imagine how big this climber is going to get. Don't put climbers too close to paths, and plant them away from children's play areas.

■ **Golden Showers** *is a fragrant, upright climbing rose.*

This chart includes just a few of the hardier climbing varieties. The word "durable" means vigorous and partially or fully disease resistant. Winter hardy refers to −15° C.

	Fragrant	Height	Repeat bloom	Durable	Winter hardy	Comments
Red/Scarlet						
Altissimo		2.2–4 m	■	■	■	
Climbing Crimson Glory	■	to 3 m		■	■	
Climbing Etoile de Hollande	■	to 6 m			■	
Dortmund		to 3 m		■	■	
Paul's Scarlet Climber		to 5 m		■	■	profuse blooms
Pink						
Aloha	■	to 3 m.	■	■	■	
American Pillar .		to 3 m.	■	■	■	
Climbing Cécile Brunner	■	to 8 m			■	good for arbours
Climbing Queen Elizabeth		3–4 m		■		
Mme. Grégoire Staechelin	■	to 6 m			■	
Morning Jewel		to 5 m		■	■	
New Dawn		4–6 m			■	
White						
Handel		to 4.5 m			■	
Mme. Alfred Carrière	■	to 6 m			■	white to pale pink
Paul's Single White		to 3 m				
White Cockade	■	to 4 m	■	■	■	
Yellow						
Lady Hillingdon		to 6 m		■		
Elegance	■	to 5 m		■	■	thorny
Golden Showers	■	2.5–4 m	■		■	few thorns
Orange/Gold						
Climbing Autumn Sunset	■	4 m		■	■	
Climbing Lady Forteviot	■	3–5 m		■	■	
Royal Sunset	■	4–5 m		■		long blooming period
Multicoloured						
Climbing Talisman		2.5–4 m		■		
Fourth of July		3–4.5 m			■	
Pinata		2.5 m				

Everything's coming up roses

IT IS IMPOSSIBLE TO COVER ALL the current and old-fashioned roses available, even in a book entirely devoted to roses. Although I've chosen to feature hybrid teas and climbers, you should have a working familiarity with some of the other rose groups. Here I've given some very, very basic descriptions and definitions.

■ **Alba Maxima** *is a large alba rose that blooms once a year.*

■ **Alba** – these are shrub roses, known to be fragrant and hardy. They grow from 2 to 2.75 metres tall. They have abundant green foliage but bloom only once.

■ **Bourbon** – these plants are vigorous, but sensitive and fragrant. They will grow up to 2 metres high and may re-bloom. They can be trained to climb.

■ **Centifolia** – also called Provence roses, these shrub roses will bloom only once but will provide huge flowers. The fragrant flowers are often seen in clusters. These plants range from 1 to 2.2 metres in height.

■ **China** – these roses range from low to tall, have clusters or single flowers, and will bloom repeatedly. They are not particularly hardy, so always try to provide adequate shelter. China roses are one of the ancestors of repeat bloomers.

■ **Damask** – rangy shrubs, these roses grow from 1 to 2.2 metres high. They are hardy, and will bloom once or twice. They bear fantastically fragrant clusters of flowers.

■ **Eglantine hybrids** – Eglantines produce fragrant single or clustered flowers on arching shrubs growing up to 4 metres. Look out for bright red hips in the autumn.

■ **Floribunda** – these plants are low growing, bushy, and hardy. They may or may not have fragrant flowers, which can either grow singly or in clusters. These roses provide nearly continuous blooms.

■ **Gallica** – Gallicas are compact, hardy shrub roses reaching about 1 to 1.2 metres high. Their large, fragrant flowers will bloom once per season. Special care for Gallicas includes watching out for suckers.

Trivia...
The Egyptian queen Cleopatra, who knew many ways to enchant her lover Mark Antony, would carpet a room with red rose petals so that their scent would rise as he strode towards her.

■ **Fantin-Latour** *is a vigorous centifolia rose with fragrant cupped or flat flowers in a delicate shade of pink.*

- **Grandiflora** – producing single or clustered large, vigorous flowers, Grandifloras grow 1 to 2 metres high. The blossoms have limited fragrance.
- **Hybrid musk** – these do well in poor growing conditions.
- **Hybrid perpetual** – hardy, vigorous, and sometimes rampant, hybrid perpetual shrubs have fragrant, large flowers. They may bloom repeatedly.
- **Hybrid rugosa** – select hybrid rugosas if you want a really tough plant. They're drought tolerant, seashore

■ **Boule de Neige** is a white Bourbon rose, often tinged pink.

tolerant, winter hardy, and have an extraordinary resistance to disease. They produce pretty red hips, and are happy to bloom repeatedly.
- **Miniatures** – although not all miniatures are small plants (some grow to 2 metres or more!), their flowers are all small.

- **Modern roses** – this designation is given to any roses that have been developed after 1867. The floribundas, hybrid teas, and miniatures are among the sub-groups of modern roses.
- **Moss** – when rubbed, the flower stalks and hips of moss rose shrubs will give off a pine-like scent.
- **Noisette** – these are climbers, and have fragrant, repeat-blooming flowers. They're not winter hardy.
- **Old roses** – these include the sub-groups alba, gallica, and tea roses, among others. These are plants developed before 1867.
- **Polyantha** – shrub roses in this group are low growing and very hardy. They'll have many small flower clusters in almost continuous bloom.
- **Portland** – the portlands are fragrant shrub roses. They resemble the bourbons but have smaller flowers.
- **Ramblers** – these are characterized by their very long, slender, pliable canes. Ramblers produce large clusters of small flowers once a season.
- **Species** – these are wild roses, and can be either climbers or shrubs. They are often fragrant and very hardy, and most bloom once a season.

■ **Henri-Martin** is a strong, upright moss rose. Its rosette-shaped, purple-crimson flowers have a light scent.

- **Tea** – available in both climbing and shrub form, tea roses prefer a mild climate. They have fragrant, large, repeat-blooming flowers.
- **Tree roses** – these are also known as standard roses. Floribundas, grandifloras, and hybrid teas can all be pruned and trained into tree form.

■ **Veilchenblau** *is a rampant rambler rose. It produces clusters of violet flowers streaked with white.*

Trivia...
..."and may there be a road before you and it bordered with roses"...
(an Irish blessing).

A simple summary

✓ Do a little homework before you purchase roses. Know the type of rose you want, and why, prior to going shopping.

✓ To simplify the selection process, make a list of the characteristics you desire in order of importance before you buy.

✓ Although a few will tolerate some shade, most roses need ample sun.

✓ Don't forget to water your roses. They need adequate water to look their best.

✓ Plant roses where they'll get good air circulation, but do not place them in windy areas.

✓ Take the time to dig a spacious planting hole, and backfill with good soil.

✓ Consider the plant's needs for water, air, and the right soil when you plant it.

✓ Fertilize roses in the spring.

✓ Give climbing roses good support as they can easily blow over in strong winds.

Chapter 11

Vivacious Vines

THERE ARE LOTS OF GREAT REASONS to include some climbers in your garden planning. One is to beautify a barrier, such as a fence or wall, that doesn't add much to the visual appeal of your garden. Another is to hide an eyesore, such as the dustbins, by growing climbers over a free-standing support. A climber-laden arch makes a lovely entrance from one part of your garden to another. Best of all, by planting vines you can erect a barrier to create more privacy in your garden.

In this chapter...
✓ *Keep it up*
✓ *Get a grip*
✓ *Annual vines*
✓ *Flowering fence covers*
✓ *Vines for fragrance*
✓ *Clingers for concrete*

BOSTON IVY SCALING A WALL

Keep it up

MOST CLIMBERS HAVE *no way to defy gravity and need some type of support system. For some of the lighter annuals, such as black-eyed Susan (Thunbergia alata) or morning glory (Ipomoea), a length of string fastened here and there to the nearest support will suffice. For others with a thicker stem, you'll need a heartier support, such as crisscrossed wires, a fence, latticework,* **trellis**, **arbour***, or* **pergola***.*

DEFINITION

A **trellis** *is a wooden frame with crossing strips. An* **arbour** *is an overhead trellis under which one can pass. Essentially, a* **pergola** *is an elaborate arbour covered by a roof or latticework on which vines grow. An unadorned pergola resembles the climbing frame you may have had in your school playground, except it is made of wood and is, therefore, a good deal more attractive.*

Support systems

Gardeners who are good at DIY can construct all types of support systems. If you're only marginally good at it, you can buy arches and pergolas in kit form that you simply put together. Or you can just have the supports you like delivered and set up for you.

I've tried to be creative in using different types of supports for different plants. I've placed chicken wire along my fences to hold up tendril climbers, used bamboo and metal uprights to guide smaller twining climbers in the proper path, and put up Y-shaped trellises to display others.

■ **A pergola** *makes an ideal focal point. There are many different styles to suit every garden, from simple or rustic to elaborate and ornamental.*

It's my goal eventually to have an archway between one section of the garden and another, either to display a fragrant climber or to try again – hopefully with more success – for grapes.

I used to worry about how to support a U-shaped arch without having to dig a trench and set posts inside concrete. Then I saw a garden where the innovative person used two large, deep, steel buckets just set on top of the ground, one for each side of the archway. She set the bottoms of the archway into the buckets, and then filled each almost to the top with sand. They appeared to make a quite solid base for a large clematis. You could paint the buckets to make them more attractive.

Get a grip

HAVE YOU EVER WONDERED how climbers cling and clamber? Well, they use more than one technique to scramble over just about anything they come across. A simple overview of the various climbing mechanisms follows.

Tendril grabbers

Tendril grabbers, such as grape vines (*Vitis*) and passionflowers (*Passiflora*), reach out to hold onto vertical or horizontal support items, including tree branches, adjacent plants, and latticework. These spiral tendrils are flexible, so when the wind blows, the vine just shifts with the action. The tendrils may also be quite difficult to dislodge. I find it easier to cut them with secateurs rather than to try to pull them off.

TENDRIL GRABBERS

DISC ATTACHMENTS

Disc attachments

A bit like the discs on an octopus' tentacles, these small, circular plant discs are at the end of a tendril reaching out for support. The discs attach themselves to the support with a quite sticky substance. To remove, I've always had to yank the vine off; the little discs stay there as reminders to be careful of what I plant.

There are also climbers that don't have any sort of holding mechanism, and need your help. I attach screw-in cup hooks to my wooden fence and attach the stems with green yarn or wire. There are masonry hooks for brick walls, and special ties available at garden centres.

193

Holdfast rootlets

Also called clinging aerial rootlets, holdfast rootlets are minuscule roots along either side of a plant's stem. These grab onto any type of roughened surface, including concrete. The rootlets don't feed on the holding material – it is almost like they staple themselves into it. They can pull cladding off a house, so use only on brick, concrete, or stone walls, if you must. Ivy (*Hedera helix*), trumpet vines (*Campis*), and evergreen wintersweet (*Euonymus fortunei*) are examples of plants that adhere and climb using holdfast rootlets.

HOLDFAST ROOTLETS

Twiners

Morning glories (*Ipomoea*), clematis (*Clematis*), and wisteria (*Wisteria*) are among the twiners. Twiners wrap themselves around a support, which can be anything that can be wrapped around, including the plant's own stem.

TWINERS

ESPALIERS – FUN FOR CLIMBER FANS

INTERNET

www.msucares.com/pubs/publicatons/pub456.htm

The Mississippi State University Extension Service offers advice on espaliers, including suggested plants for espalier use, planting tips, espalier patterns, support, and training methodology.

You may, from time to time, hear the fancy word "espalier". This is a French word that derives from the Italian *spalliera*, which means something to rest your shoulder on, or from *spalla*, which means against. At one time, it meant a framework for the plant to lean against. Today it refers to plants that have been trained to stand flat against a wall or other vertical site, generally affixed to a trellis.

Espaliers are often trimmed into lovely designs, from informal, such as a fountain shape, to intricate, such as a diamond pattern. Fruit trees were among the earliest to be espaliered for the purpose of catching reflected sun off a wall. Newcomers often begin by working with pyracantha.

If you're interested in this art, there's a lot of advice available in books and on the Internet. As with all other plant projects, make certain you know the growth habit and ultimate size of the plant you are planning to espalier.

Annual vines

ANNUAL CLIMBERS ARE A FINE WAY to find out whether you want a climber in a particular spot, and if so, what type of climber you want. They are also useful if you are in rented property and don't want to put too much energy into a perennial climber, but still want fence cover or patio ornamentation. You may see some climbers here that are perennials where you live, but in most climates they're treated as an annual.

Do be aware that most annual climbers do not transplant well, so put them where they are to grow. Put in their support system – trellis, arbour, or strings along a fence – at the same time that you plant them.

Black-eyed Susan

Plant seeds for this climber in early spring, once the chance of frost has passed. This fast-grower is also called clockvine, and black-eyed clockvine. It does well in full sun or semi-shade, but needs moist, well-drained soil. If given a satisfactory site, it will reach 1.5 to 2.5 metres, hanging onto a trellis or other support by twining stems. Its funnel-shaped flowers are bright yellow or orange with dark centres. Easy to grow, black-eyed Susan (*Thunbergia alata*) does well in hanging baskets. If you have a sunny windowsill indoors, try it in hanging baskets there, too.

BLACK-EYED SUSAN
(*Thunbergia alata*)

Morning glory

Morning glory (*Ipomoea tricolor*) seeds are available at any garden centre and most seed racks in supermarkets. Soak the large, round seeds for a few hours in warm water to speed germination. The flowers are up to 7 centimetres across, and colours are plentiful, including shades of pink, blue, red, and white, as well as striped varieties. In the spring, plant morning glories in average soil. Over-rich soil will give you lots of heart-shaped green leaves but limited flowers. Give these plants full sun.

Plants reach 3 to 6 metres, wrapping around a support mechanism as they grow. Give them a trellis or multi-branched tree to hold onto. Morning glories, true to their name, have showy flowers in the morning that close in the afternoon. For variety, try the night-blooming morning glory called the moonflower (*Ipomoea alba*), which has a white flower. Moonflowers have a pleasant, light perfume that attracts night-flying moths.

Scarlet runner bean

■ **The scarlet runner bean** (Phaseolus coccineus) *climbs quickly to smother a tripod.*

If you have a small, open area with good air circulation and full sun, but not too much wind, this is a great temporary cover. Quite hardy if you water it regularly, scarlet runner bean (*Phaseolus coccineus*) climbs quickly to 4 metres using tendrils equipped with tiny suction discs. It is perennial in some areas, but it has always died back at summer's close for me. Medium red, pea-shaped flowers are profuse in small, drooping clusters. In addition to full sun, this plant needs rich, moist, well-drained soil.

After the flowers have come and gone, long, dark green pods will appear, and these can be eaten. The bean-sized seeds are fun for children to plant, as something usually grows even in less-than-ideal conditions. Pink- and white-flowered varieties are also available, but they are harder to find. Try growing scarlet runner beans with a few sweet peas (see below) for a colourful display.

Sweet pea

A native of Italy, this annual climber shoots upwards using tendrils to eventually reach about 2 metres in height. Sweet peas (*Lathyrus odoratus*) look great as a long temporary hedge. Put up a lengthy wire trellis and let them meander along it. Sweet peas do need some care and attention if they are to produce a good display. Start out with very rich, organic soil in a well-drained site. For best results, sow them indoors in peat pots and then move them outside. Their preferred growing area has a good deal of sun. The soil for sweet peas must be kept moist at all times. There are now bush varieties of sweet peas as well as vines. The bushes grow to up to 60 centimetres high. Butterfly-shaped flowers, some with fragrance, appear in spring or summer, depending on the variety.

Some people have phenomenal luck with sweet peas, which seem to thrive if their owners just smile at them. Then there are others who, despite servitude, can't get them to survive at all. But it's worth a try because the flowers are so sweet smelling.

More annual vines:

■ Balloon vines (*Cardiospermum halicacabum*)
■ Cup-and-saucer vines (*Cobaea scandens*)
■ Nasturtium (*Tropaeolum majus*)

Trivia...

The original sweet pea was a Sicilian wildflower that was discovered by a Franciscan monk. Father Cupani sent seeds to England in the early 1700s. At the time, sweet peas, while fragrant, were quite plain. But gardeners began making improvements, particularly the gardener to Earl Spencer of Althorp Park, who developed a wavy-flowered variety. It was named Countess Spencer. If the name seems familiar, think of Princess Diana, a relative.

Flowering fence covers

ALMOST ALL VINES will cover a fence. Some are fairly delicate covers, others cover the fence and all the neighbouring property. Before installing a fence-cover vine, read on to discover some exceptional choices.

Chilean potato vine

The Chilean potato vine (*Solanum crispum* Glasnevin) is, as it name suggests, a member of the potato family. Vigorous and semi-evergreen, it can be grown as a climber very successfully in a sheltered garden, reaching up to 6 metres tall. It needs to be planted in full sunshine and fertile, well-drained soil. Water regularly, but sparingly in winter. The vine has lilac to purple, fragrant flowers with distinct yellow centres, which are borne in clusters during the summer.

For an unforgettable display, give the Chilean potato vine a grid of close-spaced, plastic-coated wires or trellis and a generous dose of slow-release fertilizer in spring and again in mid-summer.

CHILEAN POTATO VINE
(*Solanum crispum* Glasnevin)

If you like white flowers, and you live in an area with a mild climate, then you could try growing the more tender, white-flowered potato vine, *Solanum jasminoides* Album. This is also semi-evergreen and will respond well to the same treatment, but bear in mind that because it originates from Brazil, it does need a warm, sunny spot. Clusters of starry flowers appear on the current year's shoots from July to September, and it will form a great wall or fence covering of 6 metres high and across.

Clematis

Another popular choice is clematis (*Clematis*), with a range of varieties flowering at different times. The roots should be well spread out in rich, moist soil with super drainage. It's a good idea to place mulch over the entire root area. Fertilize clematis monthly during the growing season. There is a great deal of diversity among the various clematis species and varieties. Some want more sun than others, so it is always sensible to research the needs of the type you choose. If you haven't, the general rule is tops in the sun, roots in the shade.

Another issue is the general climate favoured by particular clematis plants. For example, sweet autumn clematis (*C. terniflora*), which has white, star-shaped flowers and a lovely fragrance, does well by the sea.

Clematis flowers, which can be up to 25 centimetres wide, are quite lovely. Colours include purple, white, lilac, pink, blue, and some multi-coloured varieties. While most appear in mid-summer, some will re-bloom in early autumn. Because they bloom at different times, if you want continuing flowers from late spring until late autumn, select accordingly.

Clematis does not have a strong self-support system. When you first plant it, include a tall bamboo stake or similar support, tying it with gardener's string. These vines cling to objects by twining around them, so you must provide a trellis, or even netting along a wall or fence. Lean the stake towards the trellis to encourage the direction of growth. The plant's ultimate size will depend on which variety you purchase. *C. jackmanii*, one of the easiest to grow, can reach 3 metres in one spring-to-summer season, and often grows to 5 metres. Others grow as high as 8 metres.

■ **A vigorous climber,** *this clematis* (Clematis viticella *Etoile Violette*) *will clamber to 3.5 metres high and cover a wide area with masses of violet-purple flowers.*

While most varieties of clematis are deciduous, which means you won't have that privacy screen or fence cover throughout the year, a few are evergreen. If evergreen interests you, look for *C. armandii*, a fast-growing vine with white fragrant flowers.

As a rule, clematis does extremely well in containers if you meet the soil, water, and light requirements.

Honeysuckle

There are several honeysuckles (*Lonicera*) available, some more controllable than others. The most aggressive is the semi-evergreen Halliana, a variety of *L. japonica*. You'll have to work at keeping this rapidly growing vine on the fence or trellis and off the ground, where it may root at its leisure, creating an extemporaneous ground cover. If you want a honeysuckle that quickly covers a wide expanse, this could be just what you are seeking. Halliana has light yellow, very fragrant flowers in June and blooms intermittently until the first frosts.

Trivia...
An old-fashioned European and American custom was honeysuckle sipping. If the base of the flower is removed, there is a teensy drop of nectar within.

TRUMPET HONEYSUCKLE
(*Lonicera sempervirens*)

For less haste, coral honeysuckle (*L. sempervirens*) will reach 4 metres, climbing by twining stems. Its tubular flowers have yellow interiors and scarlet exteriors. They are very pretty indeed. The flowers are followed by short-lived orange berries. This vine works nicely on a small trellis or a section of fence. *L. henryi* grows quickly to 10 metres, and although an evergreen in mild areas, is deciduous where winters are very cold. This climber has pretty, but not striking, purple-red flowers and long-lasting clusters of blue-black berries that are adored by birds.

Honeysuckle will grow in fairly good soil, shade or sun. If you want prolific flowers, however, you should plant it in a sunny area. Regular watering is needed, at least to get it started, but soggy conditions will not be tolerated.

Wisteria

Most often with violet-blue flowers, this prolifically flowering, deciduous climber draws attention, particularly older specimens, which can cover house walls and sometimes the roof. On average, wisteria (*Wisteria*) will grow to 10 metres tall. The flower clusters are quite conspicuously displayed because they may appear before new leaves develop in spring. Japanese wisteria (*W. floribunda*), with drooping flower clusters up to 30 centimetres long, has a spicy scent. It is tolerant of both seaside and city conditions. Chinese wisteria (*W. sinensis*) has blue-violet, white, or pink drooping flower clusters, often reaching 32 centimetres in length. Following the flowers are long, green, bean-like seed pods that last through the winter. Pests seldom bother this hardy vine.

Although slow to get started, wisterias eventually demand a large growing space. If you don't provide it, you will be forever pruning. Fortunately, pruning, even rather dramatically, doesn't seem to bother wisteria. Wisterias also need solid support. This is a heavy climber. Give your wisteria well-drained, average soil.

JAPANESE WISTERIA (*Wisteria floribunda*)

Vines for fragrance

IF YOU TRAIN a fragrant climber over an arbour or pergola, your reward will be a fabulous scented tunnel to walk through or sit under. A long pergola smothered in wisteria can be a heady experience, and it looks stunning, too. Another idea is to train a fragrant climber around your front door; this provides a wonderfully welcoming entrance to your home.

Chilean jasmine

In early summer, white or rich pink trumpet-shaped flowers bloom profusely on this deciduous, woody, twining climber. There may be a second flower display in early autumn. The fragrance of these flowers has been compared to that of gardenias. Many gardeners like to place Chilean jasmine (*Mandevilla laxa*) in hanging baskets. It's a tropical plant so must be given frost protection.

Chilean jasmine is often purchased in containers, but you can try growing this vine from seed, or even from stem cuttings rooted in a sterile medium, such as vermiculite. Eventually it will grow to about 5 metres.

Easter lily vine

Also called Herald's trumpet, the fragrant 7- to 12-centimetre-long trumpet-shaped white flowers do resemble Easter lilies. Flowers appear from spring through summer on this enthusiastically growing evergreen vine, which has attractively glossy deep green leaves when mature. This plant may twine up to 10 metres high and equally wide. It's important to give this plant good soil, ample water and fertilizer, full sun, and a strong support system. Prune Easter lily vines (*Beaumontia grandiflora*) back after flowering has ended. Should it be apparently frost killed, don't despair. It just may return from the roots.

EASTER LILY VINE (*Beaumontia grandiflora*)

Poet's jasmine

Also called common jasmine, poet's jasmine (*Jasminum officinale*) will surround you with scent from its small white flowers. These very fragrant flowers will bloom from early summer until autumn. As a deciduous vine, poet's jasmine will reach 10 metres, but you can also grow it as a mounding shrub, placing it near a window or patio door. Another option, should you not have room for the lengthier version, is to look for yellow jasmine (*J. mesnyi*), which only reaches about 2 to 3 metres, or dwarf jasmine (*J. parkeri*), which is a 30-centimetre-high shrub. All jasmines need full sun to partial shade and good, well-drained soil.

POET'S JASMINE (*Jasminum officinale*)

Star jasmine

Also called confederate jasmine, the white, clustered flowers of star jasmine (*Trachelospermum jasminoides*) have a fragrance that envelops gardens throughout the world (in addition to its star status in the perfume industry). Eventually, this pleasantly growing vine will reach 3 to 8 metres, starting slowly at first and then picking up the pace. Purple flower buds precede the flowers in early summer. You can also use star jasmine as groundcover. Put it near a sitting area, since the fragrance is appreciated best on warm still evenings. Give regular water, good soil, and mostly full sun.

STAR JASMINE
(*Trachelospermum jasminoides*)

Chinese trumpet vine

One of the finest varieties of this woody-stemmed, clinging climber is the orange-red Chinese trumpet vine called *Campsis ¥ tagliabuana* Madame Galen. This produces pairs of large, up-thrusting trumpet blooms from August to October. It also has attractive dark green leaflets and can grow as much as 10 metres tall. As it's a scrambler, you must prune it regularly to keep it tidy and flowering freely. Simply shorten every stem to within two buds of the main framework in early spring. Plant it in a warm sunny site and keep it well watered in summer.

More fragrant vines:

- Carolina jessamine
  (*Gelsemium sempervirens*)
- Chocolate vine
  (*Akebia quinata*)
- Climbing hydrangea
  (*Hydrangea petiolaris*)
- Evergreen clematis (*Clematis armandii*)

- Honeysuckle (*Lonicera*)
- Jasmine (*Jasminum polyanthum*)
- Madagascar jasmine
  (*Stephanotis floribunda*)
- Moonflower
  (*Ipomoea alba*)
- Wisteria (*Wisteria*)

Clingers for concrete

IF YOU WANT TO COVER CONCRETE *and keep it hidden forever, you can plant one of the following vines. They attach by adhesive discs or holdfast rootlets to upright surfaces, including concrete, stone, wood, brick, and the like. However, there are potential problems with these plants to be aware of before you start. These vines can envelop a multi-story building. Attractive over a small front wall or tool shed, they are a pain if they lodge into your roof. It's one thing to prune a low vine and another to climb on a ladder and prune a second storey.*

There's always the temptation to purchase something that grows quickly, but keep in mind that this attribute can be a liability as well as an asset.

Ercilla

Ercilla (*Ercilla volubilis*) is an unusual self-clinging climber from temperate North and South America. It has pale green rather leathery leaves, and in spring bears short spikes of pinkish-white flowers. Although it is rather slow to get started, once established it'll grow quite vigorously. As a result it is better suited to a house wall than a low wall or fence.

Ercilla is only marginally frost hardy, which means it'll need to be well sheltered from strong and cold winds, and it is best either in full sun or part shade. To keep its growth under control, pruning should be done after flowering has finished.

Ercilla shouldn't be grown on a north-facing wall because it won't do well if it gets too cold.

Climbing hydrangea

Of all the climbers, climbing hydrangea (*Hydrangea petiolaris*) is one of the prettiest. It attaches to vertical surfaces by holdfast rootlets, reaching an eventual 15 metres by 15 metres. Clusters of small white flowers appear in summer. As with most hydrangeas, this deciduous vine needs rich soil, ample water, and some afternoon sun protection.

Cross vine

Climbing rapidly to 10 metres using adhesive discs and tendrils, cross vine (*Bignonia capreolata*) is planted by some people to cover unsightly poles. In a comfortable site, it can also reach 18 metres, covering trees and fences. Unlike some of the other clingers, it doesn't become overly thick. Cross vine's glossy dark green leaves turn purplish in winter. Although an evergreen in most areas, the leaves will drop off in very cold climates. In summer, clustered, small, trumpet-like, reddish-brown or apricot flowers appear, followed by pod-like fruit.

■ **The climbing hydrangea** (H. petiolaris) *is one of the most attractive plants for covering a fence or wall. Once established, it grows quite quickly.*

Ivy

INTERNET

ivy.org

This site is brought to you by the American Ivy Society, a not-for-profit organization dedicated to ivy education and promotion. The site provides membership information, ivy care, ivy sources, and general ivy information.

There are many kinds of ivy (*Hedera*). Some are used as pretty and tidy container plants, others as topiary, and still others as thick, ever-spreading, 45-centimetre-high ground cover useful for controlling soil erosion. On walls and other upright surfaces, some ivies, such as Boston ivy (*Parthenocissus tricuspidata*), will climb using adhesive discs. Others, such as common ivy (*Hedera helix*), will climb by means of holdfast rootlets. The Boston ivy, which prefers a semi-shady or shady spot, has striking autumn colours that make it a popular choice; once the leaves have fallen, however, your wall or fence is no longer covered.

There's a great choice of colours. Ivies with green leaves are very shade tolerant, while those with variegated or yellow leaves prefer a situation with more light.

Once in place, vigorous ivies such as common ivy can be difficult to eradicate, both for you and any affected neighbours.

I admit to a bias, having spent years trying to eradicate common ivy from a nextdoor garden that kept crawling through my fence and trying to take root in mine. Thick ivy is also a snail haven and a rodent hideaway. It will smother small plants and take over trees. However, those that are not thick – and that is most varieties – can be quite satisfactory. There are advocates whose entire gardens are created around yellow, white, green, or variegated ivy. Just be aware of the possible eventual impact of your choice.

COMMON IVY (*Hedera helix*)

Most ivies are easy to grow in average garden soil. They do well in full sun if the weather doesn't get overly hot. Otherwise they should be kept in partial shade. Regular watering is necessary, at least until the plant gets a head start. Trim ivy as necessary to shape. For ground-cover ivies, light mowing may be possible if done with great care, or use hedge shears. Each variety has its own tolerance of cold, so once again it's important to look into the needs of the type you like.

EVERGREEN BITTERSWEET (*Euonymus fortunei*)

Evergreen bittersweet

An evergreen climber, *Euonymus fortunei* will creep or crawl up a wall by holdfast rootlets. Depending on the variety, it may climb as high as 12 metres, or may grow only to 1 metre. To establish on a wall, spray the wall with a garden hose from time to time, especially during warm weather. By dampening the wall, you help the rootlets cling. If they still need help attaching themselves to the wall, use pieces of sticky tape placed across the stem to hold them in place. Plan on pruning.

The most familiar varieties of *Euonymus fortunei* are Emerald 'n' Gold with its dark green leaves with gold vareigations, and Silver Queen, which has paler leaves, broadly edged with silver and tinged pink in winter. Both of these are very useful plants to brighten up a dark shady corner of the garden.

A simple summary

✓ Vines serve to enhance the beauty of vertical surfaces and to cover those that are less attractive. A vine-covered arbour is a pretty addition to almost any garden.

✓ Vines' climbing mechanisms include twiners, tendril grabbers, holdfast rootlets, and disc attachments. Most vines need some type of strong external support on which to grow.

✓ There are annual vines, which must be re-planted each year. Many self-seed, and others have large seeds that are fun for children to plant and grow.

✓ Some vines are perennial, but aren't very hardy, so they are grown as annuals.

✓ Fragrant vines add a touch of scented luxury to a pergola or transform an arch.

✓ Vine growth varies widely. While some vines are gentle, others are rampant and will cover the side of a garage or even an entire house in no time at all.

PART FOUR

SWEET BASIL, READY FOR PICKING

EXPLORING EDIBLES

T HERE'S ABSOLUTELY NOTHING in the garden gourmet world more delightful than eating a fruit or a vegetable you have nurtured yourself. If you can pick it off the tree and crunch into it while basking in the summer warmth, you may feel as if the whole world is yours at that moment.

Visions of vegetables, fruit trees, and berries may make you think of the farm. But there's no need for hectares of land. Smaller versions of just about everything have been created by hybridizers. Tomatoes indoors and on patios, 2-metre-high dwarf fruit trees, tiny carrots, and berries that grow on 60-centimetre-high bushes are just a small part of your decorative yet edible garden. Tuck in a few home-grown herbs here and there, and you send out an invitation to pollinators, butterflies, and birds. Best of all, you can also season the delicacies you *create* with your home-grown produce.

Chapter 12

Volumes of Veggies

YOU REALLY DON'T NEED a green thumb to have a successful vegetable garden. What you do need is a simple understanding of how to arrange your vegetable plants and the fundamentals of planting and maintaining your little crops.

In this chapter...

✓ Shopping for veggies

✓ Arranging the vegetable garden

✓ Terrific tomatoes

✓ Carrots for crunching

✓ Please pass the peas

✓ Perfect peppers

✓ Prime potatoes

Shopping for veggies

GOOD ADVICE ON *where and how to shop for your garden vegetables essentially applies to all of your plants. I've chosen to elaborate on catalogue shopping in this chapter because so many people use mail order, and rely on catalogue descriptions to purchase their garden edibles.*

■ **Home-grown vegetables** *are rewarding to grow and they always seem to taste so much better than their shop-bought counterparts.*

If you do decide to shop at a garden centre or nursery, be sure to buy bare-root plants and bulbs early in the season – that is, when they first appear at the retailer.

Do not buy vegetable plants with veggies already on them, as they don't transplant well.

Winter reading

In winter, the catalogue companies get busy. There is nothing more cheering during a miserable, cold, wet winter than looking through catalogues just bursting with plants that will make your garden resemble Eden. Most catalogues offer seeds, but there are some that offer plants already growing in small or medium-size containers.

I do not wish to think about all the plants I have ordered that are totally unsuitable for my little suburban mild-winter space. But I love catalogues, have zillions of them, and still order regularly. On occasion I even try to be sensible. But this is a challenge, as I do love greenery, especially greenery that claims to flower fragrantly, or attract birds, butterflies, and beneficial insects, or give me a fruit or a vegetable I can eat.

Decoding descriptions

I am also particularly attracted to the word "easy", which seems to have various meanings, depending on the author of the catalogue text. Some of the descriptive phrases you'll find in lovely catalogues include:

a **Hardy:** *This means that the plant will survive out of doors all year round without protection. However, in the UK a plant that's labelled as "hardy" may struggle in the longer and harsher winter conditions that prevail in more northern counties.*

b **Requires winter protection in cold, frost, etc. areas:** *In cold climates you must either bring it under shelter or cover it with something that conserves heat.*

c **Disease tolerant/disease resistant:** *The word "tolerant" means the plant may get the disease but the disease doesn't bother it very much. The word "resistant" means the plant usually doesn't get the disease. Diseases you may see mentioned are anthracnose, aster yellows, blight (many types), downy mildew, fireblight, fusarium wilt, leaf spot (many types), mosaic virus, peach leaf curl, powdery mildew, red core, root rot, rust, scab, tobacco mosaic virus, and verticillium wilt. In Chapter 21 you'll get more information on some of the more common plant diseases. There are books and Internet sites that deal entirely with plant diseases. I seldom worry about these plant problems, but do try to purchase disease-resistant plants, especially vegetables and fruit trees.*

d **Hybrid:** *A mixture of two usually well-known proven plants of the same type that have been combined to obtain their best qualities, such as one with large fruit and one that is vigorous. Hybridization is an art form done by specialists, but you can try it in your garden too.*

e **Cool-season or overwintering plants:** *Plants that thrive in cool weather, such as asparagus, beetroot, broad beans, broccoli, cabbage, carrots, cauliflower, celery, chive, leek, lettuce, onions, peas, radishes, and spinach. Plant these crops as early in the spring as the soil will allow. Most overwintering crops have matured by May.*

f **Warm-season plants:** *Plants that do well in warm weather, such as green beans, sweetcorn, cucumbers, melons, peppers, pumpkin, squash, and tomatoes. Warm-season crops should be planted after the last sensible frost threat has passed. Nowadays, with all the wonderful hybridization going on, you will find crops designed to cross these seasonal barriers. For example, there are now numerous tomatoes that will grow in cooler weather, as well as broccoli that thrives in warmer weather.*

g **Short-season vegetables:** *These plants will germinate, grow, and produce quickly. Beans, beetroot, carrots, lettuces, and radishes are short-season plants.*

h **Long-season plants:** *Plants that take a while to grow, flower, and produce a crop. Long-season plants include sweetcorn, cucumber, melons, pepper, and squash.*

i **Prize-winning or award-winning:** *Usually a superior variety judged against others of its kind for good growth, production, vigour, and other strong points. Look for the Royal Horticultural Society award-winners. They're the cream of the crop.*

Catalogues vary greatly in their descriptions of plants and it's fun to read a whole batch of them before you decide on anything. You will see many of the same plants offered again and again, each with a different nuance. Names of catalogue/mail order companies are provided in the Appendices.

Arranging the vegetable garden

ONCE AGAIN, the essential advice here is to plan ahead. For the best results, you'll need to have a good idea of what you want to plant, when you should plant it, and where you should plant it. It's really very simple!

Design

Novice gardeners tend to plant too much too close together. Well, it's a live-and-learn world. Just as using graph paper is helpful in designing a flower garden, it is useful in figuring out your vegetable garden. Outline the area you have available, and remember it must have plenty of sunshine. After you have decided what you are going to plant first, begin marking rows on the graph paper.

Try using the little sticky multi-coloured dots sold at stationers to represent veggies on your graph paper. The dots come in various sizes, which allows for great flexibility. Place the colour-coded dots at the approximate spacing recommended for your vegetable.

Mark all your trees and large shrubs on your graph. Keep your vegetable garden as far away from them as possible, as they block sun, and wide-ranging root systems are bossy about who owns soil nutrients and moisture.

Spend one day making note of how the sun travels across your garden. When you make your graph design, you want rows of vegetables that run north and south, so they get the best sun exposure. The taller vegetables should be at the rear of the garden. These include climbing beans and peas, cordon tomatoes, and sweetcorn. The shorter veggies, such as bush varieties, can be in the middle, and the little ones, such as spinach and salad greens, should be placed at the front where they won't be shaded.

■ **In a cottage-style garden** *every inch of space is used in a seemingly random way. Screens and wigwams made from canes support beans and peas.*

Out in the garden, don't forget to identify each row of vegetables with indelible pen on plastic labels or ice lolly sticks. Paper labels won't withstand the rain, and are a popular snack for snails, slugs, and bugs.

DEFINITION

Farmers have long been known to **rotate crops***. When crops are rotated, different plants are grown in one spot during each growing season. Why not plant the same crops in the same space? Because annoying crop-specific bugs and diseases like to hang around for another opportunity to flourish. Crop rotation helps decrease that phenomenon.*

Sequential crops

To make the most of your space, grow vegetables in sequence. Check the maturity date of the vegetable you want to grow on the seed packet. If it says, for example, 52 days, you've selected a short-season crop. In that case, you may want to plant a second crop of something else. Leaf lettuce and radishes may be followed by carrots, spinach followed by lettuce, and the like. For long-season crops, you have to decide how much ground you want to devote to them for the duration.

As you can see, much of your planning will depend on the size of your planting area. However, since the best practice is to **rotate crops** whenever possible, you may have ample opportunity to grow a bit of everything eventually.

Double cropping

Double cropping, or intercropping, is the practice of planting quicker-growing crops among slower growers, giving a larger harvest. For example, you might plant radishes amid slower-growing carrots, or spring onions among cabbage.

■ **Vegetables planted** in neat, well-organized rows make the maximum use of space and allow you easy access to each crop when it's ready to harvest.

Placing your perennials

Perennial vegetables, such as asparagus and artichoke, can simply have a sunny corner of their own. Or, if you like, mingle them with your medium-sized flowering plants that get sun and enough water. Just remember where they are, so you don't dig them up in the plants' sleeping, or dormant, season.

Companion planting

Companion planting usually refers to placing specific herbs among specific plants to deter insect pests and diseases. Examples are using onion to ward off carrot root fly, using mint to deter aphids, and using pot marigold to slow down the onslaught of asparagus beetles.

Companion planting may also describe plants that grow better when grown next to each other. Examples include onion and carrots, radishes and cucumbers, and basil and tomatoes. Companion planting has both its advocates and those who scoff. It certainly won't hurt to try.

Raised beds

When it comes to veggies, planting on raised beds (an elevated mound of soil) means you can plant earlier and grow later.

Do not use any type of preservative-treated wood for vegetable gardens.

■ **Nasturtiums** *can be used near a vegetable garden both for colour and edible capers.*

Terrific tomatoes

TECHNICALLY, YES, TOMATOES (Lycopersicon lycopersicum) *are a fruit. But let's face it, you slice up tomatoes for the top of a salad. You don't slice them up to combine with grapes and chunks of watermelon. Everybody thinks of tomatoes as vegetables. So without further ado, let's make some sauce!*

PLUM TOMATO

Endless variety

You see quite a few different types of tomatoes in the supermarket, but did you know that there are at least 2,600 tomato varieties? Various types include heritage, early-season, mid-season, late-season, beefsteak, cherry, indoor, outdoor, and patio. Tomato shapes include accordion, egg, heart, oblong, pear, ribbed, round, and even square-round. If that isn't enough, tomatoes come in yellow, white, red, green, green with yellow stripes, gold, pink, brown-red, purple-brown, bicolour yellow/orange, bicolour red/yellow, and orange.

If you truly get into tomatoes, you can have an entire garden of American tomatoes, Italian tomatoes, heritage tomatoes, or hybrid tomatoes. Ninety-five per cent of vegetable gardeners grow tomatoes. It is actually easy. It's even easier if you buy them in a little container at the garden centre, but more fun if you grow them from seed. I won't say anybody can grow tomatoes, because they do take some care, but for a vegetable they are extremely cooperative.

■ **Bush tomatoes** *don't need any form of support – they simply sprawl along the ground.*

Trivia...

The original tomotl, *or tomato, is believed to have come from Peru's Andes Mountains. In the early 1600s Spanish explorers brought seeds home to Europe. In Italy, they were called* poma amoris, *or the apple of love, in France it was* pomme d'amour. *Most people, however, didn't eat them, instead using them as ornamental plants. The Pilgrims took tomato seeds to North America and the tomato later found its way into most colonial gardens.*

The North Americans believed that the tomato was poisonous. It wasn't until the French military, stationed in New Orleans, began using tomatoes in their daily meals that the tomato gained culinary acceptance there.

Starting tomato seeds

Begin with a few pots containing a multi-purpose compost, which you can buy at the garden centre or supermarket. It is best not to use garden soil because the soil may carry some insect or disease that will destroy the susceptible seeds. You can place your tomato seeds in individual plastic cups if you like; just make a little hole in the bottom for drainage and put the whole batch of cups in a waterproof tray. Poke a few seeds in a cup, just a centimetre deep. They will germinate, or sprout, in about a week if they are in a reasonably warm (about 24° C) site. A sunny kitchen windowsill is often a great spot for sprouting. If the area is only about 15° C, the sprouting can take up to 2 weeks. Don't despair if you have no sunny windowsill or if yours is already filled with plants, as mine is. Try starting them under a lamp that you leave on most of the time.

Once you see the seedlings, add water so the soil stays slightly damp. You don't want the soil to be wet, as the teeny roots drown quickly. When seedlings are about 7 centimetres high and have a few sturdy leaves, you must give them more room to grow. You can transplant them to other plastic cups or cottage cheese containers, or to something more charming, such as a 10-centimetre pot. Your new tomato plants need a good amount of sun at this point, so you may just have to rearrange your windowsills after all.

Into the garden

As the weather warms up, move your outdoor tomato plants into the garden. The tomato is strictly a warm-weather fruit. If you plant it outside too early and the temperature takes a sudden dip below 13° C, the emerging flower buds will fall off.
Each pretty yellow bud = one tomato.

I love plucking ripe, exquisitely crunchy, tiny tomatoes growing indoors, for breakfast. Try it.

You can also continue to grow tomatoes, such as the tiny cherry tomatoes, indoors. Each plant requires a nice-size pot with a drainage hole if you tend to over-water at times. A sunny site is mandatory. Provide an occasional (but skimpy) liquid fertilization when you do your other houseplants. A tomato fertilizer is best, of course, but I find these plants are not overly selective in this respect.

Transplanting tomatoes

With plants that are to go outside, place the plant, whether home-started or nursery-raised, into a soil hole that is about 15 centimetres wider and deeper than the container. Soil should be composed of 50 per cent good organic soil and 50 per cent garden compost. Some people with only one or two raised beds use them strictly for tomatoes. These are nice people to know if you want tomato gifts.

Gently remove the plant from its container. Tomatoes from the nursery may be somewhat root-bound, especially if you've bought them late in the season. If you can be extraordinarily gentle, separate the roots a bit so they move outwards instead of curling inwards. Otherwise, leave well alone. Place the plant with the lowest set of leaves at soil level. Backfill the hole with good soil, and gently firm the soil down. Give your plants a nice drink of water. Start fertilizing your tomatoes when they are about 60 centimetres tall. Fertilize every 2 to 4 weeks with a commercial fertilizer that has a big picture of a tomato on the label and says "for tomatoes".

Of course, you can sow your tomato seed right in the garden. Poke little planting holes a centimetre or so deep with a stick or an old screwdriver. Install two seeds per hole, and cover with very fine organic soil. Keep slightly moist until seedlings appear.

Support systems

There are those who like their tomatoes sprawling all over the ground and those who like their tomatoes growing neatly on some type of support. I am a lazy gardener, but I now support my tomatoes. I usually do it on plastic shoe racks, but there are a multitude of choices, from tomato cages to 1 to 2 metre stakes of anything you have around or is cheap to buy. Put stakes in the ground before you install your tomatoes. If you decide to do it later, you'll have to hammer the stakes through the root system. As the vines grow, tie them to your support system with strips of soft cloth – a good use for clean rags.

The goal of the support system is to keep the tomatoes off the ground, because the part that's in contact with the soil may get discoloured or a bit rotten, especially as the tomato matures. In general, tomato plants should be placed about 1 metre apart, but of course, each type has its own preference.

■ **Staking tomatoes** *need to be trained, or tied to support stakes or wires as they grow, to ensure that all the fruits receive enough sunlight.*

Patio pots

Tomatoes have a long, wide root system, and if you want to grow tomatoes on your patio make sure the pot is big enough. Even the roots of cherry tomatoes can develop heartily.

The most critical care you can give all tomatoes, and patio tomatoes in particular, is to water them regularly, preferably at soil level.

Without adequate water, patio tomatoes develop leaf wilt quickly. If you notice early signs of leaf wilt, give some water and the plant will probably resuscitate without major harm. A few days of untreated leaf wilt and you'll have to go back to the nursery or garden centre. Regular under-watering causes blossoms to drop, and you'll end up with misshapen and/or undersized fruits.

Note that although tomato plants self-fertilize, each flower does need to be pollinated. If you live in a wind-free area, your patio is well enclosed, or you're growing the plants indoors, not enough pollen will naturally meander from one part of the flower to the next. Play matchmaker and brush the blossoms gently with your hand a few times.

Tomatoes of all types

It's so much fun looking through garden catalogues trying to decide which tomato to grow, from itsy-bitsy grape tomatoes to huge monsters. To help you choose among the many types, the following list sets out the qualities of some delicious tomatoes.

The phrase "determinate" indicates a sort of stalky plant that stops bearing fruit when it reaches a determined size. The fruit of these plants tends to ripen all at the same time, which is a benefit if you want to bottle or preserve them.

■ **Here, tumbling bush** *tomatoes share a hanging basket with French marigolds, grown as a companion plant.*

All of the large tomatoes are "indeterminate", which means they continue to grow and bear fruit until frost kills the plant. Large tomato plants may need support and the sideshoots should be pinched out. The supported single stems are known as cordons.

Bush tomatoes don't need support, and pinching out of the sideshoots isn't necessary either. However, the fruit tends to be hidden, making picking it a little more difficult than on a cordon.

Trivia...

Some sellers will describe particular types of tomatoes as "mild", particularly the lighter-hued varieties. This may or may not be quite accurate, as a "mild" tomato may have a high sugar content that masks the acidity. I mention this because some people don't tolerate highly acidic foods, such as tomatoes.

Tomatoes for greenhouse or garden

- **Ailsa Craig** – widely available, popular variety with a good reputation, produces a heavy crop of medium-sized brightly coloured fruits that have an excellent flavour.
- **Alicante** – well-known cordon type of tomato, producing a heavy crop of high-quality medium-sized fruits, an ideal variety for beginners.
- **Gardeners' Delight** – heavy-cropping cordon cherry tomato producing fruit on long trusses, sweet tangy flavour, well suited to being grown in containers.
- **Golden Sunrise** – cordon tomato with well-shaped, medium-sized golden-yellow fruits, sweet fruity flavour.
- **Moneymaker** – very popular cordon variety, produces large trusses of medium-sized fruits, flavour tends to be a little on the bland side.
- **Tigerella** – cordon tomato, early maturing with medium-sized red- and yellow-striped fruits, good flavour, produces a good crop.
- **Sweet 100** – cordon cherry tomato with fruit on long rope-like stems, up to 100 very sweet and tangy tomatoes on each, long harvesting period.
- **Tumbler** – bushy cherry tomato, grows well in patio pots or a hanging basket, produces a fast-ripening and heavy crop on pendant stems.
- **Green Grape** – new novelty cherry tomato, green when ripe, has a unique sweet flavour.
- **Baby Heart** – unusual, heart-shaped, seedless cherry tomato, produces up to 50 fruits per truss, good sweet flavour.

CHERRY TOMATOES

Tomatoes for the greenhouse

- **Shirley** – excellent variety well worth trying, resistant to a range of diseases and disorders such as greenback, virus, and leaf mould, matures early and produces heavy crops of fruit.
- **Dombito** – a true beefsteak with large, red, tasty fruits weighing around 340 grams each!

Heritage tomatoes to try

- **Christmas Grapes** – a cherry tomato.
- **Lemon Tree** – an unusual variety with lemon-coloured and lemon-shaped fruits.
- **Tangella** – orange fruits with good flavour.

BEEFSTEAK TOMATO

219

Harvesting hints

Once you have eaten a home-grown tomato, supermarket tomatoes tend to taste like cardboard. Why? Because they are usually picked while green and ripened artificially. You just can't wait to pick your first tomatoes, but leave them on the plant as long as possible. Try not to tear the fruit when you pick it off. Store extra fruit at room temperature, out of direct sunlight.

■ **Yellow tomatoes** *turn a golden-yellow colour when ripe.*

To maintain the fresh taste of your tomatoes, don't store them in the fridge.

Carrots for crunching

CARROTS (Daucus carrota) *actually grow in a variety of colours, including purple, red, yellow, white, and, of course, orange. The orange carrot originated in the 1700s, but the wild carrot, which was branched rather than conical, was around long before that and was often used as food for cattle. Today, carrots are favoured for their health-giving properties and high vitamin A content.*

Planting carrots

Sow carrot seeds where they are to grow every 2 weeks from February through to August. Those planted from July to mid-August will provide the winter harvest. The seeds may take up to 3 weeks to germinate. It is better to sow them thickly and then thin out the extras. Because the seeds are so small, mix them with some sand before sowing.

■ **Thin seedlings** *to 2½ centimetres apart for early carrots and 3 to 5 centimetres apart for late carrots to give them room to develop.*

Gardeners often mix 20 per cent radish to 80 per cent carrot seed when sowing. The radishes mark the site of the slower-germinating carrots, and are ready long before carrots need their full space. Early carrots will be ready for picking about 3 months after they're sown; late carrots will take about 4 months.

If you want long carrots, your soil should be fine, sandy loam. If you have clay or other heavy soil, plant short carrots. The longer ones will be tough and misshapen from trying to drill their way downward. Raised beds work well for growing carrots. They may also be grown in a container, using commercial potting compost. Below are some favourite types of carrots.

Early-season carrots

These carrots have round or short, stumpy roots that mature more quickly early in the year. Early carrots are eaten as soon as they are pulled, or can be frozen.

- **Amini** – miniature carrot with smooth skin.
- **Amsterdam Forcing** – one of the earliest to mature, good for successional sowing, has cylindrical root with blunt end and small core, excellent for freezing.
- **Early Nantes 2** – has slightly longer roots than Amsterdam Forcing, good for successional sowing every 2 to 3 weeks, tender, good for freezing.
- **Ingot F1** – very sweet, tasty, deep orange roots, excellent raw or cooked, good for freezing.
- **Mokum** – high yield, very juicy, crisp and sweet.
- **Pariska** – small, rounded roots with no core, often sold as a mini vegetable.

EARLY-SEASON CARROTS

Main-crop carrots

Main-crop carrots are good all-rounders for the average garden. Pull up young carrots for immediate consumption, and leave the rest to mature for winter storage.

- **Autumn King** – long carrots with distinctive stumpy ends, extremely hardy, can stay in the ground over winter.
- **Chantenay Red Cored** – originated in 1829, good harvest over a long period, stores well, deep orange colour with smooth skin.
- **Fly Away** – good taste, resistance to carrot fly, medium to long in shape, small, central sweet core.
- **James Scarlet** – good reputation for all-round performance.
- **Juwarot** – deep orange, sweet-flavoured roots, high in Vitamin A. Great eaten raw or for juicing.

MAIN-CROP CARROTS

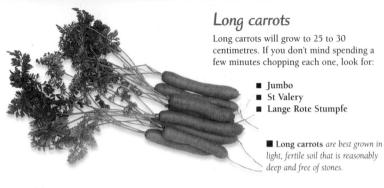

Long carrots

Long carrots will grow to 25 to 30 centimetres. If you don't mind spending a few minutes chopping each one, look for:

- **Jumbo**
- **St Valery**
- **Lange Rote Stumpfe**

■ **Long carrots** *are best grown in light, fertile soil that is reasonably deep and free of stones.*

Maintaining your carrot crop

Carrots prefer ground that is very slightly damp, so remember to water them evenly. Root cracking is too often caused by soil that swings between wet and dry. Be sure to remove weeds as they emerge, making a point to differentiate between weeds and carrot leaves that look somewhat like weeds. A hint to help you along: carrot leaves are vertical, or upright, while weed leaves tend to flop to the side. Continue to thin the plants so that the carrots intended for mature size are about 5 centimetres apart.

Your best defence against disease in your carrots is a good offence. In this case, be sure to buy the strongest type of plants. Look for the disease-resistance of your choice, which is noted on the package. The only insect of consequence to a carrot crop is the carrot root fly. The young of this insect, appearing as maggots, chomp away on the carrots. To deter these pests, try planting onions nearby to deter female adults from laying their eggs, and place fresh grass clippings around your carrots to protect them.

Harvesting

Carrots get sweeter the closer they get to maturity, and in this case the simple taste test is best. After you remove the carrot from the ground, cut off all but about 2 to 3 centimetres of the greenery, as the root continues to try to supply it with nutrients. This eventually dries out the root.

Some gardeners simply leave their carrots in the ground as a means of storage. But make a point of removing them by February before they get tough, and definitely before the ground freezes. A frozen carrot will rot. Note: if you like the look of carrot flowers, leave a few. They attract pollinators.

Please pass the peas

UNTIL THE 1800s, PEAS (Pisum savitum) were
eaten dried – unless they were boiled to make pease
pudding. Later, peas were cooked in the pod,
and, when served at the table, diners licked the
peas out of the pods. Move along a bit and
people began eating peas with a knife. I'm not
sure how they did that, since when I tried the
peas rolled off the knife. I eat mine with a
fork if they are cooked, and crunch them
out of the pod when fresh. It's considered
lucky to find a pod with a single pea in it.

■ **Best eaten soon after picking**, *peas
are a good source of protein and fibre.*

Today, 40 per cent of gardeners grow peas. There are pea types that appear early in the
season, types that appear mid-season, and others that come late. If you have enough
space, try a few of each, planted at the same time for a long harvest season.

Planting peas

Where winters are cold, you should plant peas as early in the spring as possible. They
don't mind light frosts and tolerate cold nights as chilly as -6° C. Sow a second crop
from mid-July to August. If you live in an area with mild winters, you can plant in
early spring to get a spring crop and then again in early autumn for a winter crop.
Peas are generally not heat lovers. If you plant peas in late spring or summer, and the
temperature tops 27° C, they tend to grow poorly. These pea plants are likely to have
wilted leaves, fallen blossoms, and tiny pods. They are also more prone to developing
powdery mildew problems.

Peas require full sun in a wind-free site and rich, well-drained, organic soil. Because
of the good drainage they supply, raised beds are ideal for pea plants. Dig a long
trench about 5 centimetres deep where you want to place your peas. Dwarf varieties
should be 1 metre apart and don't need trellising or support systems. Tall varieties
should be placed just over 1 metre apart. When placing the tall pea varieties, it
helps to provide some support for the tendril-climbing vine. Any type of 5-
to 10-centimetre mesh will work well.

*Because peas germinate slowly, many gardeners soak the seeds
overnight before planting.*

SUPPORTING PEAS

Peas range from 45 centimetres to over 2 metres tall and all will benefit from the support of twiggy branches known as peasticks as they are growing.

1 Push sticks into the ground

When seedlings have developed tendrils, push peasticks into the ground, as upright as possible, along the outside of the block or row.

2 Watch your peas climb

As the peas grow, the tendrils are able to wrap themselves around the peasticks and clamber upwards on the supports.

Varieties of peas

There are basically two kinds of pea plants: smooth peas and wrinkled peas. Smooth peas are generally quicker to mature than other types and are more able to tolerate poor growing conditions. Wrinkled peas tend to be less hardy than the smooth types but have the advantage of being more tasty. There is also another type of pea where the whole pod is eaten while the peas inside are immature, and these are called mange-tout peas, snow peas, or sugar peas.

Smooth peas

- **Douce Provence** – a good choice for a sweet-tasting pea, although it doesn't produce massive crops.
- **Feltham First** – an old favourite that needs little support, produces 10-centimetre long-pointed pods.
- **Fortune** – similar to Feltham First, but slower to mature, and produces a greater crop.
- **Meteor** – good reputation for succeeding in cold and exposed sites.
- **Pilot** – popular, matures early, produces a heavy crop.
- **Yushaya** – new variety, produces straight 10-centimetre pods of tender juicy peas.

Wrinkled peas

- **Alderman** – large pods with up to 11 peas in each, long harvesting season.
- **Daybreak** – good cropper, large pods and very sweet peas.
- **Hurst Green Shaft** – long pods borne in pairs, very sweet peas, produces heavy yield of about 11 peas in each pod.
- **Kelvedon Wonder** – reliable, early, can be used for successional sowing to ensure a longer cropping season, reputed to be resistant to wilt and mildew.
- **Knight** – very early maturing, large podded pea, consistently produces worthwhile late yields due to mildew resistance.
- **Little Marvel** – very sweet flavour, neat plants with blunt-ended pods borne in pairs.
- **Lord Chancellor** – late-maturing variety, producing heavy crop of dark green pointed pods.

Whole pod varieties

- **Oregon Sugar Pod** – crisp, sweet, and delicious
- **Sugar Gem** – completely stringless, crisp, and succulent pods.
- **Sugar Snap** – tender, tasty, can still be eaten whole even when the pods are turning yellow.

Easy pea plant care

Water your peas regularly so the ground doesn't quite dry out, but do not over-water. Peas seldom need any type of fertilizer, but adding mulch to the base of the plant will help conserve moisture. Because pea vines are quite delicate and can be broken easily, weed around them very carefully by hand.

Diseases commonly seen in pea plants include wilt, root rot, and downy mildew. Aphids, bean maggots, cucumber beetles, pea weevils, snails, and slugs are all pea pests, so keep an eye out for insects while your plants are growing.

Picking peas

Depending on when they are planted and what type they are, peas will bear pods from 2 to 4 months. The first pods will appear at the plant base. Pick these quickly to encourage the plant to form more pods. Harvest about every 2 days. Pick the pods when they are somewhat slim and about 5 to 7 centimetres long. As they plump up, the peas become hard and lose flavour.

Eat your harvest as quickly as possible after picking. If you must refrigerate, put the pods, in their entirety, in a plastic bag. They will last up to 1 week. Sugar and snow peas have tender, sweet pods that can be eaten pod and all when still small. Smooth peas are best for drying; wrinkled peas are best for eating fresh.

Perfect peppers

PEPPERS (Capsicum annuum, C. frutescens) are
very popular home-grown vegetables. There are so
many varieties, from sweet to phenomenally hot,
that you could plant an entire garden in
peppers and it would look just
as pretty as a flower-filled
one. Peppers grow well in
containers, too.

MIXED SWEET PEPPERS

Planting peppers

Plant peppers in spring about a week after the last frost. The preferred temperature for
sweet peppers is about 20° C, for hot peppers between 20 and 30° C. Night temperatures
below 15° C may cause blossoms to fall off. Each blossom represents one pepper.
Because their roots don't care to be disturbed, peppers grow and fruit better if you plant
them from seed. However, pepper plants are available from nurseries if you don't
want to start from scratch. Just handle young plants gently and water them
after planting.

*Do not purchase pepper plants if they have flowers or fruit. Once the
plants are at this level of maturity, they will not adjust well to
transplanting. To select, look for strong stems and dark green leaves.*

Peppers need full sun, reasonably good soil, and good drainage. Avoid placing them
in windy areas. Indoors, start peppers in peat pots so you can place the entire plant
and pot in the ground. Put about three seeds in each pot, each a centimetre deep and 2
centimetres apart, keeping the soil slightly damp. After the seeds sprout, put the containers
in a sunny window. Thin to one plant per container when the seedlings are 7 centimetres
high. Move the plants outdoors when each is about 15 centimetres high and when night
temperatures rise above 7° C. Space the plants about 60 centimetres apart.

Pepper particulars

There's a lot of diversity among peppers. There are even ornamental varieties, such as
Varingata with its variegated leaves, purple and white blossoms, and small green and
purple fruits that turn red when they mature. But assuming you plan to eat your harvest,
check out the following.

Sweet peppers

- **Bananarama** – 20 centimetres long, yellow fruit becomes orange-red.
- **Big Bertha hybrid** – 18 by 10 centimetres, dark green to red, great for stuffing and roasting.
- **California Wonder** – 10 by 10 centimetres, green to red, a good pepper for stuffing.
- **Canape** – ideal for growing outdoors on a sunny and sheltered patio.
- **Gypsy** – 10 centimetres long, matures earlier than most varieties, good-flavoured orange fruit.
- **Jingle Bells** – mini pepper that is ideal where space is limited, delicious in salads, stir-fries, stuffed, or grilled.
- **Jumbo Sweet** – often more than 15 centimetres long, vigorous, early maturing, a prolific cropper.
- **Pimiento Elite** – thick-walled oval fruits that mature to a bright red, also sweet when still green.
- **Sweet Chocolate** – early fruiting, cold-tolerant bell pepper that tastes sweet and juicy straight off the plant, a good low-calorie substitute for chocolate!

■ **Yellow peppers** *tend to have the sweetest flavour of all sweet peppers.*

Hot peppers

Note that hot peppers get even hotter as they mature.

- **Anaheim** – about 15 centimetres long, green to dark red, mildly hot, good fresh, pickled, dried, or in stews.
- **Apache** – compact plant for a windowsill or patio, prolific fruits turn red when ripe, the higher the temperature as fruit develops, the hotter the pepper.
- **Cherry Bomb** – especially high yielding, large-fruited cherry pepper with super thick walls to absorb more pickling brine.
- **Firecracker** – compact, well-formed plants producing lots of miniature upright peppers in a range of inferno colours, appropriately named, as the peppers are very hot!
- **Habanero** – 5 centimetres square, silvery green, short, wrinkled fruits turn orange, extremely hot.
- **Heatwave** – beautifully ornamental with a mix of red, yellow, and orange fruits. Mind-blowing hot flavour.
- **Hero** – strong, vigorous, copes well with poor conditions.
- **Jalapeño** – about 7 centimetres long, dark green to dark red, hot!
- **Prairie Fire** – these look small but certainly make up for their size in pepper flavour – atomic!
- **Thai Dragon** – tiny, cone-shaped fruit on a very small plant, looks good as a houseplant provided it's kept away from children and pets, not for the faint-hearted.

JALAPEÑO

Pepper plant care

Water your peppers regularly. Water stress causes blossoms and growing fruit to drop off, so don't let the soil totally dry out. Fertilize the plants about every 3 weeks with a vegetable fertilizer. Fertilizing is most important just as blossoms are becoming fruit.

If you plant sweet peppers too close to hot peppers, cross-pollination can occur and you may bite into a hot sweet pepper.

Diseases often found in pepper plants include tobacco mosaic virus, mildew, and bacterial leaf spot. Aphids and caterpillars are common insect pests. Peppers need good drainage, and too much rain can stunt plants. Unfortunately, there's absolutely nothing you can do about bad weather.

Picking peppers

Cut peppers off the vine with scissors or secateurs. Most peppers will begin ripening in July and in some areas will continue until early winter. Many of the sweet and hot peppers become sweeter or hotter as they ripen. But if you leave too many on the vine, new peppers won't develop.

If your hands are sensitive, wear gloves when harvesting hot peppers.

Harvest all peppers before any frost is predicted. They cannot tolerate even a light freeze and are damaged by cold rain. Hot pepper plants can be hung upside down so that the fruit dries slowly. Fresh peppers will keep in the refrigerator for about 2 weeks.

■ **Harvest hot peppers** *once the fruits have swollen. Wash hands after harvesting. Contact with peppers can cause a burning sensation. Avoid rubbing the eyes.*

Prime potatoes

POTATOES (Solanum tuberosum) are a main staple of our diet and a great favourite in many a vegetable plot. The potato was brought to Europe from the Americas by Spanish explorers in the 16th century, and was originally a delicacy eaten only by the rich. It has since become a staple part of the Western diet.

Potato planting

Potatoes are grown from seed potatoes saved from the previous year's crop or bought from garden centres or seed merchants. Early in spring, about six weeks before planting, seed potatoes are sprouted, or chitted, indoors to start them into growth. Place your seed potatoes in a shallow tray in a cool, light position, such as on a windowsill or in a greenhouse. Make sure that the place you choose is frost free but not too warm, so that the tubers can develop short, strong shoots.

■ **To chit seed potatoes,** place them in a box or tray in a single layer with the end of the potato containing the most "eyes" uppermost.

Potato shoots will be damaged by frost, so the time for planting will depend on the last frost in your area, but generally mid-March to mid-April will be about right. Plant about 15 centimetres deep and about 60 to 75 centimetres apart. If your potatoes do sprout before the last frosts, protect the early growth by covering the plants with horticultural fleece, or pulling some earth over the emerging shoots to provide them with some insulation when frost is forecast.

■ **To plant potatoes,** make a drill about 8 to 15 centimetres deep and place the tubers in the bottom, sprouts uppermost. Cover them carefully with soil. Plant early potatoes 30 centimetres apart and main-crop potatoes about 40 centimetres apart.

Potato varieties

There are several types of potatoes to choose from and all are grouped according to the time that they crop: first earlies, second earlies, and main-crop potatoes. First earlies are dug and eaten as new potatoes before they have grown to their full size, and are generally not stored. Because these potatoes have not formed a thick skin, they can be scraped rather than peeled. New potatoes are followed by the second earlies. Main-crop potatoes are left to mature before being lifted. They will have formed a thick skin, and will last for some time if properly stored. The last category of potato is the salad potato, where the tubers are generally either scraped like new potatoes or scrubbed, and then cooled after boiling. They are delicious eaten with salad.

With a little planning, you can still enjoy some new potatoes in the winter. All you need to do is to plant a few tubers in the middle of summer and then cover them with a *cloche* in autumn to give them some protection. Your new potatoes should be ready for digging up several weeks later.

> *Trivia...*
>
> Potatoes are part of the Solanaceae family, related to tomatoes and capsicums or peppers. After flowering, the potato plants develop small fruits that look just like small green tomatoes. Potatoes are also related to deadly nightshade!!

> **DEFINITION**
>
> A **cloche** is a small, portable structure made of clear plastic or glass, usually within a metal framework, that's used to protect early crops on open ground and to warm the soil before planting.

First earlies

- **Concorde** – waxy flesh, heavy cropper, oval white tubers, suitable for all soil types.
- **Foremost** – white tubers, resistant to slug attack, can be stored.
- **Maris Bard** – white tubers, good for early lifting.
- **Pentland Javelin** – white skin and flesh, good for boiling and salad potatoes.

Second earlies

- **Nadine** – round white tubers, ideal for baking whole.
- **Maxine** – red-skinned tubers with waxy white flesh, heavy cropping.
- **Kondor** – red-skinned with white flesh, high yielding with good disease resistance.
- **Maris Peer** – medium-sized, white-skinned tubers.

EARLY POTATOES

Main-crop potatoes

- **Maris Piper** – white skinned, good all-rounder.
- **Valor** – resistant to tuber blight and good for storing, round white tubers ideal for mashing and roasting.
- **King Edward** – red and white skin, floury flesh. A good potato for baking, mashing, or chipping.
- **Desiree** – disease resistant, excellent flavour, good all-rounder for cooking.

Salad potatoes

- **Charlotte** – early maturing, delicious eaten hot as new potatoes, or cold as salad potatoes.
- **Pink Fir Apple** – knobbly tubers, ready in late summer, delicious nutty flavour, best eaten as young tubers when they can be scraped, or as autumn salad potatoes, cooked after scrubbing the tubers.

■ **Maris Piper** *is a popular white-skinned main-crop potato. It's very versatile but is especially good for baking and roasting.*

Maintaining your crop

As your potatoes grow, they will need to be "earthed up". This involves moving soil up around the stems of the potatoes to cover any forming tubers. If the weather is dry, water early potatoes generously every 10 to 12 days. Delay watering main-crop potatoes until they are at least the size of marbles, and then water generously – but just the once.

■ **Draw up the soil** *around your potato plants when the foliage is about 23 centimetres high. Also known as "earthing", this prevents tubers that form near to the surface from turning green and being unfit to eat.*

Harvesting

You can start digging up early, or new, potatoes just as soon as the plants begin to flower, which is when the tubers should be forming. Just dig up one plant to start with, so that you can check that the potatoes are the size you want. If they are not large enough, simply leave the rest of the crop and start lifting them a week or so later.

Main-crop potatoes should be left until the stems and leaves (or haulms) die down. Choose a dry day, and allow the tubers to dry in the sun before using them or storing them in paper or hessian sacks. They do need to be kept frost free and dark (to stop them turning green). Also, they must be kept cool – if they get too warm they will start to sprout.

Potato blight

The main disease affecting potatoes is potato blight, a fungal infection that can ruin a year's crop and make it entirely inedible. Blight tends to occur during a warm, damp summer, as it is encouraged by humid weather. The first sign of blight is dark patches on the foliage, which then dies, and infected tubers will rot. If you spot blight on your potatoes then the crop is best dug up and burnt. You can try to prevent it by spraying regularly with a fungicide, and rotate your crops.

■ **Store your good potatoes** in a light-proof paper sack. Don't keep any that are damaged because they'll cause the remainder to rot.

Alternative ways to grow potatoes

You can grow extra early potatoes in a cool or unheated greenhouse, but don't grow potatoes in the same soil for two seasons running. The chitted tubers can be planted as early as February and harvested in May, when potatoes planted outside will only just have reached the surface. You can also grow potatoes in pots on the patio if you have only a small amount of space, or in among the flowers in your border if you have a gap.

Trivia...

For potatoes with a difference there are unusual varieties, such as the purple potato Edzell Blue. This actually has purple skin and mauve flesh, so if you like different colours on your plate, try purple mash!

To save yourself a great deal of digging, you can also grow potatoes under black plastic to save having to earth them. The tubers form just under the sheet of plastic, which gives them ample protection. Alternatively, grow them in amongst a thick layer of straw. When the potatoes are ready to harvest, the plastic or straw can be easily removed and the potatoes collected.

A simple summary

✓ Determine the boundaries of your vegetable growing area before you buy plants or seeds.

✓ When buying vegetable seeds by mail order or through catalogues, read all descriptions carefully. If you have time, read several catalogues, and see how they compare before deciding to buy.

✓ Plan the layout of your vegetable garden carefully so that you maximize your harvest.

✓ Because vegetables tend to need good drainage, consider planting in raised beds.

✓ Make certain you have enough sunlight for the types of vegetables you want to grow.

Tomatoes and peppers, in particular, need plenty of warm sunshine in order to ripen.

✓ Remember to fertilize and water plants as often as necessary – given the right care and attention your vegetables should reward you with a bumper crop.

✓ You can help to protect your vegetables by placing companion plants among them, or those plants, such as herbs, that are known to deter pests and diseases.

✓ Make sure you visit your vegetables on a frequent basis. You'll want to pick them at exactly the right time to enjoy them at their best.

Chapter 13

It's the Berries

THERE ARE ONLY TWO WAYS to get really fresh berries: Either grow them yourself or buy them from a farm where they're raised. I used to fool myself into thinking those pricy berries in the little plastic containers at the supermarket were the "real thing" (despite the fact that the ones on the container's bottom were either soggy or growing mould). Then I went berry picking and eating, and it was a revelation.

In this chapter...
- ✓ *Culinary currants*
- ✓ *Grapes galore*
- ✓ *Bountiful blackberries*
- ✓ *Gorgeous gooseberries*
- ✓ *Rolling in raspberries*
- ✓ *Succulent strawberries*

Culinary currants

WHITE AND REDCURRANTS (Ribus rubrum)
*are easy-to-grow, attractive bushes that don't take up
too much space in a small garden. Redcurrants are a
popular dessert garnish and are a vital ingredient of
summer pudding. Blackcurrants (Ribus nigrum)
usually need more room but their flavour is unsurpassed
for eating raw, cooking, or making drinks, and they're
very high in vitamin C, so are well worth growing.*

■ A host of delicious
summer *berries provides a
feast for the eyes, as well as
tempting the palate.*

Growing currants

White and redcurrants are grown in much the same way as each other because the
white version is just a colour variant of the red. Both currants are grown as bushes on a
short stem developing a permanent framework of branches. White currants are less
vigorous than the red, but have sweeter tasting fruit.

*Birds are especially fond of currants, so you will need to net the
bushes or invest in a fruit cage.*

Blackcurrants are grown slightly differently. Since they fruit on wood made the
previous summer, you'll need to remove a proportion of the older stems each
year to make sure that they produce plenty of young growth. Blackcurrants have a
distinctive flavour, and are more tolerant of the cold than the red or white currants.

Planting currants

All currants prefer an open sunny position and well-drained soil, although
blackcurrants will tolerate heavier soils. Dig plenty of well-rotted manure into the soil
before planting and always buy your bushes from a reputable supplier to ensure that
your young currants are free from viruses.

In autumn, plant currants approximately 1.5 to 2 metres apart. Once planted, the
currants will start to produce good crops after two years and will continue to provide
delicious fruit for many years to come.

Plants to include in the same area of the garden, if you have the space, are gooseberries
and jostaberries. Jostaberries have both blackcurrants and gooseberries in their parentage,
and have fruit similar to extremely large blackcurrants, but a flavour all their own.

Blackcurrants

- **Ben Connan** – an early ripening variety, ready from early July, with large berries.
- **Ben Lomond** – ripening at the end of July, this variety is late flowering and resistant to cold. Requires only light pruning.
- **Ben More** – mid-season fruiting
- **Ben Sarek** – a good variety, with compact bushes and frost resistance. Slightly later cropping than Ben Lomond.
- **Jet** – very late cropper.
- **Laxton's Giant** – ripening early to mid-season, this variety produces some of the largest fruits.
- **Seabrook's Black** – mid-season ripening, resistant to big bud mite attack.
- **Wellington XXX** – mid-season ripening.

■ **Ben Sarek** *has large acid berries and is a compact bush that's suitable for small gardens.*

Redcurrants

- **Jonkheer van Tets** – an early ripening variety, with heavy crops of large, full-flavoured berries.
- **Junifer** – fruits on both 1- and 2-year-old wood, so produces a good yield. Disease resistant and early cropping.
- **Laxton's No. 1** – early to flower and fruit, produces tasty, medium-sized currants.
- **Raby Castle** – hardy, produces a prolific crop.
- **Redstart** – very late cropping, but yields are high and consistent.
- **Red Lake** – fruits on long, easy-to-pick trusses.
- **Rovada** – late cropper, ready from late July, disease resistant.
- **Rondom** – late to ripen, produces a heavy crop of large berries.
- **Stanza** – smallish fruits are darker than other redcurrants, this is a late flowerer so less at risk from frost damage.
- **Wilson's Long Bunch** – late fruiting.

■ **Jonkheer van Tets** *is an early fruiting variety that produces a good heavy crop of fruits with a lovely sharp flavour.*

Whitecurrants

- **Blanka** – reliable Dutch variety, August-cropping.
- **White Dutch** – produces long trusses of pale golden fruits, on a rather untidy spreading bush.
- **White Grape** – mid-season, with large berries of good sweet flavour.
- **White Versailles** – large, light yellow, almost transparent fruit, ready from early July.

Harvesting

It's easier to harvest currants if you wait until the whole sprig is ripe, but remember to protect the ripening bushes with netting, or fruit cages – otherwise the local bird population will strip your bushes of berries before you have a chance to get to them. Fruit cages, available from good garden centres, are generally made of metal, are about 1.8 metres high, and should also be covered with netting. Once you have picked ripe bunches of fruit, you can remove the fruit by combing the currants from the stems with a table fork.

> ### Trivia...
> Blackcurrant coulis is easy to make – simply sieve the fruit with some sugar and if it isn't sweet enough for you add more sugar. It's a great accompaniment to summer puddings and ice cream (preferably home made)

■ **Thin your blackcurrant bush** *in the centre by cutting out one in every 3 or 4 stems, getting rid of the oldest and least productive (those with fewest sideshoots).*

Pruning blackcurrants

In the first year, prune blackcurrants hard to stimulate new shoots to grow and encourage the bush to develop a multi-stemmed shape. Once they are established, prune your blackcurrants in the autumn by removing about a third of the older wood, cutting the stems off close to the ground. Take out stems that are growing close to the ground and those that are crossing or causing congestion in the centre of the bush. You want to stimulate blackcurrants to grow plenty of strong, new stems because they will produce the best crops from 1-year-old wood. Give your blackcurrants plenty of nitrogen-rich fertilizer – they are greedy plants that enjoy lavish feeding.

■ **Cut back any low branches** *or those that spread out over the ground, as when laden with fruit, they will brush the soil and the fruits will be spoiled.*

Pruning red and white currants

Prune white and redcurrants after fruiting, or in the autumn by trimming the tips from all of the main leading branches, cutting to a bud and cutting back all of the sideshoots to one bud from the branch. Aim to create an open framework of permanent stems, so that air can circulate in the centre of the bush. Side shoots should then be pruned each autumn to 2.5 centimetres long. Cut out any diseased branches and allow new shoots to replace them. It's a good idea to mulch these plants with well-rotted manure in spring, and give them a good feed with fertilizer to encourage fruit production.

Grapes galore

■ **Grapes need** *plenty of sunshine to help the fruits develop.*

HAVING A FRUIT-LADEN *grape vine is many a gardener's dream. Although dessert grapes (Vitis) need warm, long summers to ripen outside, it is possible to reap a harvest in less reliable conditions, especially if you choose an early or mid-season variety. At the very least, a vine will form a stunning wall of foliage if trained vertically. It can be grown over a sturdy support such as a pergola, or in a greenhouse.*

Getting started

If you have a greenhouse, you should be able to provide the warmth needed to ripen grapes. If not, try growing them in a sunny position on a sheltered wall equipped with horizontal wires every 30 centimetres or so. Even if, in a poor summer, the crop may not be up to much, the beauty of the vine will compensate for a lack of fruit.

It is best to buy a young vine (most likely a 2- or 3-year-old vertical stem) in late autumn to early winter. Site your vines in an area with ample sun and good air circulation. Without good air circulation, vines are prone to develop mildew. You will also need well-drained, good-quality soil. Grapes like somewhat acidic soil, with a pH of about 5.5 to 6.5.

Recommended grapes

Dessert grapes are usually divided into three groups: muscat, sweetwater, and vinous. Vinous grapes crop late, which makes them less suitable for cooler climes. Varieties that can be grown more successfully in the UK are:

- **Black Hamburg** – produces large bunches of juicy, sweet, dessert-quality black grapes, early October ripening.
- **Foster's Seedling** – considered the best of the sweetwater grapes, heavy cropper, good-flavoured sweet and juicy fruit.
- **Phoenix** – Heavy yielding, very large grapes that turn yellow when ready for picking in early October.
- **Regent** – very large grapes with sweet, refreshing flavour, fruit matures to a true black colour after a hot summer.

FOSTER'S SEEDLING

Good grape-keeping

Water your vines regularly, as it is important to prevent drought stress. Drooping leaves are signs of thirst, so take action. Do not feed late in the season, as this encourages growth when energy should be placed into the fruit.

Pruning the vines

Once the main stem has reached the height you want, prune in winter to 2 buds of new growth. Cut back all the sideshoots from the previous summer to one strong bud. As the vine matures, growth around these sideshoots may become congested, so you may need to saw off these woody stubs. By early summer, you should see the flower trusses that will develop into bunches of grapes. Pinch out any weak trusses to concentrate the vine's energies on fewer, larger bunches.

Trivia...

Grapes got their English name from the Old French word grappe, meaning a cluster of grapes. This word was derived from the Old High German chrapo, the small hook used in harvesting grapes. In many cultures, the grape signifies cheer, fellowship, pleasure, fruitfulness, lust, and youth.

Harvesting grapes

Examine your grapes for a slight translucence. This is a sign that they're mature. Fully ripe grapes have the best flavour, and you should taste before you pick to ensure sweetness.

It's important to avoid handling the ripe or ripening fruits, as they are easily damaged

Bountiful blackberries

ONE OF MY BEST CHILDHOOD MEMORIES *is picking wild blackberries from the hedgerows and other wild patches of land. Even in cities, blackberries will grow wild along railway embankments and in other areas of neglected land. Cultivated blackberries are altogether more luscious, and well worth growing for apple and blackberry pie and bramble jelly.*

I'd put the other hybrid berries into the same category of deliciousness, the most popular of which is the loganberry. This is a cross between the blackberry and the raspberry, with fruit characteristics in between the two. The main difference is that hybrid berries have perennial canes, unlike the raspberry's annual stem.

Choosing blackberries and hybrid berries

These plants like to sprawl and ramble, so you'll need to control them by confining them in some way, such as training them up a wall or fence, or a series of wires. If you have a small garden or limited space, choose a less vigorous variety, or one without thorns (or both). Hybrid berries are more suited to a smaller garden than blackberries, since they are generally less vigorous. Hybrid berries prefer a sunny sheltered site, but blackberries will thrive in most situations, tolerating some shade and even bad drainage. Plant the bushes in autumn or winter, and tie the canes to some form of support.

BEDFORD GIANT BLACKBERRIES

Recommended blackberries

- **Ashton Cross** – wiry-stemmed, bears a heavy crop.
- **Bedford Giant** – as its name suggests, this is vigorous and so is not suitable for a small garden.
- **Black Satin** – thornless variety propagated in the U.S.
- **Fantasia** – discovered on an allotment near London, thorny, vigorous, with very large fruits indeed.
- **Helen** – thornless, best choice for early fruit.
- **Himalaya Giant** – makes a superb windbreak, but only suitable for large gardens.
- **Loch Ness** – thornless, and a good performer in the garden.
- **Merton Thornless** – good for confined spaces, small yields, but needs very little maintenance.
- **Oregon Thornless** – reliable, thornless, with mild-flavoured fruit.
- **Waldo** – thornless.

Hybrid berries

- **Boysenberry** – a cross between the loganberry, blackberry, and raspberry. Thorned and thornless varieties are available. Fruits are long or oblong, and look more like raspberries although they taste more like wild blackberries. They ripen at the end of July.
- **Dewberry** – generally more popular in the US than in the UK, this is not a cross between other berries, but a distinct species on its own. The fruit tastes much better than it looks!
- **Hildaberry** – a new hybrid cross between a boysenberry and a tayberry, named after the plant breeder's wife. Not widely available except through specialist nursery catalogues.
- **Japanese wineberry** – This is a very ornamental plant with its arching stems covered with stiff red bristles. There's the added attraction of edible, seed-filled red berries.
- **Loganberry** – a straight cross between a raspberry and a blackberry. This plant fruits mid-season, is very popular and more widely grown than other hybrid berry varieties.

- **Marionberry** – no one knows quite how this berry came into being, although some experts believe it's a true blackberry despite its sharp loganberry flavour. Whatever its parentage, it produces fruit over a long period of time.
- **Tayberry** – another hybrid developed from the raspberry and the blackberry. Yields are good, it fruits early but is not very hardy and can suffer in harsh conditions. Very suitable for warm sites. Thorned and thornless varieties are available.
- **Tummelberry** – a new berry from the Scottish Crop Research Institute. It'll stand up to cold winters. Its hairy canes grow rather more upright than arching.

TAYBERRY

Maintaining your plants

If you have a large trellis or a wide expanse of wall to cover, then do consider a blackberry variety. Thornless varieties will grow well over arches, and all the berries described here can be grown against a series of strong wires stretched across fences, trellises or walls. A simple post and wire system will give you space for tying in canes, room to prune, and of course you'll be able to pick berries from both sides!

These fruits are much less appealing to birds so you probably don't need to net the fruit as you would for raspberries. Prune in autumn, cutting out the older, unproductive canes. Tie new canes upright to the support and in spring make sure you tie them in to your support system, spacing the canes out in a fan shape.

Harvesting fruit

These bushes have fruit that will ripen over a period of weeks, so you don't need to pick all the fruit at once, but bear in mind that none of the soft fruit will store for any length of time.

Soft fruit berries are best picked and eaten quickly, within a few days, or else preserved.

Fruit that will eventually be used for cooking can be frozen, but the berries will lose their shape and texture when they are thawed, so can't be used in the same way as fresh berries. However, they are excellent for making summer puddings. Alternatively, the fruit can be made into jams or jellies.

Gorgeous gooseberries

GOOSEBERRIES (Ribes uva-crispa var. reclinatum) *are tolerant of cold weather and have traditionally been grown in the north of Britain, where they are frequently grown for show purposes. Both red and white gooseberries like an open, sunny postion but will grow in less than ideal situations and tolerate some shade.*

WHITE GOOSEBERRIES

Culinary varieties can be grown against a north-facing wall, but dessert, or eating, varieties will have tastier fruit if grown in full sun. Plants can be grown as bushes, or as cordons. You'll need to protect your gooseberries, as birds are fond of them too.

Early season gooseberries

- **Keepsake** – when ripe, the fruit is almost white.
- **Golden Drop** – good fruit, to be used when fresh.
- **May Duke** – an old favourite, traditionally used for pies and bottling.

Mid-season gooseberries

- **Careless** – very popular green fruit, for dessert and cooking, ripens mid-July.
- **Lancashire Lad** – red, heavy cropping variety for cooking.
- **Leveller** – best flavoured dessert gooseberry, prone to mildew, ripens in late July.
- **Invicta** – ripens late July, resistant to mildew, use for cooking

Maintaining gooseberries

Apply a general fertilizer around each bush in March. Water in well, and then apply a mulch of well-rotted manure or compost to keep down the weeds. Prune your bushes in autumn or winter, maintaining an open centre to allow air to circulate. On an established bush, prune the current season's growth back to 2-4 buds. Remove older, unproductive wood, and any diseased wood .

Always wear thick leather gloves to prune gooseberries, as it's a very prickly job.

Protect gooseberries from late frosts by covering them with horticultural fleece. If a heavy frost occurs, check the plants, and firm down the surrounding soil if the fruit bushes have been lifted. Remove suckers when you see them.

Rolling in raspberries

EARLY RASPBERRIES, mixed with honey, were used more often in Greek and Roman times to cure bloodshot eyes and skin disorders than they were as a dessert. The early European raspberry, often called a brambleberry, was not too tasty back in the 18th century, and was most often used for pies, as well as to make red dye. Today, garden raspberries (Rubus idaeus) are most often eaten fresh, and the hybridizers continue to achieve marvels with bigger, tastier, and firmer berries. Of course, they can also be made into delicious jams and jellies, and they also freeze extremely well. Of all the cane berries, raspberries are the hardiest. They thrive in a cool, damp climate, which is a fair description of most British summers.

■ **Red raspberries** *are popular for their sweet, rich flavour.*

The common raspberry is red, and has a wonderfully rich flavour. But you can also find a few yellow varieties, which tend to have paler green leaves and fruit in autumn. Both yellow and red raspberries grow on upright, non-branching plants with either prickly or smooth canes. Their spreading roots develop buds, and these buds grow into new canes. Raspberries are both easy and rewarding to grow: you really don't need to put in much effort to reap the rewards of a plentiful and juicy crop.

The raspberry also has an important advantage in that it flowers late in the spring. This means that frost damage is rarely a problem. You can expect your canes to remain productive for 8 to 12 years.

Raising raspberries

Raspberries are either summer or autumn fruiting, and should be planted either in the autumn or as early as possible in the spring. They prefer a slightly acidic and well-drained soil, so you need to make sure that your chosen planting site will not become waterlogged in winter. If this is a possibility, consider creating a raised bed.

If you want to harvest raspberries over a long period, you will need to plant several different varieties, including at least one summer-fruiting and one autumn-fruiting variety. Autumn-fruiting raspberries have smaller canes and smaller yields, and they grow best in mild regions.

PLANTING RASPBERRIES

Raspberries do best in full (not scorching) sun, but will often tolerate light shade. They like a rich, organic soil with good drainage, but still plenty of moisture. With the hardier plants, you can probably try them in anything that doesn't get soggy. Make sure that you choose a sheltered spot for new plants because the young shoots are easily damaged by strong winds.

1 Put the plants in position

Dig a trench and plant the canes about 1 metre apart. Set them about 2 to 3 centimetres deeper than they were in the nursery, spread out the roots carefully, and fill in the trench with soil.

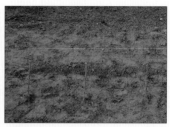

2 Trim the canes

Cut back all the newly planted canes to about 12 centimetres above the ground, except black raspberries, which you can cut almost to the ground. Finally, pat down the soil.

Berries are formed on second-year canes. After these canes fruit, they die back. But you don't have to worry about berry supply. New canes are forming while the older canes are fruiting. Summer-bearing raspberries usually produce bountiful crops in July, while autumn-fruiting types will produce berries in August and September.

Do not plant any type of home garden raspberry near blackberries, aubergines, peppers, potatoes, or tomatoes, as these plants can transmit diseases, such as verticillium wilt. Also, experts advise against planting new raspberry canes in any soil that has had raspberries growing in it within the last 7 years.

SUPPORT YOUR RASPBERRIES

Your raspberry plants will generally do
better if you give them something to
hang onto while they are growing. One
way to do it is to make a wire trellis.
Place two heavy-duty, 1½-metre-high
poles in the ground and string three sets
of wires at intervals between them.
If you don't like trellis, or you don't have
much space in the garden, you may
consider growing them up against a
sunny wall or a fence.

Summer-fruiting raspberries

- **Glen Ample** – disease resistant, thornless, good cropping, excellent flavour.
- **Glen Cova** – very popular, firm though rather small berries, ideal for freezing.
- **Glen Moy** – spine-free canes with medium to very large conical-shaped berries, well-flavoured firm fruit.
- **Glen Magna** – heavy cropping, large berries in July and August, disease resistant, fruit freezes well.
- **Glen Prosen** – round, very firm fruit, spine-free canes that are easy to control.
- **Julia** – large, firm, red berries with a good flavour, canes have small spines but fruit is well displayed.
- **Leo** – large, reddish-orange berries with a tart flavour, rather slow to establish but will produce reliably vigorous canes within a few years.
- **Malling Admiral** – numerous spine-free canes, vigorous, resistant to some common diseases, good-flavoured fruit with firm texture.
- **Malling Jewel** – reliable, tolerant of virus infection, a consistent cropper, ripening over 3 to 4 weeks with good-flavoured berries.

INTERNET

**www.focusdiy.co.uk/
advice/projects/g21
/htm**

*Go to this site for
information and advice on
growing all types of soft fruit
including black, red and
white currants, gooseberries,
logan berries, blackberries,
and raspberries.*

Trivia...

*Some people think that black
raspberries are blackberries.
These people are wrong.*

Autumn-fruiting raspberries

- **Autumn Bliss** – produces high yields of large fruit, short, sturdy canes with large red, firm berries that have a very good flavour.
- **Fallgold** – vigorous, with a large crop of yellow berries from September right through until the first frosts.
- **Heritage** – a once-popular autumn variety that has been somewhat eclipsed by Autumn Bliss.
- **September** – reliable cropper, its berries are renowned for their excellent flavour.

AUTUMN BLISS

Maintaining raspberries

It's not necessary to fertilize raspberry plants, but it does help to mulch them, especially in warmer areas. Mulch keeps the soil cool and prevents root disturbance. Raspberry roots are shallow, so be careful when cultivating the soil nearby.

Raspberries are a particularly thirsty crop. You'll have to water them regularly – especially if the weather is dry for prolonged periods and while the canes are flowering and producing fruit. Watch out for suckers that are becoming too overcrowded or growing too far away from the row. Lift these up, and sever them from the parent plant with a sharp knife.

Harvesting ripe fruit

Pick raspberries when they are fully coloured but still firm. Simply pull the raspberry gently away from the stem, leaving the stalk and plug behind. Inspect the crop regularly, and only pick the fruit when it is dry, since wet berries will start to go mouldy very quickly. Eat them as soon as you can. The smaller, slightly under-ripe fruits are the best ones for freezing.

Making new plants

You can easily make new plants by removing and replanting any suckers that appear in October and November. Only make new plants from healthy looking canes.

When choosing suckers to make new plants, ensure that they come from plants that you know are healthy and free-cropping. If you are in any doubt, it's best to buy certified virus-free canes from a specialist nursery instead

PRUNING AFTER FRUITING

Prune your raspberries each year, either when they finish fruiting or in late winter. With the yellows and reds, cut all canes that gave fruit off at their base. Thin out the new canes, leaving only the heartiest. Then cut all remaining canes to about 1.8 metres. Why do you do this? If you don't, you will have an unruly mass of raspberry bushes which may become prone to disease.

1 Cut back

When you have finished picking all your berries, cut back to ground level all those canes that have produced fruit.

2 Tie in canes

Thin out the current season's canes, keeping the healthiest. Tie these to the support wires about 10 centimetres apart.

3 Loop tall canes

At the end of the growing season, loop any tall canes over the top wire and tie them in securely.

Pruning autumn-fruiting raspberries

Prune established autumn-fruiting varieties in February by cutting down all canes to ground level. Tie in the new canes to the wires with soft twine as they grow in the spring and summer. The following spring, trim the canes to 15 centimetres above the topmost wire, cutting back any tips with frost damage.

Cutting autumn-fruiting varieties right back stimulates the growth of new canes, which will produce fruit the following autumn

Succulent strawberries

EVEN INTO HER 90s, my mother-in-law often spoke of the wild strawberries she gathered as a child in Europe, saying their flavour was beyond delicious. Today, you can grow a cultivated "wild" strawberry, the fraises des bois, or woodland strawberry (Fragaria virginiana) in your own garden. These summer-bearing plants are petite, so you need a dozen to make a true gourmet feast for the family, but they take up so little room that it's worth the effort.

■ Strawberries can be grown in pots on a sunny patio if space in the garden is limited.

Trivia...

In Latin, the strawberry is fragra, meaning fragrant. From this word was derived the French word fraise, or fragrant berry, and the species name Fragaria. Nobody is quite sure how the word "strawberry" came into being, which it did in about AD 100. One of the more common theories is that straw was used to mulch the plants during the winter. Children would pick the berries, string them on straw, and then sell them in the open markets as "straws of berries." Another common theory is that adults would string dried berries on straw and use them as decorations.

Identifying healthy strawberry plants

Always buy strawberries from a reputable nursery or from a catalogue rather than getting plants from friends. Unfortunately, strawberry plants attained through informal channels can carry disease.

Healthy dark green leaves

Even growth

Plant not yet in flower

Moist weed-free soil mix

HEALTHY STRAWBERRY PLANT

Strawberry diseases caused by a fungus include verticillium wilt, powdery mildew, leaf spot, and red core. Verticillium wilt causes one side of the plant to wilt upwards or outwards from the plant's base. The leaves turn yellow, and the plant may die. Powdery mildew causes whitish powdery patches on leaves that gradually spread to the entire leaf. The leaves become distorted and may drop. Leaf spot shows itself as tiny spots of varying colours on the leaves. The spots gradually enlarge to form blotches, and the leaves turn yellow, die, and drop off. Red core, a root rot, is generally considered the most damaging disease of strawberry plants. Plants with red core will be stunted with markedly discoloured leaves: blue-green, yellow, or red. The afflicted plant's leaves wilt, it produces only a few berries, and the plant eventually dies.

Viral diseases, transmitted to strawberry plants by aphids, cause distorted, yellow leaves and stunted plants. Few runners emerge and fruit, if present, is minimal.

When buying strawberry plants, look for healthy ones without any signs of disease. Also look for a plant's level of resistance:

LS = resistance to leaf spot

PM = resistance to powdery mildew

RC = resistance to some types of red core

V = resistance to virus

VW = resistance to verticillium wilt

POWDERY MILDEW

Planting strawberries

Strawberries are usually planted in late summer to allow them to get established before the first winter frosts. If you live in an area where the winters are mild, you can plant strawberries in early summer, early autumn, and during the winter.

Prepare the ground well before you plant strawberries, digging in lots of organic matter. Strawberries need plenty of sunlight, rich, slightly acidic soil, and lots of water.

Good drainage is absolutely critical for success with strawberries. The plants will die if the soil is too soggy.

To improve drainage, plant in raised beds about 15 centimetres high and just under 1 metre wide. Remove weeds as soon as they appear. Choose a site that is separate from any area where you have grown such plants as aubergine, pepper, potato, raspberry, or tomato. You don't want any pests or diseases from these plants to move onto your new strawberry plants. For the same reason, avoid planting strawberries in areas that were recently part of a lawn. In addition to the threat of underground lawn pests, lawn weeds will compete aggressively with shallow strawberry roots for nutrition.

When putting plants into the ground, place the crown base (the semi-pointed area where the roots converge together) at soil level. Fan out the roots, completely cover them, and firm the soil down. Some strawberry plants have *runners*, and some don't.

Strawberry selection

Constantly hybridized for quality and performance, today's garden strawberries are big and sweet. There are two common types of garden strawberries: summer-bearing, which give a single crop per season in summer; and perpetual, which give two crops per season, in summer and autumn.

The easiest way to choose strawberries is to buy those sold in your local nursery. Strawberries can be selective about where they thrive, and even a "preferred" area will vary from year to year depending on that year's climate. For the best selection, grow one or more of each kind: summer-bearing and perpetual.

But if you want to experiment or just can't find what you want locally, over the page I've listed just a few of the many varieties available.

> **DEFINITION**
>
> **Runners** *are the new baby plants that come off the parent plant via trailing stems. The stems will eventually root. Running strawberries are a fine way to multiply your strawberry bed, but they do need room. Place each prospective parent plant about 0.5 to 1 metre apart. To get larger berries from running strawberries, limit the trailing stems to four per plant, spacing them well.*

Summer-fruiting strawberries

- **Cambridge Favourite** – reliable mid-season choice, with slightly conical fruits.
- **Elsanta** – good-flavoured berries that last well after picking.
- **Elvira** – very early, especially suited to growing in a greenhouse.
- **Emily** – very heavy yields, exceptionally early, attractive, firm fruit, good resistance to diseases including mildew, may need protection from frost.
- **Eros** – Mid-season variety, heavy yields of exceptionally high quality, well-flavoured fruit.
- **Florence** – Fruits July to mid-August, firm, regular-shaped fruits with good sweet flavour, berries stay firm over a long period.
- **Honeoye** – American variety that ripens in early summer, has good flavour and is suitable for freezing.
- **Laura** – very useful late-season variety, prolonged picking period, high yield, good flavour.
- **Pegasus** – late June to August fruiting, berries with firm, glossy skin, easy-to-grow, compact plant.
- **Rosie** – new variety, early ripening, high-quality berries with glossy skin.
    - **Sophie** – new variety, early ripening, high-quality berries with glossy skin.
    - **Strawberry Darselect** – strong-growing, mid-season, suits most gardens, produces an excellent crop of juicy sweet berries from mid-June, good resistance to disease.
    - **Symphony** – resistant to most diseases other than powdery mildew, good flavour.
    - **Rhapsody** – late summer-fruiting, good for the north of the country and resistant to most diseases.

HONEOYE

Perpetual

- **Aromel** – best replanted more frequently than 3 years, but excellent flavour.
- **Bolero** – glossy, orange-red fruits, excellent flavour, cropping over 3 months.
- **Mara des Bois** – odd flavour, reminiscent of wild strawberries, good-sized fruit combined with excellent flavour.

ELSANTA

- **Perpetual strawberries** *grow best in regions with mild, frost-free autumn weather.*

Maintaining your strawberry patch

Probably the most important aspect of good strawberry plant care is to mulch. Mulching keeps the plant's shallow roots cool and moist, and it keeps the strawberries off the ground. If the weather gets really cold, cover the strawberry bed with an 8-centimetre-deep light mulch, such as straw. Remove the mulch in the spring when the plant centres are a yellowish-green. If an unexpected frost comes along just as your strawberry plants have started to flower, put the mulch back on or just cover the bed with a light blanket.

Don't put slug bait around ripening or ripe fruit. It could be harmful to birds, pets, and curious children.

Birds like strawberries as much as you do, so either you will have to plant enough to share, or cover your beds with netting. The netting is sold at garden centres, and must be held somewhat above the berries so the birds don't peck through it. If your ripe strawberries have round or elongated holes, there's a chance that slugs are enjoying your efforts. I find that picking strawberries once they become ripe helps to keep slugs away, as they seem to prefer overripe berries.

Strawberry beds don't last forever. The parent plants gradually give smaller and smaller berries. Three years is considered a long life for a strawberry plant. When a bed's berry production decreases, remove the oldest plants and thin out the younger ones. Add mulch and water well afterwards.

INTERNET

**ohioline.ag.
ohio-state.edu**

Work your way to the Ohio State University Extension Fact Sheet on strawberries. It includes info on how to grow them and the various types and their attributes.

A simple summary

✓ Familiarize yourself with the different types of berries and grapes available. Choose a type that does well in your climate and that serves your purposes in planting.

✓ Be prepared to put in a little maintenance work with berries and grapes, which need regular pruning, thinning, and mulching.

✓ Well-drained soil is a must for berries and grapes. Planting on raised beds will help plants thrive.

✓ To prevent birds eating the fruit, cover with garden netting.

Chapter 14

Fun With Fruit Trees

YOU CAN GROW PLANTS FOR YEARS without understanding their anatomical or functional details. But if you understand a bit about how fruit trees grow, you will be rewarded with home-grown delights. So I've chosen to start this chapter with a little lesson.

In this chapter...
✓ Super simple plant anatomy
✓ Fruit tree fundamentals
✓ The apples of autumn
✓ Fabulous figs
✓ Plentiful peaches
✓ Three cheers for cherries
✓ Pears for all
✓ Plant a plum

255

Super simple plant anatomy

PLANTS, WHETHER TINY HERBS OR GIANT TREES, *are basically made up of three parts: roots, stems, and leaves. Roots are the parts growing downwards into the ground. They take in part of the plant's nourishment, including water, from the soil, and they anchor the plant into the soil. Roots usually branch many times as they grow. The smaller branches are called rootlets.*

Growing upwards from the roots is a stem. At certain places along the stem, according to plant type, there are leaves. Leaves, as a group, make up the plant's foliage. The stem acts as a conduit, carrying nourishment from the roots to the leaves. Leaves also take in food from the air. These nutrients, along with the nutrients transferred to the leaves from the root system, begin to change within the leaves. When exposed to sunlight, the nutrients change into a form that the plant can actually use for its health and growth. This process is called photosynthesis.

A healthy growing plant extends its roots and rootlets further and further out into the soil. Reaching out lets it have access to more soil nutrients and more water. Meanwhile, in a healthy plant, the stem becomes longer. It develops more leaves, or sends out more branches, which in turn develop more leaves. The many leaves obtain more light and air, aiding plant nutrition. Your job as a gardener is to help each of your plants meet its growth needs.

Reproduction

In addition to roots, stems, and leaves, plants also produce flowers. From flowers come fruits. From fruits come seeds. Flowers, fruits, and seeds don't have any part in nourishing, or feeding, the plant. Their purpose is to produce individual new plants, as well as making certain, if at all possible, that the species doesn't die out and disappear from this earth. The flowers, fruits, and seeds are a plant's reproductive organs.

Flower parts

Each flower generally has four parts: calyx, corolla, stamens, and pistils. In spite of their fancy names, the jobs done by each part are quite simple. The calyx, or flower cup, usually green, partly covers the outside of the flower. It looks almost like a little cap or cup. Each piece of the calyx is called a sepal, and each sepal resembles a little leaf.

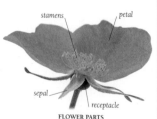

stamens · petal · sepal · receptacle

FLOWER PARTS

The corolla is what we think of when we imagine a flower; each separate piece is called a petal. The petals, besides being part of the pretty flower, have a practical purpose. They provide a protective covering for the flower's reproductive interior and they attract pollinators.

Pollination parts

Within each flower are the stamens. Each stamen is usually made up of two parts: a filament, or stalk, and an anther, or little sac, on top of the stalk. Within this little sac is a powdery substance called pollen.

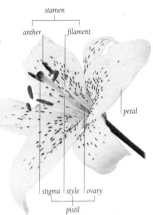

Also within each flower are one or more pistils. The pistils are in the flower centre. Each pistil has three parts: an ovary, a style, and a stigma. Don't go, we're just coming to the good part. The rounded ovary, at the bottom of the pistil, will be the seed holder. The style, a slim supporting mechanism, supports the stigma. The stigma has a sticky or furry surface.

■ **Each male stamen** *consists of an anther and a filament, while the female pistil has three parts – a stigma, style, and ovary. When pollen lands on the stigma, pollination occurs.*

When pollen is carried by the wind, or transported by bees or other pollinators, some of it may land on a similar flower's stigmas. If this happens, pollination occurs.

When the flower fades and falls, all that is usually left is the ovary of the pistil. This, if it has been properly fertilized, becomes larger and larger. Eventually it becomes a fruit, or a seed pod, or a nut, or whatever. Within the fruit are one or more seeds. If the ovary hasn't been fertilized properly, it doesn't develop. It remains a small ball that dries up and falls off. This is why you may think your cherry tree or apple tree will have lots of fruit because it has lots of flowers. But they develop into little balls, and nothing more. For some reason, fertilization has not occurred.

Fertilization

Plants can be self-fertile or require a pollinator plant. Cross-fertilization occurs with plants that rely on a pollinator plant.

When planning a fruit tree purchase, it is important to know whether the plant is self-fertile or whether it requires a pollinator. If a plant is self-fertile you need only one tree of that kind to produce fruit. If a plant requires a pollinator, you will need two trees to get fruit.

Some fruit trees are able to cross-fertilize only with specific types of similar fruit trees, so sometimes the tree's "brand name" is very important.

Plants are pollinated in a number of ways, but insects do most of the legwork. And probably the hardest worker is the honeybee. Watching a honeybee load up her pollen baskets is fun. Her body is covered with feathery hairs. Both hind legs have a hollowed-out section that acts as a basket. As the honeybee goes from flower to flower, pollen literally sticks to her. She brushes this off with leg combs into her pollen baskets. Sometimes the baskets get so heavy that the honey-bee can barely carry her load around. Eventually, heavily laden, she flies home. But in the meantime, pollen from one flower has brushed against the stigma of another flower, and perhaps a cherry, or peach, has begun. Other bee types, such as the bumblebee, act as good pollinators too.

■ **A bumblebee** *is an effective pollinator, carrying pollen from one flower to another. Yellow flowers are particularly attractive to insects.*

In addition to insects, you'll want to encourage other pollinators to visit your garden, such as butterflies. Bats are good pollinators of some plants too. I'll discuss how you can attract pollinators to your garden in Chapter 20.

Fruit tree fundamentals

IT PROBABLY SEEMS AS THOUGH the world of plants is simply a bunch of categories, each with big sub-categories and each sub-category with more sub-categories. And yes, in some ways this is true. A quick overview of the basic types of fruit trees will help you understand how the trees work, and so will help you succeed as a gardener. I've chosen to categorize them as follows.

APPLE SEEDS

Fruit with seeds

There are many types of seeded fruits, including apple, fig, pear, persimmon, and pomegranate. I'll be focusing on apple and pear trees, since they're common in British gardens, as well as figs, which are becoming popular, too.

Although they are considered very much warm-country plants, figs will do very well indeed outside in quite temperate areas and in a cold greenhouse or conservatory in cooler parts of the country. When the climate is colder, fig trees produce tiny fruits in late summer that overwinter to swell and ripen the following summer.

Stone fruits

Better known as fruit with pits, stone fruits include apricots, avocados, cherries, nectarines, peaches, and plums. Since avocados won't grow well in the United Kingdom, I'll be concentrating on giving you some good advice on growing peaches, cherries, and plums. Peaches aren't nearly as difficult to grow as their exotic nature might lead you to believe, while cherries are beautifully decorative trees, and plums will produce good crops of fruit with relatively little attention.

Trivia...
When you get involved with planting fruit trees, you'll eventually hear the terms rootstock and scion bandied about. Rootstocks, sometimes called understocks, are the roots of a tree selected for their predictable vigour, size, disease resistance, and the like. A scion is a fruiting variety that is budded or grafted onto the rootstock. The fruit from this scion is predictable for characteristics such as size, colour, taste, and hardiness. The aim is to combine the best of both for the purchaser.

■ **Fruit trees** *are really rewarding to grow, because they allow you to harvest an array of healthy, delicious produce all through the year.*

259

The apples of autumn

PROBABLY THE EASIEST TO GROW *of all the fruit trees, apples (Malus domestica) are very popular. There are well over 1,000 varieties, ranging from the antique apple to newer disease-resistant types. A few years after planting, you will have apples to eat, and apples to spare. You can even train apple trees, particularly dwarf varieties, on espaliers.*

APPLE
(Malus domestica)

Planting apple trees

Put bare-root trees into the ground in the autumn when they are dormant, or without leaves. Container-grown trees may be planted at any time when the ground is not frozen or very wet. With apple trees, you have a wide choice of sizes and a wide choice of fruiting time. Mini-dwarf trees grow from 1.2 to 2.5 metres tall and do very well in containers. Dwarf trees will grow from 2.5 to 5 metres tall, semi-dwarf trees from 4 to 6 metres tall, and standards will grow up to 12 metres. Expect semi-dwarf trees to start bearing fruit in their second or third year, and standards in the fourth or fifth year.

Choosing trees

All apple trees are deciduous. Before buying your tree, you need to think about two important factors: *rootstock* and variety. The rootstock determines the eventual size of the tree, so you need to know what you're buying. If your local nursery or garden centre can't tell you, go elsewhere. If the soil conditions in your garden are poor, you'll probably need to choose a more vigorous rootstock to compensate.

When considering variety, you'll want fruit that you enjoy eating and a variety that will do well in your area. Ask around to see whether any of your neighbours have grown apple trees, as they may be able to give you good advice. If you live in an area where late frosts are likely to occur, choose a late-flowering variety so that the blossom will not be damaged. Apple trees require a sunny, sheltered site and well-drained, average soil. If you are putting in more than one tree, place smaller trees about 5 metres apart, and larger ones up to 11 metres apart.

> ### DEFINITION
>
> *You will hear the term* rootstock, *or see it on tags at the garden centre. Apple rootstocks are prefixed by the letters "M" and "MM", which stand for Malling and Malling Merton respectively – the research stations where the rootstocks were developed. The names of some rootstocks therefore bring to mind some of our favourite motorways: there's the M27, which is very dwarfing, and the M25, which is extremely vigorous. For most gardens, the M9 is a good dwarf tree, the M26 is slightly larger, and the MM106 grows to a medium size.*

Picky pollinators

You should know whether your prospective purchase is self-fertile, or whether you need a pollinator apple tree. In fact, it's worth bearing in mind that even the self-fertile types aren't always reliable, so it may be worth having a different variety nearby anyway. Some apple trees are generic pollinators, helping just about every apple tree in sight, and other apple trees are picky pollinators. If you are buying for pollinator purposes, do a bit of homework. Of course, if your neighbours have an apple tree or two, that pollen will meander in your direction, which often helps things along.

INTERNET

**www.brogdale.
org.uk**

This is the web site of the Brogdale Horticultural Trust, which describes itself as a living fruit museum, with the largest collection of fruit cultivars in the world: more than 2,300 apples, 400 pears, and 360 plums. Here you'll find out everything you've ever wanted to know about these fruits and much more besides!

An abundance of apples

It's impossible to mention here all the apple types for your garden. Still, I've listed and categorized some to give you an idea of what is available in the nurseries and catalogues, as well as some of the characteristics you might be looking for.

Disease-resistant apples

■ **Bountiful** – cooking apple, medium-sized fruits with yellow and red stripes, sweet, juicy, keeps shape when cooked.

■ **Discovery** – eating apple, bright red fruits with crunchy flesh, often stained pink. Lovely eaten straight from the tree. Suitable for planting in the north, good pollinator.

■ **Fiesta** – eating apple, attractively coloured with a red flush on yellow ground. Cox-like flavour, scrunchy and juicy, suitable for planting in the north, good pollinator.

■ **Grenadier** – reliable, early cooking apple with a tangy, juicy, and honeyed flavour. Very good for baking and purées.

■ **Katy** – pale yellow-flushed, red fruits with white, fine-textured flesh that is crunchy and juicy. Suitable for planting in the north, good pollinator.

■ **Meridian** – excellent new Cox/Falstaff eating apple with good skin and lovely colour. Firm, juicy texture with an excellent aromatic flavour. Heavy cropping.

■ **Spartan** – eating apple, deep maroon fruits, sweet, juicy, crisp white flesh. Best left on the tree to develop colour before picking. Good pollinator.

■ **Worcester Pearmain** – scarlet eating apple with firm, juicy white flesh and a densely sweet strawberry-like flavour. Suitable for planting in the north, good pollinator.

■ **Newer varieties** *of apples have been specially bred to be more robust and less prone to disease.*

Apples for small gardens

- **Bramley Clone** – cooker with large green and red apples that cook to a cream purée.
- **Cox Self Fertile** – deliciously sweet eating apple with intensely rich aromatic flavour and deep cream flesh.
- **Discovery** – eating apple, bright red fruits with crunchy and juicy flesh, often stained pink. Lovely straight from the tree. Suitable for planting in the north, good pollinator.
- **Idared** – pale green fruit with a bright red flush, good flavour for cooking and dessert.
- **Queen Cox Self Fertile** – wonderful eating apple with a Cox-like flavour, highly coloured with deep cream flesh.
- **Red Devil** – a deep rich red-skinned eating apple with pink-stained flesh that has a slight strawberry flavour.
- **Winter Gem** – eating apple with pink blush and lovely flavour, much like Cox.

Dwarf apples for containers

- **Blenheim Orange** – eating and cooking apple, large orange-yellow crisp fruits with a sweet, nutty flavour.
- **Bountiful** – medium-sized cooker with yellow and red stripes, sweet and juicy.
- **Egremont Russet** – medium-sized eating apple, yellow-skinned russet with a delicious, nutty, dry flavour. Suitable for planting in the north, good pollinator.
- **Greensleeves** – eating apple, firm, juicy, deep cream flesh with a honeyed flavour.
- **Katy** – pale yellow-flushed red fruits with white, fine-textured, crunchy, juicy flesh. Suitable for the north, good pollinator.
- **Lord Lambourne** – eating apple, a heavy and regular cropper with brightly coloured apples that have a refreshing, sweet, and juicy flavour. Suitable for planting in the north.
- **Sunset** – eating apple like a small, early Cox with aromatic, intensely flavoured fruits. Easy to grow.

Pruning your orchard

To give your apple trees the extra nutrients they need, fertilize in the spring with a fertilizer marked "for apple trees". You might want to put off pruning while your apple tree is young. Overly enthusiastic pruning encourages growth in lieu of fruiting. However, once a tree reaches full size, an annual pruning is beneficial to keep the branch structure open. But don't cut off the old branches, as this is where fruit appears. When baby apples appear, you may have to thin out the branches so the apples are about 12 centimetres apart.

■ **Egremont Russet** apples, renowned for their sweet, nutty flavour, are ideal for growing in containers.

Thinning a fruit tree always worries me. However, when I initially didn't thin my apple tree, I ended up with lots of tiny, little fruit instead of big crunchy apples.

Apple pests and diseases

Of course you want your trees and fruit to be healthy. There are several diseases you should watch out for. Fireblight, caused by bacteria, turns the leaves black. The serious fungal disease powdery mildew makes young leaves and flower trusses appear grey in spring. Growth is stunted, diseased flowers do not set, and leaves may fall. Scab is another serious fungal disease. It produces brown spots on young fruit that gradually turn corky as the fruits grow. It's worst in warm and humid weather. Brown rot normally begins through bird pecks, insect holes, or fruit cracking, and the developing fungal spores spread rapidly.

The best way to avoid disease in your apple trees is to make sure you plant resistant varieties.

I have had my green apple tree for 20 years and never had a major problem of any kind, and I do not use chemical controls at all.

In addition to diseases, apples have their share of pests, including aphids, the codling moth (that white worm that you can find in your apple and which makes the surrounding fruit become brown and pulpy), and the apple sawfly (which eats crescent-shaped scars into the fruit).

Reaping the apple harvest

Some apples stay comfortably on the tree longer than others. If you don't have ample storage space, consider planting trees that hold apples up to 4 months. If the fruit separates easily from the branch, that's a good sign of readiness, but the taste test is the best.

Harvest apples carefully. Pick an apple when it parts easily from the branch and place it in a cloth-lined basket to avoid bruising.

Trivia...
The legendary Johnny Appleseed was born John Chapman in Massachusetts in 1774. At 23 he set out westward, planting apple trees as a way of staking a claim on land he one day hoped to own. John wanted to sell trees to other travellers, too, but realized there was no room for them on the wagons. So he collected apple seeds from local cider mills and, travelling ahead of the wagon trains, he planted thousands of them. When the wagons arrived, he sold the young trees to the settlers. John died at 70 years old, responsible for nearly all the apple orchards at the time in the new American settlements.

Fabulous figs

FIGS ARE AMONG THE OLDEST *of cultivated fruits. Records show that people have been planting figs (Ficus carica) since at least 2500 BC, but their history pre-dates that time. According to the Old Testament, while Adam was strolling around the Garden of Eden, he ate the apple Eve had given him and then had to cover his nakedness with a nearby fig leaf.*

FIG BRANCH WITH
YOUNG FRUIT

Planting figs

Figs do best in areas with a long, hot growing season. However, people do grow them successfully in regions where the winter temperature drops to −14° C. Even if cold winters kill the tree to the ground, new growth may appear in spring. You can also enhance your success with fig trees by planting in a warm, wind-protected corner where heat bounces off concrete or the house: try growing them fan-trained on a south- or west-facing wall. Alternatively, place them in a large container on wheels that can be moved to a greenhouse or conservatory as necessary. Deciduous fig trees, without leaves, do not need light, but must be moved outdoors as soon as possible in spring.

In the spring, buy fig trees as container plants. I was lucky and was given a rooted sucker from a fig tree. I now have a lovely old-timer. Figs are self-fertile, so you don't need more than one unless you want different types of figs.

Fig trees need full sun, and do best with rich, slightly alkaline, very well-drained soil. Although some fig trees are smaller than others, all need plenty of space unless you intend to prune regularly. The average fig tree grows to between 5 and 10 metres, with a wide branch spread.

Figs for the fickle

There are hundreds of fig varieties, although you may find only a few for sale. Others you must get from the suckers of friends' fig trees. The following are just a few of the more common fig trees that are available, but be aware that most have several names. For example the kadota is also called white kadota, dottato, and Florentine. In garden catalogues, the few figs offered are generally not named at all, but are described with great zeal. Unless you really like to experiment, make a point of finding out exactly what you are buying.

Favourite figs

- **Angelique** – medium, roundish fruit that are yellow with white specks. Flesh white with pink tinge. Good for pots, does well by walls in a greenhouse.
- **Brown Turkey** – the large, pear-shaped fruit are brown with occasional purple tinge. Sugary rich flesh at centre. Excellent by garden walls or in a greenhouse. Easy to force in pots.
- **Castle Kennedy** – very large fruit. Skin greenish-yellow. Tender white flesh stained red. Very early cropper.
- **Fig d'Or** – golden fruit with pink-tinged flesh. Very indented leaves. An old variety most suited to pots in a greenhouse. Strawberry flesh, rich, sweet, and good quality.
- **Kadota** – medium-sized fruit with yellowish green to white skin. Rich, sweet, amber flesh, very old variety.
- **Panachee** – striped wood and striped sweet fruit. Delicious eating. The figs look like little hot air balloons! Vigorous habit, but easily controlled.
- **Rouge de Bordeaux** – medium-sized fruit. Purple skin with violet bloom and red flesh. Excellent rich flavour. One of the best figs for greenhouse culture, border, or pot.

■ **Brown Turkey figs**
(Ficus carica) *have particularly attractive pinkish flesh and brownish-purple skins.*

A fig fitness programme

Caring for your fig trees couldn't be simpler. When the weather gets hot and dry, remember to give them plenty of water.

As with many plants, mature trees require much less water than young trees. Potted figs need regular watering at all times. A mulch will help to preserve moisture, since the fig roots grow close to the surface. Because of the shallow root system, don't plan on digging or cultivating around your fig trees.

Figs need little pruning, and most pruning should be done for size and shapeliness when the tree is young. If you are into pruning, be aware that some fig trees fruit mostly on new shoots, and others fruit on both old and new branches.

Some people advocate wrapping fig trees for the winter. A simple way is to tie the branches together to make a cylinder. Use a wire cage to enclose the branches and fill the empty spaces with dried leaves. Cover the cage with a waterproof fabric. Few insects or diseases annoy fig trees, except birds and wasps. Weeding must be thorough near trunks to prevent rodents nibbling the bark.

Harvesting figs

Figs will ripen from June to October, depending on the variety of tree and its location. Figs will not ripen after they are picked. Pick them when they're slightly to moderately soft. Eat them the same day you pick them if at all possible. Figs will keep in the fridge for a maximum of about 4 days. If you let them hang on the tree, the figs get softer and softer and birds and ants have a picnic. You probably will have lots of figs ripening at one time.

I have found that people appreciate gifts of just-ripe fresh figs more than just about any other fruit, because these are almost impossible to find at the supermarket in really good condition.

Plentiful peaches

PEACHES AND NECTARINES *are close relatives and can be grown in exactly the same way. Peaches (Prunus persica) have a soft down on their skin, while nectarines (Prunus persica var. nectarina) are hairless, slightly smaller than peaches, and have a subtly different flavour.*

■ **Choose the site** *for your peach tree carefully and you will be rewarded with plenty of ripe, succulent fruit.*

There are dwarf peach trees reaching only 1.2 to 2 metres in height and semi-dwarf trees growing from 2.2 to 2.75 metres tall. All have beautiful pink blossoms and shiny green leaves. In cold areas you'll have to bring your plant indoors in winter, and move it outdoors to a sunny, sheltered site on a south-facing wall in the spring.

Delightful dwarfs

Dwarf trees are very popular in this age of small gardens. They are also well adapted to growing in pots. Dwarf trees produce fruit of the same size and colour as standard trees. Although standards produce more peaches than the dwarf trees, it takes them longer to do so. Care is the same for dwarf and standard trees, except with dwarf trees you don't need a ladder when pruning!

Planting peaches

The best time to buy a peach tree is November for a bare-rooted tree and early autumn if it's in a container. Remember to choose a peach tree variety that is disease resistant if you don't want problems.

Don't let your peach tree's roots dry out before you plant it. This will markedly hinder its growth.

It is best not to buy trees in containers full of dry soil. If you do so, soaking the roots for about 12 hours may revitalize the tree. Always water a container well when you get it home.

When planting, you should choose your peach tree site carefully. All fruit trees need full sunlight and exquisitely drained soil. The planting hole should be slightly wider and deeper than the spread-out root system. Place the tree in the hole so the upper roots are about 2 to 5 centimetres below the soil surface. Partially fill the planting hole with a mixture of good organic soil and local soil, then water. Do this again until the soil is at the same level as it was in the container. Tamp down the soil and water well.

It's just peachy

In freestone peaches, the pit just falls out. In semi-freestone peaches, you have to wiggle the pit a bit to remove it. The pit stays in place in cling peaches.

CLING PEACH

The cling variety is the standard at the greengrocer, but these are not nearly as tasty as the others. Unless they are into preserving, most gardeners plant freestone or semi-freestone peaches.

In most instances, peach trees are self-fertile so you won't need two. However, they tend to flower early in the year, when pollinating insects are scarce, so you may have to hand-pollinate.

All types of peaches are available in early-, mid-, and late-season varieties. The fruiting season may vary according to where you live, so this is just intended as a general guideline. For the novice, it is best to ask at your local specialist nursery before you buy peach trees. They can be really very fussy about where they'll grow. There's no point in being disappointed in your purchase when you could have selected another peach tree for the same price.

Early peaches and nectarines

- **Amsden June** – the first peach to ripen, but not a heavy cropper. The creamy-white flesh inside the round fruit has a good flavour. Grow outdoors or under glass.
- **Duke of York** – good quality peach. The pale yellow flesh is very juicy with a refreshing flavour. Crops heavily and does well on a south-facing wall.
- **Early Rivers** – one of the first nectarines to ripen. Yellow flesh is juicy and the flavour is good.

EARLY PEACHES

- **Hayles Early** – this peach crops heavily and is early enough to make it a sound choice for growing outdoors, it's prolific so must be thinned out. Flesh is melting.

Mid-season peaches and nectarines

- **Elruge** – a nectarine that's best grown in a greenhouse. The nearly round fruit has almost white flesh with a good flavour.
- **Garden Lady** – dwarf form of peach. Ideal planted out in a sunny, well-drained position or in a container. Sweet, golden-fleshed fruits in August.
- **Humbolt** – a very heavy-cropping nectarine that's best grown indoors. Its fruit has golden flesh and a distinctive rich flavour.
- **Peregrine** – excellent, juicy flesh with great taste. A reliable tree with high yields that will do particularly well outdoors on a sunny wall.
- **Red Haven** – an attractive round peach, reliable in southern counties. Crops well. The yellow flesh is firm but juicy with a distinct red tinge around the stone.

Late peaches and nectarines

- **Bellegarde** – very large peach with deep yellow flesh and a good flavour. High yields, but ripens very late and so is really only suitable for a greenhouse.
- **Pineapple** – as this nectarine is a later-ripening variety, it rules itself out for growing outdoors, but does well in a greenhouse. The yellow flesh is melting in texture and it has an outstanding rich flavour, with a hint of pineapple.

Simple care for your peach crop

Water your peach trees regularly. In general, fertilize with a fruit tree fertilizer in the spring and after you harvest. Sprinkle the fertilizer evenly and keep it away from the tree trunk.

A peach tree begins forming next year's flowers at the same time as it's growing this year's fruit. This is tough work for the tree and so good watering is a must.

PRUNING AND THINNING PEACH TREES

You should prune every year, preferably while the tree is in bloom. This helps to decrease the fruit production – too much fruit will leave you with very small peaches. You also want to stimulate the growth of new wood, because new wood is where peaches form the following year. Even with pruning, you will probably have too many fruits, in which case you will need to thin them out.

1 Thin once

When the fruitlets are the size of hazelnuts, thin them to one fruit per cluster, removing first any that are growing away from the sunlight.

2 Thin again later

Once the fruits are walnut-sized, thin again to leave one fruit every 15 to 22 centimetres. Do not thin again if frost has ruined young fruit.

Peach pests

A very common disease in peach trees is peach leaf curl. Its hallmark sign is the puckering of the tree's leaves, which become quite distorted and discoloured. Where bacterial canker is affecting a plant, clearly defined areas of bark flatten and sink inwards. Amber-coloured, resin-like ooze may appear, closely associated with the injured bark. A fungal disease called shot hole looks just as it sounds. Holes develop, usually with an inconspicuous brown ring round the edge of each one. Various fungal infections can invoke this condition. Deal with the primary cause.

Watch out for pests. Peaches suffer most losses to birds and wasps. Small net or muslin bags will protect the fruit. Greenfly and red spider mite are common, and plum sawfly can also be a problem, leaving a crescent-shaped, ribbon scar on the outside of the fruit, which then makes it more susceptible to secondary disease.

Picking peaches

How do you know when the time is right? Start by feeling your peaches very gently as they mature. As they begin to soften slightly, pick a peach and taste. Is it tasty? Not yet? Wait a bit. Try again a few days later. When peaches are sweet, they are ready to be picked.

Be aware that peaches getting the most sun will ripen first, so your tasting trials should begin on the upper and outer branches. When harvesting, do so carefully, as ripe peaches bruise easily and those brown bruises start the rotting process.

The best way to remove peaches from the tree is with a little twist combined with a slight upward pull. If you do pick some that are not quite ripe, let them ripen at room temperature. They'll taste much better than peaches ripened in the refrigerator.

Three cheers for cherries

I CANNOT TELL A LIE. You are going to love growing your own cherry (Prunus) trees. They're awash with blossom in spring and look just as attractive when full of fruit, be they sweet cherries (P. avium) or sour (P. cerasus).

Planting cherry trees

Cherry trees should be planted in early spring while they're still completely dormant. The trees should not be leafing out – if they are, plant them immediately. Why? Trees that are developing leaves and trying to set down a strong root system seldom accomplish both activities well. Plant cherry trees in rich soil. They like a very well-drained area with full sunlight. There is a direct relationship between lots of sunshine and good-quality, tasty fruit.

Plant your sweet cherry trees in a site that doesn't get late frosts, because sweet cherries blossom quite early in the spring and a frost will kill the blossoms.

If you live in a mild winter area, you can also plant cherry trees, completely dormant, in the autumn. By doing so, you will give the tree's roots a chance to get comfortable for the following year.

To help prevent the roots from developing crown rot fungus damage, don't plant too deeply. Place the trees in the ground at the same soil level they were in when you brought them home from the nursery. To provide good air circulation, dwarf trees require at least 2.5 metres of growing space, and standard trees should have about 8 metres in which to stretch out.

> *Trivia...*
> *Many cherries are not dark red when ripe. Some are yellow, some are bright red, and some are almost black.*

Choosing cherries

Most sweet cherry trees require another sweet cherry tree as a pollinator. The pollinator tree doesn't have to be in your garden, but it certainly helps to have one nearby. Acid cherry trees, producing the kind of fruit used in preserves and pies, are self-fertile. The varieties I've chosen to feature are all trees producing sweet eating cherries. Some can be found as dwarf trees, such as Compact Stella, which produces more fruiting spurs and a heavy crop for its smaller size. Dwarf cherry trees are self-fertile.

Good cherries for beginners

- **Compact Stella** – this has all of the basic properties of the most popular sweet cherry. It readily forms spurs. The fruits are large, dark red, and are ready for picking around late July.
- **Early Rivers** – a variety that was introduced over 100 years ago and is still popular. The fruits are sweet, very large, and nearly black. Cropping is heavy and regular and the cherries are ready for picking around mid-June.
- **Governor Wood** – this yellow-fleshed cherry has a good flavour. Its sweet, medium-sized fruit have dark red skins, flushed yellow. They ripen in early July.
- **Merchant** – a newer variety of sweet cherry with large fruit and bacterial canker resistance. Ripens early July.
- **Merton Bigarreau** – large, black cherry with dark red firm flesh and an outstanding flavour, a heavy cropper with high vigour, it ripens around mid-July.
- **Merton Glory** – large, yellow cherry ripening in late June. It has firm, white flesh and heart-shaped, rather than round, fruit. Growth is distinctly upright.
- **Napoleon Bigarreau** – renowned for its firm, very sweet flesh, pale yellow fruits, flushed with dark red. It's a heavy cropper that's ready for picking in early August.
- **Van** – reliable cropper with sweet, large, dark red fruit and firm, dark red flesh. Not a good choice for a small garden. Is ready for picking in late July.

■ **Compact Stella** *is a late, self-pollinating cherry that has an excellent sweet flavour and lush flesh.*

Pruning cherries

Keeping your cherry trees in good shape is really simple. In summer, be sure to water regularly and deeply. Don't do any pruning until the tree has completed a season of bearing fruit. Any pruning should be very light, since cherry trees bear fruit on both new and old branches. It's best to just remove any damaged or diseased branches.

However, if you have a standard tree, as I do, it may get too tall for you to reach the cherries without a long step-ladder. Birds are delighted to get the tastiest cherries at the top of the tree, but you may want them for yourself. If you dislike ladder climbing as much as I do, you can shorten the top of the tree.

The goal of pruning is to create an open centre. Rather than have one main trunk growing upwards, you want four to five significant branches growing outwards at about a 45° angle. The branches should be separate from one another. An open centre gives each of the different areas more sun, and makes fruit easier to reach.

■ **Morello cherries** *have an excellent flavour that makes them among the best for cooking. They make particularly tasty fruit pies and jams.*

Cherry pests

Cherry blackfly can be quite devastating to your cherry tree. The leaves at the tips of shoots become curled in late spring, and dense colonies of black aphids are visible on the leaf undersides. By midsummer, some of the affected leaves will turn brown and dry up. Silverleaf is a serious disease of plums, which can also affect cherries. The first sign is a silvering of leaves, followed by dieback of shoots and staining of the stem wood. Powdery mildew produces a powdery white coating on the leaves that eventually distorts them. Bacterial canker, will be seen as oozing patches of sap.

Is it ripe yet?

Knowing when to pick your cherries could not be simpler. Let your taste buds be your guide. Pick a cherry by pulling carefully on the stem with a slight upward twist. Ripe fruit will separate easily from the stem. Be gentle when picking to avoid bruising your fruit. Eat or cook cherries right away. Don't let them pile up – one bruised cherry can cause rot in the whole batch.

Pears for all

THE PEAR (Pyrus communis) is a close relative of the apple, which means that the planting technique is identical, and many pests and diseases can move from one to the other. Pear trees can also be trained into the same range of tree types as apples – standards, cordons, and espaliers.

Trivia...
A healthy pear should live a long and happy life. Fifty years is the normal life span for an apple tree, but a pear should live for a century or more.

However, there are some distinct differences. Pears are more sensitive to frost. The blossom appears about 2 to 4 weeks before the apple, and this means that the risk of frost damage is greater. Dessert pears need more sun than apples, and an easterly wind will completely blacken young pear foliage. If you live in an exposed part of the country, then it's essential to provide your pear trees with adequate shelter.

A pear tree will tolerate a heavier soil than an apple, but will not thrive so well on a sandy soil, especially in a coastal region where the winds are salt-laden.

Pears are grown on a more limited range of rootstocks, and this has a direct effect on the final height of the mature tree. While the choice of apple trees can range from 1.5 to 7.5 metres (depending on the rootstock used), pears are grown on quince rootstocks, and most of the popular trees will grow to between 3 and 6 metres high. You can also buy dwarf tree varieties.

■ **Pears won't keep** *as well as apples once harvested but you can keep them in a cool place for a few weeks. Just remember to bring them into the warm to finally ripen 2 days before eating.*

Pollinating partners

Unless your pear tree is self-fertile, you'll need to provide it with a pollinating partner.
You can choose different varieties, but before buying check at your garden centre or
nursery that both trees flower at the same time. This will help to ensure a healthy crop
of delicious pears.

You can check whether a pear is ripe by lifting it gently in the palm of your hand and
giving it a gentle twist. If it readily parts company from the tree, it's ripe. Pears have a
limited storage life, so they are best eaten soon after being harvested. Once you have
picked the fruits, put them on a warm windowsill for a couple of days or so to allow
their full flavour to develop, then tuck in!

Varieties to choose from

■ **Beth** – good choice for amateurs, small to medium-sized fruits with soft-
textured flesh, produces a reliable crop that ripens in late August.

■ **Beurre Superfin** – long yellow pear with reddish patches, very sweet,
melting white flesh, ripens in October. This variety must be eaten soon
after picking, as it doesn't store well.

■ **Concorde** – a fairly new variety with medium to large, pale
yellow fruit and sweet, very flavoursome flesh. Partially
self-fertile, this is a late pear. Pick in September and eat
from October onwards.

■ **Conference** – prolific pear bred last century, semi self-
fertile, but much better if cross-pollinated. Long, pale
green fruit ripens in October.

■ **Doyenne du Comice** – this is the queen of pears if
you're looking for flavour since the
texture and taste are

BETH

outstanding. However, this variety is
difficult to grow in less than perfect
conditions. It needs warmth, a
good sheltered position away from any wind
and a nearby pollinating partner.

■ **Doyenne d'Ete** – small, yellow fruits
that are usually the first to ripen in
July to August, excellent flavour, very
juicy. This pear flowers mid-season,
reducing the risk of frost damage to
the blossom.

■ **Williams Bon Chretien** – this variety was
discovered in a garden in the late 1700s.
Juicy and delicious pale yellow fruit.
Ripens in September.

■ **Conference**
pears *are one of the most*
popular varieties because they are reliable
croppers and produce good-sized fruits
with an excellent flavour.

- **Robin** – a Norfolk pear with small fruits, bright red on the sunny side. Sweet and juicy. Fruiting in September.
- **Sensation** – a new red-skinned pear. The foliage has a bronzy sheen, which makes this tree a handsome sight throughout the summer months. Fruit is ready for picking in September, is juicy and will keep for several weeks in store.

Plant a plum

THE GOOD NEWS *is that plums (Prunus domestica) are very easy to grow, which is probably why they're so popular. You can grow either sweet dessert plums or the more tart culinary variety – just don't forget to check that you're choosing the type that you want at the nursery. Patience is certainly a virtue with plums, as you may have to wait until your tree is about 5 years old before it starts producing any fruit.*

The only drawback with plums is that they flower very early in the year, before many of the pollinating insects have appeared. This could result is a disappointing yield, especially if your garden is on a low and exposed site. Give nature a helping hand by hand-pollinating your plum. Simply dab the flowers gently with a ball of cotton wool or fine paintbrush, and do this every day or two from the time the buds open until the petals drop.

Plums do best in moist but well-drained soil and need a healthy spring feeding of nitrogen to give them a good start to the season. Any good garden centre will be able to provide you with a slow release granular product. Don't forget to read and follow the label instructions carefully.

November is the best month for planting plum trees. Choose the highest spot in the garden, and a position that gets lots of sun. Your best buy is a 2- or 3-year-old tree that has been partly trained. If your garden is cold and exposed, then choose a late-flowering variety.

It's important that you do not prune your plum during the winter because the wounds will take longer to heal. This will make your tree more vulnerable to an infection of silver leaf, a disease that attacks plums.

Prune your plum trees either immediately after harvesting or in early spring, just as the trees start into growth.

As a general point, if you plant a plum tree against a wall, make sure that you water it well, and regularly. Without a good supply of moisture to the roots, you could run the risk of not getting any decent plums at all.

Dessert plums

■ **Crimson Drop** – considered a first-rate plum, this has large, red, richly flavoured fruit. Ripens mid- to late September, self-fertile.

■ **Denniston's Superb** – large, apple-green fruit with yellow markings, good reputation for hardiness and reliability. A good pollinator, self-fertile.

■ **Early Laxton** – round, firm fruits with golden, juicy flesh. Should usually be picked before the end of July. This variety is sometimes used for cooking.

■ **Goldfinch** – large, yellow fruit, very juicy with sweet rich flavour. Ripens mid- to late August. Partially self-fertile.

■ **Victoria** – probably the nation's favourite tree, this mid-season flowering variety produces oval, red, good-flavoured fruit that's juicy and sweet when ripe. Pick plums before they are fully ripe for cooking in pies.

■ **Dessert plums** *can be eaten straight off the tree. The best varieties produce good-sized fruits that are sweet and juicy.*

■ **Warwickshire Drooper** – medium-sized dessert and culinary plum, deep yellow fruit with orange flesh, makes lovely jam. If using as a dessert plum, allow to hang on the tree for a little longer. Expect fruit mid-September. Self-fertile.

Culinary plums

■ **Belle de Louvain** – large culinary plum with reddish purple skin, covered with a delicate bloom. Yellow flesh has a good flavour. Ripens early August. Partially self-fertile.

■ **Blue Tit** – medium-sized blue-black fruit with a good flavour, ripens mid-August.

■ **Bountiful** – medium to large red fruit with translucent flesh. Excellent for jams. Self-fertile.

■ **Culinary plums** *can be used to make jams and preserves, as fillings for pies, or as ingredients for sauces. They can also be frozen.*

- **Purple Pershore** – medium to large purple-blue-black fruits, ripening mid- to late August, self-fertile.
- **Pershore Yellow** – one of the best culinary plums, this variety is superb for jams and bottling. A reliable cropper, producing fruit at the end of August. It is reasonably disease resistant.

A simple summary

✓ The roots anchor a plant and the stems support it. The roots and leaves work together to provide the plant with nutrition. Everything you do to help each part of a plant complete its job will make for a healthier garden.

✓ Fruit trees can be self-fertile or require a pollinator. Self-fertile apple trees are rarely reliable, so it's as well to ensure that there's a pollinator nearby to do the job if necessary.

✓ The most popular fruit trees with seeds for the home garden are the apple and the pear. Both can be grown in any garden in the United Kingdom, but it's important to consider each tree's eventual size to make sure that it has plenty of room.

✓ Peaches, nectarines, and cherries often do not ship or store well – they taste far better when grown in a home garden.

✓ Fig trees are usually associated with warmer climes, but they will grow well in most parts of the country if planted in the right position and given some protection in cold weather.

Chapter 15

Herbal Harvest

I CAN THINK OF LOTS of reasons to grow herbs. It's easy. It's fun. Herbs don't take up a lot of space and so are a great choice for people with small gardens. In fact, you don't need a garden at all to raise many herbs. You can do it in your kitchen; which will be convenient, because that's ultimately where you'll want them.

In this chapter...
✓ Herbal history
✓ Herb gardens
✓ Favourite garden herbs
✓ Easy-to-grow herbs for cooking
✓ Easy-to-grow fragrant herbs
✓ Preserving your harvest

DILL IN FLOWER

Herbal history

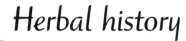

LONG BEFORE *recorded history, people enjoyed herbs. How do we know? Well, pollen grains from a long-ago relative of wild marjoram have been found in cave dwellings dating back 60,000 years. No doubt there are all sorts of stories of herbal use that we'll never know! Fortunately, there are many ancient writings about herbs.*

■ **Herbs have been** *harvested over the centuries because of their health-giving properties.*

Legendary herbs

The Mount Olympian gods of early Greek mythology ate only **herbs** and drank only herb tea. In this way, the gods remained ever youthful and healthy. These same deities washed their hair with herbal brews and washed their faces with herbal juices. They took herbal baths and consumed herbal brain tonics. All this made for beauty as well as long life.

> **DEFINITION**
>
> *The term* **herb** *generally refers to the seeds, leaves, flowers, bark, roots, or other parts of any plant used for cosmetics, dyes, flavouring, fragrance, or health purposes.*

The Greek gods, so it is told, wanted to hide these prized herbs away from common folk. So they made certain herbs grow in forests, where the ordinary mortal would not think to look for them. Diana, goddess of the hunt, was put in charge of guarding herb-growing sites. But, being a kindly sort, she felt sorry when women came begging for medicinal help, so she shared her information.

The angered gods took control of their herb garden again, later putting it in charge of Hebe, the goddess of youthfulness, warning her to keep their secret. However, Hebe felt sorry for warriors who were injured in war without any medicine to help cure them. Since her capabilities included restoring youth and vigour to gods and men, she slipped medicinal herbs into the warriors' food. Which, so the story goes, is how herbs came to be used in cooking.

The warriors, upon returning home, went seeking the source of this culinary delight. They got ample assistance from young maidens who had had brief trysts with various gods. These gods were indiscreet in their conversation. And gradually the sources of ambrosia – the food of the gods – were discovered by ordinary people.

■ **Herbal infusions** *are often soothing and refreshing.*

Get it in writing

Only a few educated people could write in ancient Greece, so information on how to grow and use herbs was passed down orally from one generation to another. Herbs were rumoured to do many things that they were far from capable of accomplishing. But at the time, medicines such as we know them didn't exist and people needed help with all sorts of problems.

A scholar named Theophrastus (c. 372–287 BC), began to compile information about herbs and put it in writing. Quite a few years later, around 65 AD, the botanist and physician Dioscorides got together detailed information on 579 medicinal herbs. His book, *De Materia Medica*, which included formulas on each herb's use, became a standard medical reference until the 1600s.

Herbal medicine

Eventually herbs took a firm place in a physician's cure-all for assorted ailments. In addition, herbs were used to season and preserve food, bring good luck to a household, discourage evil spirits, eliminate nightmares, act as love potions, and improve beauty. They were also carried to ward off the implacable stench of an unwashed world. Many people grew their own herbs, and to get the best results they listened to the advice of assorted astrologers. Herbs were planted and harvested for a particular disease or disorder according to the positions of the planets.

The Romans, bent on conquest, and therefore carrying their own body-mending kits, brought the use of herbs to Britain. Initially, monks working in monastery gardens were the chief cultivators. But before too long, every estate and small farm had a herb garden.

■ **Some herbs** grown in modern-day window-boxes would once have been essential to a physician's medical kit for treating a wide range of illnesses.

Early herbs

The knowledge of herbs and herb growing has been handed down from generation to generation for thousands of years, and some of the earliest herb gardens were planted in Egypt as long as 4,000 years ago. Favourite plants in Roman times included rosemary, bay, and myrtle, and other aromatics for incense. By the ninth century, monasteries placed special emphasis on herbs to heal the sick and also used them to liven up their dull vegetarian diet. In the days of poor sanitation, sweet-smelling herb leaves and flowers worked wonders to mask unwelcome odours.

In the sixteenth century, physic gardens became a feature of many leading universities where medicinal herbs were grown for teaching botany and medicine. During the colonial era, Europeans settled in many parts of the world, taking seeds and cuttings of their favourite herbs with them.

Herbs in print

Over the years, thousands of books and pamphlets in all languages have been written on herbal use. Some very early texts are still available today. If you go to a large bookshop or do a book search online, you'll find *Gerard's Herbal*, a book first printed in 1596. It has since been expanded several times. The author, John Gerard, grew more than 1,000 herbs in his garden. Also found on modern bookshop shelves is Culpeper's *Complete Herbal*, a reprint of a text originated by Nicholas Culpeper (1616–1654), a London physician, pharmacist, and astrologer.

Recently there has been a true resurrection of herbs for health, and shops selling health foods and treatments have shelves filled with expensive containers of St. John's wort, kava kava, echinacea, valerian root, and the like. Herbal teas have become a standard on household shelves, and if you order tea in a restaurant, chances are chamomile and peppermint teas are on the menu.

There are books on how to cook with herbs, how to dry herbs, how to stuff pillows with herbs for a good night's sleep, and how to use herbs to enhance your beauty. There are also innumerable web sites devoted to herbal information. Just type in "herbs" and see where it gets you.

■ **The striking** *flowers of echinacea* (E. purpurea).

Herb gardens

BECAUSE HERBS HAVE A SPIRITUAL NATURE to many, and perhaps to you, sit in the garden for a while before designing your herb garden. Visualize how you would like your special herbal space to appear, and think about the plants you would like to grow. You might want to visit the herb gardens at local gardens open to the public. Do you have adequate sun for what you want? With a few exceptions, herbs like at least 6 hours of sunlight per day and reasonably good drainage.

You can often create a sunny spot for a herb garden by trimming back trees and bushes, and drainage can be improved with the use of raised beds. Raised beds in a herb garden lend a very lovely rhythm to the visual scene. An alternative is to mingle herbs – here and there, in pots and in the ground – among other sun-loving plants. Some gardeners prefer to interplant herbs among their vegetables, acting on beliefs that some herbs have protective powers against pests. You can also grow a multitude of herbs on your sunny windowsills.

It is never recommended that you gather herbs from the wild. Some healthful herbs are look-a-likes of extremely poisonous varieties.

The knot garden

Popular in the 1600s, a formal English herb garden is a fun challenge to re-create. The herbs are planted in intricate geometric designs, with a specimen plant in the centre of each knot. A knot garden is often placed in full view of a patio or terrace.

■ **An Elizabethan-style** *knot garden is characterized by geometric shapes of rectangles, triangles, and circles. A popular feature of the original knot gardens was to enclose a wide variety of herbs and medicinal plants between the rows of clipped box hedges.*

You can create a traditional design for a herb garden, or design your own. A drawn-to-scale plan is a very important first step.

Then, using garden sand, mark the lines on a prepared, levelled site. Don't forget to leave pathways for strolling and care. The pathways can be left bare, or covered with a mulch such as decorative wood chips or gravel. In the traditional versions, coloured earth and pebbles are used to fill open spaces.

Herbs selected for the design of a knot garden should be compact, and it's best to go for texture variations. This type of garden is labour intensive. In order to maintain its appearance, you must clip the plants about every 2 weeks from spring to autumn to keep a uniform plant height. To lighten the work load, start by selecting plants that don't grow too wildly.

The Japanese herb garden

Often favoured by gardeners living in rocky areas, the Japanese herb garden design incorporates rocks. A true Japanese herb garden is a highly structured affair, so you must be prepared to do a lot of preparatory manual labour to set one up correctly. Of course, you can hire someone to do this for you, or contact the Japanese Garden Society (01926 632747).

A traditional garden will have formal pathways between the rocks made of stepping stone, crushed rock, or steps. Then you encircle the open space between each rock group and close it off with large pebbles or small rocks. Good organic soil will fill the open area, and this is where you will place your carefully researched purchases. Select plants that will create some tracery as they grow, but will not overwhelm their rock-rimmed site.

INTERNET

**www.herbsociety.
co.uk**

Here you'll find a reference site compiled by the Herb Society of the U.K. You can become a member and receive the society's quarterly magazine, which contains detailed information on all aspects of growing herbs and the names and addresses of reputable suppliers. The society also organizes seminars and workshops around the country.

The theme garden

Are you fond of butterflies? History? Shakespeare? Are you raising herbs just for teas? For cooking? Would you prefer a garden that includes only those herbs grown in Biblical times, such as aniseed, cumin, garlic, mint, and wormwood? Or would you like a garden with a colour theme, such as all grey leaves?

There are almost endless possibilities for theme gardens, and obviously this choice is up to you. Regardless of the theme you choose, make sure you leave a place for a bench or a comfortable garden chair within your herb garden. You deserve a front-row seat in your own special place.

Favourite garden herbs

WHEN IT COMES TO HERBS *for the outdoor garden, or for the kitchen, container gardeners have a lot of options. Among the many herbs you can grow are:*

- Aniseed *(Pimpinella anisum)*
- Basil *(Ocimum)*
- Bay *(Laurus nobilis)*
- Caper *(Capparis spinosa)*
- Caraway *(Carum)*
- Catnip *(Nepeta cataria)*
- Chamomile *(Chamaemelum nobile)*
- Chervil *(Anthriscus cerefolium)*
- Chives *(Allium schoenoprasum)*
- Coriander *(Coriandrum sativum)*
- Cumin *(Cuminum cyminum)*
- Dill *(Anethum graveolens)*
- Fennel *(Foeniculum vulgare)*
- Garlic *(Allium sativum)*
- Ginger *(Zingiber officinale)*
- Lavender *(Lavandula officinalis)*
- Lemon balm *(Melissa officinalis)*
- Lemon verbena *(Aloysia triphylla)*
- Marjoram *(Origanum majorana)*
- Mint *(Mentha)*
- Nasturtium *(Tropaeolum majus)*
- Oregano *(Origanum vulgare)*
- Parsley *(Petroselinum crispum)*
- Rocket *(Eruca versicaria)*
- Rosemary
  (Rosmarinus officinalis)
- Sage *(Salvia officinalis)*
- Savory *(Satureja hortensis)*
- Scented geraniums *(Pelargonium)*
- Tarragon *(Artemisia dracunculus)*
- Thyme *(Thymus vulgaris)*
- Watercress
  (Nasturtium officinale)

■ **Potted garden herbs** *provide an aromatic focal point. Combine interesting foliage shapes and textures with the odd flowering plant for a great effect.*

Some of the easier-to-grow varieties are reviewed in this chapter. Others, such as chamomile and thyme, are discussed in greater detail in Chapter 16 on groundcovers. You'll find more on nasturtiums in Chapter 18.

Easy-to-grow herbs for cooking

IF YOU'RE LOOKING FOR HERBS *that will grace your table (without a lot of effort on your part), try the simple plants that follow.*

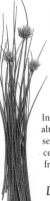

No-jive chives

Indoors or out, chives are easy to grow. If outside, give them a spot with full sun. If you want to grow chives indoors, place them in a pot of standard commercial potting compost. Use a fairly large pot to accommodate their extensive root system, and be sure to place them in good light. Gently scatter the seeds, and then lightly cover them with compost. Sprinkle with water until the compost is just damp.

In about 2 weeks, your first grass-like seedlings will appear. These are edible, although you should rinse them off first and remove the tiny roots. Thin the seedlings (you do it by simply eating them). Mature chives are from 20 to 30 centimetres tall. When you cut leaves for garnishes or to add to salads, cut from the outside.

Don't remove all the leaves unless you intend to kill the plant. Chives are a perennial plant, and once they get healthily started you can divide their expanding clumps to create more plants.

CHIVES

Gourmet garlic

Garlic may not be as attractive as other members of the lily (*Allium*) family, but if cooks were given a choice of which to grow, the smelly version would win hands down. Garlic has been cultivated practically forever. It was nurtured in Egypt while the first of the great pyramids was built, about 6,000 years ago. Labourers working on the pyramids under the hot desert sun were fed garlic to stave off heatstroke. It has had, and continues to have, numerous health-related uses, and today you can buy it packaged with and without odour.

To grow your own, you can start from seed, or, more conveniently, you can buy bulbs at any garden centre or at the supermarket. If you're planning to use lots of garlic in the kitchen, though, I'd advise investing in specially prepared virus-free cloves from an established nursery or seed firm.

GARLIC

PLANTING GARLIC CLOVES IN CELL PACKS

Garlic bulbs are made up of numerous small bulblets, called cloves. Separate the cloves and place them in the soil with the pointed side up. Use good potting compost, preferably with a little sand mixed in. Plant the cloves about 2–3 centimetres deep. Keep the soil slightly on the dry side. Do not over-water, or the bulbs will rot. I have also grown garlic indoors on a very sunny windowsill in good potting compost.

There are early- and late-season types of garlic, so try some of each. Plant them from early autumn through to late autumn, or in early spring. Garlic grows best in an open, sunny position on light soil that does not have to be very fertile. Plant cloves upright at 2 to 3 centimetres deep, or twice their own depth, and cover them with more soil. Make sure that you choose a sheltered position for the cloves.

After about 3 months, the leaves will turn brown. It is now harvest time. Remove any loose dirt and rootlets from the bulbs, and begin cooking. Dry those that you don't want to cook right away. Dried garlic will generally be stronger than fresh.

■ **Plait the leaves** *of several garlic bulbs together, tie the end with a piece of string, and hang them up to store.*

Elephant garlic (Allium ampeloprasum) is not a true garlic; it is a leek and has a relatively mild taste. Try growing some of this too.

INTERNET

gourmetgarlicgardens. com/overview.htm

Click here for a garlic overview: garlic, the sweet breath of life! If you like garlic, this is the site to visit to find out more. There are good descriptions of the garden varieties available, history, folklore, harvesting information, cooking tips, growing tips, health benefits, garlic chemistry, reference books, on-line purchase catalogues, and how to plait. Lots of fun information!

Marvellous mint

Mint can be found in many varieties, including apple, orange, peppermint, pineapple, and spearmint. All mints are perennial, and grow rapidly if they're given plenty of water.

Mints are great for places where you can keep them confined. Given good care, they may grow so rapidly, their underground root runners going this way and that, you'll wish you never saw a mint.

Culinary advocates grow a garden of mints in colourful pots. In fact, they are among the very few herbs that do nicely in pots that don't have good drainage. For mint grown in pots, it is best to pinch the tops to keep them at about 25 centimetres high.

PLANTING INVASIVE HERBS

When planting invasive herbs in open ground, you can restrict their spread by growing them in a sunken container. Old buckets, large pots or even heavy-duty plastic bags are suitable, although it is usually necessary to make drainage holes. For best results, lift and divide the plants each spring and replant young, vigorous pieces in the containers using fresh potting compost.

1 **Position your pot**

Dig a hole large enough to accommodate a large pot or old bucket. Make drainage holes in the pot, then place it in the hole and fill with a soil and compost mixture.

2 **Plant the herb**

Plant the herb in the pot, firming it in well. Add enough compost to conceal the pot's rim, and water thoroughly. Each spring, replant and replace the soil mix in the pot.

CORSICAN MINT (*Mentha requienii*)

Mints need about 3 hours of sun each day. (An exception is Corsican mint, a dense groundcover that does very well in semi-shade.) Each plant grows from 30 to 120 centimetres high, and most have small white, pink, or lavender flowers in mid-summer. To start new plants, just take a cutting from an older one and stick it in a glass of water until roots form, then plant.

Mints are high in vitamin A, vitamin C, and calcium, and also contain some niacin and potassium. They are used in teas, liqueurs, jellies, salads, soaps, to flavour chewing gum, scent perfumes, scent sweets, and in sauces. Long ago, before toothbrushes were invented, Romans chewed a paste made of mint and honey to sweeten their breath.

Parsley particulars

Parsley roots have long been prized for their medicinal value. Dried leaves were used to make tea, and the fresh leaves, chewed, help make breath fresher. There are several parsley varieties, some with curly leaves and some with flat.

Parsley is primarily a potted plant, kept either indoors or on a sheltered patio or porch. However, you can get good results outdoors if you plant in good soil and in a sheltered spot. Parsley grown indoors prefers partial sun, and will do fairly well in bright lamplight. Grow it in a commercial potting mix. Drainage must be good, so don't forget that the pot needs a drainage hole. Feed once a month with a weak-strength liquid plant food.

Trivia...

In Greek mythology, the god Pluto was king of Hades, or the underworld. Pluto was married to Persephone, but he fell in love with a beautiful young Grecian nymph named Minthe. In her jealous rage, Persephone decided to get rid of Minthe, changing her into a lowly herb easily stepped on and crushed. The legend goes that this herb is mint, which still sends out runners along the ground to seek her lover. Pluto couldn't do anything about the transformation, but gave the mint a lovely fragrance and the power to make people love her.

Trivia...

Many people think of parsley as something chefs use to garnish a steak. But aside from its decorative purpose, parsley contains vitamins A and C, calcium, magnesium, potassium, and riboflavin. So be sure to encourage everyone at the table to eat their parsley.

Growing parsley is easiest if you buy young plants in the herb section of your local garden centre. However, if you want to plant from seeds, be aware that it does take about 6 weeks for the seeds to sprout. Begin the process from March until early May. To speed it up, soak seeds overnight before planting. Eventually plants will become 15 to 30 centimetres high. Parsley is a biennial plant, and small yellow flowers appear the second year. After this, the leaves become tough and bitter, so you will need to grow new plants. Prolong your plants' productivity by cutting off flower stalks as they first form.

Easy-to-grow fragrant herbs

MANY HERBS ARE KNOWN for their wonderful aroma. Those that I've selected to discuss in detail are also known to be ideal plants for beginner gardeners who may be a bit nervous about choosing and growing herbs.

Cavorting with catnip

CATNIP (*Nepeta faassenii*)

Certainly cats like catnip, which is precisely why some people plant it. The bruised leaves give off the attractive oil. At one time, catnip was used in foods, flavouring soups, stews, and teas. It contains good amounts of vitamins A and C.

Catnip, called catmint by some, is a hardy perennial. The most common type is a 1.2-metre bush with grey leaves and spikes of small white flowers with lavender spots. However, there is also the compact *Nepeta faassenii*, which has grey-green leaves and lavender-blue flower spikes, and another type, called dawn to dusk (*N. grandiflora*), which has rose flower spikes. There is also a Syrian catnip (*N. curvifolia*), available in speciality catalogues, that has blue-purple flowers.

Catnip attracts honeybees as well as cats. Its flowers will appear in summer and may remain into the early autumn. They're excellent for cutting. You can obtain catnip from a friend who will share the roots, or grow it from seed sown directly in the garden in spring or autumn. Thin the seedlings to about 60 centimetres apart. Once the plants have become established they will self-sow.

Catnip isn't choosy about where it lives, so it's a good plant for dry, shaded, or sunny areas with poor soil. However, a sunny site and somewhat sandy soil will produce catnip with the best fragrance. To keep plants trim, cut them back each year. The only thing that seems to disturb this hardy perennial is over-watering.

Lovely lemon verbena

The leaves of this deciduous South American native give off a distinct lemony scent at the slightest touch. They were used by the Incas for stomach ailments, among other purposes. Dried lemon verbena leaves can retain their scent for years. For use in pot pourris and sachets, the best scent is obtained by picking the leaves during the flowering period.

LEMON VERBENA (*Aloysia triphylla*)

This pale green shrub gets tall and can eventually reach 2 to 3 metres high. It can be grown in a container or in a sunny garden corner where it won't overwhelm the smaller herbs. Inconspicuous white to pale lavender flowers appear from July to September.

The planting soil for lemon verbena should be moist but well drained, and this plant should be fertilized regularly. Since lemon verbena won't make it through a really cold winter, you can either dig it up or take cuttings in mid-summer. If you dig it up, first cut the plant to the ground. Find a dark place to store the roots in moist sand.

Replant your roots in spring for quick growth. If you prefer to take cuttings, the cuttings should have at least two joints: the lower joint, without leaves, will be below the soil line; the other, with just a few leaves, will be above the soil line.

Majoring in marjoram

Marjoram could be considered a true all-purpose herb. Marjoram's aroma comes from its small round bracts, which are covered with shiny oil glands. (As a reminder, the bracts are the modified leaves growing just below a flower or flower cluster.) The ancient Greeks and Romans used fragrant marjoram in perfumes, food, and medicine. They crowned young lovers and bridal couples with marjoram wreaths and planted marjoram on the graves of loved ones as a token of good feelings and remembrance. Long before we had carpets, or vacuum cleaners, homeowners would sprinkle marjoram along the ground to sweeten one's step. And of course, today we use marjoram to flavour food. If you plan to use your marjoram in cooking, you'll need to have about a half-dozen plants, as the leaves shrink quite a bit when dried.

Marjoram is a quite tender perennial that is usually grown as an annual. It will not survive a cold winter. However, it is easily grown from seeds sown in spring, or from cuttings taken in summer. If you want, you can start the seeds indoors in March, then transplant outdoors in May. The seed is slow to germinate, or sprout. When it does, thin the seedlings so that they are about 15 centimetres apart. The plant grows to about 30 to 60 centimetres, and has grey-green leaves. Like most plants from the Mediterranean, marjoram prefers a warm, sunny location in slightly alkaline soil. Flowers, appearing in late summer, are tiny, white, pink, or pale lilac.

MARJORAM
(*Origanum majorana*)

Marjoram does quite well in pots for patio use, and it makes a delightful hanging-basket plant. It will even grow indoors if given enough light. To grow marjoram inside, you'll need to use potting compost. Don't forget to water so that the soil stays slightly moist. As mentioned above, you can plant it from seed, or you can purchase marjoram in the herb section of most garden centres.

Simple scented geraniums

Scented geraniums were a choice plant during the Victorian era, rivalling ferns in popularity. There seems to be a geranium available in every scent: almond, apple, apricot, coconut, lemon, lime, mint-rose, rose, nutmeg, peach, peppermint, and strawberry, to name a few. The fragrance of geraniums is fine on a sunny day, and at all times when you gently rub the leaves between your fingers and daintily sniff. There are people who grow nothing but scented geraniums. In addition to their lovely fragrance, they also have white to rose-coloured flowers. There are also trailing scented geraniums, which are particularly nice in pots, hanging baskets, and even as groundcovers.

Trivia...

In Greek mythology, Amaracus, a young and delicate servant of the cruel King of Cyprus, accidentally dropped a precious vial of perfume containing the juice of the world's only red pearl. In his terror of the ensuing punishment, Amaracus fainted. The local gods, feeling kind, instantly changed the perfume-soaked Amaracus into a fragrant herb, amarakos. The Latin word somehow transformed into the word "marjoram," which means "joy of the mountain". The oil is still used in some perfumes.

Most geraniums will start easily, if quite slowly, from seed, but I find it much simpler to grow them from cuttings. Just take a stem that's a few centimetres long, let it dry off for an hour, then set it about 2 to 3 centimetres deep in potting compost. Or you can just stick the stem in a glass of water until the roots appear. If that isn't simple, nothing is.

Outdoors, these geraniums aren't too fussy about soil, but a good fertile, well-drained soil always helps things along. These plants prefer a slightly dry environment, but not too dry or their lower leaves will drop off. Most geraniums eventually reach from 60 to 120 centimetres in height and will grow equally wide. Pinch the top growing tips to inspire fullness rather than ranginess. Leaves for the different scented geraniums vary greatly, from fern-like to large and round. You'll also see a wide array of shades of green and some have variegated foliage.

Indoors, or in patio pots, plant scented geraniums in potting compost, and plan on fertilizing about once a month with a liquid plant food. You'll probably find a limited selection in the herb section of a garden centre, and it's likely you'll want to browse through some garden catalogues for variety.

■ **Rober's Lemon Rose** *is a scented geranium with a heady rose and lemon aroma.*

Preserving your harvest

IF YOU'RE SUCCESSFUL with your herbal efforts, which of course you will be, the chances are pretty good that you just won't be able to use all the herbs you have grown when they're fresh. Moreover, having your own herbs on hand through the winter makes the drearier months of the year pass by just a little more quickly. So here we'll explore some ways you can enjoy the fruits of your labours all year round.

Harvesting herbs

Culinary herbs harvested for their leaves should always be cut just as flower buds appear. By cutting at this time, dried herbs will have the strongest flavour. Do this first thing in the morning, right after the dew dries off the leaves, but before the sun's heat has evaporated or changed the plant's basic oils, decreasing its quality. It's best to do most of your harvesting when the weather is dry rather than damp or rainy. You can get several harvests off most of the leafy herbs, as long as you don't remove too much of the plant at one time.

Herbs grown primarily for their flowers, such as chamomile, should also be harvested right as the plant begins flowering. For both types of herbs, you will need a sharp knife or good pruning shears to harvest properly. Use a sharp spade to dig up garlic and other root crops.

If you are into seed gathering, do this as the seed heads form by cutting the flower with a short length of stem attached. Immediately place each herb group upside down into labelled brown paper bags. The seeds will fall into the bag as the plant dries. Always handle carefully when harvesting to prevent most of your seeds from dropping onto the ground. Why not let them dry on the plant? It's too chancy that the seedpods will open and disperse the seed before you collect it.

■ **Dried seeds of aromatic** *dill (Anethum) are often used for culinary purposes.*

■ **Dry seed heads** *by covering them with muslin or a paper bag, secured in place with string or a rubber band. Hang them upside down in a warm place until dry.*

HERBS IN ICE CUBES

Several different herbs can be used to flavour and enhance the appearance of ice cubes when added to drinks. Suitable herbs include borage, pineapple mint, and parsley, as shown here. Put chopped herbs, or herb flowers like borage, in ice-cube trays, adding about 1 tablespoon of water to each tablespoon of herb. This method is a good way of protecting delicate flowers like borage, which could get crushed during storage.

Freezing your herbs

Herbs with soft leaves, such as basil, chives, dill, marjoram, mint, and parsley, freeze best. If you intend to freeze your harvest, go out when the dew is still on the plants. After you bring them indoors, rinse the plants well and gently shake them dry. To freeze, put sprigs of each herb type into individual bags, and then store them in your freezer. Store frozen herbs in small quantities and don't refreeze once thawed.

Another way to freeze herbs in small amounts is to chop them into very fine pieces, and freeze them with water in ice-cube trays. Pop out the frozen cubes and place in freezer storage bags. The process of cooking will defrost frozen herbs.

Drying herbs

Proper herb drying is essential to retain as much of the original colour, flavour, and fragrance as possible. Good drying techniques remove moisture, thereby preventing chemical changes, mould, and enzyme activity that can destroy your best growing efforts. There are various methods for drying herbs. For limited amounts, use string or rubber bands to fasten the collected herbs loosely in small bunches. The fastener should be tight, because the herbs will shrink as they dry. But the bunches themselves should not be too thick, or the inner parts may rot. Hang the bunches upside down in a warm, not hot, dry, shady place that has good air circulation.

Do not allow sunlight to reach the drying herbs, as it will cause the leaves to darken considerably, even turning them black.

Drying times for each herb will vary, but on average, 1 to 2 weeks will be required. All herb bunches should be left until they are crisp to the touch, but not powdery. If you let them hang too long, some herbs begin reabsorbing moisture, making them useless for storing purposes.

Once the bunches are dry, remove the leaves, or flowers, from the stems. Store the dried leaves in dark, airtight, glass jars. Do not store in paper or plastic containers, as they will allow the herbal oils to evaporate. Preserving jars, on the other hand, are excellent for storing dried herbs. Put a dark jacket around each one, and be sure to label and date the contents. Keep the jars in a cool place out of direct light. Dried culinary herbs will keep their flavour for about 6 months.

■ **Air-dry herbs by** *spreading them on a mesh-covered rack. Leave them in a warm place until dry.*

An alternative drying method, if you have a lot of herbs, is to spread them loosely on wire mesh racks or on racks covered with paper towels, newspaper, or muslin fabric. Again, shade, warmth, and good air circulation are musts. The herbs should be stirred gently every day to encourage even drying. When the plants feel dry to the touch, they are ready. Do not wait until they crumble when you touch them.

A simple summary

✓ Herbal gardens range from the rather formal to the very expressive. They provide a great opportunity to plan your own special place.

✓ When selecting herbs, consider how many of each you'll need for a gratifying harvest. A few herbs are rampant growers, and you should know this before planting.

✓ Most herbs need full sun for good growth.

✓ Determine how much land you have to dedicate to herb use exclusively, or what sites intermingled with other plants are suitable.

✓ Decide whether you want herbs for cooking, for fragrance, for craft, or if you want a mixture of each.

✓ The majority of herbs grow well in containers, so you can have your herbal garden on your patio, or even in your kitchen.

PART FIVE

SUCCULENT HOUSELEEK

TYING IT ALL TOGETHER

EVERY GARDEN NEEDS *unifying elements* – some common thread, like a leitmotif in music, that joins your home and garden together. And bringing *harmony* to all aspects of your outdoor space means providing a nice smooth flow from one area to the next.

How do you do this? You *keep it simple*, of course. In this part I'll take a look at some of the ways you can create a complete, beautiful environment.

Chapter 16

Glorious Groundcovers

GROUND-COVER PLANTS ARE LOW-GROWING PLANTS that spread (gradually or rapidly) to form a moderate or dense cover over the soil. They are used for many purposes, such as to control erosion, to cover slopes, to unify a garden scene, to provide plantings beneath shrubs, to deter weeds, and to serve as an alternative to grass, concrete, or mulch. Some groundcovers can be walked on, others serve more decorative purposes.

In this chapter...
✓ Low-profile groundcovers
✓ High-speed groundcovers
✓ Dry climate groundcovers
✓ Beach covers
✓ Cool in the shade

GROUNDCOVER HERBS CREEPING THROUGH PAVING

Low-profile groundcovers

SOME LIKE IT SUBTLE. *If you do, consider very low-growing groundcover. Some of these recommendations are most often used between stepping stones or in other somewhat limited areas; others spread quite quickly, so they need a wider expanse. My choices are included below.*

Baby's tears

This creeping, light green, groundcover plant doesn't grow to more than 7 centimetres, and usually stays lower than that. It will root easily from any piece of stem, so you can either buy it at the garden centre or find some in a friend's garden. Place plants about 15 centimetres apart for quick cover and to deter weeds.

BABY'S TEARS (*Soleirolia soleirolii*)

Baby's tears (*Soleirolia soleirolii*), so named because of the tiny round leaves, will need regular watering and good soil, but this evergreen doesn't require a lot of sunlight. You can even try growing it in almost full shade. It is hardy to –4° C, and in perfect surroundings can be somewhat aggressive. Try it between stepping stones around the perimeter of the house. Baby's tears' little flowers are white and are not easy to see.

Chamomile

Small, yellow, button-like flowers cover the bright, medium green leaves of this perennial evergreen herb. It will grow from 7 to 15 centimetres high in ordinary garden soil. Buy seedlings in a multi-pack, and place them 30 centimetres apart. Buy several packs if you need a lot at once, because chamomile (*Chamaemelum nobile*) will meander along gradually and take its time filling up space. This ground-cover plant forms a thick enough cover that weeds don't get much of a foothold. Chamomile prefers sun. It's a good choice for areas that don't get much rainfall, as it's somewhat drought tolerant after it gets started, and likes to be kept slightly on the dry side.

Trivia...

In addition to being pretty, chamomile has a number of uses. It has long been believed to have a soothing effect. The soft, aromatic leaves, placed in a muslin bag, can be floated in the bath and are supposed to encourage relaxation. Chamomile tea recipes abound. If you're a blonde, and you want to have more fun, use this sweet-smelling herb to make a hair rinse. Put the chamomile flowers in a saucepan, and pour very hot water over them. Let it sit until it's cool, then strain.

Creeping thyme

DEFINITION

A flat is a container of about 45 × 45 centimetres wide and 5 centimetres high. It's used to hold a whole batch of ground-cover plants.

Creeping thyme (*Thymus serpyllum*) is an almost flat, dark green ground-cover plant. It is super hardy after it gets well started. Buy it in six-packs or by the *flat*, and place plants 15 centimetres apart in full sun or light shade and average soil. Small flowers, which attract bees (good for pollination!), are usually purple, but you may find some with pink, lilac, red, or white flowers. Thyme blooms from summer to autumn. Although this evergreen perennial withstands both neglect and drought, it does much better with occasional watering. There are several types of creeping thyme, but this is the hardiest and spreads the most quickly. It is also occasionally used as a seasoning, but common thyme (*T. vulgaris*) is more often the culinary choice.

Mazus

This ground-cover plant will grow from 2 to 5 centimetres high. An evergreen in areas with mild winters, mazus (*Mazus reptans*) disappears in cold climates, reappearing quickly in spring if it's protected by mulch. It likes regular water and good soil that never quite dries out. In hotter areas it will do well in part shade; otherwise you should give it full sun. The tiny flowers are purple-blue, appearing in clusters in late spring. Mazus will eventually form a dense groundcover. It roots at the joints and is easily increased by division.

MAZUS (*Mazus reptans*)

INTERNET

alpine garden society.org

This site is run by the society, which was founded in 1929 to promote interest in alpine and rock garden plants, many of which make excellent low-profile groundcovers. Click here for helpful information on these plants, and plenty of links.

More low-profile groundcovers:

- Alpine yarrow (*Achillea tomentosa*)
- Australian violet (*Viola hederacea*)
- Cinquefoil (*Potentilla*)
- Creeping Jenny (*Lysimachia nummularia*)
- Creeping speedwell (*Veronica repens*)
- Creeping wire vine (*Muehlenbeckia complexa*)
- Green carpet (*Herniaria glabra*)
- Mint (*Mentha*)
- Parrot's beak (*Lotus berthelotii*)
- Purple rock cress (*Aubrieta × cultorum*)
- Sea pink (*Armeria maritima*)
- Stonecrop (*Sedum*)
- Wall rockcress (*Arabis caucasica*)

High-speed groundcovers

WITH EXCELLENT TREATMENT *and rich soil, rapidly growing groundcovers can become rampant. However if, like me, you have hard-work soil, "rapidly growing" can actually be moderate – but it does grow, which is nice.*

Greater periwinkle

With plenty of water and light shade, this 45-centimetre ground-cover plant has been used to control highway erosion. It tolerates temperatures to –15° C, and once established it deters just about all weeds. Place the plants 45 centimetres apart. Also called big periwinkle or blue buttons, greater periwinkle (*Vinca major*) is a favourite for large, sloping areas where lots of work is difficult. It does well in sun where the summers are not very hot and long, and is also happy in quite a bit of shade. It spreads by rooting stems, with pretty blue flowers appearing among dark green leaves in both spring and autumn. A relative, lesser periwinkle (*V. minor*) grows to only 15 centimetres high. Usually seen with lilac-blue flowers, there are varieties with white, blue, pink, reddish, or purple flowers, and also some with variegated leaves. Also called dwarf periwinkle, it is somewhat less aggressive than greater periwinkle, but is still quite energetic if watered regularly.

GREATER PERIWINKLE
(*Vinca major*)

Mock strawberry

This plant gets its name from its pretty berries that resemble strawberries. But these berries are inedible, so just enjoy them for their good looks. They're preceded by petite, bright yellow flowers that bloom all spring and into the early summer. I use mock strawberry (*Duchesnea indica*) in semi-shade to blanket a hard-to-reach site. Growing only 10 centimetres high, the only problem is convincing it to stay on its site, rather than wander by trailing and rooting stems into adjacent areas of the garden. Other than occasional watering, this plant needs virtually no care. It tolerates temperatures below zero and so is good for colder climates. I've read that birds like the berries.

Serbian bellflower

There are so many campanulas that entire books have been devoted to them. Most are exquisitely pretty plants, but for difficult soil, Serbian bellflower (*Campanula poscharskyana*) is one of the best. Its dainty blue bells can appear from spring to early autumn. It likes full sun in cooler climates, but is happy in partial shade elsewhere.

Although this evergreen perennial tolerates occasional drought, it needs regular watering to thrive and form low, up to 10-centimetre-high, undulating growth. It is occasionally mislabelled as Dalmatian bellflower (*C. portenschlagiana*), its cousin. The latter has purple flowers and it is not as aggressive. Both are very hardy.

Snow-in-summer

Quite happy in dry, poor soil, this 7-centimetre-high grey ground-cover plant makes an interesting contrast to taller plants. Where it grows strongly in a suitable situation, very few weeds dare to emerge. This is one of the few ground-cover plants that does well in reflected heat from

SERBIAN BELLFLOWER
(*Campanula poscharskyana*)

concrete. Just water it enough to get started and, once underway, water occasionally. In early summer, white flowers blanket the leaves, looking almost as if they were covered with snow. Easily multiplied from segments and tolerant of low temperatures, snow-in-summer (*Cerastium tomentosum*) may even straggle along in sand.

■ **Rampant groundcover** *is furnished by snow-in-summer* (Cerastium tomentosum). *This is a very tolerant plant, happy in just about any sunny situation, provided you give it a little water when thirsty.*

More high-speed groundcovers:

- Creeping gold wallflower (*Erysimum kotchyanum*)
- Creeping Jenny (*Lysimachia nummularia*)
- Creeping speedwell (*Veronica repens*)
- Fleabane (*Erigeron*)
- Green carpet (*Herniaria glabra*)
- Ground ivy (*Glechoma hederacea*)
- Ground morning glory (*Convolvulus sabatius*)
- Ivy (*Hedera*)
- Ivy geranium (*Pelargonium*)
- Mint (*Mentha*)
- Rose carpet knotweed (*Persicaria bistorta*)
- Sage-leaf rockrose (*Cistus salvifolius*)
- St. John's wort (*Hypericum calcyinum*)
- Stonecrop (*Sedum*)
- Sweet woodruff (*Galium odoratum*)
- Trailing African daisy (*Osteospermum fruticosum*)
- Trailing gazania (*Gazania rigens*)
- Trailing ice plant (*Lampranthus*)

Dry climate groundcovers

THE ABILITY TO TOLERATE DRYNESS, or drought, is a variable. *Dry to one plant means never watering; dry to another is watered seldom. It is best to be aware of this if you are thinking of planting groundcover in an area that can't be reached by a hose or sprinkler.*

When most of us think of plants for very dry areas we think of cacti. All cacti are **succulents**, but there are many more types of succulents, including stonecrop. Stonecrops are low-growing succulents with creeping stems. Their leaves are green and come in a variety of sizes, shapes, and colours. You'll see stonecrop included in the following list of good groundcovers for arid areas:

Blue fescue

Often used in dry landscaping, the serene, blue-grey leaves of blue fescue (*Festuca ovina glauca*) accent taller, brighter perennials. Only 17 to 25 centimetres high, blue fescue develops into a tufted, mounding plant that usually displays moderate growth, expanding from individual plants that may each get to 30 or more centimetres wide. During the summer months, brownish, rather bland flowers appear on little spikes. Blue fescue markedly prefers sun, but it will also tolerate light shade. To keep it looking its best, just water it occasionally.

BLUE FESCUE (*Festuca ovina glauca*)

Silver brocade artemisia

My 15 centimetre-high artemisia (*Artemisia stelleriana*) started when a dinner guest gave me a home-grown flower bouquet made up of stems in grey. Out of curiosity, when the flowers faded I tucked the stems in a glass of water on a sunny bathroom windowsill and forgot about them. Three weeks later, the stems developed roots. The plant went into the sunny, dry spot where just about everything had refused to grow because of concrete-reflected heat. The artemisia thrived. I clipped a few stems, rooted them in water, and placed them into more tough, small areas, such as inside an ancient lorry tyre that has been transformed into a raised bed. To use artemisia as groundcover, you must place each plant about 25 centimetres apart. Expect artemisia to reach about 38 centimetres wide. This evergreen perennial has silvery-grey leaves about 5 to 10 centimetres long.

Trailing gazania

A true sun lover, the daisy-like flowers of gazania (*Gazania rigens*) close up on shady days and at night. Tolerant of pretty much any soil, they need regular watering until they settle in. With hybridization, flower colours are seemingly limitless, including pink, cream, yellow, orange, rose, and scarlet.

Although most of the gazania flowers are about 3.5 centimetres wide, there are varieties with 7-centimetre flowers. (These larger versions are better for individual placement rather than groundcover – place them 30 centimetres apart, and you have a good-natured plush carpet.) Gazania tolerates temperatures to –1° C, but really prefers warm and dry surroundings. If you want to play around a bit, you could always try raising gazania from seed.

GAZANIA
(*Gazania* Chansonette Series)

Trailing ice plant

Soil- and drought-tolerant varieties of trailing ice plant (*Lampranthus*) are most often used in planting strips that get limited water. Trailing ice plant has tiny, succulent-type, fleshy leaves, and belongs where temperatures don't drop below –4° C. Because its growth can be rather rapid, an area surrounded by concrete suits it quite well, although it is easy enough to pull up if it becomes annoying. In spring, bright purple, orange, yellow, or fluorescent pink flowers make a vivid display. Trailing ice plant grows to 15 centimetres high and is useful for erosion control, seaside gardens, and on slopes. Some people even put it in hanging baskets that aren't easy to water.

More dry climate groundcovers:

- Alpine yarrow (*Achillea tomentosa*)
- Cape weed (*Arctotheca calendula*)
- Chamomile (*Chamaemelum nobile*)
- Creeping coprosma (*Coprosma*)
- Creeping thyme (*Thymus serpyllum*)
- Euonymus (*Euonymus*)
- Ground morning glory (*Convolvulus sabatius*)
- Herringbone cotoneaster (*Cotoneaster horizontalis*)
- Hottentot fig (*Carpobrotus edulis*)
- Lavender cotton (*Santolina chamaecyparissus*)
- Purple rock cress (*Aubrieta ✻ cultorum*)
- Red valerian (*Centranthus ruber*)
- Rockrose (*Cistus*)
- Snow-in-summer (*Cerastium tomentosum*)
- Stonecrop (*Sedum*)
- Sunrose (*Helianthemum*)
- Trailing African daisy (*Osteospermum fructicosum*)
- Trailing verbena (*Verbena*)
- Woolly lamb's ears (*Stachys byzantina*)

Beach covers

FORTUNATELY FOR THOSE AT THE SEASHORE, *a good number of ground-cover plants work nicely in this environment. Try some of the following plants if your garden gets beach winds and salt sprays:*

CAPE WEED (*Arctotheca calendula*)

Cape weed

I use cape weed (*Arctotheca calendula*) in a really hot, dry, side area where nothing else wants to tolerate the living conditions. The only problem is it keeps trying to escape into an area with soil less like hardened concrete. It's aggressive enough to require vigilance, but then, that's exactly what you may need. Cape weed can grow to about 20 centimetres tall, but will hug the ground in dry situations. It can tolerate temperatures as low as –4° C and is quite useful on neglected slopes and for erosion control. If you plant it in any form of shade, it will grow with great determination towards sunlight. Cape weed's flowers are daisy-like and yellow, opening during bright days.

Hottentot fig

Hottentot figs (*Carpobrotus edulis*) have thick leaves, and each stem can reach 2 metres long. In some hot, dry areas of America it is called "freeway ice plant". It helps stabilize beach sand, and tolerates coastal soil spray and some soil salt. The large flowers are yellow and pink. Hottentot figs tolerate temperatures as low as –4° C.

Hottentot fig does have its advantages, but I don't recommend it for ordinary garden use because it has a bulky appearance and spreads rapidly. Initially lying flat, it may mound gradually as long stems pile on top of one another.

HOTTENTOT FIG
(*Carpobrotus edulis*)

Sage-leaf rock rose

There are many types of rock rose, all originating on dry, stony soil in warm climates. They are grown in parks as well as gardens, and if watered occasionally and given full sun, they'll reward you with lovely spring flowers in white, light pink, or rose pink.

Although some types of rock rose reach 1.5 metres high, sage-leaf rock rose grows to only 60 centimetres in height but has a fast-paced spread up to 2 metres wide. It has white flowers with yellow centres, and is not particular as to soil, other than the necessity for good drainage. Sage-leaf rock rose (*Cistus salvifolius*) tolerates wind, salt spray, and desert conditions, and can withstand temperatures as low as −10° C.

St. John's wort

Full of vigour, this 30- to 45-centimetre-high ground-cover plant, also called rose of Sharon, is quite aggressive, spreading by underground stems. It's better for large areas, and has been used for erosion control and on slopes. Usually evergreen, dark green leaves show off bright yellow, 7-centimetre flowers from spring through summer. Bees like this plant. Not at all particular about its soil, and often able to compete with tree roots, St. John's wort (*Hypericum calycinum*) tolerates drought well once it gets started. Plant it in full sun to light shade. It looks best if cut back every other year, after all frost danger has disappeared.

ST. JOHN'S WORT (*Hypericum calycinum*)

There are several types of St. John's wort. If you want to take St. John's wort as a herbal supplement, do not try to grow your own. Some varieties contain phototoxins and should not be ingested. Herbal St. John's wort is best purchased at the chemists.

More beach covers:

- Bergenia (*Bergenia*)
- Blue fescue (*Festuca ovina glauca*)
- Cotoneaster (*Cotoneaster*)
- Creeping coprosma (*Coprosma*)
- Dwarf rosemary (*Rosmarinus officinalis*)
- Gold dust (*Aurinia saxatalis*)
- Heather (*Calluna vulgaris*)
- Lavender cotton (*Santolina chamaecyparissus*)
- Lilyturf (*Liriope*)
- Mondo grass (*Ophiopogon japonicus*)
- Shrub verbena (*Lantana*)
- Snow-in-summer (*Cerastium tomentosum*)
- Stonecrop (*Sedum*)
- Sun rose (*Helianthemum*)
- Trailing African daisy (*Osteospermum fructicosum*)

Cool in the shade

YOU MIGHT BE LOOKING *for something to soften a shady area. If so, there are a number of lovely ground-cover plants that aren't unhappy to get a little relief from the sun. I suggest:*

BUGLE (*Ajuga reptans*)

Bugle

There are several new varieties of this long-time semi-shade favourite. The older varieties have dark green leaves and grow about 10 centimetres high. In spring and early summer, they form a carpet of blue, as each leaf rosette has a 12-centimetre-high flower spike. Among the new hybrids are those with larger, variegated pink, green, and white leaves, bronze leaves, and pink flowers. Moderately spreading by creeping stems that root, bugle (*Ajuga reptans*) will form a thick enough blanket to eliminate all but the most persistent weeds. Fertilize it in early spring and water regularly. It will survive in temperatures above –15° C.

Creeping Jenny

Also known as creeping Charlie and moneywort, this is truly a hardy, takeover plant. Flat and fast, it is sometimes called a weed. But if you have tough soil to cover, where shade and almost soggy soil forbid most else, this is a delightfully pretty perennial plant with bright green, rounded leaves and inconspicuous, bright yellow flowers in summer. I quite like it, and sunlight often helps keep this shade-lover in place. Creeping Jenny (*Lysimachia nummularia*) tolerates temperatures as low as –15° C. There is a gold-leafed variety sometimes offered, but be aware that it needs coddling.

Sweet woodruff

Give this delicate-looking, medium green, aromatic plant shade, average soil, and ample moisture, and it will thrive, spreading by rhizomes, or horizontal underground stems. It is easy to divide; space new plants about 30 centimetres apart. It tolerates temperatures as low as –15° C. While there is no fragrance when fresh, dried sweet woodruff (*Galium odoratum*) smells like newly mown hay or, some say, vanilla. In days gone by, sweet woodruff was used to make sachets for linen cupboards.

In spring, tiny, white flower clusters appear on sweet woodruff. If you want to harvest this herb, do so just before it flowers.

Wild ginger

Usually found in a friend's garden, wild ginger (*Asarum europaeum*) makes a thorough, dark green, 10-centimetre-high blanket if properly sited. Easy to get started, it tends to persist, so plant it where you want it. Apart from shade and regular watering, it is not demanding at all. Inconspicuously held under the leaves, wild ginger has minute, reddish-brown flowers.

More groundcovers for shade:

- Baby's tears (*Soleirolia soleirolii*)
- Bellflower (*Campanula*)
- Bergenia (*Bergenia*)
- Bluets (*Hedyotis*)
- Bridal wreath (*Francoa*)
- Dwarf African blue lily (*Agapanthus*)
- Greek yarrow (*Achillea ageratifolia*)
- Ground ivy (*Glechoma hederacea*)
- Japanese spurge (*Pachysandra terminalis*)
- Lilyturf (*Liriope*)
- Mint (*Mentha*)
- Mock strawberry (*Duchesnea indica*)
- Mondo grass (*Ophiopogon japonicus*)
- Periwinkle (*Vinca*)
- Plantain lily (*Hosta*)
- Strawberry begonia (*Saxifraga stolonifera*)
- Sweet box (*Sarcococca*)
- Wandering Jew (*Tradescantia zebrina*)
- Wintergreen (*Gaultheria procumbens*)

A simple summary

✓ Groundcover comprises low-growing plants that form a moderate to dense soil cover.

✓ Regardless of the soil conditions that exist where you live, there's a ground-cover plant to suit your situation.

✓ Several ground-cover plants grow extremely fast once they get started. Make sure you know the speed at which the plant you select grows, and plan your planting accordingly.

✓ Groundcover is very valuable in coordinating a landscape plan, moving the eye easily from one site to another.

✓ Some ground-cover plants grow slowly, so that weeds emerge, but they will eventually form a mat. Some do not ever grow thickly enough to shut out weeds.

Chapter 17

Luscious Lawns

A ROLLING GREEN LAWN is what a garden is all about. It's a resting place, a status symbol, sometimes even an obsession. You should know something about your planting area, and your willingness to spend time maintaining it, before you rush out to buy sacks of grass seed.

In this chapter...

✓ Getting grass off the ground

✓ Fine grasses

✓ Utility grasses

✓ Starting from seed

✓ Maintaining a lovely lawn

✓ Common lawn problems

Getting grass off the ground

ASK YOURSELF THE FOLLOWING QUESTIONS:

1. Will you, the family, the neighbours, or assorted tradespeople be walking across this area? Some grasses like a lot of foot traffic, some just tolerate it, and others are squashed beyond redemption.

2. Being completely honest and looking at your track record for this type of thing, how much time and energy are you truly going to devote to the perfect lawn? (There's a house near me that has been sold several times. Each time, the new home-owner rips out the old scraggly lawn and spends a lot of money getting it reseeded or laying down turf strips. A year later, suffering from advanced neglect, the new lawn looks like the old lawn. This isn't to say you shouldn't put in a lawn, if you like lawns. But some types of lawn grass are more good-natured than others.)

INTERNET

www.turfgrasssod.org/ lawninstitute/guide. html

Take a look at the Lawn Institute Homeowner's Resource Guide to a Beautiful Lawn, to learn about grass types, seed selection, and planting and maintainance.

3. How much water is available? Some areas have occasional droughts when water use is strictly limited. Does this happen in your area? What about your usual water bill? Is your water on a meter? Lawns can be heavy-duty water users.

4. Is your site in full sun? Partial shade? Some grasses are particular. You will soon realize this if you plant the wrong one.

5. Is the grassed area in your garden completely free from bumps and dips? If not, then your mower will have great difficulty in giving a smooth finish – the bumps will be scalped and the dips will never get a proper cut. What sort of mower do you have?

■ **Choose your grass** *with care. High-quality fine grass (top) needs good growing conditions, regular maintenance, and little use. Coarse grass (bottom) is less fussy and much more hardwearing.*

Utility lawns

Utility lawns are largely mixtures of perennial ryegrass and broad-leaved turf grasses. If you want to be able to use your lawn for outdoor living, and particularly if you have a family, utility-grade grasses are probably best because they're far more hardwearing. A utility lawn also requires less maintenance than a fine lawn, and is better able to withstand a little neglect without serious deterioration.

A utility lawn will stand up to the traffic of all aspects of daily life without showing signs of wear and tear: you'll be able to walk on it, play games on it, let the kids loose on it, and it will still spring back into shape.

Broad-leaved grasses grow quite quickly so you'll need to cut them regularly. Don't be tempted to lower the mower blades to remove more grass in one session. If you do, you risk scalping the lawn, which will kill the grass completely and leave patches of bare soil that will quickly become colonized with unwanted weeds.

Luxury lawns

Think of a lovely, smooth bowling green with its velvety, close pile. This is what a well-maintained luxury lawn looks like. The turf is composed of fine-leaved and compact grasses – called bents and fescues.

A luxury lawn is one to behold and admire, not to be walked on too often. It needs lots of care and attention to look its best and, because the fine blades of grass are vulnerable to drought, it'll need regular watering, especially in hot, dry weather.

This type of lawn is primarily ornamental, and requires intensive maintenance to keep it in pristine condition. It won't withstand heavy wear, so if you have children or animals playing in the garden, this is not the lawn for you. If you have a large garden, you might consider having a small, low-cut, high-quality lawn near the house, where its fine appearance can be enjoyed, and creating a path or steps to a utility lawn a bit further away.

Growing grass successfully

Grass needs good light and sunshine to flourish. If parts of your lawn are under the canopy of large trees, it's worth considering choosing a grass seed mix that's specially formulated for life in the shade. These generally contain less perennial ryegrass, and more creeping fescues. Any reputable garden centre will be able to supply you with a suitable product.

313

Fine grasses

*FINE-LEAVED GRASS MIXES are more expensive than utility grasses.
The difference in price is not so noticeable if you're buying seed, but if you're
looking to lay fine-leaved grass turves, cost may well be an issue. When
considering a luxury lawn, bear in mind that the site will need to be thoroughly
prepared and levelled or else you'll end up with unsightly lumps and bumps
that will spoil the overall effect.*

Browntop

The most common of the bent grasses, browntop (*Agrostis tenuis*) is a basic ingredient
of luxury seed grass mixes. It's a tufted grass with short rhizomes that's slow to
establish, but with regular mowing it forms a neat, dense turf that blends well with
other varieties of lawn grasses. It grows well in all soils, and is especially suited to dry
sandy soils.

Creeping bent

Creeping bent (*Agrostis stolonifera*) is normally used in seed mixes specially
recommended for chalky soils. It's a tufted grass that spreads quickly. With regular
mowing, it forms a dense turf, but as it is shallow-rooted, its resistance to drought
and heavy traffic is rather poor.

Chewing's fescue

Another basic ingredient of luxury lawn seed mixtures, Chewing's fescue (*Festuca rubra
communata*) blends well with other grasses. It's a densely tufted grass and is quicker to
establish than browntop (its usual partner in high-quality seed mixes). It does tolerate
close mowing, but the tips tend to discolour after cutting. This variety will grow well in
all soils, except heavy clay.

Creeping red fescue

Widely used in luxury lawns and for sports areas such as bowling greens, croquet
lawns, and golf putting greens, creeping red fescue (*Festuca rubra* var. *rubra*) is a rather
lax grower, so must be mixed with other varieties for dense and compact turf. It will
grow in all soils, except heavy clays.

Utility grasses

THE GRASS SEED SOLD IN GARDEN CENTRES is usually available with or without ryegrass. Ryegrass is coarse-textured but very resilient and fast-growing, so it's worth choosing if you require a turf that's really tough and have a site that receives plenty of sun.

Perennial ryegrass

Extremely hardwearing, tolerant of heavy soils, and quick to establish, perennial ryegrass (*Lolium perenne*) produces tufted grass, with smooth green or dark green blades. It likes lots of sun but may adapt to very light shade.

Smooth-stalked meadow grass

Smooth-stalked meadow grass (*Poa pratensis*) is especially good where the soil is sandy and shaded. It's rather slow to establish, but once it gets going, it'll spread rapidly – by seed rather than underground stems. It's resilient and resistant to drought but doesn't like regular, close mowing.

Annual meadow grass

Annual meadow grass (*Poa annua*) flourishes even in difficult situations, such as in the shade under trees. It needs plenty of water during hot weather because it can turn yellow in dry conditions and, at worst, may die.

ALTERNATIVES TO GRASS

While grass is the obvious choice for most gardeners, spreading plants, such as chamomile or thyme, are an attractive option for smaller areas.

- **Chamomile (*Anthemis nobilis*)**: this low-growing, creeping plant has ferny leaves and white, daisy-like flowers. It stands up well to being trodden on, and emits a pleasant scent when crushed underfoot.

- **Thyme (*Thymus serpyllum*)**: will grow in any soil and is tolerant of dry conditions. By choosing your variety carefully, you'll get white, pink, red, or lilac flowers.

Starting from seed

THIS WILL REQUIRE *some heavy work, and you may end up sharing some seeds with the birds. Just make sure you get enough to go around.*

Tilling the soil

If you are planting from seed, you begin by either tilling the area with a rotovator (you can rent them) or digging out the area where you'll be planting to a 15-centimetre depth. Remove all rocks, roots, and miscellaneous items.

PREPARING THE SOIL

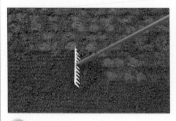

1 Rake the soil

After firming the tilled soil by treading evenly over the whole area, rake it very finely, removing any debris or weeds.

2 Check the level

To ensure you get a lovely flat lawn, check that the area is level after firming down the soil. Measure at regular intervals with a spirit level.

After making sure your soil level is even throughout, relaxation then ends, because now weed seeds, deprived of competition and given more sunshine, will begin sprouting. Let them have their way for about 3 weeks, and then *rotovate* or chop them out. Now you have to level the ground again. Buy a truckful of good topsoil, and rake this about 2 to 3 centimetres deep into the entire area. Let the topsoil fill in any low-lying areas. Smooth everything out again. You may want to rent a plastic or metal lawn roller for this purpose.

> **DEFINITION**
>
> When you **rotovate**, you dig. Also called power cultivators, rotovators have sharp rotating tines. They are also used to aerate, de-thatch, or make planting rows.

Fertilize obediently

Now, using a hand-held or other spreader, distribute a general granular fertilizer over the area. You'll get a suitable one at your local garden centre. Make sure you obey all instructions on the fertilizer container. Then, once again, add a topsoil layer, up to 15 centimetres deep, and level this out.

SOW YOUR SEEDS

1 Make a grid

For large areas, it's better to mark out a grid system before sowing, so you can be sure you spread the seeds evenly. Use stakes to divide up the site into many equal squares. Weigh out each portion of seed, scattering half of it up and down and the other half side to side.

2 Rake over the soil

Once you have finished sowing, lightly rake over the surface of the soil. Work across the whole area carefully to cover the seeds. In the following days and weeks, water the site regularly. Be sure not to walk on the area for at least 2 months.

Aftercare

You'll need to water at least twice a day using the fine mist nozzle on your garden hose. Use a sprinkler only after the seeds have germinated. Germination takes from 1 to 3 weeks, depending on the grass species. Do not let the young grass dry out – you will not be able to resuscitate it. Do not walk on it for about 2 months. Mow only after the grass is about 7 centimetres high. Fertilize again in the autumn using an appropriate autumn lawncare product.

Plugs, sprigs, or turf?

In addition to sowing grass seed, you can also establish a lawn using *plugs*, *sprigs*, or *turf*. Plugs and sprigs are generally used where the weather tends to be warm and dry, making it difficult to establish a traditional lawn. The best aspect of using turves, rather than seed, is that the lawn looks attractive straight away. You can lay turf at any time (although it's advisable to avoid frosty or very hot, dry conditions).

When using plugs or sprigs, you must prepare the area by removing any existing plants and, of course, rocks and larger detritus. When your new lawn area is ready, dig holes about 30 centimetres apart. Your plugs or sprigs, kept moist and covered until planting time, will be placed individually in the pre-dug holes. Each plug is from 5 to 10 square centimetres, so the pre-dug holes must be large enough to accommodate them easily. Water your new lawn regularly, not letting the soil dry out. Keep weeds at bay by weeding between the plants.

■ **Space the plugs** *evenly over the prepared area, planting them 15 to 30 centimetres apart. When the plugs are all planted, apply a top-dressing of soil and make sure they are kept well watered.*

Trivia...
In the Middle Ages, the word laund *was used for a woodland glade, or a place without trees. Eventually, the word "lawn" was derived from it.*

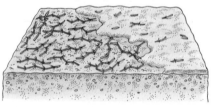

■ **Distribute the sprigs** *over the surface of the soil and then cover them with a top-dressing of fine soil. Water well.*

■ **When buying turves,** *make sure all pieces look healthy and are of good quality, and that none is showing any bare or brown patches.*

SIMPLE TURFING

1 Make a start

Begin by laying the first row of turves against a straight edge, such as a path or board, so that you can use it as a guide. Each piece should lie flat and be positioned so that it is flush against the next one.

2 Kneel on a board

Once you've finished the first row, place a board on top of it and kneel on the board. Lay the second row of turves, staggering the joins against those of the previous row. Keep going until you have covered the entire area.

3 Firm the turves down

With the back of a rake, firm down the turf to get rid of any air pockets and to create good contact between the grass roots and the soil. Or, you could use a light roller to do the job.

4 Water thoroughly

Give the newly planted lawn a good drink of water and keep watering it daily for at least 2 weeks. The roots in the turf will eventually take hold in the soil below.

Maintaining a lovely lawn

THERE'S NOTHING DIFFICULT *about keeping your lawn looking beautiful. It does take some time and some dedication, but it doesn't take an advanced degree in horticulture. Just follow these simple steps.*

Mowing made meaningful

If mowing the lawn were a complex task, you wouldn't hire a youth to do it. But there is a bit to know about mowing. For example, if your mower blades aren't sharp enough, they'll tear the grass instead of cutting it. So get them sharpened if you haven't done so in a while.

Begin mowing in the spring, as soon as the grass starts growing. Don't let grass grow too tall because it may then be traumatized by the cutting and slow down future growth. Some gardeners remove the grass clippings mechanically or with a rake after each mowing job. Others prefer to leave a light layer of grass clippings to act as a moisture-protective barrier. This might be a good idea if you live in a particularly dry area. Continue mowing until the autumn or when growth ceases. Over long grass continuing into winter is an open invitation to lawn disease.

Do not be tempted to let thatch pile up. If it gets to be a thick layer, rake it off and put it into the compost pile or the dustbin. If this layer gets more than a centimetre thick, it can keep water and fertilizer from penetrating into the lawn.

If you have the time to go over the lawn with a heavy-duty garden rake every few weeks, you can easily deter thatch build-up. Otherwise, remove it with a special de-thatching rake sold at most garden centres, or hire a

power de-thatcher. De-thatching is best accomplished in early spring to remove winter debris and to lift weed stems for efficient cutting.

DE-THATCHING RAKE

■ **Pull the rake** *vigorously when de-thatching, pushing the tines well down into the surface to aerate the lawn and get rid of any build-up.*

Fertilizing facts

Lawns are big nitrogen users and must be fed regularly. Use a lawn fertilizer that has a nitrogen content of about 20 per cent. Fertilize during the season when lawns are most capable of absorbing the nutrients.

That means feed in the spring and early summer, but stop feeding in August, otherwise the grass will be too "soft" to survive winter.

An energizing meal in March and April is extremely important, because a rapidly growing lawn quickly uses up soil nutrients. Snow thaws and spring rain will dissolve the fertilizer and help transport it downwards through the soil. Apply fertilizer evenly, preferably on a calm day. Otherwise there will be dark green sections you have fertilized, and yellowing areas that have been deprived. A broadcast spreader is most helpful in getting even coverage.

Be water-wise

If possible, water the lawn early in the morning on days when there is no wind. Water only when the lawn is dry. Do not over-water. If you are seeing runoff, the ground may be soaked. One of the more common over-watering problems is caused by not adjusting a sprinkler system for cooler weather or rain. We have all seen sprinklers going full spurt ahead when it's been raining all day. Drowned roots do not produce healthy lawns. It is also possible that the water pressure or amount is excessive, with more water being applied than the soil can absorb at one time, so it runs off. Underneath the top layer, the soil may be dry.

Before you decide that you're over-watering, check out whether the water is actually sinking in. If it's not, you'll need to try a more moderate approach to watering.

Under-watering can be a problem too. Grass roots will only survive with some moisture. If there isn't enough, the grass may be unable to withstand drought. Check your sprinkler system as the seasons change. The heat of summer is simply going to require more water for your lawn. Check how deeply the water has been absorbed with a spade, digging to about 15 centimetres. The soil should be damp. Check several spots, as absorption on slopes or in hollows will differ. If you don't like digging, buy a lawn-water measuring gadget.

■ **Grass roots** *soon show the signs of a lack of water. If roots remain too close to the surface (top), it means they're just not getting enough moisture down in the soil where they need it. To ensure healthy roots (bottom) make sure that water is getting to a depth of at least 10 to 15 centimetres.*

Weeding wisely

Patience is most definitely a virtue when it comes to picking out weeds from pretty green lawns. Among the many perennial and annual weeds you may encounter are bindweed, black medic, clover, celandine, dandelion, and plantain. The most effective weed deterrent is a healthy, dense lawn that is well fertilized, watered, and has plenty of air circulation and the sunshine it needs. Always mow to the recommended height. If you mow too short, low-growing weeds have more space to thrive. Pull weeds out consistently so as not to let them get a foothold and just use herbicides on the areas where pulling just won't do the job. There are some organic weed sprays on the market, but you may have to look in specialist catalogues. Chapter 21 covers the use of herbicides in detail.

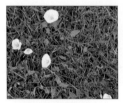

BINDWEED

CLOVER

PLANTAIN

Common lawn problems

THERE ARE A THOUSAND REASONS *why your lawn could drive you crazy – or to the poorhouse. I'll address the most common ones here.*

Too much fertilizer

Fertilizer or other chemical overdoses cause irregular yellowing areas with a dark green border. Water well, and if your grass doesn't recover, remove it and replant with new grass in the afflicted spot.

Wandering Weimaraners

It's a fact of life that passing dogs peeing on your grass won't do much to improve its appearance. When canines wander onto your lawn, you'll probably notice characteristic browning areas. Female dogs squat when they urinate, so they are the likely suspects if you see canine-caused round lawn circles. Male dogs lift a leg, so shrubs at favourite corners can turn brown or yellow. Grass by these areas will also be affected.

What's in animal urine that's so disturbing? Urine contains nitrogen, and the fertilizer you buy also contains nitrogen. An overdose of either will cause lawn damage or death.

What to do? Water well. Try to keep dogs off your lawn (which may be impossible). You can try fencing off your lawn, or planting a border of something less welcoming (if you can figure out what plant life is unattractive to your neighbour's dog). Some grass types, such as fescue and perennial ryegrass, are more resistant to urine burns than others. Finer-leaved grasses are less tolerant.

Diseases and pests

Most lawn diseases are caused by fungi, and some of them, if left untreated, can be devastating. For more information on how to cope with diseases and insect pests, see Chapter 23. But if you want a quick overview, common lawn diseases include algae, dollar spot, fusarium patch (or snow mould), lichen, red thread (or Corticium disease), toadstools, and fairy rings. Pests of note are ants, birds (in their seach for food), chafer grubs, cutworms, earthworms, leatherjackets, mining bees, and moles.

A simple summary

✓ Be honest with yourself about how much time you actually have to spend on lawn care, and how willing you are to use that time for lawn work.

✓ Be aware of any water limitations in your area, current or pending.

✓ Make sure you choose the grass variety that is most suited to your area and to your site.

✓ You can plant grass with seeds, turves, sprigs, or plugs.

✓ Different grasses have different needs. Check out the strengths and weaknesses of the grasses you like so that you select the correct variety.

✓ Do not over-water, and check to make certain water is soaking down into the soil rather than running off.

✓ Fertilize your lawn regularly and in the recommended seasons. Lawns need lots of nutrients to be healthy.

Chapter 18

A Bounty of Balcony and Patio Plants

SETTING UP YOUR PLANTS in a large container on a balcony or patio can be as challenging as moving the furniture, yet again, in your living room. You may like everything orderly, so your pots are in a precise arrangement and all your plants are almost equal height. Then again, you may like the natural look where everything is helter-skelter.

In this chapter...

✔ Container choices

✔ Re-potting like a pro

✔ Potting particulars

✔ Picking plants for the patio

✔ Cacti and other succulents

✔ Seasonal sensations

✔ Basking in baskets

325

Container choices

YOU HAVE A MOST marvellous choice of containers for balcony and patio plants. You can be strictly economical, using pretty cups with broken handles for small plants, old pots for medium-size greenery, and plastic dustbins for the larger, tree-like versions. Just remember that most objects that did not start out as plant pots don't have drainage holes, so you must not over-water.

■ **Containers in groups** *provide maximum impact. Mix flower colours as well as leaf textures for a truly eye-catching display.*

Another great way to collect containers is to do your shopping at car boot sales. You'll find even the most expensive planter pots for just a few pence when people have grown tired of them or need to get rid of them because of a house move. Sometimes you even get plants in the pots for free. Reviving them might be a challenge, but a fun one.

Then, of course, there's the vast array at your nearby nursery or garden centre. What do you have to know about containers to get the best results?

■ **You'll find containers** *in just about every size, shape, and colour. It's important that your container is the right size for the chosen plant and has good drainage.*

glazed earthenware

unglazed ceramic

wooden Versailles planter

painted Versailles planter

terracotta trough

terracotta urn containing New Zealand flax (Phormium tenax)

moulded concrete urn

period-style reconstituted stone urn

Clay pots

Clay pots are everywhere. I think that they have a nice natural look, but you should know that they allow rapid water evaporation in hot weather. Cacti are quite happy in clay pots provided they have drainage holes.

Wood containers

Made of Scandinavian redwood, oak, or cedar (all long-lasting woods), wooden containers seem to become part of the plant because they are so well suited to each other. They may be square or round, small or huge. If you are going to plant a dwarf tree on your patio, consider using a wooden half-barrel as the container. At one time these were relatively cheap ... now they have become trendy and so the prices have risen. But they have a charming rustic appearance and, if properly constructed, will last a long time.

Like any large container, they are very heavy when filled. So unless you are quite certain you'll remain where you are currently living for a long time, and during that time you will never have to move that 140-kilo-plus container, consider placing it on a low wheeled platform.

There are many other types of wooden containers. Make certain they don't leak water as fast as you pour it in. Test them first, and if there seems to be a problem, line them with a sheet of heavy-duty plastic.

■ **Dwarf trees** *and trimmed shrubs, like this conical box (Buxus), look great in wooden containers.*

Plastic containers

Lightweight and not overly charming, plastic containers have the advantage of being inexpensive and usually transportable without much stress. You can get small to large pots in identical fuchsia, blue, or black colour schemes, which is nice. These pots almost always have drainage holes, and are accompanied by a little saucer that has a tendency to fall off. I usually put a larger saucer underneath to be on the safe side.

Charity shops often have a section of used kitchenware, where everything is sold for a few pence. These can be good places to find old saucers to put under plants.

Ceramic pots

Purchased for their design, ceramic pots are usually quite functional as well as attractive. Most have a drainage hole, and if they don't come with a sensible water-holding saucer, that's easy enough to remedy. The only disadvantage with ceramic pots is that they break. If you have a cat or a dog, or a boisterous youngster who might push over the pot or its stand, you may have a re-potting emergency.

Hanging pots

Both lightweight ceramic and plastic are preferable for hanging pots, because lightweight containers are less likely to fall, and if they do, they're less likely to hurt someone.

Any hanging plant container should be very firmly fixed to the overhead support, and should never be low enough to be a head bumper.

On the same safety-first note, no container filled with soil should be placed on any windowsill without being very strongly attached. On a balcony, plants are better on a solid stand away from the railing. If you insist on putting them on a wide balcony railing, they must be anchored very, very securely. A pot filled with soil can fall if given an accidental push, or in rough, windy weather. It can kill or seriously injure a passer-by.

■ **Hanging pots** *provide greenery for even the smallest patio or balcony.*

Potting tips

Unless your container is brand new, wash it out well with hot water, using a scrubbing brush, before putting in a new plant. You don't want to inherit pests or diseases from the pot's prior occupant. If the pot doesn't have a drainage hole, put in a 2.5-centimetre layer of coarse sand mixed with gardening charcoal. Despite your best efforts to avoid over-watering, water may well pool at the bottom of the container. This mixture will do a nice job of preventing the water from developing an unpleasant odour.

If your pot has a drainage hole, put a saucer underneath with a 2.5-centimetre lip at the edges. Water-holding saucers shouldn't be too shallow; they are meant to hold excess moisture, not let it flow over the rim.

Re-potting like a pro

MOVING A NEW PLANT *from its garden centre plastic container to your pretty pot can be accomplished without traumatizing the plant. Why is this important? Traumatized plants take a longer time to get going, and in a few cases don't get going at all. Be sure the plant's new container is several centimetres wider than the one you bought it in, so the roots have room to grow.*

Transplanting from six-packs

If your plants come in little black six-packs, water them lightly while they're in their original container. Doing so holds the soil together a bit, so it doesn't fall off the little plant as you remove it. After dampening, gently pinch the bottom of each cell to extract the plant. Always support the rootball with one hand and don't dangle the little plant by its delicate leaves.

Don't take all the plants out of the container at once and leave them lying around to bake in the sun as you plant. Remove each plant individually after you have prepared its new space and are ready to gently pop it in.

Transplanting from containers

Today, most nurseries put their plants in plastic containers. Once you get the plant home, wet the container soil to help keep the root ball together. After dampening, gently remove the plant. If it doesn't come away easily from the container and seems stuck, it may have overgrown roots. If the roots are overgrown, you will need to either loosen them gently so you can remove the plant, or carefully cut away the plastic pots without damaging the plant's roots.

The best way to cut roots is to cut those at the side of the plant. Cut from top to bottom, rather than chopping off the bottom roots. Only cut off what you have to, then spread the roots out carefully in your selected container. Of course, you'll try to avoid purchasing *pot-bound* plants, but it does happen. Some plants don't like having their roots disturbed, so give them a little time to adjust to their new container, taking extra care when following their particular watering and feeding needs.

> **DEFINITION**
>
> *Overgrown roots may hold tenaciously onto the pot's drainage hole, or even grow out of it and circle the pot. In gardener's language, this is a* **pot-bound**, *or* *root-bound, plant.*

RE-POTTING A CONTAINER PLANT

1 Soak the rootball

An hour or so before re-potting, and keeping the plant in its original pot, soak it in water. This reduces the impact of the move and helps to establish the roots in the new soil mix.

2 Loosen the roots

Encourage the roots to grow into the new soil mix by gently teasing out congested roots with your hands. Trim off damaged or dead roots with a sharp knife.

3 Add compost

Add some potting compost, firm lightly, and position the plant, leaving room for watering. Fill around it with more soil, firming as you go.

After planting

Water the new resident well. It is better to water directly onto the soil or into the saucer beneath the container. Watering from above can leave unattractive leaf spots caused by the water drying out on the leaves. More importantly, it can invite fungal disease. To help minimize transplant trauma, keep the plant in a shady spot for the first day or two to let it get used to its new container before it has to acclimatize to its outdoor site.

■ **Trim off any dead leaves** *and straggly or damaged stems, as this will help to encourage new growth. Give the plant a good start with some fertilizer, and water well.*

Potting particulars

IT IS ALWAYS BEST to buy commercial potting compost for any type of potted plant, including houseplants. Although it is often easier to take shortcuts and use your garden soil, this may contain almost invisible insect eggs, or the remnants of various diseases. Moreover, with clay soils it tends to form an almost impenetrable clump in the pot once it settles in.

Just like fish in an aquarium, plants in pots don't have a place to go if they don't like where they are. Potting compost may cost somewhat more than the home-dug variety, but it's less expensive than having to buy a new plant, and more cheering than watching your carefully nurtured seedlings disappear because of some inherited bug.

Compost components

Good generic potting compost may be a combination of any or all of the following:

- Peat
- Sawdust
- Leaf mould
- Bark chippings

- Sand
- *Vermiculite*
- *Perlite*

You also may want to look for compost that contains water retention crystals. These are a relatively recent invention, designed to let the user be less compulsive about watering.

Water retention crystals are tiny, whitish granules that swell up to many times their original size when water is added to them. Mixed with soil on a specific ratio, depending on the product, they very slowly release their moisture, enabling you to avoid watering for up to 2 weeks.

Each product is different, and you must be careful that you don't end up with soggy soil, the bane of so many potted plants. Check the plant's needs first, but I would urge you to test-drive an unplanted pot of compost using these crystals before using it with a favourite new plant.

> **DEFINITION**
>
> **Vermiculite** *is created from the mineral mica. The mica is heated, puffed up, and transformed into tiny, very lightweight chips that help retain soil, air, and water. It has no nutritional value for your plants.*
>
> **Perlite** *is created from volcanic rock, and is slightly heavier than vermiculite. It is used to loosen heavy soil, and help oxygen and water reach plant roots.*

Picking plants for the patio

WITH SO MANY CHOICES, you may be wondering where to begin. I'll help simplify things by offering some beautiful plants that don't grow too large for containers and will keep your patio looking good throughout the year.

■ **Group pots** *to hide ugly features or to brighten up a boring part of your garden. Try mixing permanent plants with seasonal ones that you can add to keep the display looking fresh.*

Cacti and other succulents

ALL CACTI ARE SUCCULENTS but not all succulents are cacti. Cacti are just part of the large selection offered in this fleshy-stem plant group. The Latin word succulentus means "juicy sap", and generally, cacti don't need a lot of water. Other succulents, including the sedums, need occasional water otherwise they begin to look like deflated balloons.

Can you tell a cactus when you see one? Cacti have little cushions, called areoles, dotting their shapes, and their flowers, new growth, and spines arise from these.

■ **Bold shapes and outlines** *are typical of cacti and succulents. Display them to even greater effect by choosing pots that are just as bold and dramatic as the plants.*

Cacti care

Many people buy cacti and other succulents in the winter, when they just need to buy a plant but are discouraged by cold weather. These plants are happy outdoors in sun, and you can over-winter them indoors – not too close to a very sunny window, but close enough. The greatest thing about succulents is that many grow so slowly that you can have an entire and completely varied collection in a limited area. If you think they are dull, just wait until they flower. It's like an unexpected gift.

Perhaps the second greatest thing about succulents is the minimal amount of care they require. Simply place them in compost mixed with some sand, or better yet, buy a bag of cactus compost. There's no need to fertilize. With most types of succulents, it's best to let the soil dry out briefly before you water again. Those that do like a slightly moist soil are the tropical, so-called "forest" cacti. Forest cacti include the striking Christmas cactus (*Schlumbergera*) with its deep pink, red, orange, or white flowers, Easter cactus (*Rhipsalidopsis gaertneri*), and Orchid cacti (*Epiphyllum*). But, whether they are forest or desert plants, if you over-water, it's goodbye, so all pots containing cacti must have a drainage hole.

CHRISTMAS CACTUS
(*Schlumbergera*)

It's highly advised, when touching or handling any form of succulent that has tiny prickles, or what even resembles a spine, to wear heavy-duty gardening gloves. If you forget this once, you will probably not forget it again.

Okay. Now that you know how to handle them, let's look at some pretty, popular succulents.

Delightful donkey's tail

Donkey's tail (*Sedum morganianum*) is an extremely popular hanging plant for placement in partial shade, but it's grown primarily where summers are hot and dry. The multiple long, trailing stems may grow to 1 metre, with light green, plump, small leaves overlapping one another. With age and the proper site, red or pink flowers may appear. If you don't have the climate to put this outdoors, try it indoors near a sunny window. Don't forget to water once in a while.

Easy echinopsis

The spines on an echinopsis (*Echinopsis*) look and are formidable, but that's what a cactus is all about: self-protection. Members of this genus are adaptable to temperatures from 5 to 26° C and actually enjoy some water during the hottest summer months. But let the pot soil dry out completely before you water again and do not water at all in the winter. Expect flowers, often night-blooming, in lemon yellow, peach-pink, white, pink, or dark orange in late spring or early summer. Many species will produce offsets – new plants growing off the parent. You can leave them on, or remove them and start a new potted cactus. Again, gloves, gloves, gloves.

Elusive living stones

Living stones (*Lithops*) really do look like pebbles. These brown, grey, or pale green, often mottled succulents are charming in their own container, and are even more so when bright yellow flowers emerge from what look like clefts in the pebbles. Some people grow nothing but living stones, since there are more than 40 species to choose from. They like lots of sun, and will put up with temperatures up to 49° C. Like most succulents, they aren't fond of very cold weather, but don't let that deter you. Bring the pot indoors in winter, where a house heated from 5 to 15° C suits them fine. Do keep them away from the kitchen sink or the bathroom, as these plants like the air to be pretty dry.

LIVING STONES (*Lithops*)

OLD MAN CACTUS
(*Cephalocereus senilis*)

Old man cactus

Bearing a resemblance to Rip Van Winkle, this columnar cactus can reach 12 metres high in a 200-year period, as it does in its native Mexico. Indoors, it will stay contentedly at 30 centimetres, maybe growing a couple of centimetres a year. It looks best in a vertical pot. Old man cactus (*Cephalocereus senilis*) won't flower, but it's still quite a conversation piece.

INTERNET

www.tucsoncactus.org/
htm/links.html

Visit this site for a listing of national and international cactus and succulent societies that offer growing advice, as well as a selection of related websites.

Seasonal sensations

ALMOST ANY SMALL TO MEDIUM-SIZE annual plant, and many perennials, can be grown in an appropriate-size container. The four detailed below are among the most colourful and easiest to grow, but others may be even better where you live. Some of my first choices follow:

- Alyssum (*Alyssum*)
- Busy Lizzie (*Impatiens*)
- China aster (*Callistephus*)
- Cockscomb (*Celosia*)
- Cornflower (*Centaurea cyanus*)
- Cosmos (*Cosmos*)
- Dusty miller (*Senecio cineraria*)
- Floss flower (*Ageratum*)
- Flowering tobacco (*Nicotiana*)

- Lobelia (*Lobelia*)
- Pansy (*Viola*)
- Petunia (*Petunia*)
- Phlox (*Phlox*)
- Polyanthus (*Primula malacoides*)
- Pot marigold (*Calendula*)
- Snapdragon (*Antirrhinum*)
- Sweet William (*Dianthus barbatus*)
- Zinnia (*Zinnia*)

Countless chrysanthemums

Chrysanthemums are, without doubt, the number one garden plant for the enthusiast – a true hobby plant. There are innumerable varieties with a dazzling array of colours. You'll hear different names for their flowerhead forms, such as *anemone*, **pompom**, spray, charm, **spider**, and **spoon**, among others.

Those that flower before the end of September can be grown outdoors, but the later ones, which may bloom from October to December, need to be grown in a greenhouse. Some chrysanthemums are suitable for growing in pots as houseplants.

There are other daisy-like flowers that people often include in the chrysanthemum family. These include the ox-eye daisy (*Leucanthemum vulgare*), shasta daisy (*L. ¥ superbum*), costmary (*Tanacetum balsamita*), and feverfew (*T. parthenium*).

POMPOM CHRYSANTHEMUM

> **DEFINITION**
>
> *The flowers of chrysanthemums can be found in many shapes. The* **anemone** *form is a semi-double flower with a raised, pillow-like centre. The* **pompom** *form is fully rounded. The* **spider** *is a double flower with long, tubular, graceful florets. A* **spoon** *flower's florets expand slightly into a spoon shape at the end.*

335

The feverfew chrysanthemum is not much to look at, but it thrives in the garden corner where my dogs pee, so it is a wonderful plant indeed.

Caring for chrysanthemums is a piece of cake. Just give them a sunny spot, self-respecting soil, fairly regular water, and good drainage. Good drainage means 'mums like life a bit on the dry side. Fertilize your chrysanthemums occasionally.

Colourful coleus

These partial-shade-loving plants are grown for their absolutely brilliant leaves: reds, oranges, greens, yellows, scarlets, sometimes all together on one tidy, 30-centimetre plant.
Tropical natives, coleus (*Coleus blumei*) require rich, loose soil (potting compost is the best choice), plus a warm, protected growing site. Soil should be kept a little damp, and the plants should be fed fertilizer once a month. Clay pots absorb heat and lose water too quickly for coleus, so find a pretty alternative. If you don't treat them courteously and they get too much shade or too much sun, they will become straggly, lose their colour, and wither. Plant several together in a large pot for maximum impact from spring to early autumn. To get bushier coleus, pinch out the tops so the sides grow wider.

Coleus act as annuals in most areas, so expect to replant them the following year. They are relatively easy to grow from seed started in the late winter or spring. You can also *propagate*, or start new plants, by putting some stem cuttings in water at any time. They will form roots. If you've got a favourite coleus leaf colour scheme, keep some to grow indoors in a window where the light filters in.

■ **Coleus come in** *an infinite variety of colours, often with strikingly contrasting margins to the leaves.*

DEFINITION

With the exception of starting seeds, all plant **propagation** *is called vegetative propagation, where you use a part of the original plant as the basis for the new one. Propagation techniques include stem cutting, budding, dividing, and grafting.*

Miraculous marigolds

From the plethora of marigolds (*Tagetes*) that festoon balconies and patios from early spring until autumn, it seems just about everybody has at least one specimen. The most commonly seen are the annual French marigolds (*T. patula*), probably because of their compact size on sturdy, upright stems. Colours range from yellow to almost mahogany red, including the spectrum in between. Flowers are found in single and double varieties. Give marigolds full sun with regular water and they will bloom until the autumn, especially if you pluck off fading flowerheads.

Marigolds are reasonably easy to start from seed. Just make certain to use good potting compost and don't let it dry out while the seeds are trying to sprout. As a note, some people don't like the musty close-up aroma of some marigolds, but in organic gardening, French marigolds are considered great company for vegetables.

MARIGOLD
(*Tagetes erecta*)

The marigold's aroma reportedly masks the odour of vegetables, so pests just fly on by. Try marigolds around your patio tomatoes, making an even prettier picture while performing a scientific experiment.

Nasturtiums – naturally

Somebody recently told me they couldn't get nasturtiums (*Tropaeolum*) to grow. I was astounded. Nasturtiums are just about the easiest annual to grow, and once happy, will drop their large, brown, wrinkly seeds all about and give you nasturtiums all over the sunny place. Nasturtiums demand full sun. They are not fussy about soil, and like life slightly on the dry side after they get started. Never fertilize, or you'll get lots of nice, medium-green leaves and few flowers. There are low-growing varieties, from 15 to 25 centimetres, and climbers, reaching 2 metres high. Flowers are found in yellow, white, red, rose, orange, and mahogany, and some are bicoloured. If they don't start out that way, the next generations may provide their own colour. Because nasturtiums don't transplant well, sow in place – pot, windowbox, or ground – in early spring to get late-spring to autumn colour. Sometimes during the season aphids tend to appear, so it's time to remove the plant, saving the seeds if you want. You can just push them a couple of centimetres into the container soil and, come the warm weather, they'll give you new nasturtiums.

NASTURTIUM (*Tropaeolum speciosum*)

Basking in baskets

THERE'S SOMETHING *wonderfully carefree about hanging plants –*
they're like a little bit of bohemia right on your own balcony. I've narrowed this
list down to my basket bests:

Awesome asparagus fern

Don't let the words "asparagus" or "fern" throw you: this plant is neither. Very long
(1 to 2 metre) waterfall-style, draping stems have green, needle-like leaves. In winter,
small, bright red berries dot the stems; in summer, very fragrant, tiny, white flowers appear.

Plant asparagus fern (*Asparagus sprengeri*) in good potting compost in a reasonably large
container, as it has thick, fleshy roots that will crowd a smaller pot. Asparagus fern does
well in partial shade, but can deal with full sun in cool-summer areas. Fertilize in the
spring, and water regularly. If you live in a frost-free area, this perennial stays green and
fluffy all year long. A really cold spell will decimate the greenery, but it usually returns
come warmer weather if you water it.

Fuchsia forever

Fuchsias (*Fuchsia hybrida*) look great pruned as small trees,
grown as shrubs, or placed in a hanging basket to delight
the eye with ballerina blossoms. There are so many types
available, complete colour palettes with a great variety of
ruffled petals, that it's pick and choose at your leisure. A bit
fussy, especially in hanging baskets, they require rich,
organic soil, regular fertilization, and regular watering to
keep the soil slightly damp. Although not prima donnas,
fuchsias dislike the cold and they dislike hot, humid
weather too. They do like partial sun, fog, or other forms of
cool air moisture, and a wind-protected site. Give them
their wishes, and you will have a great display from early
spring until the frosts.

FUCHSIA (*Fuchsia hybrida*)

Excelling with ivy geranium

All of the geraniums are good patio and balcony plants. Some grow in a mounding form,
others are draping. Ivy geranium (*Pelargonium peltatum*), in spite of its name, isn't an
ivy mimic. It only grows to 1 metre long, and is very well behaved, producing white,
pink, red, lavender, and purple-pink flowers in spring and summer. In warmer climates,
you may see flowers intermittently throughout the year.

When purchasing ivy geraniums, don't go for the longest plant; select the one with the most stems coming from the base. This is the one that will give you a nice, plump, hanging plant.

It's best to purchase when this hardy plant is in flower – with all the different colours, you'll want to know ahead of time what you'll be getting. Care is the same for almost all geraniums: place in a mostly sunny spot and water regularly. They'll be happy in average soil.

More hanging plants for baskets:

- Busy Lizzie (*Impatiens balsamina*, New Guinea Group)
- Canterbury bell (*Campanula isophylla*)
- Donkey's tail (*Sedum morganianum*)
- Parrot's beak (*Lotus berthelotti*)
- Sapphire trailing lobelia (*Lobelia erinus*)
- Surfinia petunia (*Petunia x hybrida*)
- Tuberous begonia (*Begonia tuberhybrida*)

A simple summary

✓ All potted plants should be placed in commercial potting compost if at all possible. Soil from your garden may harbour unwanted pests and diseases.

✓ Many container types are available. Place your plant in a container that is 2 to 5 centimetres wider than the container you bought it in.

✓ Containers should have drainage holes. If they don't, add 2 to 3 centimetres of sand mixed with gardener's charcoal at the base.

✓ Balcony plants are safer standing back from the railing. If you do put a plant on a wide railing, anchor it firmly. This also goes for hanging plants. A plant dropping on someone could kill or injure them.

✓ The rims of the saucers around potted plants should be high enough to prevent water spillage.

✓ Potted plants are at your mercy. If you give too much or too little water, the plant has no recourse.

✓ Select the best patio and balcony plants for your growing environment and for your willingness to give proper care.

PART SIX

EASY-TO-GROW SUNFLOWER SEEDS

GARDENING CHALLENGES

ONCE YOU HAVE BEGUN your garden, whether it's a small patio or half a field, you may decide that you want to take a *special direction*, experiment, or learn some more techniques. A special direction might include planting a garden for the birds, butterflies, or  beneficial insect *pollinators*. A new technique might include starting plants from seed, either indoors or out, or dividing your daffodils or irises correctly.

Because any garden will get insect and weed pests from time to time, there's information here about which pests may bother you most, and what to do about them, if anything. Before you use chemicals in the garden, read the section on pesticides in Chapter 21 so you *control* them appropriately and safely.

Chapter 19

Making Your Own Plants

I T IS QUITE SIMPLE to grow your own plants from seeds or cuttings, or by dividing a favourite plant. Growing your own plants saves money and is fun, and a home-grown plant makes a wonderful gift for garden-loving friends. A small, or not-so-small, bonus is that plant parenting can often be done in late winter, when it looks like spring will never come dancing around the corner.

In this chapter...

✓ *Starting seeds indoors*

✓ *Starting seeds outdoors*

✓ *Making plants from cuttings*

✓ *Dividing garden plants*

NASTURTIUMS, IDEAL FOR NOVICE GARDENERS

Starting seeds indoors

A PACKET OF 100 OR MORE SEEDS *costs only about £1.99. That's about 2 pence a plant. If you wait until a nursery has started the seeds for you, each young plant can cost £2 or more. Nature starts seeds every day, and with a little skill, you can too.*

Smart seed buying

Most seeds are purchased in little paper packets. Do not buy or use commercial seed packets with last year's date printed on them. They were meant for last year's use. Fresh seed germinates well. Old seed, or improperly stored seed, does not.

When you buy a seed packet, put it in a container and store it in a cool, dry place. To help hasten germination, some people like to put flower and vegetable seed packets in the fridge (not the freezer) for a week before sowing. You can always try a test packet and see what happens.

If you're concerned about the easiest seed to nurture indoors, look for those packets stating that seeds will germinate within 10 days. Anything longer than that requires extra vigilance.

Trivia...

By the mid-1800s, many intrepid plant hunters were sending rare seed back to baker-turned-botanist, William Thompson of Ipswich. His reputation for successful propagation of exciting new plants gained him the friendship of eminent scientists Joseph Hooker, Michael Foster, and Charles Darwin. Thompson founded the seed house Thompson & Morgan in 1855 and it remains in his family to this day.

Start with the right soil

Always use sterile potting compost for your seeds. Ordinary garden soil contains a host of bacteria and fungi that cause damping-off and other miserable seed and seedling disorders. You can buy seed compost ready-made in a bag, or purchase sterile soil components. A satisfactory generic mixture is 25 per cent vermiculite, 25 per cent perlite, 25 per cent horticultural sand, and 25 per cent sphagnum moss or peat.

Containers

You can start some seeds in something as plain and simple as a polystyrene cup or yogurt pot that is ¾ full of sterile compost, or in sturdier and more aesthetically pleasing containers.

PEAT POT

Containers for seed starting must be at least 5 centimetres deep, and should have drainage holes at the base. You can buy starting trays, or little *peat pots* (the simplest solution), at garden centres. Peat pots should definitely be used for vining plants, such as tomatoes.

If you're re-using containers that previously contained soil, each must be thoroughly cleaned to prevent the transmission of bacterial and fungal diseases that can communicate via just one small leftover lump of soil. While a good hot water and detergent solution will do if the container is rinsed very well, an even better way is washing with hot water to which about 2 tablespoons of bleach have been added. Again, rinse well.

You're now ready to plant your seeds (see pp.346-7). To avoid shifting the seeds about when watering them, place a sheet of paper towel over each seed container and lightly sprinkle water onto this.

You must never allow seeds to dry out at any time after you have planted them.

Allow the soil to drain, remove the paper towelling and place sheets of cling film over each container. Don't let the cling film touch the soil. Label each container with a waterproof marker, stating both the plant's name and the planting date.

Now place your containers near a window, but out of direct, hot sunlight. If a sunny window is all you have, cover it with a net curtain. Seedlings may grow towards any light source, so rotate the containers regularly. Keep the soil moist at all times but don't let the soil become soggy, or the small seeds will drown.

DEFINITION

Peat pots *are little pots made of pressed and dried peat. When you use them, you can place the pot and plant directly into the garden soil for transplant, without damaging the root system.*

When you see the sprouts

After the seeds germinate, or sprout, remove the cling film covering. Place the container in a sunny indoor site. If the site really gets hot, give the seedlings a little paper covering during the warmest part of the day. If you don't have a sunny indoor site, you can create your own sunshine using plant growth lights, which can be bought at most garden centres and DIY stores. A 2-tube fluorescent fixture holding 40-watt bulbs is a standard variety. Place the lights about 15 to 20 centimetres above the seedling containers. To avoid burning the delicate seedlings, raise the light fixture as the seedlings grow. You can leave the lights on full time, or use a timer to provide about 12 hours of light a day.

PLANTING SEEDS

When starting seed, the indoor temperature should be between 18 and 21° C. Fill your containers with seed compost. It is important to moisten the soil and let it drain before inserting seeds. After adding the seeds, note their size before covering with soil. Seeds the size of pepper grains, such as foxglove, petunia, and snapdragon, should not be covered with soil. Seeds the size of rice grains, such as zinnia, need only a light covering, while large seeds, such as morning glory, sunflower, or sweet pea, should be covered firmly but just enough so that you cannot see them.

1 **Firm the soil**

Fill a planting container with soil and then firm it down to about 1 centimetre below the rim of the pot. You can do this by hand, or by using a presser. Moisten the soil.

THINNING SEEDLINGS

When seedlings reach 2 to 3 centimetres high, thin them out a bit, using your fingers to extract them by the roots. With the point of a pencil, poke holes about 2 to 3 centimetres apart in a new pot and put the removed seedlings in the pre-moistened hole, filling and firming around the roots. When seedlings are about 5 centimetres high, they are ready to move into the garden if the last spring frost has already occurred. You will need to **harden them off**.

DEFINITION

Hardening off *a plant means making it a bit tougher so it can withstand cold, wind, or other outdoor natural weather conditions. You do this by gradually exposing it to the harsher outdoor environment.*

1 **Harden the seedlings off**

Cover your seedlings with glass or clear plastic and place the pots in a sheltered spot outside for a few hours each day for about a week.

2 Sprinkle the seeds onto the soil

Use a folded piece of paper to hold the seeds and help ensure an even distribution. Scatter the seeds sparingly over the surface of the compost.

3 Sieve soil over the pot

Once you have distributed the seeds, gently sieve a shallow layer of compost over the surface of the pot, taking care not to dislodge the seeds.

2 Pot on the seedlings

When the seedlings are 5 centimetres high, move them into a bigger container. Lift the seedlings out by the leaves, as the stems are very delicate.

3 Plant outdoors

When the seedlings have grown into small plants with good, strong roots, you can either transplant them again or plant them outdoors.

COLD FRAMES – TRANSITIONAL HOUSING FOR YOUNG PLANTS

A cold frame is a transitional place where small young plants can harden off before they are placed directly in garden soil. Cold frames are particularly helpful in areas with late spring frosts. They are used for interim seedling transplants, rooted cuttings of deciduous and evergreen trees and shrubs, softwood cuttings of such plants as chrysanthemums, pelargoniums, and fuchsias, and leaf cuttings of rex begonias and African violets.

Cold frames use the sun's heat. Soil within the box is warmed during the day and gives off its retained warmth at night, keeping the plants comfortable. If you live in a cold winter climate, you can surround your cold frame with straw or another protective material to insulate it from the outside air and increase heat retention.

The basic cold frame is nothing more than a bottomless box with a removable top. The box is usually made of wood pieces (either 1 metre by 1.2 metres or 1 metre by 1.75 metres) that are about 2 to 3 centimetres thick. My favourite design has a wooden back about 45 centimetres high, and a front that is 30 centimetres high. The sides should be cut diagonally to accommodate this 15-centimetre slope.

The top is usually made of glass or clear plastic, such as clear plastic sheeting. If you have good drainage, you may place the frame directly on top of the soil. If not, you must dig down about 15 centimetres. Fill the dug-up area with coarse sand or gravel. Pack this down firmly and water well. Then, place the cold frame over the dug-out area and fill it with a commercial sterile compost. If you use garden soil you risk bringing in all the fungi and bacteria that eliminate seedlings.

■ **Protect your young plants** *from the elements by keeping them in a garden cold frame.*

Your cold frame should not be sited where it gets baking sun, or its interior will become an oven. Where this is unavoidable, put a covering over the glass, and/or ventilate the cold frame by opening the top slightly. You can also buy more elaborate cold frames with glass tops that open and close automatically to keep the air temperature constant.

Starting seeds outdoors

BECAUSE OF SEED PREDATORS, such as snails, slugs, cutworms, and birds, sowing seeds outdoors can be something of a challenge. However, with vigilance and some pre-planting preparation, you can be quite successful. Fortunately, there are some seeds that tend to provide good results, regardless of the experience of the gardener.

> Trivia...
> An old-time farmer's ditty
> about seeds:
> "One for the rook,
> one for the crow.
> One to die
> and one to grow."

Good choices for beginners

Maximize your chances of success by starting with plants that tend to do well when they're sown outside. The easier annual flower seeds to grow include:

- Common sunflower (*Helianthus annuus*)
- Forget-me-not (*Myosotis sylvatica*) (a perennial usually grown as an annual)
- Marigold (*Tagetes*)
- Morning glory (*Ipomoea*)
- Nasturtium (*Tropaeolum*)
- Sweet alyssum (*Lobularia maritima*)
- Zinnia (*Zinnia*)

■ **Pretty blue** *forget-me-nots are ideal plants for novice gardeners to grow.*

349

Among perennial flowers, the easiest
seeds to grow include:

- Columbine (*Aquilegia*)
- Coneflower (*Rudbeckia*)
- Delphinium (*Delphinium*)
- Four o'clock (*Mirabilis jalapa*)
- Shasta daisy (*Leucanthemum* x
  superbum)
- Snow-in-summer (*Cerastium
  tomentosum*)

CONEFLOWER (*Rudbeckia hirta*)

SWEET PEPPERS (*Capsicum annum*)

Finally, the easiest vegetable seeds to grow
are:

- Courgette (*Cucurbita pepo*)
- Peppers (*Capsicum*)
- Pumpkin (*Cucurbita moschata*)
- Tomato (*Lycopersicon*)

Shortcuts with seed tapes

If you're looking for a shortcut, you can buy seed tapes at
some garden centres and nurseries. The tapes are about 5
metres long, with seeds integrated into them. You can cut
them into smaller segments if you want. Place the seed
tapes along the area where you want these particular
plants to grow, and you get straight rows and correct,
even spacing. Seed tapes are more expensive than seed
packets, but they do make sowing easier. It's a relatively
novel idea in Britain, so don't expect too many different
varieties but you can get beetroot, carrot, lettuce, spring
onions, parsley, and radish to experiment with.

SEED TAPE

Sowing successfully

Preparing the soil properly is as important as obtaining fresh seeds. You cannot just dump seeds on the ground and expect them to survive. If you need a refresher course on how to improve your soil so that it's ready for planting, look again at Chapter 2.

Be sure to read through the instructions on your seed packet. They will recommend the best time to sow.

Before planting, you must have some idea of when the last frosts have usually occurred. This information is important because a sudden frost will quickly kill almost all emerging seedlings.

Check on the packet to see if the seeds need sun, semi-shade, or shade. This will affect where you place your seeds. A final, and important, instruction is how deep to plant the seeds, so always check on the package. Seeds that are planted too deep do not get enough light and will not germinate. Seeds that are planted too shallow will get too much light and will not germinate.

Seed in the hole

When you're ready to plant, make a series of small indentations in the ground. I use my finger, but a pencil makes a nice, tidy dent too. Sprinkle the area lightly with water. Insert your seed at the proper depth.

Some seeds are exceedingly small. You can finger-pinch the seeds into your planting hole. You may get several seeds in one planting, but you can always thin the seedlings out later.

Mix very small seeds with horticultural sand, about ½ a cupful per seed packet, right before sowing. This is a little haphazard, but it beats dumping all your tiny seeds in one place, as often happens to people such as myself who lack great finger dexterity. The lighter-coloured sand displays where you are putting the seeds.

Planting in furrows

An alternative method of sowing is to make shallow, V-shaped furrows about 10 to 15 centimetres apart along your planting area. Water the furrows and allow the water to soak in. Now make a cone of your seed envelope, and gently shake the seeds out along the furrows. Alternatively, you can use the mix of seeds with sand, put some in a used envelope, and shake out the results from the corner of the envelope.

Cover the seeds with a sterile compost and press it down firmly with your hands or another solid object. Label your plantings with ice-lolly sticks or pre-purchased plastic or metal tags – whatever garden creatures won't eat. Slugs will often munch on paper labels, such as seed packets.

Seedling care

Never let the newly planted area totally dry out. In warm climates, you may want to cover the seeded area with newspaper held in place at the edges with rocks or the like.

Use a fine mist from the hose to keep the area slightly damp. Of course, you don't want to flood the planting site with water, which will drown seeds and seedlings, or use a strong spray from the garden hose, which will wash the seeds hither and thither.

When the emerging seedlings are about 5 centimetres high, remove any covering and begin thinning. Thinning is best done using your fingers, because you can feel what you are doing. Hopefully, you won't mind getting your hands dirty. If you're worried about your manicure, you can gently use a kitchen fork or the tip of a butter knife to remove seedlings, or you can snip off the excess seedlings with a slim pair of scissors. You can try transplanting rooted seedlings to another prepared area. Remember, they do best when taken out of the ground with some soil around the roots. Protect transplants with a light covering, such as a box, for a day or two if the weather is really hot. Be sure to water these transplants regularly.

■ **Be sure to water seeds well** *after planting. Use a watering can or hose with a nozzle that provides a very light spray so that you don't dislodge the seeds from the soil.*

Trivia...
From time to time you may find flowers and trees starting in your garden, even if you haven't planted them. Seeds travel to a garden in many ways. They arrive on the wind, with the rain, and in bird droppings. Your pet may also deposit seeds that have become attached to its fur after a walk. Seeds stick to clothes, socks, and shoes, and you might bring them home from the woods, or even the garden centre.

Making plants from cuttings

THERE ARE FOUR basic types of cuttings: softwood, hardwood, leaf, and root. For the novice gardener, softwood and leaf cuttings are the easiest to work with. The advantage of cuttings of all types is that the offspring are identical to the parent plant. This is not true when plants are started from seed, especially from the seed of hybrid plants.

DEFINITION

Softwood cuttings are those taken from the stems of perennial plants before they become hard and woody. These cuttings are usually best taken during spring or early summer when the plant is actively growing, and preferably has finished blooming. The cutting should be about 15 centimetres long and should develop roots within 3 weeks. **Hardwood** cuttings are those taken from mature wood, and must be taken when trees are dormant. Some trees, such as fruit trees, will not develop roots from cuttings.

Softwood cutting choices

Some of the easiest perennial flowering plants to multiply from softwood cuttings are:

- Aster (*Aster*)
- Balsam (*Impatiens*)
- Bedding begonia (*Begonia*)
- Chrysanthemum (*Chrysanthemum*)
- Coleus (*Solenostemon scutellarioides*)
- Fuchsia (*Fuchsia*)
- Geranium (*Pelargonium*)
- Lavender (*Lavandula*)
- Penstemon (*Penstemon*)
- Sage (*Salvia*)

GERANIUM (*Pelargonium*)

Get your cuttings going

Softwood cuttings are usually taken in spring when the parent plant has almost fully developed new shoots on it. The cuttings are easy to grow, provided you give them clean, healthy compost, the right amount of light, and water them regularly. Cuttings deprived of water tend to keel over very quickly. Always plant up several cuttings in one go, as this reduces the chances of failure. If you lose them, try again later in the year.

It's important to use a sharp implement to make cuttings, because a dull blade squashes the cutting base, damaging the growing cells.

Trivia...
The ancient Romans dipped their plant cuttings in ox manure to encourage a strong root system.

Containers for cuttings

Once you have made your cutting, proceed promptly with potting it up. You will need containers that are about 12 centimetres deep, have a drainage hole, and are ¾ filled with cutting compost. Poke holes in the planting mix with a pencil or with a screwdriver. Remove the leaves from the lower third of each cutting.

TAKING SOFTWOOD CUTTINGS

Always select a strong, healthy plant from which to take your cuttings. Make your cuttings early in the morning before the sun becomes too hot and the plant begins to lose water. If the parent plant has nodes, or eyes, which are little growing bumps along the stems, try to obtain about 3 to 5 nodes per selected cutting.

1 Take a cutting

Make an angled cut on the stem, taking approximately 7 to 15 centimetres. Use a sharp knife or sharp-edged secateurs.

2 Give it a trim

Remove the lower leaves from the cutting and trim the stem just below a node. You should be left with a nice, clean stem.

Lightly dip the bottom of the cutting into plant-rooting hormone powder. The powder, although not absolutely necessary, is a great help in stimulating quicker and stronger rooting. It is available at all garden centres. Bear in mind that the cuttings you've taken have no roots, and therefore, for the time being, they don't need nourishment such as fertilizer. Instead, they need to form roots as quickly as possible.

Insert the cuttings gently into the prepared holes so that the lower leaves are just above soil level. Firm the cutting compost around each cutting, and water lightly.

Softwood cutting care

Cover the cuttings with plastic bags. Place the cuttings in a well-lit but not overly sunny area, with a temperature of about 21° C. Check your cuttings at the 3-week mark. They should not be wilted. If you tug lightly, the newly formed roots should hold a cutting in place. If your test cutting resists a bit, lift it out of the soil. You should see thread-like white roots.

The clear plastic bags you get in the supermarket fruit and vegetable section are great for covering cuttings.

3 **Plant up cuttings**

Place several stems into a pot of cutting compost. Water well and then cover the pot with a plastic bag to encourage the roots to grow.

4 **Divide plants**

After the cuttings have developed strong and healthy roots, separate them by gently pulling each cutting away from the clump.

Repot cuttings

You can now repot all the cuttings into their own individual pots, as each cutting has become a separate plant. Water well.

SOFTWOOD CUTTINGS IN WATER

1 Remove a stem

With your hands, scissors, or secateurs remove a piece of stem about 10 centimetres long from the growing tip of the plant. Take off all the leaves except the three topmost ones.

2 Place in water

Fill a tall glass or jar about ¼ full of tap water. Place up to 3 stems in the glass, depending on their size and width. Ensure the stems are covered with the water.

3 Allow roots to form

Keep the cutting in a semi-shaded spot for about a week, and then move it to a semi-sunny site. You will be able to see how well the roots are forming in just a few weeks.

4 Plant your cutting

Half fill a pot with compost, lower the softwood cutting into the pot and add more soil. Gently firm the soil around the newly developed roots and water well.

Softwood cutting choices for water

Some indoor plants are incredibly easy to multiply in water. These include:

- Angelwing begonia (*Begonia coccinea*)
- Corn palm (*Dracaena fragrans*)
- Dumb cane (*Dieffenbachia*)
- Golden pothos (*Epipremnum aureum*)
- Goosefoot (*Syngonium podophyllum*)
- Ivy (*Hedera*)
- Philodendron (*Philodendron*)
- Ribbon plant (*Dracaena sanderiana*)
- Wandering Jew (*Tradescantia zebrina*)
- Wax plant (*Hoya carnosa*)

You can also take dangling offshoots of spider plant (*Chlorophytum comosum*) or piggyback plant (*Tolmiea menziesii*) and root them in water.

Many of the plants I've just listed will thrive for quite a while in their watery home, but eventually the roots will fill the glass and you will have to plant the cutting.

WAX PLANT (*Hoya carnosa*)

CORN PALM (*Dracaena fragrans*)

LEAF STALK CUTTINGS

Leaf cuttings are best begun in the spring and summer. Have ready a container ¾ full of horticultural sand. Cut 5 centimetres of leaf stalk off the original plant using a razor blade or a pair of scissors. Make a slanted cut. Dip in water, and then lightly in plant-rooting hormone powder, shaking off any excess.

1 Planting a cutting

Insert the leaf stalk (here an African violet) in moistened sand, right up to the leaf base.

2 Cover with plastic

Water the stalks well and cover with a plastic bag. Place in a well-lit but not too sunny, hot site.

■ **Always keep the soil** *slightly moist. When tiny leaves appear, you can either transplant the leaf cutting into a permanent pot, or leave it where it is.*

GETTING YOUR LEAF CUTTINGS GOING

1 Remove leaf and stalk

Remove a large leaf from the parent plant (here a rex begonia leaf) and remove the central stalk, using a sharp cutting knife.

2 Cut through main leaf veins

Turn the leaf upside down, so the veins are showing. With a sharp knife, make some straight cuts in a few of the main leaf veins.

The best plants for leaf cuttings

Houseplants that you can multiply via leaf cuttings include:

- African violet (*Saintpaulia*)
- Christmas cactus (*Schlumbergera*)
- Florist's gloxinia (*Sinningia speciosa*)
- Peperomia (*Peperomia*)
- Piggyback plant (*Tolmiea menziesii*)
- Rex begonia (*Begonia rex* group)
- Sansevieria (*Sansevieria*)
- Wax plant (*Hoya carnosa*)

Sedums do well too, if you let the leaves dry for 24 hours before you put them into soil.

INTERNET

www.gardeningdata.co.
uk/plants/plant_
propogation.htm

This site lists links for plant propagation information and techniques including air layering for large houseplants, hydroponics, and summer cuttings from garden shrubs.

AFRICAN VIOLET (*Saintpaulia*)

3 Place leaf onto soil

Place the leaf, topside upwards, onto the soil in the growing container. You might need to weight the leaf down with a few small pebbles.

4 Divide the new plants

New plants will form where the cut leaf veins touch the soil. These new plants can be lifted, divided, and then repotted.

Dividing garden plants

PERENNIALS THAT GROW IN GROUPS *originating from a single plant, such as aster, primrose, and Shasta daisy, often get rather sad looking in the centre, start producing smaller flowers, or just grow too large for the site. When this happens, it may be time to divide. There is a continuing discussion on the best time to divide clumps of roots. I recommend dividing in the early spring, just as the plant starts rapid growth. My second choice would be after the plant has flowered. For bulbs, divide after the flowers have come and gone.*

DIVIDING BEARDED IRIS

Every type of iris has a preferred planting time. If you don't know the best time for your iris type, look for when the bulbs or rhizomes appear in your local garden centre. At this time, lift and divide overcrowded clumps in your garden. Lift the entire clump with a spade or garden fork and shake off the soil.

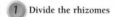

1 **Divide the rhizomes**

Cut the rhizomes apart with a sharp knife. Each of the sections should have green leaves, as well as roots. Discard the old and leafless centre sections.

2 **Transplant the sections**

Cut the leaves to about 7 centimetres high, removing any discoloured parts. Transplant the sections 25 centimetres apart. Firm into place, with the rhizomes just below the soil surface.

Dividing clumps

Divide shallow-rooted plants, such as chrysanthemums or violets, by lifting the entire clump with a spade or a garden fork. Gently break off rooted sections. If the roots are entangled you can cut them apart carefully with a sharp knife or secateurs. If extracting the entire clump from the ground is difficult, just slice it with a spade and lift out a cut-off section. Do not make the divisions too small. Leave or place one section in the original site, and place the other sections elsewhere, ensuring each has roots. Water the new plant well, but do not over-water.

Dividing bulbs

Divide bulbs after flowering has finished and the leaves die back and turn yellow. Dig carefully, to avoid bruising the bulbs, as this encourages disease. Do not cut off the leaves. You may see little bulblets on the plant, which you can gently pull off and replant in groups (but not as deeply as the parent bulbs). Alternatively, store the bulblets in a dry, cool site for the winter, and replant in early spring. The bulblets will mature and bloom the second or third year.

■ **Separate the bulbs** *by gently breaking the clump apart. If the bulbs have bulblets, pull them off carefully and replant for new plants.*

A simple summary

✓ The easiest seeds to grow usually sprout within 10 days.

✓ Start seeds indoors to get a head start on plant growth and an earlier harvest for vegetables.

✓ Use potting compost for indoor planting. Prepare soil thoroughly.

✓ Don't let seeds or seedlings dry out. They will die rapidly without water.

✓ When transplanting seedlings, water the area first so that a little soil remains on the roots.

✓ Late winter is a good time to start houseplant cuttings. Many can be easily rooted in water.

✓ Early spring is the best time to divide overgrown perennial clumps. Divide bulbs after the flowering and when leaves have turned brown or yellow.

Chapter 20

Wonderful Wildlife

E VEN IF YOU HAVE a tiny garden in the city or the suburbs, you can still design it to attract birds, butterflies, and beneficial insects. A bird enjoying a feast on the bird table you have placed in your garden is a marvellous sight on any lovely day.

In this chapter...

✓ Attracting birds with berries and seeds

✓ Beckoning bats

✓ Harbouring hedgehogs

✓ Bird feeders

✓ Bringing in butterflies

✓ Attracting beneficial insects

Attracting birds with berries and seeds

IT IS AMAZING the variety of birds attracted to your garden if you invite them with a plenitude of food and shelter plants. Food plants are those providing berries or other fruit, nuts, or seeds. Shelter should include some evergreens, especially in cold winter areas. First, we'll take a look at the berries birds love.

Barberry

Barberry (*Berberis thunbergii*) is an attractive garden shrub that bears berries well into winter. Although it's a deciduous plant, shedding its canopy along with the autumn leaf drop, there'll be a guaranteed supply of small berries to last through the worst part of the winter, providing food for resident and visiting birds. The barberry's spiny leaves also provide good protection for nesting birds during the spring and summer. If the plants are being used as a hedge, trim them back in late summer or early autumn if necessary.

Pyracantha

Glossy, small-leaved pyracantha is as good to look at as it is beneficial to local wildlife. During the spring and early summer, it produces masses of delicately scented white flowers, which then go on to produce thick bunches of bright berries. During the cold

BARBERRY (*Berberis thunbergii*)

winter months, small birds will find shelter within its thick evergreen canopy, and the long-lasting bright yellow, orange, or bright red berries provide a ready supply of food for hungry birds.

Pyrcantha grows well in either full sunshine or partial shade, and is a good plant for a north- or east-facing wall. No garden should be without at least one pyracantha.

Cotoneaster

There are many different varieties of this berry-producing plant. All are excellent for birds, and offer a range of potential uses to the wildlife gardener. A word of caution: birds find cotoneaster berries extremely tasty but parts of the plant, including the berries, are mildly poisonous to humans. If you're worried about young children being tempted by the shiny berries, plant them where they're out of reach.

Cotoneasters thrive in ordinary garden soil, preferably in a sunny site. After planting, remove the tips of the shoots to encourage bushier growth. Evergreen varieties provide valuable winter shelter for garden birds, and a dense canopy of leaves allows for secure nesting in the spring, as well as food on tap during autumn and early winter.

Mountain ash

The mountain ash (*Sorbus aucuparia*) is a much-loved and widespread native tree of woodlands, moors, and mountains. As a result, it's extremely tolerant of exposed sites. It produces frothy clusters of spring flowers followed by distinctive berries that make it popular with birds. In fact, they can hardly wait for the berries to fully ripen before tucking in, so there won't be too many left for the winter. There is a choice of ornamental varieties in the *Sorbus* family that will provide berries in a range of colours, from ivory to white, yellow, and orange.

Bringing in birds with berries

To bring birds to your garden, plant any or many of the following shrubs with berries:

- Alder buckthorn (*Rhamnus frangula*)
- Barberry (*Berberis*)
- Bearberry (*Arctostaphylos*)
- Beautiberry (*Callicarpa*)
- Bilberry (*Vaccinium*)
- Cherry laurel (*Prunus laurocerasus*)
- Cornelian cherry (*Cornus mas*)
- Cotoneaster (*Cotoneaster*)
- Elder (*Sambucus*)
- Firethorn (*Pyracantha*)
- Flowering currant (*Ribes*)
- Hawthorn (*Crataegus*)
- Holly (*Ilex*)
- Oregon grape (*Mahonia aquifolium*)
- Privet (*Ligustrum*)
- Rose (*Rosa*)
- Sargent crabapple (*Malus sargentii*)
- Snowberry (*Symphoricarpos*)
- Viburnum tinus (*Viburnum*)

■ **Birds just love elderberries –** *the tiny clusters of dark berries that appear on elder shrubs after flowering.*

In addition to berries, birds are also partial to the delectable seeds that are produced by your flowers.

Lovely love-lies-bleeding

Also called tassel flower, this annual plant is quite aptly named after its tiny, bright red flowers that appear in long, cascading, tassel-like clusters surrounded by green or red leaves. The grain-like seeds that follow often produce more plants, if the birds don't nibble them all first. Give this plant full sun, wind protection, and slightly below average amounts of water. Even in relatively poor soil, expect love-lies-bleeding (*Amaranthus caudatus*) to grow from 1 to 1.5 metres high, and to provide a long-lasting sea of dangling red strands from summer to autumn.

Pretty purple coneflower

Place this daisy-like perennial plant among your taller sunflowers for an eye-catching flower border. Purple coneflowers (*Echinacea purpurea*) will reach from 1 to 1.5 metres tall. They'll expand in diameter from 75 centimetres to 1.5 metres, so be sure to leave enough room between plants when planting. Purple coneflowers bloom from July to September, and there are reddish-purple as well as white varieties.

LOVE-LIES-BLEEDING
(*Amaranthus caudatus*)

The name derives from the conical purple or brown centre. This plant is drought and wind tolerant.

Sunflowers for supper

The sunflower (*Helianthus*) is the ultimate in seed producers for birds. I buy sunflower seeds by the huge bagfull at the supermarket and pet shop, both the bigger striped sunflower seeds for the jays and the smaller black seeds for just about every other bird that crowds the feeders. There are huge, old-fashioned sunflowers that reach almost 3 metres high (these gangly plants will require staking), and also smaller sunflowers about 30 centimetres high. If you have bird-feeding stations near sunflowers, your visitors will leave behind mementos in the form

SUNFLOWER (*Helianthus*)

of a sprinkling of sunflowers growing here and there in sunny sites. Although you may remember the yellow-petalled, brown-centered sunflower from childhood, there now are ivory, orange, brown, rose, and maroon, single and double-flowered varieties. All sunflowers require full sun, and do better in good soil. They must have regular water and well-drained soil, or they will droop and then die.

Zoom in on zinnias

Zinnias (*Zinnia*) are easy-to-grow annuals that can be found in a wide selection of flower shapes and colours. They may have button-size flowers on 30-centimetre-high plants or dinner-plate-size flowers on 1-metre plants. Because zinnias bloom in late summer when other annuals are getting ready for winter shutdown, they provide a special treat for the gardener. You can plant entire sections in one colour – apricot, cream, violet, or red – or you can mix and match as you like. Zinnias are strictly warm-weather plants and they do best when placed in rich soil. Plenty of water is a must. To keep them happy, water them with a soaker hose or something like it. Don't water them from above, as doing so encourages the growth of mildew.

ZINNIAS (*Zinnia*)

Bringing in birds with seeds

Birds love seeds. Here are a selection of those they like best:

- Aster (*Aster*)
- Black-eyed Susan (*Rudbeckia hirta*)
- California poppy (*Eschscholzia*)
- Columbine (*Aquilegia*)
- Cornflower (*Centaurea cyanus*)
- Cosmos (*Cosmos*)
- Floss flower (*Ageratum*)
- Forget-me-not (*Myosotis*)
- French marigold (*Tagetes patula*)
- Globe thistle (*Echinops*)
- Love-in-a-mist (*Nigella*)
- Marigold (*Calendula officinalis*)
- Mexican sunflower (*Tithonia*)
- Nasturtium (*Tropaeolum majus*)
- Pincushion flower (*Scabiosa*)
- Rose moss (*Portulaca*)
- Sea lavender (*Limonium*)
- Sweet alyssum (*Lobularia*)
- Tickseed (*Coreopsis*)

Beckoning bats

BATS MAY NOT BE everyone's idea of a furry friend, but they're having a hard time. Many species are becoming rare, to the point of near extinction, because they are gradually losing their natural habitats and roosting sites. In cities and intensively farmed areas, their food supply of insects is also becoming depleted. A thriving garden with lots of insects will provide bats with a rich night-time hunting ground, ridding you of insect pests such as midges and maintaining your garden's natural balance. If you're batty about the idea of bats visiting your garden, read on …

In 1992, the mouse-eared bat finally became extinct after many years of struggling for survival. It was the first British mammal to become extinct for 250 years.

Bats traditionally roost in hollow trees or in caves, but they've adapted to using buildings. Bats move around to roost in different places throughout the year. In the winter they look for a well-insulated spot where the temperature will remain fairly constant for their hibernation. In spring they'll search out a safe place in which to give birth and rear their young. In summer they may choose a cooler spot to roost, and in autumn a slightly warmer one.

Building boxes

If there are old trees in your garden, they may well be inhabited by bats already. If not, then the neighbourly thing to do would be to provide them with a bat box. Boxes should be sited at least 3 to 5 metres above the ground, on a tree, a post, or even on the wall of a house. Try to ensure that the bats have a clear flight path by removing overhanging branches or other obstructions.

INTERNET

wildlifetrust.org.uk

Click here to find out more about the work of the Wildlife Trusts, a nationwide network working for the conservation of Britain's wildlife.

INTERNET

english-nature.org.uk

To find out more about bats and their protection, click here to visit the site of English Nature.

You can inspect the boxes for droppings or other signs of habitation, but do so carefully so as not to disturb any bats that may be inside. If bats come to roost, you must contact English Nature to apply for a licence to continue checking. Bats and their roosts are protected by law, and it's an offence to disturb them. If you already have bats in the roof of your house, cellar, or any other part of your property not used as a living area, you should contact English Nature.

Harbouring hedgehogs

HEDGEHOGS ARE ANIMALS that any gardener should be delighted to accommodate. Their diet sheet reads like a checklist of garden vandals, such as slugs and snails. Although the occasional hedgehog may be seen during mild winter weather, they are usually out and about from April to October. For the rest of the year these prickly creatures are usually fast asleep under a thick blanket of leaves, under your shed, or hidden in an old pile of logs.

INTERNET

software-technics.co.uk/bhps

Visit the site of the British Hedgehog Preservation Society for advice on attracting hedgehogs to your garden and caring for them.

The obvious signs that hedgehogs are about are the sounds of grunts and rustling leaves as these animals forage for food. The name hedgehog or "hedgepig" is well deserved, and not only because of its characteristic snuffling and snorting. When hurt or when courting, the hedgehog will even squeal like a pig. Fortunately, hedgehogs are fairly resilient. They'll often climb walls and wire fences and, on reaching the top, simply roll into a ball and drop down to the other side, their flexible spines cushioning the fall perfectly.

Providing a snack

During a hot, dry summer, a hedgehog's regular diet of slugs, snails, and worms can be hard to come by. It is at this time that babies are being born and the females are suckling, so they are unable to travel far to find food. Give hedgehogs a helping hand by putting out a little tinned pet food and a saucer of water.

Don't give hedgehogs bread and milk – this will upset their digestive systems.

If hedgehogs are to have a permanent place in your garden, they'll need a dry, secure place for hibernation from late autumn to early spring. A pile of dead leaves or garden prunings heaped into a corner will often be acceptable. A word of caution: if you decide to have an autumn bonfire, check carefully amongst the debris that a hedgehog hasn't taken up residence.

■ **Hedgehogs are no slouches:** *they'll often travel a kilometre or more during their nightly forage for food.*

Bird feeders

MANY PEOPLE THINK of bird feeders for winter use, when snow is on the ground and plants are dormant. But placing food out throughout the year brings birds that you might not see otherwise. In spring, especially, that extra supply of edibles might encourage birds to build their nests in your garden, perhaps in view of a window that looks out onto the garden.

Perfect placement

Birds have many predators, including household cats. All feeders must be placed within 3 metres of protective cover so the birds can seek quick shelter if threatened.

You may not think that birds need to be protected from predators, as feeders tend to be placed high in a shrub or tree. Even though the feeders are high, seeds will fall to the ground, where many birds prefer to dine.

To get the largest variety of bird visitors, use different types of feeders scattered throughout the garden. Place the feeders at various levels and distances from the house. Feeders should not be in a windy site, and you might want to screen off wind with a plant barrier or a fencing arrangement. Most birds prefer to eat in a sunny area.

■ **Position a hopper feeder** where you want to attract birds. These dispensers re-fill automatically.

Hopper feeders

Hopper feeders keep seed in enclosed bins that have a seed tray at the base. Birds feed from the base, which is automatically replenished from the bin. Hopper feeders may be hung, or attached to trees, poles, or windowsills. Hopper feeders may attract blue tits, bullfinches, great tits, greenfinches, nuthatches, siskins, and sparrows, among other types of birds.

Platform or tray feeders

Platform feeders are trays or shallow pans used for birds that like fruit, suet, and nuts, as well as grains and seeds. They may be mounted on flat sites such as retaining walls, poles, and tree stumps. Platform feeders attract a very wide variety of birds, including bullfinches, chaffinches, collared doves, dunnocks, goldfinches, greenfinches, house sparrows, jays, long-tailed tits, magpies, nuthatches, robins, tree sparrows, and wood pigeons.

Suet feeders

Suet feeders are mesh or wire holders for suet, peanut butter, or various mixtures that are compacted together in a cake. You can place them on tree stumps or on poles. It's best not to place them directly against a tree, as the birds' pecking can result in some nasty damage to the tree. Birds that love suet include chickadees, flickers, jays, mockingbirds, sapsuckers, titmice, and woodpeckers.

SUET BALL

Tube feeders

INTERNET

rspb.org.uk

Visit the Royal Society for the Protection of Birds' site for advice on all aspects of bird care, from providing nesting boxes to getting the most from a bird table.

Tube feeders are usually made of plastic and are suspended from trees. Perches for the birds are attached near the holes. Tube feeders will attract any birds that don't mind performing acrobatics while eating.

Nesting time

If the ground is frozen during March or April, continue feeding birds as normal. However, if the weather is fair, reduce feeding as nesting begins. Hard bread and peanuts are harmful to newly hatched birds, so restrict the supplies on the bird table to soft fat or grated cheese. Cutting back on the amount of food you put out will also encourage the adults to start feeding on emerging insects.

Birdbaths

Concrete birdbaths are more stable than the plastic or ceramic types. Birds like to stand in the birdbath, so the water shouldn't be too deep. To control water height, add pebbles to the bottom. All birdbaths must have clean water. Do not place them under shedding trees unless you clean and re-fill the bath daily. Provide some type of high protective cover within 1.5 to 3 metres of the birdbath, and do not place a birdbath near or over shrubbery where predators can hide.

■ **Attract birds** *by setting up a birdbath in your garden. Not only will they drink from it, but they will also, literally, take a bath.*

Bringing in butterflies

BUTTERFLIES ARE PARTICULAR *about their food and residence. Many will starve rather than feed from just any plant. They are also extremely selective as to where they place their eggs. Butterflies avoid shaded sites and need shelter from the wind. If you live in a windy area, plant windbreaks that are also butterfly food, such as butterfly bush. A mud or sand puddle will provide water.*

■ To attract *butterflies to your garden, you need to consider three elements: colour, shape, and fragrance.*

Colour

Butterflies prefer feeding on purple, violet, orange, and yellow flowers. They are guided to the flower nectar by light patterns that we cannot see.

Shape

Although butterflies fly easily, they do not hover in one place very well. They therefore must have a place to perch. Large bloom clusters, *umbels*, and daisy-like flowers are good landing pads.

> **DEFINITION**
>
> *Flowers sprouting from stalks that spread from a common centre, similar to umbrella ribs, are known as* **umbels**.

Fragrance

Butterflies have a very acute sense of smell. They are most strongly attracted to heavily scented flowers. Sadly, many pretty hybrids, bred for colour and size, have had the fragrance bred out of them. When buying plants to attract butterflies into your garden, seek out old-fashioned varieties that still have their own heady fragrance.

Beckon with butterfly weed

This perennial, also called butterfly milkweed (*Asclepias tuberosa*), gives rise to 1-metre-high stems topped with 5-centimetre-wide clusters of bright orange, red, or yellow nectar-rich flowers. The flat-topped flower clusters present perfect landing fields for butterflies in summer and autumn. Narrow seedpods follow the flowers, each containing flat brown seeds with long, silky hairs that aid wind distribution.

BUTTERFLY MILKWEED
(*Asclepias tuberosa*)

Butterfly weed also attracts bees. It requires full sun, good drainage, and moderate amounts of water. Not only does it make a great garden plant, but it also is a long-lasting cut flower, and the dried pods look charming in winter bouquets.

As a warning: parts of the butterfly weed plant may be poisonous if eaten, and the milky sap can irritate the skin.

Butterfly bush bonus

This well-known butterfly attractor was named after the Reverend Adam Buddle, a noted amateur English botanist of the 17th century. Clustered flowers can be pink, blue, purple, magenta, or white. Shop for plants that are in bloom to be sure you end up with the flower colour you like. Older varieties grow to 4 metres tall, and the newer dwarf varieties will grow to about 1.5 metres. Every garden should have a butterfly bush (*Buddleja davidii*), and the smaller ones fit snugly in a large patio pot. Give this attractive semi-evergreen shrub full sun and regular water. Members of the *Buddleja* genus do well in coastal areas and will tolerate some air pollution. The bush may die down in cold winter climates, but it generally returns in the spring.

BUTTERFLY BUSH (*Buddleja davidii*)

Do your own butterfly count

You can use the garden's butterfly bushes to carry out your own butterfly species count. It's remarkable how many will visit the sweet-smelling flower spikes on a warm summer's day.

If you're unfamiliar with the names of the many different visitors, borrow or buy a pocket guide to Britain's insect life, and you'll soon find that names such as Peacock, Red Admiral, Tortoiseshell, Brimstone, Comma, Holly Blue, and Speckled Wood, will become very familiar to you. If you're really lucky, lesser-known species such as Painted Lady and Wall Brown may grace you with an appearance.

Summoning shrub verbena

This is a delightful shrub, usually growing from 60 centimetres to 2 metres high. Depending on the variety, shrub verbenas (*Lantana camara*) may have quite a wide spread, possibly reaching 2.5 metres. In warm climates, shrub verbena will serve as an evergreen, but expect it to act like an annual in frosty areas. Numerous 1½-centimetre flowers, usually in two-colour pairings such as orange and yellow, or magenta and yellow, form multiple, 2-centimetre-wide bouquets from spring until autumn. The tiny black fruits that appear after the flowers are gone are poisonous – do not eat them! Shrub verbenas require a sunny site, good soil, and lots of water in the summer. You will need to move them into a greenhouse during the winter.

INTERNET

butterfly-conservation.org

For fascinating information on butterflies, how to attract them, and how to join a butterfly society, visit the site of the British Butterfly Conservation Society.

Beckoning butterflies

Butterflies are most drawn to gardens with generous patches of a nectar flower. Butterflies' favourite plants for nectar include:

- Aster (*Aster*)
- Bee balm (*Monarda didyma*)
- Black-eyed Susan (*Rudbeckia hirta*)
- Butterfly weed (*Asclepias tuberosa*)
- Cosmos (*Cosmos bipinnatus*)
- Goldenrod (*Solidago*)

- Lilac (*Syringa*)
- Mexican orange blossom (*Choisya*)
- Purple coneflower (*Echinacea purpurea*)
- Red valerian (*Centranthus ruber*)
- Viburnum (*Viburnum*)
- Yarrow (*Achillea*)

Caterpillars feed on plants to gain strength for their metamorphosis into butterflies, and adult butterflies tend to stay around areas where their caterpillar foods can be found. You

must plant enough plants so the caterpillars have a continuing meal. Great host plants to help them along are:

- Borage (*Borago*)
- Dill (*Anethum*)
- Hollyhock (*Alcea*)

- Parsley (*Petroselinum crispum*)
- Red clover (*Trifolium pratense*)

Moths are generally night-flyers and feeders, and so they like flowers that open in the evening. The best plants for attracting moths include:

- Four o'clock (*Mirabilis jalapa*)
- Hyssop (*Hyssopus*)

- Lavender (*Lavandula*)
- Tobacco plant (*Nicotiana*)
- Zinnia (*Zinnia elegans*)

FLOWERING TOBACCO (*Nicotiana*)

Attracting beneficial insects

IF YOU HAVE A GARDEN set up for birds and butterflies, chances are your garden is a haven for beneficial insects too. Beneficial insects include bumblebees, hover flies, ground beetles, honeybees, lacewings, ladybirds, and parasitic wasps. To keep these wonderful garden helpers around, you must provide shelter, water, and flowers. They prefer many of the same flowers as butterflies do.

Of course you should not use pesticides of any kind in your garden if you want beneficial insects, including butterflies, to thrive.

Hover flies

Also called syrphid flies, these insects are striped like bees, but are much slimmer. Adults have only one pair of wings, never buzz, and hover over flowers seeking nectar and pollen. They are good pollinators as they move from blossom to blossom. The young, resembling tiny, light-brown caterpillars, feed on pest aphids and mealybugs. To encourage hover flies plant:

HOVER FLY

- Baby blue eyes (*Nemophila menziesii*)
- Black-eyed Susan (*Rudbeckia hirta*)
- Cosmos (*Cosmos bipinnatus*)
- Marigold (*Tagetes*)
- Spearmint (*Mentha spicata*)
- Tickseed (*Coreopsis*)

Ground beetles

I love ground beetles because they eat slugs and snails. Ground beetles are plain, usually shiny black, fast-crawling beetles, about 2 centimetres long, with a small head, short antennae, and long legs.

GROUND BEETLES

Ground beetles also feed on cutworms and root maggots, among other nuisances. I encourage ground beetles by giving them some log pieces to hide under. They prefer sheltered sites during the day, emerging after dark, and occasionally will meander indoors.

Shoo ground beetles outside, but do so wearing gloves, because a few species will try to protect themselves by giving off a skin-irritating fluid.

Lacewings

These insects are about 2 centimetres long, green or brown, and have lacy, long wings. Lacewing larvae, or young, can each devour 60 aphids per hour, and also feed on leafhoppers, mites, thrips, and other small pest insects. The adults feed on flower nectar and pollen. To encourage lacewings into your garden, plant:

- Archangel (*Angelica archangelica*)
- Butterfly bush (*Buddleja davidii*)
- Campion (*Lychnis*)
- Common tansy (*Tanacetum vulgare*)
- Goldenrod (*Solidago*)
- Red cosmos (*Cosmos*)
- Tickseed (*Coreopsis*)
- Yarrow (*Achillea*)

Ladybirds

Most ladybirds are shiny red, orange, or yellow with black markings. Each adult ladybird is about 7 millimetres long. The wrinkled larvae, or young, are orange and black. Both adults and larvae feed on aphids, mites, whiteflies, and scale insects. Ladybirds emerge in spring, just as the aphids descend, and eat hundreds of these insects a day, making them a true gardener's friend. To encourage ladybirds, plant:

- Butterfly weed (*Asclepias tuberosa*)
- Marigold (*Tagetes*)
- Spindle tree (*Euonymus*)
- Yarrow (*Achillea*)

LADYBIRDS

Trivia...
The Vedalia ladybug beetle (Rodalia cardinalis) was the first successful predator to be introduced into a country for the control of a pest insect. In 1885 an outbreak of cottony-cushion scale threatened to destroy the California citrus industry. Once introduced, the beetles began chomping on the cottony-cushion scale.

Archangel ecstasy

This tropical-looking biennial plant, sometimes called angelica, offers bright green, deeply divided leaves and fragrant greenish-white flowers in large clusters. A rapid grower, it does best in rich, damp, soil planted in partial shade. In medieval times, archangel was believed to be sent by angels. It provided a cooked vegetable for the dinner table, candied stalks for dessert, kept evil spirits from entering the body, and offered protection from the plague. Archangel (*Angelica archangelica*) can grow to 2.5 metres high. The seeds may self-sow for next year's garden.

Cosmos companions

Cosmos (*C. bipinnatus*), sometimes called Mexican aster, can be found in perennial and annual varieties. The annuals may be white, pink, lavender, crimson, or bicoloured, but it's the white cosmos that is most attractive to beneficial insects. Ranging in height from 1 to 2 metres, cosmos prefer full sun, average soil, and moderate water.

Glorious goldenrod

These easy-to-grow plants are popular with beneficial insects. Although the wild species can be invasive, hybridizers have produced several goldenrods (*Solidago*) suitable for the home garden, including the seaside-happy *S. sempervirens*, the groundcover *S. sphacelata* Golden Fleece, and the clumping, 1-metre-high *S. rugosa* Fireworks. True to its name, goldenrod's flowers are bright golden-yellow, and provide lovely colour into the autumn.

Tempt them with common tansy

All species in the *Tanacetum* genus prefer full sun and well-drained, dryish soil, but will thrive in anything that's not soggy. They are hardy plants, quite frost tolerant, and a good perennial for areas where the growing gets tough. In really comfortable surroundings, some, such as common tansy (*Tanacetum vulgare*) and costmary (*T. balsamita*), may become slightly invasive. Others, such as painted daisy (*T. coccineum*), tend to behave themselves quite well. The common tansy is the one that ladybirds like best.

INTERNET

www.harmsy.freeuk.com/veggie/

Find out how to improve garden habitats for both people and wildlife, and how to attract useful predators.

A simple summary

✓ Even a small urban garden can attract butterflies, birds, and beneficial insects.

✓ If you have room, plant shrubs or trees, including evergreens, for winter bird shelter.

✓ Birds like plants with berries or other fruit, nuts, and seeds.

✓ Bird feeders will attract a nice variety of birds. Place a feeder where you can easily see it, but away from where a cat can hide.

✓ Welcome bats and hedgehogs to your garden and they'll make a meal of several highly irritating insects and pests, including midges, slugs and snails.

✓ Bring butterflies to your garden with nectar plants, particularly those that have orange, yellow, and purple flowers.

✓ If you want beneficial insects, including butterflies, to thrive in your garden, it is essential that you do not use any pesticides.

Chapter 21

Garden Nasties

THE SIMPLEST WAY to avoid having to read this chapter is to buy and maintain healthy plants. When your plants are in the right site and get the right nourishment, they'll be more resilient to pests. But even the accomplished gardeners have problems with disease, weeds, and the like.

In this chapter...

✓ *Hole punchers*

✓ *Sap suckers*

✓ *Fruit and veggie varmints*

✓ *Tree and shrub shredders*

✓ *Common plant diseases*

✓ *Weed world*

✓ *Pest controls*

✓ *Animal visitors*

Hole punchers

SOME PESTS DO NOT SEEM TO BE PARTICULAR *about what part of a plant they eat, but you'll know they've set up shop from the holes you see in leaves, flowers, fruit, and so on. Some of the most common hole punchers are earwigs, flea beetles, snails and slugs, and weevils.*

Earwigs

Earwigs are pincer-tailed insects. They usually eat decaying fruit or other garden litter. Occasionally you may get large earwig populations in the garden, and they'll snack on flowers or ripe fruit, creating small ragged holes. No chemical controls are usually necessary if you clean up garden debris and eliminate (to the extent possible) the bugs' hiding places.

Flea beetles

If you find very tiny black beetles jumping around your plants when disturbed, your plants have flea beetles. Their hopping movement is similar to that of the fleas that bother dogs and cats. They eat dozens of tiny round holes in leaves, preferring vegetable seedlings and young plants. These holes cause the leaves to quickly lose moisture, and the rapid drying may kill seedlings. No chemical controls are usually necessary. If an infestation is truly annoying, spray with an insecticidal soap, following the directions on the product.

Sneaky snails and slimy slugs

Not all garden pests are insects. Snails and slugs, which are molluscs, are frequent garden visitors. Although there are many different types of snails and slugs, they share a common feature: thousands of "teeth" on their tongue. The teeth act somewhat like a rasp, grinding food into bits before making it a meal.

Both snails and slugs prefer seedlings, young plants, and damaged plants. Usually working at ground level, they will also crawl up trees to feed on fruit. These creatures feed mostly at night, and

Trivia...

Unlike most other insects, earwigs are good parents. After both the male and the female create an underground nest, the female chases the male out. She then takes good care of the tiny white eggs, licking them clean to make sure no destructive fungus takes hold. When the babies emerge, the female earwig makes certain they stay close to home until they are ready to fend for themselves.

BROWN SNAIL

you'll see silvery slime trails in the morning as one clue to their nocturnal appearance. The other clue will be large, ragged holes in leaves, or possibly a total disappearance of your vegetable seedlings.

Snails and slugs hide in dark places during the day. Natural predators are frogs, snakes, and ground beetles. You probably don't want to lure snakes to your garden, but you might want to encourage ground beetles as a way to keep these pests in check.

If you can face it, you can just pick the snails and slugs up with your hand, place them in sealed containers or bags, and discard. Another option is to buy one of the many compounds available at garden centres that kill snails and slugs. These products have to be reapplied regularly, especially after rain.

INTERNET

www.ext.colostate.edu/ pubs/insect/05515.pdf

For more information on slugs, their history, habits, cultural controls, traps, barriers, and baits, click here.

Be cautious – all slug- and snail-killing compounds can cause serious illness or death if ingested. Keep children and pets away from areas treated with these products, and store products in a secure, locked place.

Weevils

Irregular notches on your plant leaf margins are telltale signs that your plant roots may have a family of vine weevil grubs living among them. An adult vine weevil can lay up to 100 eggs in the soil, close to the crown or stem of a plant.

Pot plants are particularly vulnerable. A healthy plant can collapse overnight through the root chomping actions of vine weevil grubs. Often, by the time you notice a plant in this sorry state, it's too late to save it.

VINE WEEVIL

If you suspect the presence of vine weevil grubs, tip the compost out of the pot, pick the grubs out and destroy them. With every grub you dispose of, you are preventing a future infestation of vine weevils.

For complete control of vine weevil, a parasitic nematode soil has proved to be the most effective method. Seek specialist advice on its use from your local garden centre.

Sap suckers

INSECTS THAT SUCK SAP from leaves can infest annuals, perennials, and
many other plants. Sap-sucking insects include aphids, leafhoppers, mealybugs,
scales, spider mites, thrips, and whiteflies.

*Sap-sucking insects have mouth parts adapted both for piercing and
sucking. Imagine, if you can stomach it, one or two needles surrounded
by a few straws. The mouth parts puncture the leaves, and then the insect
sucks up leaf sap or juices.*

The insect gorges itself, while the plant loses its nutrition. A severely infested plant
loses vigour and blossoms or fruits poorly. Some sucking insects may carry a plant virus
in their saliva, which they inject into the plant.

Aphids

Aphids are also called blackfly or greenfly, but can also be
yellow, grey, brown, or pink. Different species of aphids can be
found on flowers, buds, stems, leaves, and on plant roots. They
multiply with extraordinary speed, and are normally found in
clusters all over the growing tip of a plant, where it's easier to
feed on fresh new cells. A heavy infestation will distort buds and
flowers, and make leaves curl and go yellow. A sticky substance
on the plant, called honeydew, means that aphids are around.

■ **Black aphids** *infesting
an allium plant.*

I ignore the infestation if it's on my roses. If my nasturtiums
are infested, it's usually time to pull them up. Systemic insecticides (described in detail
in the next chapter) may be used to control massive aphid infestations, but choose a
formulation that will not harm beneficial insects.

Leafhoppers

LEAFHOPPER

There are different leafhoppers that live on rhododendrons, roses,
apples, strawberries, raspberries, potatoes, and a whole variety of
flowers grown in the greenhouse. Most adult leafhoppers are between
2 and 3 millimetres long and live on the undersides of leaves. You'll
probably only notice them as they jump and fly briefly when
disturbed. The wingless nymphs feeding causes a coarse, pale
mottling of the upper leaf surface. Leaf edges may turn dark brown,
and leaves may drop early. Some leafhoppers transmit plant viral
diseases. For severe infestations, use an insecticide spray.

Read the container label carefully to be absolutely certain your plant can withstand the insecticide. You can do more damage with the wrong insecticide than the leafhoppers do.

Mealybugs

These powdery, whitish insects are the bane of many outdoor garden plants. Mealybugs are usually found in groups, initially clustered within leaf-stem junctions and at fruit-stem junctions. If not controlled, they will take over an entire plant. Each female can deposit as many as 600 eggs, and there may be three generations each year.

A severe infestation may require a systemic spray or a biological control. You must treat the entire plant, including stem and leaf undersides.

Do not treat fruit trees when they are blooming, as you will kill the bees that are pollinating the trees for you.

MEALYBUG

Mites

All plant pest mites are extremely small – less than 1 millimetre long. Each mite puncture results in a little white dot where sap, containing chlorophyll, has been removed. Infested plants gradually become speckled, and then begin to yellow and shrivel. On plants that are heavily infested with spider mites, the leaves may be covered by webbing.

Houseplants are vulnerable to red spider mites as they are often kept in a dry atmosphere. Mist the leaves regularly with a fine spray of water to minimize the risk of mite infestation.

SPIDER MITE

There are pesticides that will slow down the mite population, but before you try them, see if you can decrease the mite infestation by hosing down the plants with a fairly heavy water stream from the garden hose.

Whiteflies

If you disturb a plant and a cloud of white flies start flying about, you've got whiteflies. Whiteflies suck sap from many annuals, perennials, fruits, and vegetables, and the plant leaves may become yellow and curled. They excrete a waste substance called honeydew. A sooty fungus grows on the honeydew, turning the area black. Many beneficial insects feed on whiteflies, so try an insecticidal soap before resorting to stronger chemicals.

Fruit and veggie varmints

IF YOU LOVE A JUICY, *sweet plum picked right off the tree, you're not alone. Some insects attack fruit crops with the same sort of gusto you might apply to a bowl of fruit salad. If you plan on growing fruit, look out for codling moths, pear midge, pear and cherry slugworm, and sawflies. There are also many unwanted vegetable visitors including caterpillars, cutworms, carrot root flies, and pea moths.*

Apple sawfly

The adult sawfly lays eggs in fruitlets just at flowering time, and on hatching, a grub leaves a characteristic ribbon-shaped scar on the apple surface, before tunnelling its way into the heart of the fruit to feed on the central core. This normally causes the fruit to drop in June or July. When the larva is fully fed, it'll depart via an exit hole, crawl into the ground to pupate, and emerge later as an adult.

Once sawflies are within the fruit, they are protected from all chemical controls. So it's not worth spraying the fruit. You will not harm the insect, but the spray might harm anyone who eats the fruit.

Pick off and destroy fruitlets showing signs of damage before the larvae escape into the soil. If infestations are severe, spray the tree branches with an appropriate insecticide, reading the instructions carefully.

Cherry blackfly

Leaves at the tips of cherry shoots become curled in late spring, and dense colonies of black aphids are clearly visible on the leaf undersides. Leaves are distorted and growth is severely checked. Foliage can be covered in a sticky honeydew, and by mid-summer, some of the affected leaves may turn brown and dry up completely. This insect will affect both flowering and fruiting cherry varieties. During the summer time, if you think the blackflies have stopped, don't be fooled. They've only flown off to take up temporary summer residence on other plants, particularly in the brassica family, for the adults to return in October to lay more eggs!

Spray fruit trees in winter with a tar oil wash, which should control any eggs laid near buds in October and due to hatch in March. Keep a sharp look out for aphids on new growth from mid-spring and spray with a product containing malathion. If you use a stronger acting systemic product, normally recommended for killing aphids, it could damage the sensitive cherry foliage.

Codling moths

The most common cause of wormy apples, these whitish-pink moth larvae also feed on pears. When the codling moths have invaded, you'll see small holes in the fruit skin with dark brown, crumbly matter around the holes. As if the larvae damage wasn't bad enough, the holes are perfect sites for bacterial and fungal growth. The larvae drop to the ground or crawl down the tree trunks when they are ready to spin cocoons. They may over-winter under tree bark or in garden litter. Severe codling moth infestations can totally destroy a fruit crop. Damage is worse in years that have warm, dry spring-time weather, because the moths lay more eggs.

To protect your garden, clean up garden fruits as they fall, and place rejects in a covered container for eventual disposal. Remove weeds and other debris to eliminate larvae hiding places.

Pear and cherry slugworms

Black slimy 'strips' on pear tree leaves signal the presence of the pear and cherry slugworm. These are small, shiny, slug-like larvae that feed on pear, cherry, apple, almond, hawthorn, and rowan leaves from late spring to mid-autumn. The larvae are up to 10 millimetres long, are swollen at the front end, and graze on the upper surface of the leaf only, leaving the skeleton behind. Apart from the cosmetic damage they cause, the tree goes hungry because it relies on its leaves as a food factory. Control this pest by spraying with an insecticide containing malathion as soon as the young larvae are seen.

Pear midges

The early symptom of the pear midge is when small fruitlets become deformed and blackened and fall off the tree in late spring and early summer. With a bad infestation, all the fruit can be lost. On splitting the fruit, you'll see a large central cavity and numerous tiny white grubs up to 2 millimetres long. On small trees, pick off and destroy infested fruitlets before the maggots complete their feeding. You can stop the adult flies laying eggs by spraying with an appropriate insecticide at the white bud stage of the tree, which is when you can see the petal colour but before the flowers have started to open.

Tortrix moths

The leaves of fruit trees are spun together with silk webbing, or are rolled into a tube to give the small caterpillar of the tortrix moth protective cover while it grazes on the inside layer of leaf, causing the rest of the leaf to go brown and dry up. The easiest way to control this pest is to pick off the rolled up leaves, or give them a quick squeeze to squash the caterpillar inside. Spraying will only work if you're prepared to really drench the tree.

Carrot fly

The first sign of this common pest is reddish leaves on your carrot crop that wilt in sunny weather. Closely related plants such as parsley, parsnip, and celery are also susceptible. The female adult, drawn to the soil by the strong carroty scent, lays clusters of small eggs that hatch in about a week. When you're thinning out your crop, take care not to bruise the leaves, as this makes the carrots smell more strongly and so attracts these pests. Planting a row of onions in between your carrots is supposed to throw the female off their scent. It's a perfect arrangement as the smell of carrots is said to deter the onion fly from laying her eggs too! Pull up carrots as soon as they are ready and don't leave any to over-mature in the ground.

CATERPILLAR HOLES

Caterpillars

Caterpillars of the large cabbage white butterfly will eat big ragged holes in the outer leaves of cabbage, broccoli, Brussels sprouts, and cauliflower, and caterpillars of the small cabbage white will feed mainly in their hearts. Infested plants wilt during warm days even if they are watered; they will eventually turn yellow.

Keep a regular check on your brassicas from early summer to early autumn. If you're not squeamish, you can pick the caterpillars off the plants as you see them. Otherwise, try the bacterium *Bacillus thuringiensis*, an organic method of destruction. Spray as soon as cabbage white butterflies are seen in the spring.

Cutworms

The soil-dwelling caterpillars of some moths feed above soil level on many vegetables and flowers, often attacking at night and severing stems to the ground. They may also eat leaves and roots and burrow into potatoes and carrots. Plants are most at risk during June and July. Cutworms tend to work their way along a row of crops, so if you find a decimated plant, it's worth tilling the soil nearby to expose the culprits. Older cutworms tend to be insecticide resistant, so a nematode drench is often used to get rid of them. Ask at your local garden centre for advice on appropriate pest-control products.

Pea moths

Caterpillars up to 6 millimetres long live inside pea pods, feeding on developing peas. Damage is most severe from July to August. The adult female emerges from the soil in early June, and lays eggs while the pea plants are in flower. There is only one generation of this pest per year, so time your sowing to prevent its attack. Sow well before March or well afterwards to avoid the plant being in flower during the moth's flight period.

Thrips

Of all the species of thrips, the western flower thrip is one that can attack a wide range of plants from houseplants to cucumbers, tomatoes, and other greenhouse plants, and is also a serious menace in the outdoor garden. On some plants, it feeds mainly on the leaves, producing a silvery mottling on the upper leaf surface. With chrysanthemums, violets, streptocarpus, verbenas, gloxinias, and fuchsias, it's mainly the flowers that are attacked. The added "value" is that these thrips can transmit tomato spotted wilt virus, which causes dieback and distorted growth on many plants. This pest was unknown in U.K. before around 1986. Chemical control is very difficult as it has a fair degree of resistance to many insecticides, and is quite secretive in its habits.

Tree and shrub shredders

APHIDS, BARK BEETLES, BORERS, capsid bugs, gall mites, leaf hoppers, leaf miners, mealybugs, sawflies, scales, and spider mites are some of the undesirables that may visit your trees and shrubs. You don't want a close up and personal encounter in your garden, so let's do it here instead.

Bark beetles

Adult bark beetles lay their eggs in tunnels that they have eaten under tree bark. The emerging white larvae, often called borers, continue making tunnels. These tunnels destroy a vital layer of the tree's inner bark, which is responsible for trunk and limb growth. The resulting damage is seen in the form of dead twigs and branches, or worse, in the form of dead trees or shrubs.

There are many different species of bark beetles, and most of them are harmless as they are secondary pests on plants that are already dying from other causes. Bark beetles prefer unkempt trees and those suffering from drought, over-watering, transplant shock, or mechanical injury such as that caused by lawnmowers. However, the most notorious bark beetle to us in the U.K. is the elm bark beetle. These breed in dying elm trees, including those infected with Dutch elm disease, and they have helped to spread this killer disease.

As with most pests, the best defence is good vigilance. Keep your ornamental, evergreen, and fruit trees healthy. Plant them in appropriate sites in the first place to avoid unnecessary stress, fertilize them regularly, and water them deeply during dry spells. Insecticides are not appropriate to use, as for much of the year the bark beetles are protected under the bark.

Capsid bugs

Chrysanthemums, fuchsias, roses, hydrangeas, and forsythias are among the plants affected by capsid bugs. They pierce the plant using a needle-like stylet, inject saliva and feed on the sap. Most of the actual damage is done in late spring or early summer. As the plant grows, the leaves begin to look increasingly tattered. Capsids tend to be rather elusive and so control is not always easy. It's a good idea to tidy under the plants in winter by raking out leaf litter and other accumulations of plant debris that may provide over-wintering niches for the bugs. Early in spring, spray with a systemic insecticide to give your plants some protection.

Gall mites

These microscopic animals can be found on many garden trees and shrubs. They feed mainly on leaves, and secrete a chemical that encourages the host plant to make an abnormal growth, in a variety of shapes of blisters, cylinders, and small cauliflower-like structures. You may see these on acers, lime trees, mountain ash, and pear and plum trees. With a few exceptions, most gall mites are totally harmless and can live on their host plants with little or no effect.

Leaf miners

The larvae of some insects spend their entire feeding lives tunnelling in the cell tissues between the upper and lower leaf surfaces. Some of the tunnels made are in straight lines, others in circular or blotch patterns, and some are complete freehand meandering paths. The pattern adopted is specific to the particular insect group. Among the plants often affected are apple trees, pyracanthas, laburnums, hollies, azaleas, and lilacs.

A quick-fix remedy is to pick off the affected leaves and dispose of them carefully. However, because most plants are relatively tolerant of leaf miners, control measures are often unnecessary.

Mealybugs

Mealybugs are soft-bodied, greyish-white or pink creatures, measuring up to 4 millimetres long. They are most commonly found on houseplants and plants grown in a greenhouse, but can affect other plants in the open garden such as New Zealand flax. Mealybugs are difficult to treat as they produce a fluffy wax that protects the insect's body and also hides the eggs.

There are also mealybugs that feed specifically on plant roots, and plants growing in containers are particularly vulnerable. Root mealybugs are difficult to eliminate. Try drenching the potting compost with a spray-strength solution of malathion. With a severe infestation, it's better to carefully dispose of the affected plant altogether.

Scales

Scales, resembling little brown or grey bumps on plant stems, are found on just about every type of outdoor fruit, ornamental, and evergreen tree. There are two types of scale insects: soft-shelled scales, and hard-shelled or "armoured" scales with a hard, brown or grey shell.

HARD-SHELLED SCALE INSECT

INTERNET

uidaho.edu/so-id/
entomology/scale_insect
_and_mealybugs.htm

*Click here for descriptions,
photographs, and information
on how to cope with scales
and mealybugs.*

The shell, often made up of waxy fibres and cast-off skins, protects the soft-bodied insect underneath from almost all forms of chemical control. Accordingly, scales are difficult to eliminate once they find a home. Chemicals are generally useless in the home garden.

The best scale control is to encourage beneficial insects to inhabit your garden. They will either feed on young scales before the pests can form their protective shell, or will pierce the shell and deposit eggs that feed off the scale beneath.

Common plant diseases

THERE IS A SEEMINGLY *infinite number of viral, bacterial, and fungal diseases that may affect plants. Some of them you truly can't do anything about. Others are treatable, but you have to be quite knowledgeable about the proper treatment. By using the wrong spray or by using the right spray incorrectly, you can injure the plant without distracting the disease in the least.*

If you want to be a plant doctor, my recommendation is to go to an established nursery or large garden centre, take with you a sample of the damaged plant, and ask for help.

If you choose to treat your plants in any way, follow the instructions on the container to the letter. Always make sure the label lists your plant as appropriate for treatment.

The following diseases are quite common, and will give you an idea of the variety that can visit your garden. But don't really worry. If you keep healthy plants growing in a suitable site, you will probably have few problems.

MOULD AND MILDEW

You've probably seen mould on household edibles left to linger too long. (Or, if you're like me, the bread you buy seems to develop it on the way home from the shop.) Let's look at the most common moulds and mildews.

Grey mould

Unfortunately, the fluffy grey fungus covering your garden strawberries can occur at any growth stage, including when they are just getting tasty and ripe. This mould may be preceded by light tan spotting on the berries. Destroy infected fruit as soon as you see it. Do not let berries become overripe. Avoid overhead watering, because fungi thrive in cool humid weather. When planting the following year, leave enough space between plants for good air circulation and rapid drying.

Sooty mould

This blackish fungus grows on honeydew, and on the sugary waste material deposited by aphids, mealybugs, scales, whiteflies, and other sap-sucking insects. The leaves and fruit of a plant with sooty mould appear dirty, but the mould can be wiped off. You may want to control whatever insect is causing the problem.

Downy mildew

This is an infection that is confined to the undersides of leaves, although you'll also see corresponding yellow or discoloured patches on the upper surface. A bad dose can cover the whole leaf and literally kill it off. Downy mildew thrives in hot, damp weather and is especially common on young plants. Your plant will be vulnerable if you've been feeding it with a plant food that's high in nitrogen, as this encourages soft, sappy, new growth which the fungus finds easy to penetrate. Ensure that plants are not overcrowded and remove weeds and debris promptly.

Powdery mildew

Powdery mildew usually occurs after May. Powdery white patches appear on leaves, stems, buds, and even on flowers. Leaves may turn yellow and/or purple and can drop off. Affected buds may never open. Plants growing in dry, sheltered sites, such as against a wall, are vulnerable. The disease thrives in hot weather. Pick off and destroy affected leaves and water affected plants regularly, but not from overhead.

Bacterial soft rot

I love bearded irises, and it bothers me when one develops yellowing, dying leaves.
If I pull it up, the rhizome is mushy, rotted, and stinky. Bacterial soft rot has infected the
plant, entering by iris slug holes or other wounds – some of them possibly incurred
during planting. This disease isn't limited to irises; it also affects melons, cacti, flower
bulbs, carrots, and other plants. On potatoes, the slimy texture and vile stink are
easy-to-recognize symptoms.

There is no cure, so prevention is critical. Make sure your soil is well drained, and avoid
over-watering and overhead watering. Buy healthy plants, because just one unhealthy
bulb can bring this bacteria into your garden soil. Try not to damage bulbs and
rhizomes during planting, and place all bearded irises in a sunny site.

Fireblight

A bacterial disease, fireblight destroyed several of my towering pyracantha, almost
overnight. The bushes turned black as if they were completely scorched by fire, and
there wasn't a green leaf left. The interesting thing is that fireblight attacks some of the
pyracanthas and skips the others. I don't know why, although I've read that *Pyracantha
coccinea* Lalandei and *P. fortuneana* aren't as badly affected by the bacteria.

In addition to pyracantha, fireblight seriously affects cotoneaster and is fond of ruining
apple, pear, plum, cherry, and hawthorn trees, among others. There is no cure for
fireblight. Avoid planting fruit trees in heavy, poorly drained soil, and avoid over-
feeding, both of which are said to increase a tree's susceptibility. If fireblight strikes,
remove the plant and replace it with another that is not prone to this disease.

Peach leaf curl

If you have a peach tree and if your springtime weather is cool and wet, every so often
you will probably have to endure peach leaf curl. Caused by a fungus, it is one of the
worst diseases infecting peach trees. Peach leaf curl causes new leaves to pucker and
curl up. The leaves develop red or yellow areas, over which a white coating may appear.
If fruit forms, it is deformed and usually falls before it is ripe. After a while, the leaves
darken and fall. The leaf loss causes nutritional deprivation, and the tree becomes
weaker. Although a tree will survive a year of severe peach leaf curl, several years in
succession will kill it.

There is no cure for peach leaf curl. If you see
it developing, remove and destroy infected
leaves. There is a preventive spray available
for use in autumn after the leaves drop, or
in the spring before the buds open. The
entire tree must be treated.

PEACH LEAF CURL

Weed world

WEEDS SEEM TO THRIVE *with much more ease than our favourite plants. Weeds are basically any plants that grow where they are not wanted. They tend to be on the vigorous side, which is no surprise, inasmuch as they sprout in our gardens with no help from us. Some weeds are found all over the country, but others are fairly climate specific. Details follow on some weeds that seem to grow just about anywhere.*

Couch grass

Couch grass (*Elymus repens*) is a difficult weed to control, because it possesses an extremely efficient root system. If you dig this one out and leave even a minute amount of root in the soil, it'll regenerate itself with remarkable speed. It is best controlled with a systemic chemical, which uses the plant's vigorous growth system to eradicate itself!

The trick is to apply the herbicide during the months when the plant is actively growing, so that it is absorbed through the leaves and deep into the heart of the root system where it acts as a food blocker. The plant is not poisoned, it's literally starved to death.

Dandelion

The dandelion (*Taraxacum officinale*) tap root easily extends 1 metre down in the soil, and may go even further than that. The

■ **Dandelion roots**
must be pried out carefully – or they will grow again.

tap roots are quite thick, in larger plants almost resembling a whitish, skinny carrot. If, when removing the tap root, you leave even a trace of root, the entire plant will regrow. This, among other factors, accounts for dandelions' continued existence in lawns and anywhere else the sun shines. Yellow flowers appear in spring and persist until frost. The flowers are followed by the familiar white puffballs. Each feathery strand acts as a parachute for the seed at its base. A strong wind carries seeds for miles. Herbicides are available to control dandelions.

Trivia...
Dandelions have been used as a food source and as a medicine for at least 1,000 years. The name apparently originated from a German surgeon's commentary that each leaf of the plant resembled a lion's tooth, or dens leonis in Latin. The French were soon calling the plant dent-de-lion. Dandelion greens were used for salad and tea, roots were served as a vegetable course, or were dried and used as a coffee substitute. The flowers of this plant were used to concoct dandelion wine, and to make a yellow dye for wool.

Ground elder

Ground elder (*Aegopodium podagraria*) is a serious weed in anyone's book, and the irritating thing is that it can pop up just about anywhere in the garden. Getting rid of it may take time and a good deal of patience. There is little point in trying to dig it out, as if you leave in even a tiny piece of the root, before you have time to turn around it has regenerated into another invasive plant. There is a systemic weedkiller that will get rid of it, but it must be used with great care.

Mouse-ear chickweed

Bothersome around vegetable and flower gardens, lawns, trees and shrubs, and unplanted areas, this dense, low-growing weed can crowd out your plants. It thrives in sunny areas where the soil is poor and damp. This plant's stems root wherever their joints touch the soil, starting more chickweed (*Cerastium fontanum*), and its seeds are present from the spring until autumn, also starting more plants.

It is difficult to control mouse-ear chickweed. If you pull it up by hand, be sure to remove all plant parts including the roots, which will otherwise re-sprout. There are herbicides available for control.

More garden weeds:

- Annual meadow grass (*Poa annua*)
- Annual nettle (*Urtica urens*)
- Bindweed (*Convolvulus arvensis*)
- Broad-leaved dock (*Rumex obtusifolius*)
- Cleavers (*Galium aparine*)
- Coltsfoot (*Tussilago farfara*)
- Common chickweed (*Stellaria media*)
- Common ragwort (*Senecio jacobaea*)
- Creeping buttercup (*Ranunculus repens*)
- Creeping cinquefoil (*Potentilla reptans*)
- Creeping thistle (*Cirsium arvense*)
- Creeping yellow cress (*Rorippa sylvestris*)
- Curled dock (*Rumex crispus*)
- Fat hen (*Chenopodium album*)
- Groundsel (*Senecio vulgaris*)
- Hairy bittercress (*Cardamine hirsuta*)
- Hedge bindweed (*Calystegia sepium*)
- Horsetail (*Equisetum arvense*)
- Japanese knotweed (*Fallopia Japonica*)
- Knapweed (*Centaurea nigra*)

- Knotgrass (*Polygonum aviculare*)
- Lady's thumb (*Polygonum persicaria*)
- Lesser celandine (*Ranunculus ficaria*)
- Nightshades (*Solanum sp.*)
- Nipplewort (*Lapsana communis*)
- Oxalis (*Oxalis corymbosa*)
- Perennial sow-thistle (*Sonchus arvensis*)
- Pineappleweed (*Matricaria matricaroides*)
- Red dead-nettle (*Lamium purpureum*)
- Rosebay willow herb (*Epilobium*)
- Scented mayweed (*Matricaria recutita*)
- Shepherd's purse (*Capsella bursa-pastoria*)
- Silverweed (*Potentilla anserina*)
- Smooth sow-thistle (*Sonchus oleraceus*)
- Spear thistle (*Cirsium vulgare*)
- Speedwell (*Veronica filiformis*)
- Sun spurge (*Euphorbia helioscopia*)
- White dead-nettle (*Lamium album*)

NIGHTSHADE
(*Solanum sp.*)

Pest controls

YOU MAY, FROM TIME TO TIME, *think about using some type of* **pesticide** *in or around your garden. You will probably go to the garden centre nearest you and ask a staff member what to do about the leaves curling on your fruit tree, the green bugs on your roses, or some obvious damage to a plant. Of course, the level of knowledge of staff members at a garden centre or even a specialist nursery will vary. They may point you to a certain product and say this will take care of your problem. It may, or may not.*

The use of pesticides is a science, one that has been made much easier for the novice with the constant work of chemists and other researchers working for manufacturers. But it still requires attention on your part. Some plant treatments may be effective at one time of the year, but ineffective at others. Some plant treatments may work on one plant but be harmful to another. Let's look at how pesticides work.

> **DEFINITION**
>
> *Of course you know that a* **pesticide** *is a pest control mechanism. But pesticides are not just toxic sprays coming out of airplanes. "Pest" is defined by the Environmental Protection Agency as a living organism causing damage or economic loss, or that carries or causes diseases. So a pesticide can be for use against animals, insects, or weeds.*
> *Specifically, a pesticide designed for use against insects is called an insecticide. A pesticide designed for use against fungi is called a fungicide. A pesticide designed for use against weeds is called an herbicide.*

Organic pesticides

Organic pesticides are composed of natural products, but should be used only as necessary. They may kill some beneficial insects as well as harmful ones. Generally, plants should be treated with organic pesticides either early in the morning or late in the afternoon, when bees are not busy pollinating.

BT (*Bacillus thuringiensis*): This is a bacterial insecticide formulated as a spray containing live fungal spores and a toxin. Leaf-feeding caterpillars ingest the spray residues and are quickly poisoned.

Insecticidal soap: This is a spray-on mixture sold in almost all nurseries. It has been used since at least the 1700s. Insecticidal soaps act to paralyze insects and must contact the insect's body to be effective. Target pests include aphids, leafhoppers, mealybugs, mites, young scales, red spider mite, thrips, and whiteflies.

Organic pesticides are short-lived and work by contact with the pest. This means they must be sprayed or dusted directly onto the pest to be effective, and you must be prepared to repeat applications regularly.

Bordeaux mixture: This fungicide is used to control rust on blackcurrants and gooseberries, leaf spot on celery, and canker on edible apples. It is non-systemic, which means that it is not absorbed by the plant through its roots or leaves. It works by coating the leaves and remains active for up to several weeks. Use it with great care because it's harmful to animals and fish.

Derris: Derived from the roots of a tropical plant, the active ingredient is a powerful alkaloid called rotenone. It's used as a dusting powder to control aphids, red spider mite, weevils, and caterpillars. It won't harm animals but will kill bees and fish, so never use it near a garden pond.

Pyrethrum: This is made from the flowers of the pyrethrum daisy (*Tanacetum cinerariifolium*), and can safely be used on all edibles to control greenfly, blackfly, strawberry aphids, thrips, sawfly, weevils, leaf hoppers, flea beetles and capsids. It is harmful to fish, ladybirds, ladybird larvae, and bees.

Sulphur: Flowers of sulphur, dusted on overwintering tubers, helps to prevent them from going rotten while in store.

Organic traps: These can be easily constructed to deal with a number of pests. Earwigs can be trapped in inverted flower pots filled with straw, while slugs are drawn to shallow trays filled with beer. In greenhouses, whiteflies (which are attracted to the colour yellow) can be caught on a piece of yellow card smeared with grease. Inspect these traps regularly and dispose of the pests.

Synthetic pesticides

When using any chemical in the garden, always read the label. Read the label before you buy the product, before you mix it, every time you use it, before storing it, and again before discarding it. Every label will tell you what ingredients are in the product, how hazardous the product is, any special use precautions, and the directions for use.

Follow the instructions on pesticide labels to the letter.

When applying a pesticide, wear gloves, goggles, and a covering garment. Wash your hands thoroughly after use, and wash clothing separately from other laundry. Discard or store all chemical products with the utmost safety.

■ **Always wear protective** *rubber gloves when applying insecticide sprays.*

INTEGRATED PEST MANAGEMENT

Integrated pest management (IPM) is a phrase you will hear frequently used among professional garden people. IPM uses multiple controls to try to manage garden pests, beginning with those that are the least harmful to the environment. Education is the key to successful use of IPM techniques. The more you understand about pests, the more successful you will be at getting rid of them. Many insects are beneficial for your garden. Although there certainly are harmful insects, some damage is merely unsightly and doesn't truly hurt the plant.

Practitioners of IPM often find they don't have to use chemicals. If they do need to use an insecticide, they probably will first try an organic product. When used correctly, organic insecticides are usually safer for people and pets than those that are made from synthetic chemicals. They also cause less environmental chaos.

The various methods used by IPM advocates include:

- **Physical controls:** Hand-picking pests from plants and screening off plants to keep pests away.

LADYBIRD

- **Cultural controls:** Selecting the right plant for the right spot, planting disease, and pest-resistant varieties, pruning at the correct time of year, using proper pruning tools and techniques, and proper watering and fertilization practices.

- **Biological controls:** Taking advantage of living organisms that naturally eliminate pests. They are often present in your garden of their own accord, if the use of pesticides, insecticides, and herbicides hasn't killed them off.

Parasitoids are organisms whose young develop in or on a pest insect, usually causing the pest insect's death.

Biological controls include predators and parasites. Beneficial insects such as hover flies, lacewings, ladybirds, and ladybird larvae will devour aphids, while frogs, hedgehogs, and birds will eat many pests including slugs and snails, woodlice, millipedes, and wireworms. Spiders do their bit, too, by trapping and eating larger flying pests. The parasitic wasp (*Encarsia formosa*) deals very nicely with whiteflies, and there are a couple of species of microscopic nematodes (especially *Phasmarhabditis hermaphrodita*) that attack slugs as well as vine weevil grubs (*Heterohabditis megidis*).

It is extremely important when considering the use of any pesticide in a garden that you do not use it on or near food plants unless the label specifically states that it is safe to do so.

The label will state what, if any, food plants may come into contact with the product. The label will state treatment times, and how long you must wait to harvest after treatment. All garden pesticides can be extremely hazardous to health, and some are suspected carcinogens. It is much better to prevent problems by good garden care and proper plant selection.

■ **Store all chemicals** *safely out of reach of children and animals – preferably in a locked cupboard.*

Synthetic insecticides

Some chemical insecticides work on contact, and others have a systemic action. Contact insecticides must come in direct contact with the insect to have any effect. Contact insecticides for garden use are sold as a dust, spray, liquid concentrate, or soluble powder. When using a contact pesticide, you must thoroughly treat all parts of the plant, because some insects live primarily on the undersides of leaves. Systemic pesticides are those that will travel throughout the plant. An insect feeding on any plant part will ingest the systemic chemical that will kill it.

It is possible for some pests and fungal diseases to build up an immunity or tolerance to chemicals, so that a pesticide that was once effective no longer works. Continual use of the same chemical is not to be recommended. Different insecticides contain different active ingredients, so it's a good idea to rotate these regularly. All pesticides are poisonous to people, animals, and birds, and some will harm beneficial insects.

Synthetic herbicides

It is quite tedious to pull out weeds over and over again. Many gardeners find it easier to use a herbicide or weed killer to do the job. There are four common types of synthetic herbicides: pre-planting, pre-emergent, post-emergent, and sterilizers.

Pre-planting herbicides are used after you have prepared the soil, before you plant your seeds. They destroy weed seeds in the soil. After you have followed the directions, plant the seeds. Pre-emergent herbicides are used to destroy seeds as they germinate. They do not affect established plants or weeds. Post-emergent herbicides are used after the grass or other plants are established and you want to eliminate growing weeds. These products, usually sprays, may kill any plant on which they land. Sterilizing herbicides kill all plants they come into contact with. If sprayed on a plant, they will kill the leaves and then attack the roots and kill them. Avoid using these on a windy day.

Herbicides have their practical uses, but they can be quite poisonous to people, pets, wildlife, fish, birds, and insects. Read and follow the instructions on the container.

Synthetic fungicides are used as preventives, not as cures. If your plant has a fungal disease, a fungicide will probably not cure it, but it may prevent the spread of the disease. When using a fungicide, always read the label and apply it as directed.

Animal visitors

AS OUR HOMES IMPINGE ON NATURE, *many animals have learned to adapt and even to use the garden as a food depot. Some people find this nice, others find it cute, and some get quite annoyed. Animal visitors you may come across include birds, badgers, cats, deer, hedgehogs, squirrels, mice, moles, rabbits, rats, and foxes.*

Being patient with badgers

Badgers are shy creatures, so you'll be lucky to see them in your garden, even though there might be plenty of evidence that they've been there. They can be a nuisance when they start to dig around in lawns and flower beds for their favourite foods of chafer grubs, leatherjacket larvae, and other insects. They are fairly weighty animals, so if there's a fence in their way, they're quite likely to barge their way through it. Badgers will sometimes feed on garden crops such as strawberries, raspberries, and gooseberries. They also like vegetables, particularly potatoes, carrots, and sweetcorn.

Badgers are an endangered species and are protected by law. If their presence in your garden is causing persistent damage, contact the RSPCA Wildlife Department in Horsham, West Sussex for advice.

Bothersome birds

Most birds are welcome in gardens, and are even invited with bird feeders and birdbaths. On the other hand, some birds are a nuisance, such as blackbirds, crows, house sparrows, magpies, pigeons, and starlings. Birds can get to your ripe fruit before you do, making little holes as they peck hungrily away. If you have just planted seeds, seed-eating birds seem to know and can scratch away at the soil looking for titbits that were intended to be vegetables. To keep your seeds in the ground, you can put 1-centimetre mesh cover over them, but remember to remove it as the plants begin growing.

To protect fruit trees and bushes, try covering them with netting. Or you may be able to scare the birds off (for a while, at least) by dangling strips of shiny aluminium foil from the branches so that they sway in the breeze. Regardless of the number of trees you have, it is wise to pick fruit as it ripens. Don't leave over-ripe fruit lying around, as this serves as an invitation, and once the birds become accustomed to using your garden as a dining venue, it will be very difficult to convince them to go elsewhere.

INTERNET

rspb.org.uk

Click here to find out how to deal with other bird problems, such as putty pecking and collisions with windows, as well as for tips on looking after birds.

Coping with neighbourhood cats

It can be extremely annoying if cats from the surrounding neighbourhood are using your garden as a convenience. Cats like freshly turned over and dry soil, so one quick remedy would be to keep the regularly visited area as damp as possible – they just don't like getting their feet dirty!

Repellant substances based on pepper dust, naphthalene, or ammonium are available, but few can claim more than a temporary solution to this vexing problem. Ask at your local garden centre for advice on the products available. Alternatively, you could opt for a very traditional deterrent. According to folklore, the one scent that cats cannot abide is orange and garlic. Grate some up and sprinkle the mixture on any ground where you do not wish cats to tread!

Foxing those foxes

Foxes may visit your garden from time to time, especially in towns and suburbs where they have learned that dustbins provide plenty of ready food. You may even find them making dens under your garden shed! Although largely nocturnal, foxes do wander around in broad daylight, causing damage by digging up or trampling on plants.

Male foxes mark out their territories, and this can create an unpleasant nuisance. Foxes are very agile, and it is extremely difficult to prevent them from entering your garden. The one thing you can do is to avoid using bone meal or dried blood products as plant fertilizers. The smell of these encourages foxes, who are led to believe that a decent meal is buried in your garden.

Meddlesome moles

These furry animals do considerable damage in a garden, not only because their tunnelling results in unsightly molehills, but because it can also result in collapsing soil under your shrubs, causing their roots to die. You can discourage moles from spoiling your garden by depriving them of their primary source of food – earthworms.

Moles have an acute sensitivity to sound and smell. This means that you can discourage them simply by sticking a head of garlic or an onion firmly down their runs.

Another method of deterring moles is to bury bottles up to their neck in soil. The loud humming caused by any breeze across the open bottle neck is very unpleasant to moles' highly sensitive ears.

Ravenous rabbits

Many people like to see rabbits hopping about the garden, but because they have a taste for many garden plants as well as rather large appetites, they can wreak havoc. As well as enjoying a good nibble of your prize vegetables, rabbits will gnaw the bark from the base of young trees. They especially like apples, and in some severe cases, this consistent gnawing can kill a tree.

You can try excluding rabbits from your garden by surrounding it with 1-metre-high, 3-millimetre-thick wire fencing – however, unless the wiring can be concealed with plants, this is hardly an aesthetic solution! If rabbits are a serious problem in your area, you might like to try growing plants that they don't like. These include rose of Sharon (*Hypericum calycinum*), hedgehog – or Japanese – rose (*Rosa rugosa*), any deciduous azaleas, Mexican orange blossom (*Choisya ternata*), philadelphus, butterfly bush (*Buddleja davidii*), daphne, hydrangeas, magnolias, and weigelas.

Squirrel problems

Squirrels are very mobile creatures and it's a fact of life that once you get rid of one lot, you're guaranteed to get a new crowd moving into the vacated territory! Squirrels are interested in young trees, flower buds, and nuts. They gnaw at bark, and eat flower buds and ripening fruits. You can use netting to protect fruits and flowering shrubs such as magnolia and camellia during periods when squirrels are showing interest in them.

If you are using permanent structures such as fruit cages, make sure that they are made from wire, rather than plastic, as squirrels can easily chomp through plastic. You can also place wire netting over the soil where bulbs and corms have been planted. This will deter the squirrels from digging them up. If you want to feed garden birds, but not attract squirrels, you can buy squirrel-proof bird feeders from most good garden centres.

A simple summary

✓ A well-planned, well-tended garden, clean started with healthy plants, is the simplest way to prevent disease and to deter unwelcome wildlife.

✓ If you are going to treat plants with any type of pesticide, make sure the product is designed to address the specific problem that your plant has, and that it is safe to use on the afflicted plant.

✓ Always follow the directions on the label of all pesticides.

✓ Organic pesticides are readily available and generally less toxic to the surrounding environment than synthetic pesticides.

✓ To deter unwanted animals and birds, remove dropped fruit and pick fruit when ripe.

✓ Generally, insects are good for gardens. They pollinate flowers and feed birds. Some insects are pests. There are beneficial insects that eat these pests.

✓ Pesticides of any kind, organic or chemical, kill beneficial insects as well as harmful ones.

✓ Use a control method designed for use against the insect. If you're not sure, have a professional help you identify it.

✓ Use good garden hygiene. Clean up all garden debris and remove rotting leaves promptly, as this is where fungi or pests often lurk.

✓ Never use a pesticide directly on fruit. If a pest insect is inside, no control will reach it, and someone eating the fruit might become ill.

✓ Never spray fruit trees in bloom, as you will kill pollinating bees.

✓ Keep your water source clean so that it does not harbour diseases.

✓ Water your plants appropriately, use the correct amount of fertilizer, and plant them where they will get the proper amount of sunlight.

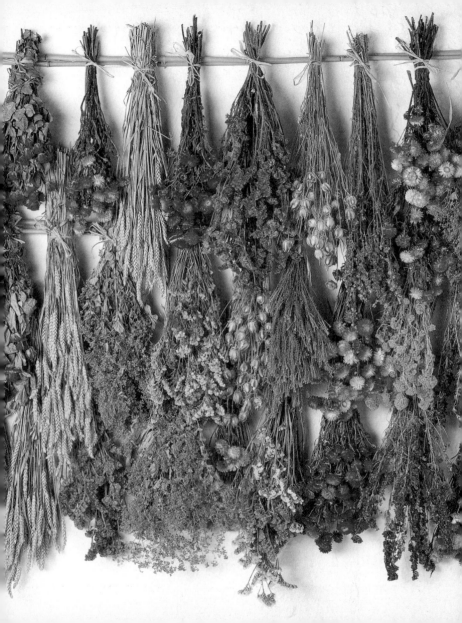

Chapter 22

A Time to Every Purpose

THERE IS SOMETHING to do in an outdoor garden throughout the year. It's easy in the spring, when just the thought of blossoms draws you outdoors. Summer is a lazy time, but a warm day with a breeze is ideal for a visit to the garden centre or a day spent playing in the soil. Autumn is clean-up time. In winter, you can order catalogues to peruse, admire your indoor plants, and by January, start deciding which roses to choose.

In this chapter...
✓ *Projects for spring*
✓ *Special projects for summer*
✓ *Autumn activities*
✓ *Whiling away the winter*

Projects for spring

IT'S NEVER TOO EARLY to get busy. In February, plan your vegetable garden and plant bare-root roses. (February may not really be spring; your roses might go in a month later.) In March, begin installing summer-flowering bulbs. After the last frost, prune rose bushes for shape. In April, fertilize the lawn and plant annuals and vegetables. See where you can use time-saving ground-cover plants and perhaps purchase plants for a water garden. You might need to check and refurbish supports for your climbers. You can always try some fun projects indoors, such as the ones that follow.

Start a lemon tree

To grow a lemon tree (*Citrus limon*) inside, begin with three seeds taken from different lemons. Soak the seeds overnight and then let them dry. Fill three containers with sterile potting mix. The containers can be polystyrene cups or something more elaborate, as long as they have a small drainage hole in the base. Place each container on an old dish or pie pan. Put a seed in each container, pushing it 1 centimetre into the soil, and cover with soil. Water lightly, so that all the soil becomes damp. Shelter the containers loosely using a sandwich bag. Place the containers in a warm, not hot, place. You can place them near, but not under, a table lamp that is on for about 3 hours a day. Water the containers whenever the soil feels slightly dry.

In a few weeks, small plants will appear. Uncover the containers and put them in a sunny site. Continue to water lightly. When the trees reach about 10 centimetres, move them to larger pots and keep them in the sun.

Don't forget to water your lemon tree, but don't over-water.

Fertilize the soil every 6 weeks with a citrus fertilizer. As your trees grow, you will have to move them into larger pots. Eventually you may want to move them into the garden. Depending on the conditions, your trees should bloom in 3 to 5 years. You can also try orange, mandarin orange, lime, and grapefruit seeds.

Grow a sweet potato vine

If you have an organic fruit and vegetable shop near you, buy your sweet potatoes (*Ipomoea batatus*) there. If the only choice is the supermarket, buy several sweet potatoes, because many of these have been treated not to sprout. Look for those that have started little white roots, or have little purple root bumps sticking out.

Fill three large glass jars or three clear vases with tap water. Place four toothpicks around each sweet potato. The containers should be large enough to hold the sweet potato dangling in place, without its sides or bottom touching the glass. Taller containers allow more room for root development. The water in the container should reach halfway up the sweet potato. Keep the containers in a warm, shady place. Add lukewarm water to keep the level at the halfway mark. If you don't see any white roots emerging, or if the container water starts to smell after about 2 weeks, you'll have to discard it.

If the plant grows, you will see green stems that will develop ivy-like leaves. It will grow nice long vines for several months. Remember to keep water at the halfway mark in the container. When the vines start to die down, you can add them to your compost pile.

Create a display of vegetable greenery

This project is fun for children. Start with a bowl about 10 to 15 centimetres high. Uproot from your garden, or buy, some large carrots, several radishes, and perhaps a few parsnips. Place the whole radishes in the bowl. Cut off the top 5 centimetres of the carrots and parsnips and put these in the bowl, cut side down. Add pebbles to hold them in place. Add water until it reaches the halfway mark on the vegetables. Place your bowl in a bright site and wait for the foliage to grow. Keep the water at the halfway mark.

CARROT AND
PARSNIP TOPS

Grow hyacinths in a glass

Hyacinth bulbs (*Hyacinthus*) are available in October or November. After a few months they'll provide fragrant blossoms. You will need a hyacinth glass to grow them in water. This is a container shaped like an hourglass. The bulb sits in the top and roots form at the base. Keep the roots covered with water. Alternatively, put the bulbs in sterilized all-purpose potting compost in a pot. Cover with soil so just the tip is visible. Place in a cool site (5 to 10° C) for 6 to 8 weeks. Keep the soil slightly moist. When leaves appear, move the pot to a brighter site.

Trivia...

In ancient Greek mythology, Hyakinthos was the god of spring flowers. The god Apollo adored Hyakinthos, but killed him by accident. The hyacinth flower sprang up from the blood of the dead youth. The hyacinth is symbolic of sorrow, sadness, and resurrection.

When the flower buds begin to display colour, put the pot in a sunny window at about 16° C. Do not overheat. When flowering is over, cut off faded flowers but keep the soil moist. Let the greenery die back and plant the bulbs outdoors in early spring.

HYACINTHS

Special projects for summer

OF COURSE, YOU'LL HAVE PLENTY to do in the garden during the summer. Start in May, making sure your plants are kept as healthy as possible so they can resist insect pests that thrive in this season. If necessary, re-seed or re-turf the lawn. Plant shrubs and hedges that provide berries and shelter for birds. Plant your annual vegetables and flowers. During June, fertilize azaleas, camellias, and rhododendrons. This is also a good time to fertilize the lawn. July is for planting autumn-flowering bulbs and for buying colourful perennials to liven up special garden sites. Read on for more fun ways to spend the summer months.

Make pomander balls

Pomander balls have been used to scent closets for hundreds of years and they make super home-made gifts. The original pomanders had an apple base (*pomme* is the French word for "apple"). You can still make a pomander ball from a small, hard apple, but lemons, limes, or oranges are much longer lasting. It'll take a visit to your greengrocer to get lots of fruit to use for this project, which will provide plenty of fun for the whole family. Children especially love to try making pomanders.

You'll need a fork, one or more containers of whole cloves, some allspice or ground cinnamon, and, of course, your citrus fruits. Poke shallow holes in the fruit with your fork. Either use a random pattern of poking, or opt for a design featuring a cross shape of holes around the fruit. Push a clove into each hole until the citrus is covered with cloves. Don't push too hard or the clove will disappear. You want it to stud the citrus exterior. When the cloves are in place, sprinkle the pomander ball with allspice or cinnamon. Poke a hairpin in the citrus centre, leaving the rounded tip exposed so that you can pull it out and insert a ribbon.

The citrus should dry for at least 2 weeks in a dry, sunny spot. Turn the fruit occasionally, so the bottom gets some air, or place it on an elevated rack. The citrus will gradually shrink and become quite hard. This shrinkage holds the cloves in place. To complete the pomander, either insert a pretty ribbon into the hairpin and tie it in a loop, or tie a ribbon round the ball, as shown here. Use the ball as a wardrobe freshener or as a Christmas decoration. Some people cover their pomander balls with colourful netting, tying it with bright ribbon. Pomander balls should last for years.

■ **Fragrant pomander balls** *make a pretty home-made gift for a friend – or even for yourself.*

Dry some herbs

On a warm afternoon, when the plants have not been recently watered, gather cut stems with leaves on them just before the flowers open. Place the cut stems, a bit apart from each other, on an elevated screen located in a shady, warm spot. Leave the stems and leaves on the screen until they're dry. Turn them from time to time to hasten drying.

■ **Dry flower** bunches by tying them up and hanging them upside down.

If you're drying more than one type of herb, label each group. Unless the weather is really humid, drying should take about 6 days. If the stem snaps easily, the herbs are dry and it's time to pick them. The flavour diminishes if you wait too long. Strip the leaves from the stems and store in a well-closed jar.

Dry some lavender

The best lavenders for drying are common lavender (*Lavendula angustifolia*), L. intermedia, and French lavender (*L. dentata*). For the best results, use the darkest-coloured flowers you can find. Cut long spikes with pruning shears or a pair of scissors just as the blossoms are opening up. Remove all the leaves from the cut plant and hang the stems in loose bundles of about 12 stems, grouped together with a rubber band. The stems should be hung in a warm, dry, dark place – a garage is ideal. The flowers should dry out in about 2 weeks. When they have, strip them from the stems to use in *potpourri* and other fragrant crafts.

LAVENDER

> **DEFINITION**
>
> A *potpourri* is made up of dried flower petals and spices. But it also can contain sweet-smelling seeds, stems, and roots. Its scent comes from the aromatic oils found within each plant.

Dry some rose petals

On a hot, dry late afternoon, gather fully open roses in good condition. Select those with a really great fragrance, as they make the best potpourri. Old roses are particularly good for the job. In a dry place, such as a garden shed, put a piece of fine mesh on top of some blocks or bricks, so that it is raised about 5 to 7 centimetres off the floor or surface. Sprinkle the petals singly, so that they don't touch each other, over the mesh and leave them for about 2 to 5 days, or until they are dry to the touch but not crumbly. If the petals touch, the overlapping parts might develop mildew, which will ruin the scent. Other petals are dried in the same way.

> **INTERNET**
>
> www.make-stuff.com/gardening/lavender_wand.html
>
> *How to make pretty, sweet-smelling lavender decorations.*

Make your own potpourri

It's fun and inexpensive to make your own potpourri. First, find a large wide-mouth jar that can hold about 2 litres and has a lid. These jars can often be found at car boot sales or food wholesalers. If you can't locate a nice big jar, a smaller one will do.

Put in the jar about 1 cup each of dried lavender flowers and dried rose petals. Add ½ cup dried marjoram leaves and ¼ cup of dried leaves from two of the following: lemon balm (*Melissa officinalis*), lemon verbena (*Aloysia triphylla*), mint, orange, or rose-scented geranium (*Pelargonium graveolens*). You can also try concoctions with dried fragrant petals of carnation, chamomile, heliotrope, honeysuckle, lilac, lily-of-the-valley, mignonette, or tuberose. Add 1 tablespoon of dried orange peel, ½ teaspoon cloves, and ½ teaspoon cinnamon. You can substitute ½ teaspoon allspice or ½ teaspoon nutmeg for the cloves and cinnamon. Seal the jar for 4 to 6 weeks. Shake the jar well, and, if possible, stir the mixture just about every day. Shaking and stirring encourages good interaction between all the ingredients. This mixture will smell lovely for quite a while when placed in pretty, open containers.

To make potpourri last a long time, many people add a fixative before letting it blend in the sealed jar.

A fixative absorbs the aromatic oils and slowly releases them. A common fixative is orris root, made from dried iris rhizomes.

To add a fixative, put about 1 tablespoon in each large jar of potpourri. There are several other fixatives available, and you might want to enquire at a local chemist or craft shop. An alternative is the dried and ground leaves of clary sage (*Salvia sclarea*), a pretty aromatic perennial for the garden. Or you can sprinkle dried pickling salt on your potpourri as a fixative. This is a non-iodized salt, which is available at some specialist groceries.

■ **Displays of potpourri** *cheer up the home in the winter months when fresh flowers are scarce.*

To keep ingredients for a potpourri all year round, separate the dried leaves and flowers in their own containers and keep them tightly sealed until you're ready to mix and place out around the house.

INTERNET

www.frontiercoop.com/ ac/botcraft/potpourri. html

You'll find complete details about potpourri fragrance and how to make and use potpourri. This site provides potpourri history and lore, fragrance classifications, equipment, fragrant ornaments for any season, fragrant wreaths, skin allergy tests, and sources of essential oils used in perfume.

Autumn activities

WHEN AUTUMN ARRIVES, the gardener has a host of jobs. September is one of the most important times of the year in your lawn care programme, and any time spent now on basic maintenance will pay dividends next year. It's time to plant spring-flowering bulbs and to start the annual clean out of the greenhouse before all your precious half-hardy plants are brought in out of the winter cold.

Decorate your home with daffodils

Paper White and Soleil d'Or are exquisite, tiny daffodils (*Narcissus*) that can be started indoors in water. The bulbs are usually available in September, and will bloom within 2 months. Paper White has white petals surrounding a yellow centre, and Soleil d'Or is a golden colour. Set bulbs about 2.5 centimetres apart in an attractive container about 12 centimetres deep. Surround the bulbs with small pebbles or coloured gravel. These are available in garden centres or pet shops that sell tropical fish. About half of each bulb should be visible. Add water to the container until it covers about 2.5 centimetres of the bulb base. Put the container in a dark, cool site, at 10 to 18° C, checking on it from time to time to make sure it has enough water for root development.

In about 3 to 4 weeks, when the plants have developed a sturdy root system, put the pots in a sunny, warm site. These water-grown daffodils will never re-bloom indoors, but if you live in a relatively warm-winter area, you can let the foliage die back naturally and plant the bulbs outdoors after they have finished blooming.

Cut dried flowers

Every garden should have a little space put aside for growing plants suitable for making dried flowers. You don't have to grow lots in a special place, a few plants of straw flower (*Bracteantha* or *Helichrysum*), statice (*Limonium sinuatum*), sunray (*Helipterum*), and safflower (*Carthamnus tinctorius*), dotted among the bedding and mixed borders are all that's needed. Other flowers suitable for drying include delphinium, love-in-a-mist (*Nigella*), hydrangea, sea holly (*Eryngium maritimum*), roses, and Chinese lantern (*Physalis*). The easiest way to prepare them for the house is by air drying them.

It's best to cut the flower stems just before the centres of the blooms open. This way they keep their shape and colour better, and are less likely to fall apart on drying. Most types are best cut early in the morning. Gather about half a dozen stems in a bundle with an elastic band or string. Stagger the flowerheads so that they don't touch one another and become damaged. Hang them upside down in a dark, warm, and airy place.

Create some apple dolls

After a few years, your apple tree will give you more apples than you need for cakes, pies, juice, and everyday munching. Experiment with making apple dolls. Making apple dolls is a true art form, and it takes experience to get the best results. But it all begins with the first apple.

If you don't have extra apples, buy several large red apples at the supermarket. Try different kinds if you want, to see what works best. Peel the apples, leaving just a little circle of skin at the top and bottom. Carve little holes where you want the eyes. To keep the apples from turning brown, squeeze lemon juice on them, making certain to cover well. You will have to hang the apples up to dry. Inserting a piece of rustproof wire, such as picture wire, through each apple from bottom to top gives you a hanging mechanism. Make a hanger-type loop at the top of the wire and knot the bottom. Place the drying apples in a cool, dark, draught-free site. Let them dry for about 3 weeks. Use white glue to add seeds, beads, or buttons for eyes. A red marker makes rosy cheeks. Cut a smiling mouth with a small pair of scissors and use a red marker or red felt pen to accentuate it. To keep the head shiny and well preserved, cover it with some glossy acrylic varnish from a craft shop.

You can make the bodies out of just about any container. A plastic container works nicely and won't break. Small, empty washing-up liquid bottles are a good size. All containers should be filled with sand. Push the holding wire into the container, then glue on the apple head. You can make arms with pipe cleaners pushed through cuts in the container. Design clothing as you please and glue it to the container. Use cotton wool balls or plain cotton wool to form hair.

Pretty placemats from autumn leaves

This project is fun and educational. Collect pretty autumn leaves of various shapes and place them, about 2 centimetres apart, in a single layer, between several sheets of newspaper. Change the paper after 24 hours. You can make multiple layers of leaves and newspaper, placing one on top the other. Put an old telephone book, board, or other heavy weight on top of the pile, and check that all areas are pressed down. Leave for about a month.

Cut a rectangle of clear sticky-back plastic of about 25 by 35 centimetres. Peel the backing off carefully and lay it on a table with the sticky side up. Place the dried leaves carefully in a design of your choosing. Once they're placed they can't be moved, so you might make an image of the design before setting the leaves on the sticky paper. Cover your arrangement with white or beige paper, letting it stick to the contact paper. You now have a placemat or a decorative picture.

■ **Collect attractive** *leaves in early autumn, before they dry and shrivel.*

Whiling away the winter

THE DARK DAYS OF WINTER *are a good time to get ready for the year
ahead. As early as November you can start preparing your garden. This is a
good time to prune your shrubs and to spray fruit trees for insect and
disease prevention. You'll also want to remove any dead and diseased
wood from your trees before the cold weather really sets in. In
December and January, start shopping! You can begin looking
for bare-root roses and fruit trees at garden centres. It's a good
idea to prune your rose bushes so they'll be pretty come
flowering time. Browse through garden catalogues and buy
some gift plants for the holidays.*

INTERNET

**ag.ohio-state.
edu/~ohioline/hyg-
fact/1000/1248.html**

*Try this site for detailed
instructions on how to get a
poinsettia to re-bloom
indoors a year after you have
received it.*

The Christmas gardener

During the Christmas season, there's a good chance you'll be giving
and receiving some pretty gift plants. Although not all gift plants
will thrive forever, some may last quite a while in your home, and
a few may even do well if transplanted properly outdoors. Some of
the traditional Christmas gift plants have problems surviving long term because they've
been forced to flower way out of their normal season by growers using severe light
alterations. It is difficult for the plant to recover from this shock, but not impossible.

Whether you are the giver or the recipient, you can keep Christmas plants looking great
with just a bit of simple care. The saucer-like containers underneath the colourful foil
wrapping of most plants are often a bit shallow and might leak. Put a plate or other
larger saucer under the plant package to protect your furniture and carpets. To prevent
root rot, empty the saucer and the surrounding foil regularly. Gift plants you'll most
likely be tending include azaleas (*Rhododendron*), Christmas cactus (*Zygocactus
truncatus*), florist's cyclamen (*Cyclamen persicum*), Jerusalem cherry (*Solanum
capsicastrum*), and poinsettias (*Euphorbia pulcherrima*).

Maintaining azaleas

There are evergreen and deciduous azaleas, but gift plants are more commonly the
evergreens. With care, these are rather easy to place outside in rich, somewhat moist,
well-drained soil. They like a semi-shady site outside. Indoors, give your gift plant
plenty of bright light (but not direct sun), and keep it at a room temperature of about
18° C. Never let the plant's soil dry out, and avoid draughty sites. A warm draught for
more than a few hours will cause almost total leaf drop and can kill the plant.

The gift plant may continue to flower for almost a month if you remove faded flowers promptly. Feed it with a liquid fertilizer for houseplants every 2 weeks if you intend to place it outdoors. When all the flowers are gone, acclimatize it outdoors in a sheltered site, and then plant it directly in soil.

The leaves of azaleas are poisonous. Don't let your kids or your pets chomp on them.

Keeping florist's cyclamen

Place the gift pot in a cool, well-lit area, but not in direct sunlight. Do not let the plant touch a cold glass window. Keep the plant at a room temperature between 10 and 15° C, and keep the soil slightly moist. When watering, use lukewarm water and try to keep it off the leaves. With good care, the flowers won't completely fade until February.

I've had success placing the gift pot outdoors in a sheltered, lightly shaded spot until it acclimatizes, then transplanting it carefully into very rich soil when the weather is consistently pleasant. Plant the cyclamen where the drainage is excellent, or the tuberous roots will rot.

The joys of Jerusalem cherry

Also called Christmas cherry and winter cherry, the pretty scarlet berries of this plant are poisonous, as is every other part of the plant. Outdoors, it is an evergreen with white, star-shaped flowers in the spring, followed later by the bright berries. It can slowly reach about 1 metre in height. Indoors, keep the plant in a cool, sunny site, at about 10° C. If the room is warm or draughty, the leaves and fruit will quickly drop. If you want a challenge, dry and store their seeds until the spring, then put them in a mix of 50 per cent sand and 50 per cent peat moss. Keep them warm until they are about 7 centimetres high, then transplant them to a larger pot. Put outdoors in summer in a semi-shaded site, watering when the soil feels slightly dry, and fertilizing lightly.

■ **Keep Jerusalem cherry** *away from children and animals who might be tempted to touch them.*

Poinsettia perfection

The most popular of Christmas plants, poinsettias can last for months indoors. Place your semi-tropical gift plant in a sunny site, preferably keeping it at a temperature between 15 and 24° C. Although you may need to place it near a window for the sunshine, keep the leaves from touching a cold window, as this will cause leaf damage.

Poinsettias are big water users. Keep your plant's soil just slightly moist at all times or the leaves will wilt and drop if it's too dry. Check the saucer under the pot, and if water is pooling there, drain it. Stagnant water will injure the plant's roots and start to smell unpleasant. Eventually the leaves will turn yellow and drop. Indoors it is difficult to maintain a poinsettia so that it re-blooms the following year. While the red-flowered poinsettias are most common, there are also white, pink, yellowish, and speckled red and white varieties.

■ **Poinsettias will last** *well into the New Year if cared for properly. Try to place them away from vents that blow out heat, as these plants dislike draughts, be they warm or cold.*

Poinsettia flowers appear to be composed of the plant's bracts, or modified leaves, that resemble petals. But the actual flowers are the little yellow centres surrounded by the bracts.

Once the poinsettia fades, put it outdoors in a sheltered, sunny spot, keeping the soil moist. In spring, you can transplant it into prepared soil. Keep the soil moist and you may eventually have a 3-metre-high shrub. You can also make cuttings in late summer. Some people have a skin reaction to the sap, so it's best to wear gloves when handling poinsettias.

A simple summary

✔ There are still garden chores to be done in the winter and there is garden fun to be had throughout the year, both indoors and out.

✔ Many indoor gift plants can be transplanted outdoors after the flowers fade. Place them outside in a sheltered spot while still in their container. Water the plants as needed, and replant appropriately in the spring.

✔ You can use the plants you grow to make lovely personal gifts, such as handmade dolls and your own potpourri.

413

More resources

Books

I have more than 400 garden reference books, some quite antique. I love book shops, the kind that have stacks of dusty books, because I often find a treasure with new titbits of information, or a self-published book written by a devotee of this or that plant, or just something with scrumptious detail on a subject I love.

From my garden library, I have here compiled a list of the books I go to first when I have a garden question. Some of them are available in most book shops or via the Internet, but others you must hunt for in independent book shops, or in the shops adjoining botanical gardens across the country. It's so much fun – a learning adventure. Enjoy yourself!

The Royal Horticultural Society's Pests & Diseases
by Pippa Greenwood and Andrew Halstead, Dorling Kindersley, 1997.

The Royal Horticultural Society's Propagating Plants
by Alan Toogood, Dorling Kindersley, 1999.

The Royal Horticultural Society's Pruning & Training
by Christopher Brickell and David Joyce, Dorling Kindersley, 1996.

The Royal Horticultural Society's A–Z of Garden Plants
by Christopher Brickell, Dorling Kindersley, 1997.

The New Lawn Expert
by Dr. D.G. Hessayon, Transworld Publishers, 1997.

The New Rose Expert
by Dr. D.G. Hessayon, Transworld Publishers, 1997.

The Fruit Expert
by Dr. D.G. Hessayon, Transworld Publishers, 1995.

The Kitchen Garden, Month by Month
by Andi Clevely, David & Charles, 1996.

The New Houseplant Survival Manual
by Jane Bland and William Davidson, Ward Lock 1995.

Know your Common Plant Names
by Brian Davis and Brian Knapp, MDA Publications, 1992.

Plant Names Simplified
by A.T. Johnson and H.A. Smith, Hamlyn Publishing, 1972.

The Herb Garden, Month by Month
by Barbara Segall, David & Charles, 1994.

The Conservatory, Month by Month
by Barbara Abbs, David & Charles, 1997.

The Plant Hunters
by Toby Musgrave, Chris Gardner, and Will Musgrave, Cassell & Co, 1999.

Complete Fruit Book
by Bob Flowerdew, Kyle Cathie Ltd, 1995.

How to Build a Wildlife Garden
by Chris Baines, Frances Lincoln, 2000.

The Royal Horticultural Society's Encyclopaedia of Herbs
by Deni Brown, Dorling Kindersley, 1995.

Ornamental Grasses, Bamboos, Rushes & Sedges
by Nigel J. Taylor, Ward Lock, 1994.

Directories of great gardens

Gardens of England & Wales
  The National Gardens Scheme
  Hatchlands Park
  East Clandon
  Guildford
  Surrey GU4 7RT
  01483 211 535

Gardens of Scotland
  Scotland's Gardens Scheme
  31 Castle Terrace
  Edinburgh
  Scotland EH1 2EL
  0131 229 1870

The Royal Horticultural Society Gardeners' Handbook 2001
  P.O. Box 313
  London
  SW1P 2PE
  020 7821 3000

Magazines for the gardener

It's almost too easy to find magazines devoted to gardening. Go to any large newsstand or bookstore and you'll find dozens of titles to appeal to gardeners at all levels. Alternatively, there's a wealth of webzines on the Internet. A sampling of popular gardening magazines include:

Amateur Gardening
BBC Gardeners' World Magazine
The English Garden
Essential Water Garden

The Garden
Garden Answers
Gardens Made Easy
Garden News
Gardening Which?

Gardens Illustrated
Kitchen Garden
Organic Gardening
The Mediterranean Garden
Water Gardening

Gardening societies

Alpine Garden Society
AGC Centre, Avonbank
Pershore
Worcs WR10 3JP
01386 554 790
www.alpinegardensociety.org

British & European Geranium Society
4 Higher Meadow
Clayton-le-Woods
Chorley
Lancs PR5 2RS
01772 453 383
www.begs.org.uk

British Cactus & Succulent Society
15 Brentwood Crescent
York
YO10 5HU
01904 410 512
www.cactus-mall.com/bcss

British Clematis Society
4 Springfield, Lightwater,
Surrey GU18 5XP
01276 476 387

British Fuchsia Society
P.O. Box 1068
Kidderminster
Worcs DY11 7GZ
01562 66688

British Hosta & Hemerocallis Society
Toft Monks, The Hithe
Rodborough Common
Stroud
Glos GL5 5BN
www.casarocca.com/bhhs/html

British Iris Society
1 Sole Farm Close
Great Bookham
Surrey KT23 3ED
01372 454 581

British Orchid Council
P.O. Box 1072, Frome
Somerset BA11 5NY
01373 301 501

British Pelargonium & Geranium Society
75 Pelham Road
Bexleyheath
Kent DA7 4LY
01322 525 947
www.bpgs.org.uk

Cottage Garden Society
Hurstfield House
244 Edleston Road
Crewe
Cheshire CW2 7EJ
01270 250 776
www.alfresco.demon.co.uk

Cyclamen Society
Tile Barn House
Standen Street
Iden Green, Benenden
Kent TN17 4LB
www.cyclamen.org

Delphinium Society
Summerfield
Church Road
Biddestone
Chippenham
Wilts SN14 7DP
www.delphinium.demon.co.uk

Hardy Plant Society
Little Orchard
Great Comberton
Pershore
Worcs WR10 3DP
01386 710 317
www.hardy-plant.org.uk

Heather Society
Denbeigh, All Saints Road
Creeting St. Mary
Ipswich
Suffolk IP6 8PJ
01449 711 220
www.users.zetnet.co.uk/heather

Hebe Society
Rosemergy, Hain Walk
St Ives
Cornwall TR26 2AF
01736 795 225
www.hebesoc.vispa.com

Herb Society
Deddington Hill Farm
Warmington
Banbury
Oxfordshire OX17 1XB
01295 692 000
www.herbsociety.co.uk

Japanese Garden Society
Groves Mill, Shakers Lane
Long Itchington
Warwickshire
CV23 8QB
01926 632 747

National Begonia Society
33 Findern Lane
Willington
Derbys DE65 6DW
Tel: 01283 702 681

National Chrysanthemum Society
George Gray House
8 Amber Business Village
Amber Close
Tamworth
Staffs B77 4RD
01827 310 331

National Council for the Conservation
of Plants & Gardens (NCCPG)
The Stables Courtyard
RHS Garden
Wisley
Woking
Surrey GU23 6QP
01483 211 465
www.nccpg.org.uk

National Dahlia Society
19 Sunnybank
Marlow
Bucks SL7 3BL
01628 473 500

National Sweet Pea Society
St. Anne's
The Hollow
Broughton
Stockbridge
Hants SO20 8BB
01794 301 490

Royal National Rose Society
The Gardens of the Rose
Chiswell Green
St. Albans
Herts AL2 3NR
01727 850 360
www.roses.co.uk/harkness.rnrs/rnrs.htm

Saintpaulia & Houseplant Society
33 Church Road
Newbury Park
Ilford
Essex IG2 7ET
020 8590 3719

Gardening on the web

THE INTERNET IS A HUGE RESOURCE for gardeners. You can find out anything you need to know about gardening, join clubs and societies online and order other supplies you need- all without going beyond your garden gate!

www.alfresco.demon.co.uk
Promoting the conservation of worthwhile old-fashioned garden plants, this site encourages owners of small gardens to garden in the informal cottage style.

www.alpinegardensociety.org
This society caters for anyone interested in rock gardening or alpine plants, with pictures and information on these plants and the chance to join a seed exchange scheme and use its advisory service.

www.botanical.com
This site features information on many medicinal herbs. On the home page, click on "word search", and then type in the name of the plant you want information about.

www.british-trees.com
Visit the British Trees web site for a guide to native trees and a picture gallery, plus details of other tree organizations.

www.bulb.com
This is the site of the Netherlands Flower Bulb Information Centre; you'll find plenty of facts about tulips and other bulbs grown commercially in Holland.

www.cactus-mall.com/bcss
Find out more about cacti and other succulents, including advice on choosing and growing these plants, at this British Cactus & Succulent Society web site.

www.cyclamen.org
Based in the U.K., the Cyclamen Society has an international membership. Its work includes research and conservation.

www.delphinium.demon.co.uk
As a new member, you'll receive a packet of seed, and all members can buy the society's hand-pollinated seeds of garden hybrids and species. The illustrated *Year Book* is a unique source of information about the genus.

www.dspace.dial.pipex.com/town/square/gf86/
The site of the Lawnmower Museum in Southport, Lancs. It displays the largest collection of vintage lawn mowers in the world, as well as town lawnmowers and lawn mowers of the rich and famous.

www.frontiercoop.com./ac/botcraft/potpourri/index.html
This site provides a rundown on potpourri history and folklore, fragrance classifications, equipment, fragrant ornaments for any season, fragrant wreaths, skin allergy tests and sources of essential oils used in perfumes.

www.gardenlinks.org.uk
A handy guide with lots of links to sites dealing with all aspects of gardening, from societies to tools, lawncare to garden centre and nursery listings.

www.grasses.co.uk
A site that's dedicated to growing ornamental grasses, featuring news, slide shows and tips on choosing, growing, and propagating these plants.

www.hardy-plant.org.uk
The Hardy Plant Society has its own garden in the grounds of Pershore College of Horticulture. There are six special interest groups – grasses, hardy geraniums, half-hardy plants, peonies, and variegated plants.

www.herbsociety.co.uk

This comprehensive site will tell you all you ever wanted to know abut herbs. Plus you can join the society to receive a quarterly newsletter; and seminars and workshops are arranged nationwide.

www.nationaltrust.org.uk

Visit the National Trust's site for full details about this organization, which has more than 2.7 million members and protects more than 248,000 hectares of land.

www.nccpg.org.uk

The National Council for the Conservation of Plants and Gardens (NCCPG) is a national body that works to preserve individual plants and endangered gardens. The society's most successful innovation has been the establishment of more that 600 national collections. Click here to find out more about its work.

www.ngs.org.uk

This National Gardens Scheme site features hundreds of gardens that are open to the public to raise money for charity. There's also a listing of garden events nationwide.

www.nhm.ac.uk/science/projects/fff

Developed by Flora for Fauna with the Natural History Museum, this is an invaluable resource for anyone who wants to find out which plants grow naturally in their area. Search by postcode or by any of 2,670 postal districts to get information on plants, plus birds and mammals.

www.rhs.org.uk

The site of the Royal Horticultural Society, where you can find out about the RHS gardens at Wisley, Rosemoor and Hyde Hall, plus much more on horticulture in general.

www.roses.co.uk/harkness/rnrs/rnrs.htm

This is the site of the Royal National Rose Society whose main aim is to promote the love of roses. In its Gardens of the Rose, you'll see more than 1,700 different roses. There are always hundreds of new roses on trial for awards, and there's a full advisory service.

www.soilassociation.org

The Soil Association's site features plenty of helpful advice on soil testing, improving your soil, and organic issues, plus lots more.

www.thompson-morgan.com

One of the best seed sites on the Web, this is a comprehensive online seed catalogue. There is also a good range of new plants, bulbs and sundries to buy, together with an A-Z search bar and illustrated references along with detailed sowing instructions.

Catalogues for gardeners

UNLESS SPECIFIED, catalogues listed here are of general interest. The inclusion of the following catalogues is for informational purposes only and does not serve as an endorsement of a particular vendor. There are many fine suppliers of seeds and equipment that are not mentioned here.

Johnsons Seeds
Maltmore Gate
Spalding
Lincs PE11 2PN
0800 614 323

S.E. Marshall & Co Ltd
Wisbech
Cambs PE13 2RF
01945 466 711

Reads
Hales Hall
Loddon
Norfolk
NR14 6QW
01508 548 395
www.readsnursery.co.uk

Gardening Direct
FREEPOST CL 4097
Kelvedon Park
London Road
Rivenhall
Witham
Essex CM8 3ZA
01376 575 575
www.gardeningdirect.co.uk

Thompson & Morgan (UK) Ltd
Poplar Lane
Ipswich
Suffolk IP8 3BU
01473 695 225
www.thompson-morgan.com

Chiltern Seeds
Bortree Stile
Ulverston
Cumbria
LA12 7PB
01229 581 137

Two Wests & Elliott
Carwood Road
Chesterfield
S41 9RH
01246 451 077
(Greenhouse and propagating equipment)

Unwins Seeds
FREEPOST 324
Cambridge
CB4 4ZZ
01945 588 522

Chempak Products
Geddings Road
Hoddesdon
Herts, EN11 0LR
01992 441 888
Plant foods & gels

Bakker Holland
P.O. Box 105
Spalding
Lincs
PE11 3WD
01775 715 500
(Bulbs)

John Chambers Wild Flower Seeds
15 Westleigh Road
Barton
Seagrave
Kettering
Northants
NN 15 5AJ
01933 652 562

The Vernon Geranium Nursery
Cuddington Way
Cheam
Sutton
Surrey SM2 7JB
020 8393 7616
www.geraniumsuk.com

The Organic Gardening Catalogue
Riverdene Business Park
Molesey Road
Hersham
Surrey KT12 4RG
01932 253 666
(Official catalogue of Henry Doubleday Research Association)

Mr Fothergill's Seeds
Gazeley Road
Kentford
Newmarket
CB8 7QB
01638 751 161

Simpsons Seeds
267 Meadowbrook
Old Oxted
Surrey RH8 9LT
01883 715 242
(Tomato seed specialist)

Ken Muir
Honeypot Farm
Rectory Road
Weeley Heath
Clacton on Sea
Essex CO16 9BJ
01255 830 181
(Fruit specialist)

Wolf Garden Ltd
  Crown Business Park
  Tredegar
  Gwent
  NP22 4EF
  (Garden tools & powered garden products)

Hozelock Ltd
  Waterslade House
  Haddenham
  Aylesbury
  Bucks
  HP17 8JD
  01844 292 002
  (Garden watering equipment, pond pumps, & water gardening products)

Gardena UK Ltd
  27-28 Brenkley Way
  Blezard Business Park
  Seaton Burn
  Newcastle upon Tyne
  NE13 6DS
  0191 217 1537
  (Lawn & garden care products)

Alitags Plant Labels
  21 Bourne Lane
  Much Hadhan
  Herts
  SG10 6ER
  01279 842 685
  (Plant labelling systems & sundries)

Town & Country
  Whitwick Business Park
  Stenson Road
  Whitwick
  Leics LE67 4JP
  01530 830 990
  (Garden workwear & accessories, including tool carrying equipment)

Agralan Garden Products
  The Old Brickyard
  Ashton Keynes
  Swindon
  Wilts SN6 6QR
  01285 860 015
  (Non-chemical plant protection)

Stapeley Water Gardens Ltd
  92 London Road
  Stapeley
  Nantwich
  Cheshire
  CW5 7LH
  01270 623 868
  (Indoor fountains, water pumps, books, & aquatic sundries)

Spear & Jackson
  Atlas Way
  Atlas North
  Sheffield
  North Yorks
  S4 7QQ
  0114 281 4242
  (Garden tools)

Glowcroft Ltd
  Unit K2 Innsworth Technology Park
  Innsworth Lane
  Gloucester
  GL3 1DL
  01452 731 300
  (Water storing granules, controlled release fertilizer, basket liners, & other useful gardening sundries)

Netlon Sentinel Ltd
  Apollo House
  Neepsend Lane
  Sheffield
  North Yorks
  S3 8AW
  (Garden products, nets, mesh, fencing, timber, & accessories)

A simple glossary

Anemone A semi-double flower with a raised, pillow-like centre.

Annual A flowering plant that will grow, flower, make seeds, and die, all within the same year.

Anther The portion of a flower at the tip of a stamen, containing pollen grains.

Anvil-type shears A set of shears with a single cutting blade and a solid, non-cutting opposing part.

Arboretum A tree garden.

Arbour An overhead trellis under which one can pass.

Bare-root plant A dormant plant sold with no soil mass around the roots.

Bicolour A flower with two very distinct colours, each appearing once on a blossom.

Biennial A plant that takes 2 years to complete a life cycle, growing from seed to leafy plant in the first year and flowering in the second year.

Bract A group of modified leaves at the base of a flower.

Bud union On a tree, the place where the trunk joins the roots.

Budwood Strong young stems that have buds suitable for use in budding, whereby buds are inserted into cuts made in the bark of rooted cuttings.

Bulb Bulbs are usually rounded, with a pointy tip, a round base, and an interior made of layers, similar to an onion. Mature bulbs – those that have been in the ground more than a season – reproduce by a dividing process within the parent bulb.

Cane A long, slender branch that usually originates directly from a plant's roots.

Cloche A small, portable structure made of clear plastic or glass, usually within a metal framework. Used to protect early crops on open ground or to warm the soil before planting.

Corm Corms are rounded, and are small to medium size and are solid all the way through. After a season, corms may produce cormlets around the parent corm. Each contains the ingredients to make a new plant exactly like the parent.

Crop rotation To use a piece of land to grow a different plant than was grown there previously. Crops are rotated to discourage the likelihood of infestations by crop-specific insects and of crop-specific diseases.

Cultivar A contraction of "cultivated variety". It's the progeny of a deliberate breeding effort, which is known only in cultivation and reproduces plants with predictable, uniform characteristics.

Damping off An incurable fungal disease also known as seed rot and seedling rot, whereby fungi residing in the soil attack and destroy young plants.

Deciduous A plant that loses its leaves in autumn.

Dieback The death of a shoot beginning at its tip, usually a result of disease or damage.

Double dig To dig down about 60 centimetres rather than the usual 30 centimetres. Performed to provide roots with a greater amount of good quality soil.

Double flower A flower that has three or more whorls of petals.

Drip line An imaginary circular area around a tree based on where the tips of the outermost branches end and where rainwater normally drips.

Exfoliate To come off in pieces, such as bark from a tree.

Fishmeal An organic product used to release nitrogen slowly to plants.

Flat A shallow box used to hold a batch of ground-cover plants.

Fungicide A pesticide designed for use against fungus.

Graft The deliberate combination of two plants to create one plant, whereby a shoot of one plant is inserted into a slit in another plant.

Granule The form of several gardening aids, particularly fertilizers. Granules used in the garden are generally about the size of bath crystals.

Hardening off a plant Making the plant a bit tougher so it can withstand cold, wind, or other outdoor natural weather conditions. You do this by gradually exposing it to the harsher outdoor environment.

Hardwood cutting A cutting taken from mature wood, made in order to produce a new plant. Hardwood cuttings must be taken when plants are dormant.

Herb The seeds, leaves, flowers, bark, roots, or other parts of any plant used for cosmetics, dyes, flavouring, fragrance, or health purposes.

Herbicide A pesticide designed for use against weeds.

Hybridize To cross or interbreed different plant varieties to produce a new plant, called a hybrid.

Insecticide A pesticide for use against insects.

Invasive plant A plant that grows aggressively, tending to take over the surrounding territory.

Nutrient An element necessary for a plant's survival, such as nitrogen, potassium, and phosphorus.

Parasitoids Organisms whose young develop in or on a pest insect, usually causing the pest insect's death.

Peat pots Little pots made of pressed and dried peat

moss. When you use them, you can place pot and plant directly into the garden soil for transplant, without damaging the root system.

Perennial A flower that has roots that survive from year to year, sending out new growth in the spring.

Perennial grown as an annual A perennial plant that has a very short life span and is usually replaced every year.

Pergola An arbour covered by a roof or latticework on which vines grow.

Perlite A soil component that is created from volcanic rock, and is slightly heavier than vermiculite. It is used to loosen heavy soil, and help oxygen and water reach plant roots.

Pesticide A pest control mechanism. Insecticides, fungicides, and herbicides are all pesticides.

Pinch To pick off the end bug of a twig or stem with the fingers in order to enhance growth.

Pinnate leaf A leaf with little leaflets running along both sides of a main axis.

Plug Cut-out section of good growing lawn inserted into prepared ground.

Pompom A fully rounded flower.

Pot-bound A potted plant with overgrown roots, also known as a root-bound plant.

Potpourri Dried flower petals and spices kept in a jar. May also contain sweet-smelling seeds, stems, and roots.

Propagation The deliberate creation of new plants from seed or other means.

Rhizome swollen section of an underground, horizontal plant stem. Roots grow from the underside of this stem, and plant buds develop on top of the stem.

Root hair A small, tubular outgrowth from a growing root that absorbs water and nutrients dissolved in water.

Rotovate To dig a lawn in preparation for seeding. A rotovator's rotating tines dig into the ground as the mechanism is pushed. Also used to aerate, de-thatch, and to make special planting rows.

Runner The trailing stem of a parent plant that generates a new, baby plant.

Semi-double flower A flower with two or three whorls of petals.

Single flower A flower with a single whorl of two to six petals.

Softwood cutting A cutting from the stem of a perennial plant, made in order to produce a new plant.

Specimen plant A single plant, usually medium-size or larger, that is placed so as to provide a focal point.

Spider A double flower with long, tubular, graceful florets.

Spoon A flower with florets that expand slightly into a spoon-shape at the end.

Sprig An individual grass plant used for lawns.

Stamen A slim stalk inside a flower's petals that serves as a pedestal for the flower's pollen.

Succulent A plant that stores water in its leaves, roots or stems. Generally easy to keep in very dry areas.

Sucker A shoot springing below the ground, typically from a plant's roots, instead of from its stem.

Tap root A strong centre root that grows straight down the soil.

Terrarium A self-contained environment for animals or plants.

Thatch A layer of dead roots and stems that builds up between growing grass and the soil.

Topiary A tree or shrub clipped into an ornamental shape.

Trellis A wooden frame with crossing strips, used to support climbing plants.

Tuber A swollen, underground stem or root that stores buds for a new plant.

Turf Mature grass with roots set in good soil that is laid in large pieces to create a lawn.

Umbel A flower that sprouts from stalks spreading from a common centre, similar to umbrella ribs.

Understock A rooted cutting, usually from a plant with a hardy root system, that serves as the host plant for budwood.

Variegated Streaks or patches of different colours.

Vegetative propagation The creation of new plants from another plant, such as through stem cuttings, dividing, and grafting.

Vermiculite A soil component that is created from mica, a mineral that has been heated, puffed up, and transformed into tiny, very lightweight chips that help retain soil, air, and water. It has no nutritional value for your plants.

Weed Any plant that is growing where it's not wanted.

Index

KEEP IT SIMPLE SERIES

GUIDE TO

Gardening

L. PATRICIA KITE

Foreword by Monty Don

A Dorling Kindersley Book

LONDON, NEW YORK,
MUNICH, MELBOURNE, DELHI

Editorial Director: Valerie Buckingham
Managing Editor: Maxine Lewis
Managing Art Editor: Heather M^CCarry
Project Editor: Caroline Hunt

Jacket Designer: Neal Cobourne
Picture Researchers: Richard Dabb, Charlotte Oster,
Melanie Simmonds, Romaine Werblow
Production: Michelle Thomas

Produced for Dorling Kindersley
by **Cooling Brown**
9–11 High Street, Hampton,
Middlesex TW12 2SA

UK Gardening Consultant: Valerie McBride-Whitehead
Senior Designer: Tish Mills
Designers: Pauline Clarke, Hilary Krag
Senior Editor: Amanda Lebentz
Editor: Jo Weeks

First published in Great Britain in 2001 by
Dorling Kindersley Limited,
80 Strand, London WC2R 0RL
A Penguin Company

2 4 6 8 10 9 7 5 3 1

This edition published in 2004

A CIP catalogue record for this book is available from the British Library

ISBN 0 7513 4865 1

Colour reproduction by ColourScan, Singapore
Printed and bound by Printer Portuguesa, Portugal

Discover more at
www.dk.com